BEING HUMAN

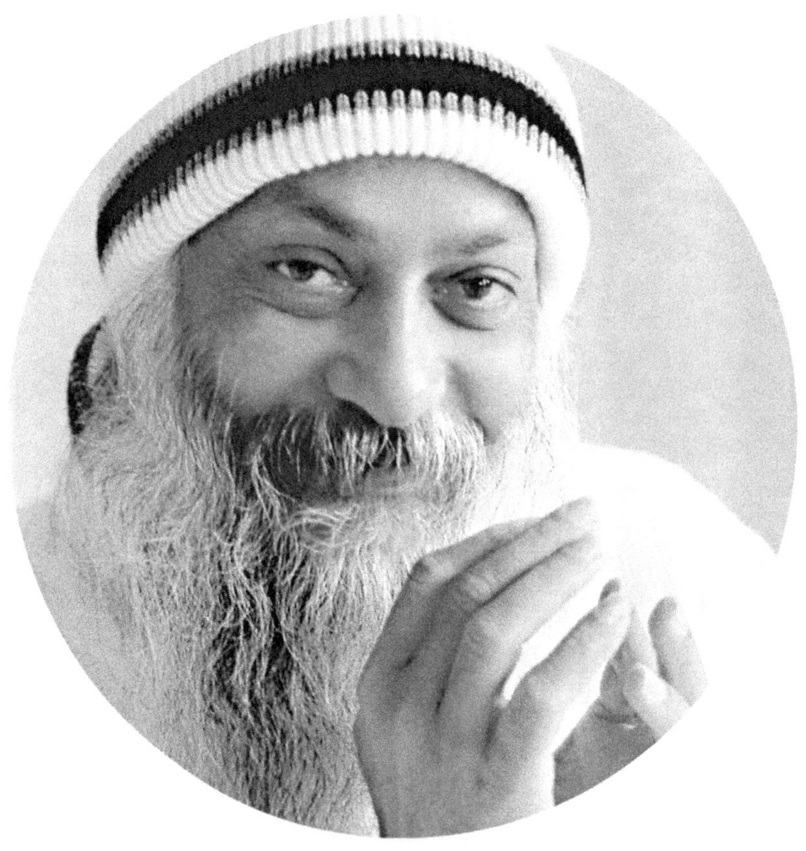

OSHO

Maturing from Sex to Love to Enlightenment

Constitution of the United States of America, Article 1: "Congress shall make no law respecting an establishment of religion, or prohibiting the free exercise thereof..."

This book contains experiential religious insights and may be copied or reprinted *for free distribution* without permission from the publisher. Otherwise, all USA and International rights are reserved.

Copyright © 2021 Osho and Swami Shunyo Mahom.

Since 1981 Swami Shunyo Mahom has been a disciple of the Enlightened Master, Osho. Swami Shunyo Mahom reserves his International and Constitutional religious right to provide excerpts from Osho discourses and his personal experience as Osho's disciple to illustrate how the Master-disciple relationship helps a disciple to mature from sex to love to enlightenment. Osho is the essential author of the Invitation and Conscious Maturing sections of this book since these sections describe Shunyo's experiments with Osho's guidance.

Enjoy!

Swami Shunyo Mahom Publishing
www.shunyo.org

"Being Human" by Osho – First Edition ISBN 978-0-578-88923-8

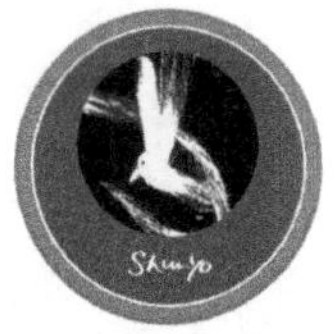

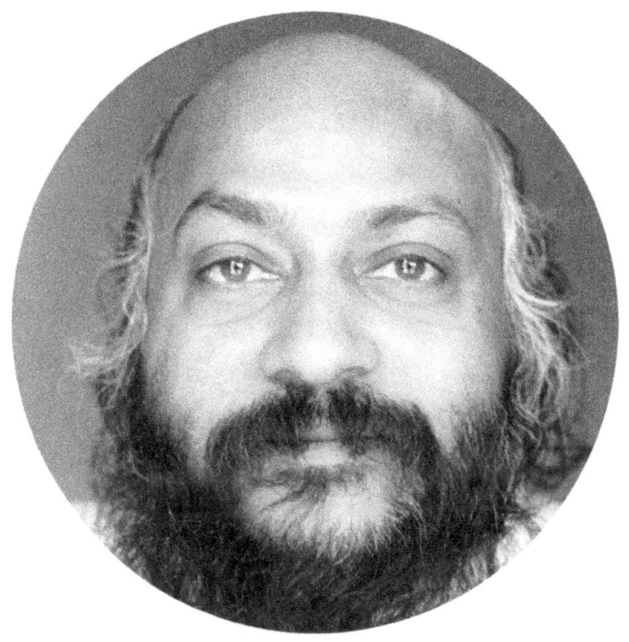

Osho is an enlightened Master whose vision encompasses the spiritual wisdom of the East and the highest potential of Western science and technology. His unique meditation techniques are designed to allow the release of accumulated stress in the body, mind, and heart to make it easier to experience the thought-free state of meditation.

Osho's books, audios, and videos are sourced from spontaneous discourses before live audiences. You can download all the excerpts from Osho discourses in this book free at oshoworld.com.

The title of the Osho discourse from which each excerpt in this book has been taken is included to encourage you to silently listen to the full audio discourse.

Silently listening to Osho's voice can be a deep meditation.

CONTENTS

AN INVITATION
by
Swami Shunyo Mahom

"One can become an animal, or one can become divine. But one thing is certain: to remain a human being is not man's destiny. To be a human being is to be in crisis. Man is not the end. Rightly understood, man is neither animal nor godly. He is unable to be an animal because he has passed through the animal stage, and he is unable to be godly because he has yet to reach up that far. Man is simply an existence that swings between godliness and the animal."

Osho – From the Book, "Inner War and Peace"

"Being Human" by Osho is an invitation to explore the multi-dimensional mystery of life and death by experimenting with Osho's insights in your life.

Personally, as a disciple of Osho, being human has been an ongoing process of consciously maturing through meditation and creative life changes over 75 years.

How is the conscious maturing process happening?

Osho is an enlightened Master who left his physical body in 1990. He was alive in 1981 when I was 36 and I experienced an awakening during which surrendering to Osho as his disciple spontaneously happened. Later I heard an audio recording of a public discourse in which Osho shared this joke:

A young woman is walking through a forest when a ragged man jumps out from behind a tree and begs her: "Lady, you've got to help me! My wife is crazy, and I don't know how to help her."

The woman tries to ignore the wretched man, but he implores her: "Lady, please, I'm desperate. You have to help me. My wife thinks she is a chicken."

"A chicken?" the woman asks. "How long has she been like this?"

"Two long years," he laments.

"Two years! Why didn't you get help before this?"

"I needed the eggs."

By age 36 I had failed to "achieve" happiness and contentment by following Western society's egoistic roadmap to happiness. I had followed a dark road and needed help.

I needed the eggs…

It took at least 25 years after I became Osho's disciple to mature into a human being, with the heart as the master and the mind a servant. Why? Because I had been emotionally and mentally crippled by a phony religious educational system which was neither religious nor educational. I needed 25 years to heal the wounds.

The Latin root of the word 'religion' means '*to re-connect, to bring together*'. But I had been conditioned by a pseudo-religion which *divided* me into a saint or sinner, to be accepted into heaven or condemned to eternal hell fires. Priests and nuns terrorized my vulnerable young mind with visions of a torturous hell. I became a phony, strong 'good boy' on the outside so I could hide the natural, sensitive 'bad boy' within.

The Latin root of the word 'education' means 'to draw out, as water from a well'. But rather than *drawing out* natural merits and strengths within me, the 'religious educational' system I was forced to experience *stuffed* moralistic unnatural ideals upon me, causing me to unconsciously repress natural sexual energy and love within. I was an emotional mess by the time I graduated from college.

I wasn't taught that human beings are born with natural animal survival instincts like fear, sex, anger, and violence - wasn't taught that even a small child can transform these natural states with awareness and experiential understanding into love, friendliness, and forgiveness. It took me 25 years to heal and let go of my sick conditioning and begin to spontaneously live moment to moment as a free human being.

I was born a male in the USA, where intellect, logic, and science ruled over qualities of love, intuition, and acceptance of nature's illogical dialectical ways. I graduated from a university and worked as an engineer in the corporate industrial world for 5 years before I realized that the intellect I was taught to value over a loving heart was a false substitute for real intelligence.

Only when I left the security of the corporate world at 26 and went into the uncharted sea of the unknown did my intelligence and creativity begin to flower. I began to see how intellectual knowledge and science without a loving heart had created a polluted insensitive inhuman world around me and that nuclear energy had become the supreme example of how technology had run amuck and needed to be balanced by educating humans on the loving ways of the heart.

How specifically has science run amuck? Three examples:

On April 26, 1986, at the Chernobyl, Russia, Atomic Energy Station, a nuclear reactor explosion killed 31 workers. As of 2005, as many as 5,000 additional cancer deaths were projected *locally* - among the 25,000 extra cancer deaths Europe-wide. 1,838-plus square miles were declared uninhabitable for thousands of years.

Following the Tohoku earthquake and tsunami in Japan on 11 March 2011, a series of equipment failures and nuclear meltdowns caused huge releases of radioactive materials from the Fukushima I Nuclear Power Plant into the Pacific Ocean. According to a 2012 Yomiuri Shimbun survey, 573 deaths have been certified as "disaster-related" by 13 municipalities affected by the Fukushima nuclear disaster. As of 2021 the Tokyo Electric Power Company has been unable to release the 1,200,000 *tons* of radioactive water kept in nearly 1,000 tanks at the Fukushima center. Where do you think they plan to release this contaminated radioactive water? Of course, into the Pacific Ocean.

On August 3, 2018, another nuclear disaster almost happened at the San Onofre Nuclear plant between San Diego and Los Angeles. Southern California could have been contaminated by nuclear waste for thousands of years.

There are still 3,600,000 pounds of nuclear waste stored at the San Onofre site! The facility is right near earthquake faults. The radioactive waste is stored *on the beach!* - a short distance from the ocean. Over time with sea level rise, the ocean can inundate the fuel and spread it worldwide. This deadly waste has to be isolated from the human environment and no one knows how to permanently do that for 50,000 years.

Nuclear power developed along with the creation of nuclear bombs and has been a destructive idea since its conception because there cannot be a safe way to permanently dispose of nuclear waste. Who is going to live for 50,000 years to actually do that? Not me. You?

50 years of power, 50,000 years of deadly radioactive waste! We get the power and future generations are left with the mess. Where is the intelligence and love in that?

The San Onofre incident was the straw that broke the camel's back, the impetus for creating this book. In this book Osho details how there *is* a healthier, more intelligent, and loving way to live, a way for the human animal to consciously evolve into a loving human being. I know this to be true from experience, thanks to Osho. I became Osho's disciple 10 years after I had left the false security of my past conditioning and had begun to explore what it means to be an authentic human being.

Science can be creative if evolved with the help of a loving heart, and I was fortunate to live at a time when science had evolved audio and visual media which documented Osho's enlightened discourses on the spiritual wisdom of the East and the highest potential of Western science and technology.

I tested Osho's transmissions on love and the healing power of meditation in my life and experienced love, bliss, and creativity. I selected the Osho discourses in this book to inspire you to journey into the unknown and unknowable realms of superconsciousness that is our birthright.

The Master-disciple relationship is an Eastern phenomenon, and my relationship with Osho is a personal love affair, not part of an organized religion, although I have lived with thousands of Osho disciples in 9 communes around the world.

Anyone who has a sincere longing to experience the truth of being human can be a disciple of Osho, and there are many Osho sannyasins and meditation centers throughout the world. An authentic seeker will find devotees of Osho with whom they can explore Osho's insights into love, meditation, creativity, and celebration.

> A disciple goes where love grows:
> from a seed to a tree,
> a tree to a flower,
> a flower to a fragrance,
> to the Master inside.

I invite you to keep a journal while reading this book and make notes on how your intellectual understanding of Osho's words can become personal experiences.

A Conscious Maturing section and a list of Osho meditation centers and resources are offered at the end of this book to support sincere seekers of Truth to integrate Osho's enlightened insights into their life.

OSHO

I SALUTE THE BUDDHA WITHIN YOU

I salute the Buddha within you. You may not be aware of it, you may not have ever dreamed about it - that you are a Buddha, that nobody can be anything else, that buddhahood is the very essential core of your being, that it is not something to happen in the future, that it has happened already. It is the very source you come from; it is the source and the goal too. It is from buddhahood that we move, and it is to buddhahood that we move.

This one word, buddhahood, contains all - the full circle of life, from the alpha to the omega. But you are fast asleep, you don't know who you are. Not that you have to become a Buddha, but only that you have to recognize it, that you have to return to your own source, that you have to look within yourself.

A confrontation with yourself will reveal your buddhahood. The day one comes to see oneself, the whole existence becomes enlightened. It is not that a person becomes enlightened - how can a person become enlightened? The very idea of being a person is part of the unenlightened mind. It is not that I have become enlightened; the 'I' has to be dropped before one can become enlightened, so how can I become enlightened? That is absurdity.

The day I became enlightened the whole existence became enlightened. Since that moment I have not seen anything other than Buddhas - in many forms, with many names, with a thousand and one problems, but Buddhas still.

So I salute the Buddha within you. I am immensely glad that so many Buddhas have gathered here. The very fact of your coming here to me is the beginning of the recognition. The respect in your heart for me, the love in your heart for me, is respect and love for your own buddhahood. The trust in me is not trust in something extrinsic to you, the trust in me is self-trust. By trusting me you will learn to trust yourself. By coming close to me you will come close to yourself. Only a recognition has to be attained. The diamond is there - you have forgotten about it, or you have never remembered it from the very beginning.

There is a very famous saying of Emerson: "Man is God in ruins." I agree and I disagree. The insight has some truth in it - man is not as he should be. The insight is there but a little upside down. Man is not God in ruins, man is God in the making; man is a budding Buddha. The bud is there, it can bloom any moment: just a little effort, just a little help. And the help is not going to cause it - it is already there! Your effort is only going to reveal it to you, help to unfold what is there, hidden. It is a discovery, but the truth is already there. The truth is eternal.

Let it be there in your heart that you are a Buddha. With this soil, with this vision in the mind, that you are a Buddha, that you are a budding Buddha, that you are potentially capable of becoming one, that nothing is lacking, all is ready, things just have to be put in the right order, that a little more awareness is needed, a little more consciousness is needed.

The treasure is there; you have to bring a small lamp inside your house. Once the darkness disappears you will no longer be a beggar, you will be a Buddha; you will be a sovereign, an emperor. This whole kingdom is yours and it is just for the asking; you have just to claim it.

But you cannot claim if you believe that you are a beggar. You cannot claim it, you cannot even dream about claiming if you think that you are a beggar. This idea that you are a beggar, that you are ignorant, that you are a sinner, has been preached from so many pulpits down through the ages that it has become a deep hypnosis in you. This hypnosis has to be broken. To break it I start with: I salute the Buddha within you.

Let it be declared to your every cell of the body and every thought of your mind; let it be declared to every nook and corner of your existence, that "I am a Buddha!" And don't be worried about the 'I'. We will take care of it. 'I' and buddhahood cannot exist together. Once the buddhahood becomes revealed, the 'I' disappears, just like darkness disappears when you bring a light in.

Osho – "The Heart Sutra", Discourse 1

LIGHT AND DARKNESS

Let us first meditate a little on the nature of darkness. It is one of the most mysterious things in existence, and your life is so much involved in it. You cannot afford not to think about it. One has to come to terms with the nature of darkness because the same is the nature of sleep, and the same is the nature of death, and the same is the nature of all ignorance.

The first thing: if you meditate on darkness, it will be revealed to you is that darkness does not exist. It is there without any existence. It is more mysterious than light. It has no existence at all; rather, on the contrary, it is just an absence of light.

There is no darkness anywhere, you cannot find it, it is simply an absence. It is not in itself, it has no 'in-itself' existence, it is simply that the light is not present. If the light is there, there is no darkness; if the light is not there, there is darkness, absence of light; it is not a presence of something. That's why light comes and goes, darkness remains. It is not, but it persists. Light you can create, light you can destroy, but you cannot create darkness and you cannot destroy darkness. It is always there without being there at all.

The second thing, if you contemplate, you will come to realize that because it is non-existential, you cannot do anything to it. And if you try to do anything to it, you will be defeated. Darkness cannot be defeated. How can you defeat something which is not? And when you will be defeated you will think: "It is very powerful because it has defeated me." This is absurd! Darkness has no power. How can a thing have power which is not?

You are not defeated by the darkness and its power; you are defeated by your foolishness. In the first place you started fighting – that was foolish. How can you fight with something which is not? And remember, you have been fighting with many things which are not; they are just like darkness.

The whole morality is a fight against darkness, that's why it is stupid. The whole morality, unconditionally, is a fight with darkness, fighting with something which in itself is not.

Hate is not real. It is just the absence of love.

Anger is not real. It is just the absence of compassion.

Ignorance is not real. It is just the absence of buddhahood, of enlightenment.

Sex is not real. It is just the absence of *brahmacharya* (living like a god).

The whole morality goes on fighting with that which is not. A moralist can never succeed, it is impossible. Finally he has to be defeated – his whole effort is nonsense.

And this is the distinction between religion and morality: morality tries to fight with darkness, and religion tries to awaken the light which is hidden within. It doesn't bother about the darkness; it simply tries to find the light within. Once the light is there, darkness disappears; once the light is there, you need not do anything to darkness – simply it is not there.

This is the second thing: that nothing can be done to darkness directly. If you want to do something with darkness, you will have to do something with light, not with darkness. Put the light off and the darkness is there; put the light on and the darkness is not there. But you cannot put on and put off darkness; you cannot bring it from somewhere, you cannot push it out. If you want to do something with darkness, you have to go via light, you have to go in an indirect way.

Never fight things which are not. The mind is tempted to fight, but the temptation is dangerous: you will waste your energy and life and dissipate yourself.

Don't be tempted by the mind; simply see whether a thing has a real existence or is just an absence. If it is an absence then don't fight with it, then seek the thing of which it is the absence – then you will be on the right track.

The third thing about darkness is that it is involved deeply with your existence in many millions of ways. Whenever you are angry, your light within has disappeared. In fact, you are angry because the light has disappeared: the darkness has entered. You can be angry only when you are unconscious, you cannot be angry consciously. Try it: either you will lose consciousness and anger will be there, or you will remain conscious and anger will not arise – you cannot be angry consciously.

What does it mean? It means the nature of consciousness is just like light, and the nature of anger is just like darkness – you cannot have both. If the light is there, you cannot have darkness; if you are conscious, you cannot be angry.

People come to me continuously and ask how not to be angry. They are asking a wrong question – and when you ask a wrong question it is very difficult to get the right answer. First ask the right question.

Don't ask how to dispel darkness, don't ask how to dispel worries, anguish, anxiety; just analyze your mind and see why they are there in the first place. They are there because you are not conscious enough.

So ask the right question: How to be more and more conscious?

If you ask how not to be angry, you will become the victim of some moralist. And if you ask the question how to be more conscious, so anger cannot exist, so lust cannot exist, so greed cannot exist, then you are on the right track, then you will become a religious seeker.

Morality is a false coin; it deceives people. It is not religion at all. Religion has nothing to do with morality, because religion has nothing to do with darkness. It is a positive effort to awaken you.

It does not bother about your character; what you do is meaningless and you cannot change it. You may decorate it, you cannot change it. You may color it in beautiful ways, you may paint it, but you cannot change it.

There is only one transformation, only one revolution, and that revolution comes not by being concerned with your character, by your acts, by your doings, but being concerned with your being. Being is a positive phenomenon; once the being is alert, awake, conscious, suddenly darkness disappears. Your being is of the nature of light.

And the fourth thing: Sleep is just like darkness. It is not accidental that you find it difficult to sleep when there is light; it is simply natural. Darkness has an affinity with sleep; that's why it is easy to sleep in the night. Darkness all around creates the milieu in which you can fall into sleep very easily.

What happens in sleep? You lose consciousness by and by. There comes an interval period in which you dream. Dreaming means half-conscious, half-unconscious; just on the midway, moving towards total unconsciousness; from your waking state you are moving to total unconsciousness. On the path dreams exist.

Dreams mean only that you are half-awake and half-asleep. That's why, if you dream continuously the whole night, you feel tired in the morning. And if you are not allowed to dream, then too you will feel tired – because dreams exist for a certain reason.

In your waking hours you accumulate many things: thoughts, feelings, incomplete matters hang in the mind. You looked at a beautiful woman on the road and suddenly a desire arose in you. But you are a man of character, manners, civilized; you simply push it down, you will not look at it, you will go on with your work – an incomplete desire hangs around you. It has to be completed, otherwise you will not be able to fall into deep sleep. It will pull you back again and again. It will say, "Come up! That woman was really beautiful, her body had a charm. And you are a fool, what are you doing here? Seek her – you have missed an opportunity!"

The desire hanging there will not allow you to fall into sleep. The mind creates a dream: again you are on the road, the beautiful woman passes, but this time you are alone without any civilization around you. No manners are needed, no etiquette is needed. You are like an animal, you are natural, no morality. This is your own private world; no police constable can enter into it, no judge can judge it. You are simply alone, there will not be even a witness. Now you can play with your lust: you will have a sexual dream. That dream completes the hanging desire, then you fall into sleep.

Dreams are a necessity for you. You are so illusory, your whole existence is such an illusion – what Hindus have called *maya* – that dreams are needed. Without dreams you cannot exist: dreams are your food, dreams are your strength, without dreams you will go mad. Dreams are a release of madness, and once the release happens you fall into sleep.

From waking you fall into dreaming and from dreaming you fall into sleep.

Every night a normal person has eight cycles of dreaming, and just a few moments between two dreaming cycles he has of deep sleep. In that deep sleep all consciousness disappears, it is absolutely dark. But still you are near the boundary, any emergency will awaken you. The house is on fire, you will have to run back to your waking consciousness; or you are a mother and the child starts crying, you will run, rush, towards waking – so you remain on the boundary. You fall into deep darkness, but remain on the boundary.

In death you fall exactly to the center. Death and sleep are similar, the quality is the same. In sleep, every day, you fall into darkness, complete darkness; that means you completely become unconscious, the very opposite pole of buddhahood. A buddha is totally awakened, and every night you fall to total unawakened state, absolute darkness.

In the Gita, Krishna says to Arjuna that when everybody is fast asleep, the yogi is still awake. That doesn't mean that he never sleeps: he sleeps, but only his body sleeps, his body rests. He has no dreams because he has no desires, so he cannot have incomplete desires. And he has no sleep like you – even in deepest rest his consciousness is clear, his consciousness burns like a flame.

Every night you fall into sleep, you fall into deep unconsciousness, a coma. In death you fall in a deeper coma. These are all like darkness. That's why you are afraid of darkness, because it is deathlike. And there are people who are afraid of sleep also, because sleep is also deathlike.

I have come across many people who cannot sleep, and they want to sleep. And when I tried to understand their mind, I came to realize that they are basically afraid. They say they would like to sleep because they feel tired, but deep down they are afraid of sleep – and that is creating the whole trouble. 90% insomnia is fear of sleep; you are afraid. You are afraid of darkness; you will be afraid of sleep also, and the fear comes from the fear of death.

Once you understand that these are all darkness and your inner nature is that of light, things start changing. Then there is no sleep for you, only rest. Then there is no death for you, only a change of clothes, of bodies, only a change of garments. But that can happen only if you realize the inner flame, your nature, your innermost being.

You may have been wandering in darkness for millions of lives, but it cannot destroy your inner light because darkness cannot be aggressive. It is not. Something which is not, how can it be aggressive? Darkness cannot destroy light. How can darkness destroy light?

Even a small flame, darkness cannot destroy it, darkness cannot jump on it, cannot be in conflict with it. How can darkness destroy a flame? How can darkness shroud a flame? It is impossible, it has never happened because it cannot happen.

But people go on thinking in terms of conflict: they think darkness is against light. This is absurd! Darkness cannot be against light. How can the absence be against that of which it is the absence? Darkness cannot be against light: there is no fight in it; it is simply the absence, sheer absence, sheer impotency – how can it attack?

You go on saying, ”What could I do? I had an attack of anger.” It is impossible. ”I had an attack of greed.” It is impossible. Greed cannot attack, anger cannot attack: they are of the nature of darkness – and your being is light; the very possibility doesn’t exist.

But anger comes; that shows only that your inner flame has been completely forgotten, you have become completely oblivious of it, you don’t know it is there. This forgetfulness can shroud it, but not darkness.

So the real darkness is your forgetfulness. And your forgetfulness can invite anger, greed, lust, hate, jealousy – they don’t attack you. Remember, you send the invitations first and they accept it. Your invitation is there – they cannot attack, they come as invited guests. You may have forgotten that you ever invited them. You can forget because you have forgotten yourself, you can forget anything.

Forgetfulness is the real darkness. And in forgetfulness everything happens. You are just like a drunkard: completely forgotten yourself, who you are, where you are going, for what you are going. All direction is lost, the very sense of direction is not there. You are like a drunkard. That's why all basic religious teachings insist on self-remembering.

Forgetfulness is the disease, then self-remembering is going to be the antidote.

You don't know how deep is your forgetfulness. You will not be able to do it for one minute continuously: not a single thought coming in and disturbing your self-remembering. This is the real darkness.

If you remember, you will become light. If you forget, you become dark. And in darkness, of course, all sorts of thieves come, all sorts of robbers attack you, all sorts of mishaps happen. Self-remembrance is the key.

Try to remember more and more, because whenever you try to remember more and more, you become centered, you are in yourself; your journeying mind falls back to one's own self. Otherwise you are going somewhere: the mind continuously creating new desires, and you are following and chasing the mind simultaneously in many directions. That's why you are split, you are not one, and your flame, inside flame, goes on wavering – a leaf in a strong wind.

When the inner flame becomes unwavering, suddenly you are going through a mutation, a transformation, a new being is born. That being will be of the nature of light.

Right now you are of the nature of darkness; you are simply an absence of something which is possible. In fact, you are not yet, you are not yet born. You have taken many births and many deaths, but you have not yet been born.

Your real birth is still going to take place, and this will be the work: that you transform your inner nature from forgetfulness to self-remembering.

Osho – "Tantra the Supreme Understanding", Discourse 3

I am reminded of the fateful day of 21 March 1953. For many lives I had been working upon myself, struggling, doing whatsoever can be done - and nothing was happening. Now I understand why nothing was happening. The very effort was the barrier, the very ladder was preventing, the very urge to seek was the obstacle.

Not that one can reach without seeking. Seeking is needed, but then comes a point when seeking has to be dropped. The boat is needed to cross the river but then comes a moment when you have to get out of the boat and forget all about it and leave it behind. Effort is needed, without effort nothing is possible. And also only with effort, nothing is possible.

Just before 21 March 1953, seven days before, I stopped working on myself. A moment comes when you see the whole futility of effort. You have done all that you can do and nothing is happening. You have done all that is humanly possible. Then what else can you do? In sheer helplessness one drops all search.

And the day the search stopped, the day I was not seeking for something, the day I was not expecting something to happen, it started happening. A new energy arose out of nowhere. It was not coming from any source. It was coming from nowhere and everywhere. It was in the trees and in the rocks and the sky and the sun and the air. It was everywhere. And I was seeking so hard, and I was thinking it is very far away. And it was so near and so close.

Just because I was seeking, I had become incapable of seeing the near. Seeking is always for the far, seeking is always for the distant - and it was not distant. I had become farsighted; I had lost the near-sightedness. The eyes had become focused on the far away, the horizon, and they had lost the quality to see that which is just close, surrounding you.

The day effort ceased, I also ceased. Because you cannot exist without effort, and you cannot exist without desire, and you cannot exist without striving. The phenomenon of the ego, of the self, is not a thing, it is a process. It is not a substance sitting there inside you; you have to create it each moment. It is like pedaling a bicycle. If you pedal it goes on and on; if you don't pedal it stops. It may go a little because of the past momentum, but the moment you stop pedaling, in fact the bicycle starts stopping. It has no more energy, no more power to go anywhere. It is going to fall and collapse.

The ego exists because we go on pedaling desire, because we go on striving to get something, because we go on jumping ahead of ourselves. That is the very phenomenon of the ego - the jump ahead of yourself, the jump in the future, the jump in the tomorrow. The jump in the non-existential creates the ego. Because it comes out of the non-existential it is like a mirage. It consists only of desire and nothing else. It consists only of thirst and nothing else.

The ego is not in the present, it is in the future. If you are in the future, then ego seems to be very substantial. If you are in the present the ego is a mirage, it starts disappearing. The day I stopped seeking...and it is not right to say that I stopped seeking: better will be to say the day seeking stopped. Let me repeat it: the better way to say it is the day the seeking stopped. Because if I stop it then I am there again. Now stopping becomes my effort, now stopping becomes my desire, and desire goes on existing in a very subtle way.

You cannot stop desire; you can only understand it. In the very understanding is the stopping of it. Remember, nobody can stop desiring, and the reality happens only when desire stops. So this is the dilemma. What to do?

Desire is there and Buddhas go on saying desire has to be stopped, and they go on saying in the next breath that you cannot stop desire. So what to do? You put people in a dilemma. They are in desire, certainly. You say it has to be stopped - okay. And then you say it cannot be stopped. Then what is to be done?

Desire has to be understood. You can understand it, you can just see the futility of it. A direct perception is needed, an immediate penetration is needed. Look into desire, just see what it is, and you will see the falsity of it, and you will see it is non-existential. And desire drops and something drops simultaneously within you.

Desire and the ego exist in cooperation, they coordinate. The ego cannot exist without desire, the desire cannot exist without the ego. Desire is projected ego, ego is introjected desire. They are together, two aspects of one phenomenon.

The day desiring stopped, I felt very hopeless and helpless. No hope because no future. Nothing to hope for because all hoping has proved futile, it leads nowhere. You go in rounds. It goes on dangling in front of you, it goes on creating new mirages, it goes on calling you, "Come on, run fast, you will reach." But howsoever fast you run you never reach.

That's why Buddha calls it a mirage. It is like the horizon that you see around the earth. It appears but it is not there. If you go it goes on running from you. The faster you run, the faster it moves away. The slower you go, the slower it moves away. But one thing is certain: the distance between you and the horizon remains absolutely the same. Not even a single inch can you reduce the distance between you and the horizon.

You cannot reduce the distance between you and your hope. Hope is horizon. You try to bridge yourself with the horizon, with the hope, with a projected desire. The desire is a bridge, a dream bridge - because the horizon exists not, so you cannot make a bridge towards it, you can only dream about the bridge. You cannot be joined with the non-existential.

The day the desire stopped, the day I looked and realized into it, it simply was futile. I was helpless and hopeless. But that very moment something started happening. The same started happening for which for many lives I was working and it was not happening.

In your hopelessness is the only hope, and in your desirelessness is your only fulfillment, and in your tremendous helplessness suddenly the whole existence starts helping you. It is waiting. When it sees that you are working on your own, it does not interfere. It waits. It can wait infinitely because there is no hurry for it. It is eternity. The moment you are not on your own, the moment you drop, the moment you disappear, the whole existence rushes towards you, enters you. And for the first time things start happening.

Seven days I lived in a very hopeless and helpless state, but at the same time something was arising. When I say hopeless I don't mean what you mean by the word hopeless. I simply mean there was no hope in me. Hope was absent. I am not saying that I was hopeless and sad. I was happy in fact, I was very tranquil, calm and collected and centered. Hopeless, but in a totally new meaning. There was no hope, so how could there be hopelessness? Both had disappeared. The hopelessness was absolute and total. Hope had disappeared and with it its counterpart, hopelessness, had also disappeared. It was a totally new experience - of being without hope. It was not a negative state.

I have to use words, but it was not a negative state. It was absolutely positive. It was not just absence, a presence was felt. Something was overflowing in me, over-flooding me. And when I say I was helpless, I don't mean the word in the dictionary sense. I simply say I was selfless. That's what I mean when I say helpless. I have recognized the fact that I am not, so I cannot depend on myself, so I cannot stand on my own ground; there was no ground underneath. I was in an abyss, bottomless abyss. But there was no fear because there was nothing to protect. There was no fear because there was nobody to be afraid.

Those seven days were of tremendous transformation, total transformation. And the last day the presence of a totally new energy, a new light and new delight, became so intense that it was almost unbearable - as if I was exploding, as if I was going mad with blissfulness. The new generation in the West has the right word for it - I was 'blissed out,' stoned. It was impossible to make any sense out of it, what was happening. It was a very nonsense world - difficult to figure it out, difficult to manage in categories, difficult to use words, languages, explanations. All scriptures appeared dead and all the words that have been used for this experience looked very pale, anemic. This was so alive. It was like a tidal wave of bliss.

The whole day was strange, stunning, and it was a shattering experience. The past was disappearing, as if it had never belonged to me, as if I had read about it somewhere, as if I had dreamed about it, as if it was somebody else's story I have heard and somebody told it to me. I was becoming loose from my past, I was being uprooted from my history, I was losing my autobiography. I was becoming a non-being, what Buddha calls *annata*.

Boundaries were disappearing, distinctions were disappearing. Mind was disappearing; it was millions of miles away. It was difficult to catch hold of it, it was rushing farther and farther away, and there was no urge to keep it close. I was simply indifferent about it all. It was okay. There was no urge to remain continuous with the past.

By the evening it became so difficult to bear it - it was hurting, it was painful. It was like when a woman goes into labor when a child is to be born, and the woman suffers tremendous pain - the birth pangs.

I used to go to sleep in those days near about twelve or one in the night, but that day it was impossible to remain awake. My eyes were closing, it was difficult to keep them open. Something was very imminent, something was going to happen. It was difficult to say what it was - maybe it is going to be my death - but there was no fear. I was ready for it. Those seven days had been so beautiful that I was ready to die, nothing more was needed. They had been so tremendously blissful, I was so contented, that if death was coming, it was welcome. But something was going to happen - something like death, something very drastic, something which will be either a death or a new birth, a crucifixion or a resurrection - but something of tremendous import was around just by the corner. And it was impossible to keep my eyes open. I was drugged.

I went to sleep near about eight. It was not like sleep. Now I can understand what Patanjali means when he says that sleep and samadhi are similar. Only with one difference - that in samadhi you are fully awake and asleep also. Asleep and awake together: the whole body relaxed, every cell of the body totally relaxed, all functioning relaxed, and yet a light of awareness burns within you, clear, smokeless. You remain alert and yet relaxed, loose but fully awake. The body is in the deepest sleep possible and your consciousness is at its peak. The peak of consciousness and the valley of the body meet.

I went to sleep. It was a very strange sleep. The body was asleep, I was awake. It was so strange - as if one was torn apart into two directions, two dimensions; as if the polarity has become completely focused, as if I was both the polarities together. The positive and negative were meeting, sleep and awareness were meeting, death and life were meeting. That is the moment when you can say 'the creator and the creation meet'.

It was weird. For the first time it shocks you to the very roots, it shakes your foundations. You can never be the same after that experience; it brings a new vision to your life, a new quality.

Near about twelve my eyes suddenly opened. I had not opened them. The sleep was broken by something else. I felt a great presence around me in the room. It was a very small room. I felt a throbbing life all around me, a great vibration - almost like a hurricane, a great storm of light, joy, ecstasy. I was drowning in it. It was so tremendously real that everything became unreal. The walls of the room became unreal, the house became unreal, my own body became unreal. Everything was unreal because now there was for the first time reality.

That's why when Buddha and Shankara say the world is *maya*, a mirage, it is difficult for us to understand because we know only this world, we don't have any comparison. This is the only reality we know. What are these people talking about - this is *maya*, illusion? This is the only reality. Unless you come to know the really real, their words cannot be understood, their words remain theoretical. They look like hypotheses. Maybe this man is propounding a philosophy: "The world is unreal".

When Berkley in the West said that the world is unreal, he was walking with one of his friends, a very logical man; the friend was almost a skeptic. He took a stone from the road and hit Berkley's feet hard. Berkley screamed, blood rushed out, and the skeptic said, "Now, the world is unreal? You say the world is unreal? Then why did you scream? This stone is unreal? Then why did you scream? Then why are you holding your leg and why are you showing so much pain and anguish on your face. Stop this? It is all unreal."

Now this type of man cannot understand what Buddha means when he says the world is a mirage. He does not mean that you can pass through the wall. He is not saying this - that you can eat stones and it will make no difference whether you eat bread or stones. He is not saying that. He is saying that there is a reality, and once you come to know it, this so-called reality simply pales out, simply becomes unreal. With a higher reality in vision the comparison arises, not otherwise.

In the dream, the dream is real. You dream every night. Dream is one of the greatest activities that you go on doing. If you live sixty years, twenty years you will sleep and almost ten years you will dream. Ten years in a life - nothing else do you do so much. Ten years of continuous dreaming - just think about it - and every night. And every morning you say it was unreal, and again in the night when you dream, dream becomes real.

In a dream it is so difficult to remember that this is a dream. But in the morning it is so easy. What happens? You are the same person. In the dream there is only one reality. How to compare? How to say it is unreal? Compared to what? It is the only reality. Everything is as unreal as everything else so there is no comparison. In the morning when you open your eyes another reality is there. Now you can say it was all unreal. Compared to this reality, dream becomes unreal. There is an awakening - compared to that reality of that awakening, this whole reality becomes unreal.

That night for the first time I understood the meaning of the word *maya*. Not that I had not known the word before, not that I was not aware of the meaning of the word. As you are aware, I was also aware of the meaning - but I had never understood it before. How can you understand without experience?

That night another reality opened its door, another dimension became available. Suddenly it was there, the other reality, the separate reality, the really real, or whatsoever you want to call it. Call it God, call it Truth, call it *Dhamma*, call it Tao, or whatsoever you will. It was nameless. But it was there - so opaque, so transparent, and yet so solid one could have touched it.

It was almost suffocating me in that room. It was too much and I was not yet capable of absorbing it. A deep urge arose in me to rush out of the room, to go under the sky - it was suffocating me. It was too much! It will kill me! If I had remained a few moments more, it would have suffocated me - it looked like that.

I rushed out of the room, came out in the street. A great urge was there just to be under the sky with the stars, with the trees, with the earth...to be with nature. And immediately as I came out, the feeling of being suffocated disappeared. It was too small a place for such a big phenomenon. Even the sky is a small place for that big phenomenon. It is bigger than the sky. Even the sky is not the limit for it. But then I felt more at ease.

I walked towards the nearest garden. It was a totally new walk, as if gravitation had disappeared. I was walking, or I was running, or I was simply flying; it was difficult to decide. There was no gravitation, I was feeling weightless - as if some energy was taking me. I was in the hands of some other energy.

For the first time I was not alone, for the first time I was no more an individual, for the first time the drop has come and fallen into the ocean. Now the whole ocean was mine, I was the ocean. There was no limitation. A tremendous power arose as if I could do anything whatsoever. I was not there, only the power was there.

I reached to the garden where I used to go every day. The garden was closed, closed for the night. It was too late, it was almost one o'clock in the night. The gardeners were fast asleep. I had to enter the garden like a thief, I had to climb the gate. But something was pulling me towards the garden. It was not within my capacity to prevent myself. I was just floating. That's what I mean when I say again and again "float with the river, don't push the river". I was relaxed, I was in a let-go. I was not there.

It was there. Call it 'God' - God was there. I would like to call it It, because God is too human a word, and has become too dirty by too much use, has become too polluted by so many people. Christians, Hindus, Mohammedans, priests and politicians - they all have corrupted the beauty of the word. So let me call it It. It was there and I was just carried away...carried by a tidal wave.

The moment I entered the garden everything became luminous, it was all over the place - the benediction, the blessedness. I could see the trees for the first time - their green, their life, their very sap running. The whole garden was asleep, the trees were asleep. But I could see the whole garden alive, even the small grass leaves were so beautiful.

I looked around. One tree was tremendously luminous - the maulshree tree. It attracted me, it pulled me towards itself. I had not chosen it, God himself has chosen it. I went to the tree, I sat under the tree. As I sat there things started settling. The whole universe became a benediction.

It is difficult to say how long I was in that state. When I went back home it was four o'clock in the morning, so I must have been there by clock time at least three hours - but it was infinity. It had nothing to do with clock time. It was timeless. Those three hours became the whole eternity, endless eternity. There was no time, there was no passage of time; it was the virgin reality, uncorrupted, untouchable, unmeasurable.

And that day something happened that has continued - not as a continuity - but it has still continued as an undercurrent. Not as a permanency - each moment it has been happening again and again. It has been a miracle each moment.

That night...and since that night I have never been in the body. I am hovering around it. I became tremendously powerful and at the same time very fragile. I became very strong, but that strength is not the strength of a Mohammed Ali. That strength is not the strength of a rock, that strength is the strength of a rose flower - so fragile in his strength, so fragile, so sensitive, so delicate. The rock will be there, the flower can go any moment, but still the flower is stronger than the rock because it is more alive. Or, the strength of a dewdrop on a leaf of grass just shining in the morning sun - so beautiful, so precious, and yet can slip any moment. So incomparable in its grace, but a small breeze can come and the dewdrop can slip and be lost forever.

Buddhas have a strength which is not of this world. Their strength is totally of love. Like a rose flower or a dewdrop, their strength is very fragile, vulnerable. Their strength is the strength of life not of death. Their power is not of that which kills; their power is of that which creates. Their power is not of violence, aggression; their power is that of compassion.

But I have never been in the body again; I am just hovering around the body. And that's why I say it has been a tremendous miracle. Each moment I am surprised I am still here; I should not be. I should have left any moment, still I am here. Every morning I open my eyes and I say, "So again I am still here?" Because it seems almost impossible. The miracle has been a continuity.

I am fragile, delicate and sensitive. That is my strength. If you throw a rock at a flower nothing will happen to the rock, the flower will be gone. But still you cannot say that the rock is more powerful than the flower. The flower will be gone because the flower was alive. And the rock - nothing will happen to it because it is dead. The flower will be gone because the flower has no strength to destroy. The flower will simply disappear and give way to the rock. The rock has a power to destroy because the rock is dead.

Remember, since that day I have never been in the body really; just a delicate thread joins me with the body. And I am continuously surprised that somehow the Whole must be willing me to be here, because I am no more here with my own strength; I am no more here on my own. It must be the will of the Whole to keep me here, to allow me to linger a little more on this shore. Maybe the Whole wants to share something with you through me.

Since that day the world is unreal. Another world has been revealed. When I say the world is unreal I don't mean that these trees are unreal. These trees are absolutely real - but the way you see these trees is unreal. These trees are not unreal in themselves - they exist in God, they exist in absolute reality - but the way you see them you never see them; you are seeing something else, a mirage.

You create your own dream around you and unless you become awake you will continue to dream. The world is unreal because the world that you know is the world of your dreams. When dreams drop and you simply encounter the world that is there, that is the real world.

There are not two things, God and the world. God is the world if you have eyes, clear eyes, without any dreams, without any dust of the dreams, without any haze of sleep. If you have clear eyes, clarity, perceptiveness, there is only God. Then somewhere God is a green tree, and somewhere else God is a shining star, and somewhere else God is a cuckoo, and somewhere else God is a flower, and somewhere else a child and somewhere else a river - then only God is. The moment you start seeing, only God is.

But right now whatsoever you see is not the truth, it is a projected lie. That is the meaning of a mirage. And once you see, even for a single split moment, if you can see, if you can allow yourself to see, you will find immense benediction present all over, everywhere - in the clouds, in the sun, on the earth.

This is a beautiful world. But I am not talking about your world, I am talking about my world. Your world is very ugly, your world is your world created by a self, your world is a projected world. You are using the real world as a screen and projecting your own ideas on it. When I say the world is real, the world is tremendously beautiful, the world is luminous with infinity, the world is light and delight, it is a celebration, I mean my world - or your world if you drop your dreams. When you drop your dreams you see the same world as any Buddha has ever seen. When you dream you dream privately.

Have you watched it? - that dreams are private. You cannot share them even with your beloved. You cannot invite your wife to your dream, or your husband, or your friend. You cannot say, "Now, please come tonight in my dream. I would like to see the dream together." It is not possible. Dream is a private thing, hence it is illusory, it has no objective reality.

God is a universal thing. Once you come out of your private dreams, it is there. It has been always there. Once your eyes are clear, a sudden illumination - suddenly you are over-flooded with beauty, grandeur and grace. That is the goal, that is the destiny.

Let me repeat: Without effort you will never reach it, with effort nobody has ever reached it. You will need great effort, and only then there comes a moment when effort becomes futile. But it becomes futile only when you have come to the very peak of it, never before it. When you have come to the very pinnacle of your effort - all that you can do you have done - then suddenly there is no need to do anything anymore. You drop the effort. But nobody can drop it in the middle, it can be dropped only at the extreme end.

So go to the extreme end if you want to drop it. Hence I go on insisting: make as much effort as you can, put your whole energy and total heart in it, so that one day you can see - now effort is not going to lead me anywhere. And that day it will not be you who will drop the effort, it drops on its own accord. And when it drops on its own accord, meditation happens.

Meditation is not a result of your efforts, meditation is a happening. When your efforts drop, suddenly meditation is there, the benediction of it, the blessedness of it, the glory of it. It is there like a presence, luminous, surrounding you and surrounding everything. It fills the whole earth and the whole sky. That meditation cannot be created by human effort. Human effort is too limited. That blessedness is so infinite. You cannot manipulate it. It can happen only when you are in a tremendous surrender. When you are not there only then it can happen. When you are a no-self: no desire, not going anywhere - when you are just here-now, not doing anything in particular, just being, it happens. And it comes in waves and the waves become tidal. It comes like a storm, and takes you away into a totally new reality.

But first you have to do all that you can do, and then you have to learn non-doing. The doing of the non-doing is the greatest doing, and the effort of effortlessness is the greatest effort.

Your meditation that you create by chanting a mantra or by sitting quiet and still and forcing yourself, is a very mediocre meditation. It is created by you, it cannot be bigger than you. It is homemade, and the maker is always bigger than the made. You have made it by sitting, forcing in a yoga posture, chanting "Rama, Rama, Rama" or anything - "blah, blah, blah" - anything. You have forced the mind to become still. It is a forced stillness. It is not that quiet that comes when you are not there. It is not that silence which comes when you are almost non-existential. It is not that beatitude which descends on you like a dove.

It is said when Jesus was baptized by John the Baptist in the Jordan River, God descended in him, or the holy ghost descended in him like a dove. Yes, that is exactly so. When you are not there, peace descends in you, fluttering like a dove, reaches in your heart and abides there and abides there forever.

You are your undoing, you are the barrier. Meditation is when the meditator is not. When the mind ceases with all its activities - seeing that they are futile - then the unknown penetrates you, overwhelms you. The mind must cease for God to be. Knowledge must cease for knowing to be. You must disappear, you must give way. You must become empty, then only you can be full.

That night I became empty and became full. I became non-existential and became Existence. That night I died and was reborn. But the one that was reborn has nothing to do with that which died, it is a discontinuous thing. On the surface it looks continuous but it is discontinuous. The one who died, died totally; nothing of him has remained.

Believe me, nothing of him has remained, not even a shadow. It died totally, utterly. It is not that I am just a modified transformed form, transformed form of the old. No, there has been no continuity. That day of March twenty-first, the person who had lived for many, many lives, for millennia, simply died. Another being, absolutely new, not connected at all with the old, started to exist.

Religion just gives you a total death. Maybe that's why the whole day previous to that happening I was feeling some urgency like death, as if I am going to die - and I really died. I have known many other deaths but they were nothing compared to it, they were partial deaths. Sometimes the body died, sometimes a part of the mind died, sometimes a part of the ego died, but as far as the person was concerned, it remained, renovated many times, decorated many times, changed a little bit here and there, but it remained, the continuity remained.

That night the death was total. It was a date with death and God simultaneously.

Osho – "The Discipline of Transcendence", Volume 2

"I AM JUST AN ORDINARY MAN"

Question: *Osho, I believe that you are one of the greatest men who has ever lived. Am I right?*

You are absolutely wrong – there are no great men. If you have a hero, look again: you have diminished yourself in some way.

This is the truth! This is it! There are no hidden meanings. I am just an ordinary man – as you are, as everybody else is. The difference is not that I am great and you are not great, the difference is that I am awake and you are asleep. But that does not make you small, that does not make me great either. Nobody is great. This whole nonsense has to be dropped.

Don't start looking on me as a hero. I am still alive! You can do whatsoever you want to do when I am dead because then I cannot prevent you, but right now I won't allow such things!

Question: *Osho, Did Gautam the Buddha and Jesus the Christ have any idea that you would be here one day on earth?*

I suspect so. Gautam the Buddha used to say that after 25 centuries there would arise one awakened man whose name would be Maitreya. Maitreya means the friend. Now for 25 centuries it has been thought that this would be the name of the awakened person, but my own interpretation is that Buddha is not talking about the name, he is talking about the quality of the person. He is saying that he will be the first Master who will be the friend, who will not pretend to be the Master, who will simply say, "I am your friend." And that's what I am saying to you: I am your friend.

Osho – "Walking in Zen, Sitting in Zen", Discourse 14

FOUR STAGES OF HUMAN EVOLUTION

Teilhard de Chardin divides human evolution into four stages. The first he calls geosphere, the second, biosphere, the third, noosphere, and the fourth, christosphere. These four stages are immensely significant. They have to be understood.

The geosphere. It is the state of consciousness which is absolutely asleep, the state of matter. Matter is consciousness asleep. Matter is not against consciousness, matter is a state of consciousness asleep, not yet awakened. A rock is a sleeping Buddha; one day or other the rock is going to become a Buddha. It may take millions of years - that doesn't matter. The difference will be only of time, and time does not matter much in this eternity. That's why in the East we have been making statues out of stone - that's very symbolic: the rock and the Buddha are bridged through a stone statue. The rock is the lowest and Buddha is the highest. The stone statue says that even in stone is hidden a Buddha. The stone statue says that Buddha is nothing but the rock come to manifestation; the rock has expressed its whole potential.

This is the first stage: geosphere. It is matter, it is unconsciousness, it is sleep, it is pre-life. In this state there is no freedom, because freedom enters through consciousness. In this state there is only cause-and-effect. Law is absolute. Not even an accident is possible. Freedom is not known. Freedom enters only as a shadow of consciousness; the more conscious you become, the more free. Hence Buddha is called a *mukta* - utterly free. The rock is utterly in bondage, fettered from everywhere, from all sides, in all dimensions. The rock is the soul in imprisonment, Buddha is the soul on wings. There are no longer any chains, any bondages, any imprisonments; no walls surround Buddha. He has no borders to his being. His being is as vast as existence itself. He is one with the whole.

But in the world of the geosphere, cause-and-effect is the only *dhamma*, the only law, the only Tao. Science is still confined to the geosphere, because it still goes on thinking in terms of cause-and-effect. Modern science is a very rudimentary science, very primitive, because it cannot conceive of anything more than matter. Its conception is very limited, and hence it is creating more misery than it solves. Its vision is so finite, its vision is so tiny, small, that it cannot reconcile itself with the totality of existence. It is looking from a tiny hole and thinks that's all. Science is still confined to the geosphere. Science is still in bondage, it has not yet got wings. It will get wings only when it starts moving beyond cause-and-effect.

Yes, little sparks are there. The nuclear physicist is entering into the world which is beyond cause-and-effect, crossing the boundary. Hence, the principle of uncertainty is arising, arising with great force. Cause-and-effect is the principle of certainty: you do this and this is bound to happen. You heat the water to a hundred degrees and the water evaporates - that's cause-and-effect. The water has no freedom. It cannot say, "Today I am not in the mood, and I am not going to evaporate at a hundred degrees! I simply say no!" No, it cannot say that; it cannot resist, it cannot fight against the law. It is very law-abiding, very obedient. Some other day, when the water is feeling very happy, it cannot say, "You need not bother too much. I am going to evaporate at fifty degrees. I am going to oblige you." No, that is not possible.

The old physics, the old science, had no glimpse about the principle of uncertainty. The principle of uncertainty means the principle of freedom. Now, little glimpses are happening. Now they are not so certain as they used to be. Now they see that at the deepest, in matter too there is a certain quality of freedom. It is very difficult to say whether the electron is a particle or a wave: it behaves both ways, sometimes this way, sometimes that way. And there is no way to predict it. It is a quanta. And not only that - its freedom is such that sometimes simultaneously it behaves like a wave and like a particle. That is utterly impossible for the old scientist even to conceive or understand. Aristotle would not be able to understand it, Newton would not be able to understand it. That is impossible to see. That is saying that something is behaving like a line and a dot simultaneously; it is illogical. How can something behave like a dot and a line? Either it is a line or it is a dot.

But now the physicist is starting to have glimpses of the innermost core of matter. In a very, very roundabout way they are stumbling on one of the greatest factors of life: freedom. But in the geosphere it doesn't exist. It is *sushupti*.

The word *sushupti* means absolute sleep - not even a dream stirs. The rocks are not even dreaming, they cannot dream. To dream they will have to be a little more conscious. The rock is simply there. It has no personality, it has no soul - at least not in actuality. It cannot even dream; its sleep is undisturbed. Day, night, year-in, year-out, it goes on sleeping. For millennia it has slept, and for millennia it will sleep. Not even a dream disturbs it.

In yoga we divide consciousness into four stages. They are very, very relevant to de Chardin's division. The first is *sushupti*, deep sleep. The geosphere corresponds to that. The geosphere is more like death than like life. That's why matter appears to be dead. It is not. It is waiting for its life to grow, it is like a seed. It appears dead: it is waiting for its right moment to explode into life. But right now it is dead. There is no mind. Remember, in the last stage also there will be no mind again. A Buddha is in a state of no-mind, and the rock is also in the state of no-mind. Hence the significance of a stone statue: the meeting of two polarities.

The rock being in a state of no-mind means the rock is still below mind. Buddha is in a state of no-mind: that means Buddha has gone beyond mind. There is a similarity, just as there is a similarity between a child and a saint. The child is below mind, the saint is beyond mind. The rock will have to go through all the turmoil of life the Buddha has passed through. He has gone and gone and gone, and gone beyond, utterly beyond. But there is a similarity: he again exists in a state of no-mind. He has become so fully conscious that the mind is not needed. The rock is so unconscious that the mind cannot exist. In the rock the unconscious is absolute, hence the mind is not possible. In the Buddha the consciousness is absolute and the mind is not needed. Let me explain it to you; it is one of the most important things to learn, to understand.

Mind is needed only because you are not really conscious. If you are really conscious, then there is insight, there is no thinking. Then you act out of insight, you don't act out of your mind. Mind is not needed then. When you see a thing as true, that very seeing becomes your action.

For example, you are in a house and the house is on fire. You see it - it is not a thinking. You simply see it, and you jump out of the house. You don't wait, you don't ponder, you don't brood over it. You don't inquire, you don't consult books, you don't go to ask somebody's advice about what to do.

You are coming from an evening walk, and just on the road you come across a snake. You jump! Before any thinking enters, you jump. It is not out of thinking that you jump, it is out of insight. The great danger is there - the very danger makes you alive, intense, conscious, and you take the jump out of consciousness. It is a no-mind jump.

But these moments are rare in your life because you are not yet ready to live your consciousness intensely and totally. For Buddha, that is his normal way. He lives so totally that the mind is never needed, never consulted.

The first sphere, the geosphere, is a no-mind sphere. There is no self, obviously, because without the mind the self cannot exist. Again, in the fourth, there will be no self - because without the mind how can the self exist? The mind needs to function out of a center, hence it creates the ego, the self. The mind has to keep itself in control, the mind has to keep itself in a certain pattern, order. It has to hold itself. To hold itself it creates a center, because only through the center can it keep control. Without a center it will not be able to keep control. So once the mind comes in, ego is on the way. Sooner or later the mind will need the ego. Without the ego the mind will not be able to function. Otherwise who will control, who will manage, who will manipulate, who will plan, who will dream, who will project? And who will be there to be referred to as a constant thing? - because the mind goes on changing. One thought after another...it is a procession of thoughts. You will be lost if you don't have any ego: you will not know who you are, and where you are going, and for what.

In the geosphere there is no mind, no self, and no time. It is below time. Time has not entered yet. The rock knows no past, no present, no future. And so is it the case with Buddha. He also is beyond time. He knows no past, no present, no future. He lives in eternity. In fact that is the real meaning of being in the present. Being in the present does not mean that space which is between past and future. In the dictionary that is the meaning given: the space between past and future is called the present. But that is not the present. What kind of present is this? It is already becoming past; it is going out of existence. This moment, if you call it 'present', the moment you have called it 'present' it is already gone into the past; it is no longer present. And that moment you were calling 'future' - the moment you called it 'future' it has become the present and is moving towards becoming a past. This present is not a real present.

The present that is between past and future is just part of past and future, of the time procession.

The present that I talk about, the now that I talk about, or the Buddha talks about, or Christ when he says, "Don't think of the morrow. See the lilies in the field - they toil not, they spin not, and look how beautiful they are. How incredibly beautiful! Even Solomon was not so beautiful arrayed in all his glory. Look at the lilies of the field..." Those lilies are living in a kind of nowness; they don't know the past, they don't know the future.

The Buddha knows no past, no future, and no present. He knows no division. That's the state of eternity. Then the now is absolutely there. There is only now, and only here, and nothing else. But the rock is also in that state - unconscious, of course.

The second sphere is the biosphere. It means life, pre-consciousness. The first sphere was matter, the second sphere is life: trees, animals, birds. The rock cannot move, the rock has no life anywhere, not visible anywhere. The tree has more life, the animal still more, the bird still more. The tree is rooted in the ground, cannot move much. It moves a little bit, sways, but cannot move much; it has not that much freedom. A little freedom is certainly there, but the animal has more freedom. He can move, he can choose a little more freedom - where to go, what to do. The bird has even a little more freedom - it can fly. This is the sphere called the biosphere, the life sphere. It is pre-consciousness; just rudimentary consciousness is coming into being. The rock was absolutely unconscious. You cannot say the tree is so absolutely unconscious. Yes, it is unconscious, but something of the consciousness is filtering in, a ray of consciousness is coming in. And the animal is a little more conscious.

The first state corresponds with Patanjali's *sushupti* - deep, deep sleep. The second state corresponds with Patanjali's *swabana*, the dream state. Consciousness is coming like a dream. Yes, dogs dream. You can see - you can watch a dog asleep and you will see he is dreaming. In dream sometimes, he will try to catch flies. And sometimes you will see he is sad, and sometimes you will see he looks happy. Watch a cat, and sometimes she is jumping on a mouse in her dream, and you can see what she is doing in the dream - eating the mouse, cleaning her mustache. You can watch the cat: dream has entered, things are happening in the world of consciousness. Consciousness is surfacing. Cause-effect is still predominant, but not so much as in a rock. A little freedom becomes possible, and hence accidents start happening. The animal has a little bit of freedom. He can choose a few things, he can be temperamental: he can be in a good mood and be friendly towards you, he can be in a bad mood and will not be friendly towards you. A little bit of decision has come into his being, but a very little bit, just the beginning. The self is not yet integrated. It is a very loose self, hodgepodge, but it is coming up. The structure is taking shape, the form is arising.

The animal is past-oriented; it lives out of the past. The animal has no idea of the future - it cannot plan for the future, it cannot think ahead. Even if sometimes it thinks ahead, that is very, very fragmentary. For example when the animal is feeling hungry it can think ahead, a few hours ahead - that he will get food. He has to wait. But the animal cannot think about one month, two months, three months into the future. The animal cannot conceive of years; it has no calendar, no time concept. It is past-oriented. Whatsoever has been happening in the past it expects to happen in the future too. Its future is more or less the same as the past; it is a repetition. It is past-dominated. Time is entering through the past, self is entering through the past.

The third sphere is the noosphere; mind, self-consciousness arises. The first was unconsciousness, the second was pre-consciousness, the third is self-consciousness. Consciousness comes, but there is a calamity with it - the self. It cannot come otherwise; the self is a necessary evil. Consciousness comes with the idea of 'I'. Reflection starts, thinking starts, personality comes into existence. And with mind comes future orientation: man lives in the future, animals live in the past.

Developed societies live in the future, undeveloped societies live in the past. Primitive people still live in the past. Only civilized people live in the future. To live in the future is a higher state than to live in the past. Young people live in the future, old people start living in the past. Young people are more alive than old people. New countries, new cultures, live in the future. For example, America lives in the future, India lives in the past. India goes on carrying five thousand, ten thousand years of past. It is such a burden, it is so difficult to carry it, it is crushing, but one goes on carrying it. It is the heritage, and one is very much proud of the past.

To be proud of the past is simply an uncivilized state. One has to reach into the future, one has to grope into the future. The past is no more, the future is going to be - one has to prepare for it.

You can watch it in many ways. The Indian mind is thrilled only by past events. Still, people go on playing the drama of Rama every year, and they are very thrilled. Thousands of years have passed and they have been playing the same drama again and again and again, and again they will play it. And they are very thrilled. They were not so thrilled when the first man walked on the moon; they were not so thrilled as they were and have always been thrilled by the drama of Rama. They know the story, they have seen it many times, but it is their heritage; they are very proud of it.

You will be surprised to know that there are Hindu mahatmas and Jaina mahatmas in India who have been trying to prove that man has not walked on the moon, that the Americans are deceiving. Why? - because the moon is a god. How can you walk on the moon? And there are people who listen to them and follow them.

A Jaina monk came to see me once in Gujarat and he said, "Support me...and I have got thousands of followers!" And he did have. And the whole thing, the theme of his life, was that the Americans have been deceiving, that those photographs are all photographic tricks that have been produced, that those rocks that have been brought from the moon have been brought from Siberia or from somewhere on the planet. Nobody has ever gone and nobody can ever go to the moon, because in the Jaina shastras, in the Jaina scriptures, it is written that the moon is a god. How can you walk on God? This is past-orientation. This is very deadening. That's why India cannot grow, it cannot evolve, it cannot progress. It is stuck with the past.

With the noosphere, with mind, self-consciousness, reflection, thought, personality, future-orientation comes into being. And the more you start preparing for the future, the more anxious, of course, you become. So Americans are the most tense people, restless. Indians are very restful, so restful that they don't have any efficiency at all. Do you know that when Indians change an electric bulb, three Indians are needed? - one to hold the bulb and two to turn the ladder. Very restful people, relaxed; they don't suffer from any anxiety, they don't know what anxiety really is.

Anxiety enters with the future, because you have to plan. You cannot just go on repeating the old ways of your life. And when you do something new there is a possibility of a mistake, more possibility of a mistake. The more you try the new, the more anxious you become. That's why, psychologically, America is the most disturbed country, India the most undisturbed.

Animals don't have anxiety. To live in the past is a lower state of mind - of course more comfortable, more convenient. And the Hindu mahatmas go on saying to the world, "Look how peaceful we are. No neurosis exists. Even if we starve, we starve very, very silently. Even if we die, we die very, very acceptingly. And you are going mad!"

But remember, progress comes through anxiety. With progress there is anxiety, there is trembling - of going wrong, of doing something wrong, of missing the point. With the past there is no problem: you go on repeating it. It is a settled past, the ways of it are perfectly known. You have traveled on them, your parents have traveled on them, and so on and so forth, backwards to Adam and Eve. Everybody has done it; there is no possibility of going wrong. With something new, anxiety, fear, fear of failure enters.

This third sphere, the noosphere, is the sphere of anxiety, tension. If you have to choose between the second and the third, choose the third, don't choose the second. Although there is no need to choose between the third and the second, you can choose between the third and the fourth; then choose the fourth. Always choose the higher.

Remember, when I condemn the Indian mind, I am not condemning Buddha and I am not condemning Krishna. They have chosen the fourth: they are also at rest, they are also relaxed - but their relaxation comes from dropping time itself, not by living in the past. They are utterly relaxed, they have no anxiety, no neurosis. Their mind is a calm, rippleless lake - but not by choosing the second but by choosing the fourth; not by remaining below mind but by going beyond mind. But that's how things go.

People have seen Buddha in India, and they have seen the silence, and they have seen the benediction of the man, and they have seen the grace, and they have seen that life can be lived in such relaxation...why not live such a life? But they have not made any effort to go to the fourth stage. On the contrary, they relapsed from the third and settled in the second stage. It gives something like Buddha's silence; but it is 'something like', it is not exactly that. It is always easier to settle in the past and become more convenient and comfortable. Buddha has not settled with the past; he has not even settled with the future. He has not settled with time itself - he has dropped time, he has dropped the mind that creates time. He has dropped the ego that creates anxiety.

Indians have chosen to drop the future because that seems to create anxiety: "Future creates anxiety? You can drop the future." Then you will slip back, you will relapse into the previous state. Drop the ego, and then you go beyond.

The third sphere is like what Patanjali calls wakefulness. The first is sleep, the second is dream, the third is wakefulness - your wakefulness of course, not the wakefulness of a Buddha. Your so-called wakefulness: eyes are open but dreams are roaming inside you; eyes are open but sleep is there inside you. You are full of sleep even when you are awake. This is the third state. And it is always helpful; if you become tired of the day, you fall into a dream - it gives you relaxation. Then you fall into deep sleep; it gives you even more relaxation. In the morning you are again fresh. You fall backwards to become restful because that is what you know already, and that is there in your system; you can go into it.

The fourth state has to be created; it is not in your system. It is your potential but you have never been in it before. It is arduous, it is going upstream, uphill. The fourth state is the christosphere - you can call it the buddhasphere, it means the same thing; you can call it the krishnasphere, it means the same. With the third state there is kind of freedom, a pseudo-freedom, the freedom known as choice. This has to be understood, it is of great importance.

At the third stage you simply have a pseudo kind of freedom, and that freedom is the freedom of choice. For example, you say, "My country is religiously free." That means you can choose: you can go to a church or to a temple, and the country and its law will not create any trouble for you. You can become a Mohammedan or a Hindu or a Christian - you can choose. 'The country is free' means you can choose your life, where you want to live, what you want to do, what you want to say. The choice of expression, the freedom - that you can say whatsoever you like, that you can do whatsoever you like, that you can choose any religious or political style; you can be a communist, you can be a fascist, you can be a liberal, you can be a democrat, and all that nonsense. You can choose. It is only a pseudo-freedom. Why do I call it pseudo-freedom? - because a mind which is full of thoughts cannot be free.

If you have lived for fifty years and your mind has been conditioned by your parents and the teachers and the society, do you think you can choose? You will choose out of your conditioning. How is it going to be a choice? First, you have been conditioned.

It is like when you hypnotize somebody. You can take somebody to our hypnotist and he can hypnotize him and tell him, "Tomorrow morning you will go to the market and you will purchase a certain kind of a cigarette, a certain brand." He can suggest this to that person in deep hypnosis. Tomorrow morning he will get up and he will not have any idea that he is going to purchase a certain brand of cigarettes in the market, because the conditioning has entered into the unconscious, has been put in the unconscious. His conscious mind is unaware. He will not even have any idea of why he is going to the market. But he will find some rationalization: he will say, "Let us go shopping today." Why today? He will say, "This is my freedom. Whenever I want to go I will go. Who are you to prevent me? This is my freedom." And he's unaware, completely unaware that this is not freedom at all. And he will go to the market with the idea that he is free, and he may not even think for a single moment that he's going to purchase a certain brand of cigarettes. Then suddenly he comes across a shop and he says to himself, "Why not purchase a packet of cigarettes? You have not smoked for so long." And he is thinking that he is thinking it! And he goes to the shop and he says, "Give me this brand of cigarettes, 555." Why not Panama? Why not Wills? Why not Berkeley? He will say, "This is my choice! I am free to choose!" And he will purchase 555, and he remains free - at least in his idea.

He's not free, he has been conditioned.

You have been conditioned as a Hindu, a Christian, as a Mohammedan, as an Indian, as a Chinese, as a German - how can you be free? You have been conditioned by your parents, by your society, by your neighborhood, by your school, college, university - how can you be free? Your freedom is pseudo. It is bogus - it only gives you the feeling of freedom and makes you happy; otherwise there is no freedom in it. When you go to the church are you going out of your freedom? When you go to the Hindu temple are you going out of your freedom? Look into it and you will find it is not out of freedom; you were born in a Hindu family.

Sometimes it can happen - you were born in a Christian family and still you want to go to a Hindu temple. That too is a conditioning - a different kind. Maybe your parents were too Christian, too much, and you could not absorb that much nonsense. There is a limit. You became antagonistic, you started rebelling against it; you became a reactionary. They used to pull you to the church. And they were powerful, and you were a small child, and you could not do anything; you were helpless. But you were always thinking, "I will show you." The day you became powerful you stopped going to church.

Now this idea, "I will show you," has been implanted by their obsession with the church. It is again hypnosis - in the reverse order, but it is still hypnosis. You are reacting, you are not free. If you want to go to church you will not be able to go, you will find yourself pulling away. You will not go because this is the church your parents used to take you to. You cannot go to this church; you will become a Hindu. You will start doing things which your parents had never wanted you to do just to show them. This is reaction. The first is obedience, the second is disobedience, but there is no freedom in either.

And one thing more: it is not only a question of conditioning that you are not free. When you choose between two things - maybe nobody has conditioned you about those two things; there are millions of things for which you have not been conditioned at all. When you choose between two things your choice is out of confusion, and out of confusion there can be no freedom. You want to marry this girl or that - how are you going to choose? You are confused.

People write to me: "We are torn apart between two women, or between two men. What should we do?"

This confusion arises because you are motivated. There is a motivation: money, music, security. There is no love; that's why you are torn apart. If love is there, intense love is there, passionate love is there, then there would be no choice. That passion itself would decide. You would not be choosing, you would not be torn apart. But people are not that intelligent and not that intense. They live very lukewarm, so-so; they don't live intensely; their lives have no fire.

Real freedom happens only when your life becomes so total in each moment that there is no need to decide; that totality decides. Do you follow me? - the totality itself decides. You are not facing two alternatives: whether to marry this woman or that. Your heart is totally with one. There is no motive so you are not divided, and there is no confusion. If you decide out of confusion you will create conflict. Confusion will take you into deeper confusions. Never decide out of confusion.

That's why Krishnamurti goes on talking about choicelessness. Choicelessness is freedom. You don't choose, you simply become totally intense. You just become absolutely alert, aware, attentive.

For example, you are listening to me: you can listen in a lukewarm way - half asleep, half awake, yawning, thinking a thousand and one things, planning, the last night still hanging around you, hangovers of a thousand and one types - and you are listening too. Then there is a question of whether I am telling the truth or not. If you are passionately listening, if you are utterly here-now, that very passion will decide. In that intensity you will know what truth is. If I say something which is true, it will immediately strike in your heart. Because you will be so intelligent, how can you miss it? Your intelligence will be so alert, how can you miss it? And if there is something which is not true, you will see it immediately. The vision will come, immediate. There will be no decision on your part: "Should I follow this man or not?" That is out of confusion. You have not listened, you have not seen me.

See the point of it! With truth you need not agree or disagree. The truth has to be heard totally, with sensitivity, that's all. And that very sensitivity decides. You see, you immediately feel the truth of it. In that very feeling you have moved into truth - not that you agreed or disagreed; not that you were convinced by me, converted by me. I'm not converting anybody; truth converts. And truth is not a belief, and truth is not an argument; truth is a presence. If you are present you will feel it. If you are not present you will not feel it.

So on the third stage, the noosphere, there is pseudo-freedom. Out of confusion, you decide; hence confusion goes on growing. Confusion brings conflict, because there are always two sides in you - to do this or to do that, to be or not to be. And whatsoever you decide, the other side will remain there and wait for its time to take revenge. Freedom happens only at the fourth stage.

The christosphere is the fourth. With the christosphere, no-mind comes into existence - the no-mind of a Buddha, of a Christ, not of a rock. With the fourth comes consciousness, without a center, with no self in it; just pure consciousness with no border to it, infinite consciousness. Then you can't say "I am conscious." There is no "I" to it, it is just consciousness. It has no name and no form. It is nothingness, it is emptiness. With this consciousness, thinking is not needed; insight starts functioning, intuition starts functioning.

Intellect lives on tuition. Others have to teach you - that's what tuition is. Intuition nobody has to teach you: it comes from within, it grows out of you, it is a flowering of your being.

This is the quality of consciousness called meditation, intuition, insight, consciousness without a center, timelessness; or you can call it the now, the present. But remember, it is not the present between past and future; it is the present in which past and future have both dissolved.

De Chardin calls it "the omega point", Buddha calls it "nirvana", Jainas call it "moksha", Christ calls it "God the Father". These are different names. This whole sutra is concerned with the movement from the third to the fourth, from the noosphere to the christosphere, from intellect to intelligence, from self-consciousness to no self-consciousness. The third is like waking, ordinary waking, and the fourth is what Patanjali calls *turiya,* "the fourth". He has not given it any name, and that seems to be very beautiful. Call it "christosphere", and it looks Christian; call it "krishnasphere", and it looks Hindu; call it "buddhasphere", and it looks Buddhist. Patanjali is very, very pure; he simply calls it "the fourth". That contains everything. He has not given it a particular name. For three he gives names because they have forms, and wherever form is, name is relevant. The formless cannot have any name - *turiya,* "the fourth".

Osho - "The Heart Sutra", Discourse 9

CONSCIOUS EVOLUTION

With man, the natural automatic process of evolution ends. Man is the last product of unconscious evolution. With man, conscious evolution begins.

Many things are to be taken into account. First, unconscious evolution is mechanical and natural. It happens by itself. Through this type of evolution, consciousness evolves. But the moment consciousness comes into being, unconscious evolution stops because its purpose has been fulfilled. Unconscious evolution is needed only up to the point where the conscious comes into being. Man has become conscious. In a way, he has transcended nature. Now nature cannot do anything; the last product that was possible through natural evolution has come into being. Now man becomes free to decide whether to evolve or not to evolve.

Secondly, unconscious evolution is collective, but the moment evolution becomes conscious it becomes individual. No collective, automatic evolution proceeds further than mankind. From now on, evolution becomes an individual process. Consciousness creates individuality. Before consciousness evolves, there is no individuality. Only species exist, not individuality.

When evolution is still unconscious, it is an automatic process; there is no uncertainty about it. Things happen through the law of cause and effect. Existence is mechanical and certain. But with man, with consciousness, uncertainty comes into existence. Now, nothing is certain. Evolution may take place or it may not. The potential is there, but the choice will rest entirely with each individual. That is why anxiety is a human phenomenon. Below man there is no anxiety because there is no choice. Everything happens as it must. There is no choice so there is no chooser, and in the absence of the chooser, anxiety is impossible. Who is to be anxious? Who is to be tense?

With the possibility of choice, anxiety follows like a shadow. Everything has to be chosen now; everything is a conscious effort.

You alone are responsible. If you fail, you fail. It is your responsibility. If you succeed, you succeed. It is again your responsibility. And every choice is ultimate in a sense. You cannot undo it, you cannot forget it, you cannot go back on it.

Your choice becomes your destiny. It will remain with you and be a part of you; you cannot deny it. But your choice is always a gamble. Every choice is made in darkness because nothing is certain. That is why man suffers from anxiety. He is anxious to his very roots. What torments him, to begin with is, to be or not to be? to do or not to do? to do this or to do that? No choice is not possible. If you do not choose, then you are choosing not to choose; it is a choice. So you are forced to choose; you are not free not to choose. Not choosing will have as much effect as any other choice.

The dignity, the beauty and the glory of man is this consciousness. But it is a burden also. The glory and the burden come simultaneously the minute you become conscious. Every step is a movement between the two. With man, choice and conscious individuality come into existence. You can evolve, but your evolution will be an individual endeavor. You may evolve to become a buddha or you may not. The choice is yours.

So there are two types of evolution: collective evolution and individual, conscious evolution. Evolution implies unconscious, collective progress, so it would be better to use the word revolution in talking about man. With man, revolution becomes possible. Revolution, as I am using the word here, means a conscious, individual effort toward evolution. It is bringing individual responsibility to a peak. Only you are responsible for your own evolution.

Ordinarily, man tries to escape from his responsibility for his own evolution, from the responsibility of freedom of choice. There is a great fear of freedom. When you are a slave the responsibility for your life is never yours; someone else is responsible. So in a way, slavery is a very comfortable thing. There is no burden. In this respect, slavery is a freedom: freedom from conscious choice.

The moment you become completely free, you have to make your own choices. No one forces you to do anything; all alternatives are open to you. Then the struggle with the mind begins, so one becomes afraid of freedom.

Part of the appeal of ideologies such as communism and fascism is that they provide an escape from individual freedom and a shirking of individual responsibility. The burden of responsibility is taken away from the individual; the society becomes responsible. When something goes wrong, you can always point to the state, the organization. Man becomes just a part of the collective structure. But in denying individual freedom, fascism and communism also deny the possibility of human evolution. It is a falling back from the great possibility that revolution offers: the total transformation of human beings. When this happens, you destroy the possibility of achieving the ultimate. You fall back; you again become like animals.

To me, further evolution is possible only with individual responsibility. You alone are responsible! This responsibility is a great blessing in disguise. With this individual responsibility comes the struggle that ultimately leads to choiceless awareness.

The old pattern of unconscious evolution has ended for us. You can fall back into it, but you cannot remain in it. Your being will revolt. Man has become conscious; he has to remain conscious. There is no other way.

Osho – "The Psychology of the Esoteric", Discourse 1

RELIGION: SCIENCE OF THE INNER

Taoism is not a religion in the ordinary sense of the term, it is not a so-called religion; it is authentically religious. But to be authentically religious it has to be basically scientific. Science and religion are separate only as far as their direction is concerned, but not in their approach. Religion can be scientific without being a science; science can be religious without being a religion. Tao is scientific without being a science.

Science means trying to know the objective world without any prejudice, without any *a priori* conclusions. The same is true about the inner world, the subjective world. One should approach it also without any conclusions. A scientist cannot be a Hindu or a Mohammedan or a Christian; if he is then he is not scientific. At least in his scientific endeavor he should put aside all his prejudices.

If Galileo remains a Christian, then he cannot discover the truth that the sun does not move around the earth. If Copernicus remains a Christian even while he is doing his scientific research, then he cannot go beyond the Bible. And the Bible is many thousands of years old; it contains the science of those days. It is very primitive – it is bound to be so.

All religious scriptures contain certain facts which they should not contain. They are not religious facts; they are concerned with the objective world. But in the old days everything was compiled in religious scriptures – they were the only scriptures. Religious scriptures have functioned in the world for thousands of years as encyclopedias: everything that was known, was discovered, was theorized, was collected in them.

The Vedas in India are called *samhitas; samhita* means a compilation, a collection. Their function was exactly that of the Encyclopedia Britannica. All kinds of things are compiled in them: the literature of those days, the science of those days, the astronomy of those days, the geography, the history, the art; everything that it was possible to know was compiled. As man has progressed, everything has become more and more specialized.

Science means the search for truth in the objective world; religion means the search for truth in the subjective world.

Just as there is a world outside you there is a world inside you, too. And, of course, the inside world is far more significant because it is your inside, it is your very being, it is your subjectivity. But about the inner world we are still very unscientific; we still live through beliefs.

About the outside world we have become a little more mature; we are ready to drop any belief. If a certain fact is discovered which goes against our older theories, we discard the older theories in favor of the new discovery. But the same is not true about the inner; to the inner we have a very deep clinging.

Tao is in that way a scientific approach to the inner – you can call it the science of the subjective, the science of being. This is one of the most significant things to remember.

The second thing to remember is that Tao is the first revelation, realization, of the fact that existence is polar. No other religion has been so clear about this tremendously significant fact. 'Existence is polar' means that existence is not logical, it is dialectical; it is not Aristotelian, it is Hegelian.

Logic is simple, logic is linear; dialectics is a little more complex. It is not simple because dialectics is possible only if the opposite is also involved in it; if the opposite is not there, there will be no dialectics. There can be no electricity without the two poles, the positive and the negative. Electricity is not logical, it is utterly illogical. It is dialectical.

There can be no humanity without the masculine energy and the feminine energy. Just think of a humanity consisting only of men or women: it will die, it will not be able to live – it will not have any energy to live. Energy is created by the friction with the opposite.

The Hegelian formulation is: thesis needs antithesis. Unless there is a thesis opposed by an antithesis there is no dynamism; life becomes stagnant. Matter is possible only if there is consciousness, and vice versa. The sky and the earth, God and existence, the day and the night, summer and winter, birth and death, these are polarities opposed to each other. But the opposition is only apparent; deep down they are complementary.

What Hegel discovered just 200 years ago Taoists had discovered almost 5,000 years before. They were the pioneers of dialectics; they were the first dialecticians of the world. They contributed one of the most important insights to existence: you will find it everywhere.

Life cannot exist even for a single moment without its opposite because it depends on the opposite. The opposition is only apparent; deep down they are complementary. They have to be – they depend on each other. Man is not man without a woman, woman is not woman without a man; they depend on each other.

Osho – "Tao: The Golden Gate", Volume 1, Discourse 5

ORDINARY ENLIGHTMENT

Centuries of wrong upbringing have completely confused your mind about enlightenment. The very word seems to be unearthly, other-worldly. The very word seems to be something which is after death or for those who are already dead. This is absolutely wrong.

If you want to be happy there is no other way than enlightenment. If you want to be ordinary, nobody has ever been ordinary without enlightenment. If you want to love and be loved, it is impossible without enlightenment.

So you will have to understand my concept of enlightenment. It is just to be ordinary, healthy, aware, whole, total.

Every mind is seeking some extraordinariness. That is what the ego is: always trying to be somebody in particular, always afraid of being nobody, always afraid of emptiness, always trying to fill the inner void by anything and everything. Every human being is seeking extraordinariness – and that creates misery. It is not possible.

Nobody-ness is your very nature. Non-being is the very stuff you are made of. Howsoever you try you will never succeed; even Alexanders fail. You cannot be somebody because that is not possible in the nature of things. You can only be nobody. But there is nothing wrong in being nobody. In fact, the moment you accept your nobody-ness, immediately bliss starts flowing from you in all directions – because misery disappears.

Misery is the shadow of the ego, the shadow of the ambitious mind. Misery means you are doing something impossible, and because you are failing in it, you are miserable. You are doing something unnatural, trying to do it and failing, so you feel frustrated, miserable.

Hell is nothing but the end result of an impossible, unnatural effort. Heaven is nothing but to be natural. You are nobody. You are born as a nobody-ness with no name, no form. You will die as a nobody. Name and form are just on the surface; deep down you are just a vast space.

And it is beautiful, because if you are somebody you will be limited. It is good that God doesn't allow anybody to be somebody; if you are somebody you will be finite, limited, you will be an imprisoned being. No, God doesn't allow that. He gives you the freedom of nobody-ness – infinite. But you are not ready…

To me, enlightenment is all about this phenomenon: to recognize, to realize, to accept the fact that one is a nobody. Suddenly you stop trying the impossible. Suddenly you stop pulling yourself up by your shoelaces. You understand the absurdity of it and you stop. And laughter spreads over your being. Suddenly you are calm and collected. The very effort of wanting to be somebody is creating trouble.

And when you try to be somebody, you cannot love. An ambitious mind cannot love. It is impossible, because he has first to fulfill his ambition. He has to sacrifice everything for it. He will go on sacrificing his love.

Look at ambitious people: if they are after money they always postpone love. Tomorrow when they have accumulated a lot of money then they will be in love. Right now it is impossible, it is not in any way practical; right now they cannot afford it. Love is a relaxation and they are running after something to achieve, a goal. Maybe it is money, maybe it is power, prestige, politics. How can they love now?

They cannot be here and now – and love is a phenomenon of here and now. Love exists only in the present; ambition exists in the future: love and ambition never meet. You cannot love. And if you cannot love, how can you be loved by anybody else?

Love is a deep communion of two beings who are ready to be together this moment, not tomorrow; who are ready to be total in this moment and forget all past and future. Love is a forgetfulness of the past and the future and a remembrance of this moment, this throbbing moment, this alive moment.

Love is the truth of the moment.

The ambitious mind is never here, he is always on the go. How can you love a running man? He is always in a race, in a competition; he has no time. Or he thinks that somewhere in the future, when the goal is achieved, when he has attained the power he seeks, the riches he desires, then he will relax and love. This is not going to happen, because the goal will never be achieved.

Ambition will never be fulfilled. It is not the nature of it to be fulfilled. You can fulfill one ambition; immediately a thousand other ambitions arise out of it. Ambition never stops. If you follow it, if you understand, it can stop right now. But if you give energy to it, how can you love? That's why people are so miserable trying to be somebody – miserable because they are not getting love, miserable because they cannot love.

Love is an ecstasy: ecstasy of a no-mind, ecstasy of the present, ecstasy of a non-ambitious state, ecstasy of emptiness. Wherever lovers are, there is nobody: only love exists. When two lovers meet they are not two. They may appear two to you from the outside, but the inside story is totally different: they are not two. The moment they meet the two-ness disappears, only love exists and flows.

How is it possible unless you are an emptiness within, a nothingness, so that there is no barrier, nothing between you and your lover? If you are somebody and your lover or beloved is also somebody, then two persons are not meeting but four: two real nobodies who are standing in the background and two somebodies – false egos shaking hands, caressing, making gestures of love. It is a drama to look at, ridiculous!

Whenever lovers meet there is nobody, and two nobodies cannot be two. How can two nothingnesses be two? Nothingnesses have no demarcation line – a nothingness is a vastness. Two nothingnesses become one. Two somebodies remain two.

Your love is an ugly affair, the ugliest. It has to be so. It could have been the most beautiful phenomenon in the world but it has become the ugliest: lovers constantly fighting, quarreling, creating misery for each other. Sartre says, "The other is hell." He is saying something about your love. Whenever you are alone you feel relaxed, whenever you are with the lover a tension arises.

You cannot live alone because the deepest nobody-ness hankers. It has a thirst, a deep hunger. So you cannot remain alone. You have to move: you seek togetherness, but the moment you are together it is a misery. All relationships create misery and nothing else. Unless you are enlightened, love becomes just a conflict, a quarrel. One by and by gets adjusted to it. That means one by and by gets dull, insensitive. That's why the whole world looks so dead, so stale. It stinks. All relationships have gone stale, they have become ugly.

So if you want really to love and be loved, that is not possible right now as you are. You have to disappear. You have to leave so that a clean nothingness is left, a fresh nothingness is left behind. Only then can the flower of love bloom. The seeds are there but the ego is like a rock, and the seeds cannot sprout on it.

If you go to the priests and to the preachers and to the organized religions and the churches, their enlightenment is different. They are against love; they are against ordinariness; they are against friendship; they are against enjoyment; they are against everything that your nature naturally seeks. They are the great poisoners.

But if you have come to me you have come to the right person – the right person in the sense that my enlightenment is of this world. I'm not saying that there is no other world. I am not saying that the earthly existence is the only existence. No, don't misunderstand me. But the other depends on this; the other world depends on this world, and the sky depends on this earth.

If you want to move higher you have to be rooted deeper here in this earth. You need roots in this life, then flowers will come in the other life. The other life is not against this life; in fact, the other life is just the flowering of this life.

God is not against the world, he is not outside it; he is in it, hidden in it. You need not go against the world to seek him – if you go you will never find him. He is hidden here and now. You have to seek, you have to go deep into this existence – and that is the only way to find him. This whole life, this whole existence is nothing but a temple, and he is hiding inside it. Don't escape from it.

Enlightenment is a man who is fully aware of his inner emptiness and is not fighting it; rather, he enjoys it, it is blissful. Through the enjoyment of his own emptiness he becomes available to others; others can enjoy, others can come and participate in his mystery. His doors are open, he invites friends and lovers, and is he is ready to share, he is ready to give.

When you give out of your emptiness you are never afraid of giving because you cannot exhaust the emptiness. You go on giving, you go on giving, you go on giving. It is always there, you cannot exhaust it. Only finite things can be exhausted, that's why they create miserliness – you are afraid to give.

A man who feels he is empty, why should he be afraid to give? He can give himself totally, and unless that is possible love is not possible. Love is a holy phenomenon, love is not profane. Every love worth the name is sacred. And when you enter into love you enter into the world of purity, innocence. When you love you enter the temple of the divine.

Enjoy! I am not for sadness and long faces. I am not here to make you more miserable – you are already too miserable. I am not here to give you more sadness. I am here to awaken you to the bliss that is your birthright, that is naturally available to you.

But you have forgotten how to approach it, and you are going in wrong directions: you seek it somewhere where it is not; you seek it outside and it is inside; you seek it far away and it is near; you seek it in the distant stars and it is just in front of you.

In English there are two words: one is 'obvious'. Obvious means just in front of you. It comes from a Latin root meaning just in front of you. And then there is another word: 'problem'. It comes from a Greek root which also means just in front of you. The root meaning of 'obvious' and 'problem' is the same.

The obvious is the problem, that which is just in front of you is the problem because you cannot see it, your eyes are wandering into distant lands. The obvious has become the problem. And enlightenment is to become aware of the obvious, and when you become aware of the obvious the problem disappears.

To live a life of no problems is to live an enlightened life. It is a totally different way of being: it has nothing to do with achievement, it has nothing to do with learning, it has nothing to do with effort, practice.

The only thing that is needed is to be a little more alert so that you can look at, see, watch that which is in front of you. The solution is closer, very much closer to you than you can imagine.

Don't seek it far away; it exists within you. Once you are settled inside, centered, rooted, I give you all freedom – go and love. Go and be in the world; now you will be able to enjoy it, you will be able to taste it, you will be able to penetrate into its deepest possibilities.

And whenever you enter into the realms of depth, always you will find the divine there. In love, go deep and you will find God. In food, eat well, with alertness, awareness, and you will find God. The Upanishads say *annam brahm,* "the food is God". And the Upanishads say that sex is just a brother, a twin brother, of the final ultimate bliss. A twin brother of the ultimate final bliss – sex! You have condemned it too much. It may be the lowest rung of the ladder but it belongs to the ladder. The highest rung belongs as much as the lowest; in fact, everything belongs to God and is divine.

This is enlightenment: to be able to see in everything the sacred throbbing. Religion is not against anything. Religion is the search to find the holy everywhere.

Osho – "Tao the Three Treasures", Volume 1, Discourse 2

EQUAL VALUE OF MALE & FEMALE PRINCIPLES

Woman came to be looked upon as inferior because she is the recipient. Then the value of the giver went up. The difference in status between man and woman all over the world arose from the fact that man considers himself the giver, the provider, whereas woman considers herself the recipient.

But who said that the receiver must necessarily be inferior? And if there were no one to receive, what use will there be for the giver? And *vice-versa*: if there is no giver, of what use will be the receiver? There is nothing superior and inferior in it. In fact, these two are complementary to each other and neither is independent of the other. They are interdependent; they are tied to each other. These are not two separate entities, but rather two sides of the same coin in which one gives and the other receives.

Normally however, the very concept of the giver raises a picture of superiority within our minds. There is no reason why the receiver should be inferior. Many things are connected with this, however, and the status of women has been accepted as second to men. Not only men but even women have accepted this position. In fact, both are first in their respective places – he as a man and she as a woman. There is no second place; both are complementary.

Now this concept has had extensive consequences in many areas and it has permeated our entire civilization and culture. That is why man went hunting, because he was aggressive. And the woman sat at home waiting for him; she accepted him naturally. He went to the fields, he harvested the crop, he worked in his shop, he flew airplanes, he went to the moon, he went out to do all these things because he was aggressive. The woman sat at home waiting for him. She also did a great many things but was not aggressive; she was receptive. She set up his house, she gathered things together, she kept everything in place.

In all cultures the principle of stability is due to women. If the woman was not there man would have been a wanderer, a vagabond; he could never set up a house. The woman acts as a peg. He wanders here and there but has to return to the peg. If the situation were otherwise he would never have settled down. Then there would have been no towns and cities. City culture came into being because woman wanted to stabilize her living in one place. She always pleads to the man, "Enough! Let us stop; let us halt. A little difficulty may come but let us not go any further."

She catches hold of the soil and grows roots into it. Then man has to make a world around her. That is how towns and cities came into being. This is how all cultures, civilizations and homes, which woman beautified and sanctified, were made. No matter what the man earned or gathered in the outside world, she saved.

Man is never interested in saving. He earns, and there the matter ends; he is no longer interested. He is eager and anxious as long as he is fighting with the world, challenging the world; his attention is always turning to other places for conquest. Whatever he brings there is someone else looking after it all, saving it all, and this individual has her own place, her own value.

She is a complementary part of the whole situation, but as she does not go out to earn, as she does not accumulate, as she does not create, it seemed to her that she was lagging behind. This feeling entered even into very small things, and everywhere she began to feel a sense of inferiority which is absolutely unfounded.

This inferiority brought evil results. As long as woman was uneducated she tolerated this inferiority, but now she will not. In order to break this sense of inferiority she has gone about doing exactly what men do. This will prove very detrimental to her. She can violate her basic personality, and this can have destructive results deep within her psyche. Now she wants to be on a level with man, but she cannot be like a man completely. She will only succeed in making herself a second-rate man; she cannot be a first-rate man. She can, if she chooses, make herself first-rate in her womanhood. There is no evaluation in this.

There will be a difference, and it will not be in spiritual practice so much as in the state of mind. For instance, when the meditation method is one and the same, even then a man will go about it aggressively, whereas a woman will go about it in a passive way. The man will attack, the woman will surrender.

The method will be the same but the attitudes will be different. When a man enters into spiritual practice he catches it by the neck, so to speak, but when a woman starts a spiritual practice she will place her head at its feet.

This difference in attitude is natural and there is no more difference between the two than this. The woman's attitude will be that of surrender: when she reaches she will not say that she has attained God; rather, she will say that she is fortunate that God has taken her unto himself. When man reaches the ultimate he will not say that God has taken him in; he feels that he has *attained* God. The difference is in their comprehension.

Doing nothing, one feels as if one is a fool. One has to do something. If you cannot do anything, at least smoke. People start smoking whenever they don't have anything to do; smoking is a complementary thing. Whenever you don't have anything to do at least you can smoke; you feel occupied.

People feel foolish if they have nothing to do. Have you not observed this phenomenon in yourself? If you are just sitting, you start feeling restless; you have to do something. If somebody comes, you will pretend to do. You will start reading the same newspaper you have read already just for show. Somebody has come, so you take the newspaper in your hand so that he knows you are doing something; otherwise, he will think you are a fool. What are you doing? A man has to do something always and always, and continuously. People pretend, they cannot just be – it is not allowed.

In the West you have the saying that "The empty mind is the devil's workshop". If somebody is not doing anything that is dangerous. In fact, the active mind is the devil's workshop. The empty mind has never done anything wrong to anybody. Hitler is not an empty mind, Buddha is an empty mind. Genghis Khan is not an empty mind, Chuang Tzu is.

A passive, inactive, empty mind has a beauty, and only in the inactive mind one comes to know what is true. The activity creates the illusion. The activity creates ripples around you and you cannot see that which is.

Inactivity...all ripples gone, the lake silent...the mind has no thought; everything disappeared, the smoke gone, and the flame burns bright.

When the consciousness burns so bright that there is no smoke and the flame is pure, then you know what is real.

The way to reality is through inaction, passivity, receptivity. The way to the real is through feminine receptivity. The way to the unreal is through male, aggressive activity.

Osho – "In Search of the Miraculous", Discourse 18

Man and woman differ basically; they not only differ, they are opposites. That's why there is so much attraction. Attraction can exist only between opposites; the similar cannot be very attractive – whatsoever you are, you are acquainted with it. For a man, the woman is the unknown. It attracts, it invokes, it invites; an inquiry arises, a curiosity arises. For woman, the man is the unknown. For man, God penetrates through this world in the shape of woman, because God is the unknown. For woman, man represents the divine because he is the unknown for her. Hence, the opposite is so significant.

So the first thing to be understood: they are different; not only different, but opposites – but they are not unequal, they are equal. Difference is there, oppositeness is there, a polarity is there, but they are not unequal, they are equal. Two opposites are always equal, otherwise they cannot oppose each other.

In the ultimate culmination, in the crescendo of spiritual being, the male becomes female as much as the female becomes male. A woman will have to transform her unconscious into conscious, her irrationality into reasonableness, her faith into an inquiry, her waiting into a movement.

And a man will have to do exactly the opposite: he will have to make his movement into a rest, his restlessness into a tranquility, into a stillness, his doubt into trust; and he will have to dissolve his reason into the irrational. Then a suprarational being is born.

From both sides they have to move: man has to move from his manhood, woman has to move from her womanhood. Because a mind which is male is half, and the half cannot know the whole; a mind which is female is half, and the half can never know the whole. Both have to move from their static positions, become liquid, melt into each other, become asexual.

Hindus are very clear about it: their term for the ultimate, *Brahma*, does not belong to either gender. In English it is difficult because there are only two genders, but in Sanskrit they have three genders: one for male, one for female, and one for one who has transcended both. *Brahma* is the third, neutral gender, and one who reaches *Brahma* becomes *Brahma*-like: male will not be male, and female will not be female, their oppositeness will disappear. And only then is being complete; then being is free, then being is liberated.

For a man like Jesus it is not a question of male or female, it is a question of becoming whole. One has to leave his part and reach the whole. So don't think that you are a male and therefore you have some priority; don't think that you are a male, so God is nearer to you; don't think that you are a male, so you have nothing to do, that you have already done much just by being a male. No, you also will have to become female, just as a female has to become male. You both have to move from your static states and become dynamic, merging into each other. You both have to go beyond the parts and become the whole.

So I would like to tell you that I will lead the males to become females, and I will lead the females to become males, so that both are dissolved, so that transcendence is achieved and sex disappears, because sex exists on the division.

Are you aware of what the word sex means? The original root in Latin means division, to divide. So when you reach God you will be neither male nor female. If you are male you are still divided – how can you reach the whole? Try to understand that the part has to be left so that you can become whole. You should not be identified with any division, so that the indivisible can enter into you.

Every male has to become like the female, because he has also to learn waiting; he has also to learn receptivity; he has also to learn nonaggression, passivity; he has also to learn compassion, love, service – all the qualities of the feminine mind. Then only, when you are whole – neither male nor female – do you become capable of entering into the kingdom. Then you are a god yourself, because God is neither male nor female – he is both, or neither.

Remember that other part of the truth also, otherwise you will miss. Nobody is more capable of entering into the divine, nobody is less capable. There are differences, but on the whole, if you take account of the whole, everybody is equally capable of entering into the divine; everybody, I say, is equally capable. But there are foolish people who will always use their negative qualities, then they cannot enter. And there are wise people who will use their positive qualities, then they can enter.

For example: the feminine mind has both qualities, the negative and the positive. The positive is love, the negative is jealousy; the positive is sharing, the negative is possessiveness; the positive is waiting, the negative is lethargy, because waiting can look as if it is waiting and it may not be, it may be just lethargy.

A man has a positive quality that he is in search of rest, and a negative quality that he is restless. Just because he is restless, there is no need for him to get identified with it. You can use your restlessness as a jumping-board to attain a restful repose. You have an energy, an urge to do something – you can use that urge to become a non-doer, you can use that urge to be a meditator.

The negative has to be used in the service of the positive, and each has both. Wherever there is a positive quality, just by the side exists the negative. If you pay too much attention to the negative you will miss; pay much attention to the positive and you will attain.

Male or female, both have to do that. Then happens the most beautiful phenomenon in the world. That phenomenon is an indivisible person, a one, a unity, an inner cosmos; a symphony where all the notes have become helpers to each other, not just a noise, but they give rhythm, color to the whole. They make the whole, they create the whole, they are not against the whole, they are not fragments anymore, they have fallen into a unity. This is what Gurdjieff calls 'inner crystallization', or what Hindus have called 'attaining to the self', and what Jesus calls 'entering into the kingdom of God'.

Osho – "Seeds of Revolution" or "The Mustard Seed", Discourse 18

MATURING

Question: *You have told me that my mind is immature. What does it mean to have a mind that is mature?*

To think that you know is to be immature. To function from knowledge, from conclusion, is to be immature. To function from no-knowledge, from no conclusion, from no past, is maturity.

Maturity is a deep trust in your own consciousness; immaturity is a distrust in your own consciousness. When you distrust your consciousness you trust your knowledge; but that is a substitute and a very poor substitute at that. Try to understand this - it is important.

You have been living, you have experienced many things; you have read, you have listened, you have thought. Now all those conclusions are there. When a certain situation arises, you can function in two ways. You can function through all the accumulated past, according to it - that's what I mean by functioning through conclusions, through experience, stale, dead - then whatsoever you do your response is not going to be a response, it will be a reaction. And to be reactionary is to be immature.

Or, if you can function right now, here in this moment, through your consciousness, through your being aware, putting aside all that you have known - this is what I call functioning through no-knowledge, this is functioning through innocence. And this is maturity.

I was reading one anecdote…

It seemed to Mr. Smith that now that his son had turned 13, it was important to discuss those matters which an adolescent ought to know about life. So he called the boy into the study one evening, shut the door carefully, and said with impressive dignity, "Son, I would like to discuss the facts of life with you."

"Sure thing, dad." said the boy. "What do you want to know?"

The mind is immature when it is not ready to learn. The ego feels very fulfilled if it need not learn anything from anybody; the ego feels very enhanced if it feels that it already knows. But the problem is that life goes on changing, it is never the same; it goes on flowing, it is a flux. And your knowledge is always the same. Your knowledge is not evolving with life, it is stuck somewhere in the past, and whenever you react through it you will miss the point because it will not be exactly the right thing to do. Life has changed but your knowledge remains the same, and you act out of this knowledge. That means you face today with your yesterday's knowledge. You will never be able to be alive. The more you function through knowledge, the more immature you become.

Now let me tell you a paradox: every child who is innocent is mature.

Maturity has nothing to do with age because it has nothing to do with experience; maturity has something to do with responsiveness, freshness, virginity, innocence. So when I use the word 'mature' I don't mean that when you become more experienced you will be more mature. That's what people usually mean when they use the word - I don't mean that. The more you gather knowledge, the more your mind will become immature; and by the time you are 70 or 80, you will be completely immature because you will have a stale past to function through.

Watch a small child...knowing nothing, having no experience, he functions here and now. That's why children can learn more than aged people. Psychologists say that if a child is not forced to learn, not forced to discipline himself, he can learn any foreign language in 3 months. Just left to himself with people who know the language he will catch it in 3 months. But if you force him to learn, it will take almost 3 years, because the more you force, the more he starts functioning through whatsoever he learns, through yesterday's knowledge. If he is left to himself he moves freely, spontaneously; learning comes easy, by itself, on its own accord.

By the time the child reaches the year 8 he has learned almost 70% of whatsoever he is going to learn in his whole life. He may live 80 years, but by the time he is 8 he has learned 70%. He will learn only 30% more, and every day his capacity to learn will be less and less and less. The more he knows, the less he learns.

When people use the word 'maturity' they mean more knowledge; when I use the word 'maturity' I mean the capacity to learn. Not to know but to learn - and they are different, totally different, diametrically opposite things. Knowledge is a dead thing; the capacity to learn is an alive process - you simply remain capable of learning, you simply remain available, you simply remain open, ready to receive. Learning is receptivity. Knowledge makes you less receptive because you go on thinking that if you already know, what is there to learn? When you already know you miss much; when you don't know anything you cannot miss anything.

The immature mind is always interested in trivia. The immature mind is always interested in things: money, houses, cars, power, prestige - all trivia, all rot. The mature mind is interested in existence, in being, in life itself. So when I say to you that you have an immature mind I mean you are still interested in things, not in persons; still interested in the outside, not in the inside; still interested in objects, not in subjectivity; still interested in the finite, not interested in the infinite.

When I say, "Be mature", I mean become a no-mind. If you act spontaneously, you will act out of no-mind. If you remain capable of learning, you will remain capable of being a no-mind again and again and again - the mind will never be accumulated. If you are capable of remaining alert and spontaneous, able to be surprised by life and by yourself, you will become by and by more and more interested in the interior-most life, in the core of life.

Once you know your supreme value, you have become mature; and once you know your supreme value, you know the supreme value of all. All beings are Buddhas - nobody is less than that; the whole of life is Divine; you are always walking on holy ground.

Osho – "Ancient Music in the Pines", Discourse 2

THE ROOTS OF VIOLENCE

The more violent a mind is, the more full of attachment it is. Violence and attachment live together, side by side. A non-violent mind transcends attachment. In fact, one who wants to be non-violent has to let go of the very idea of attachment. The very sense of 'mine' is violence, because as soon as I say 'mine', I have begun to separate myself from that which is not mine. As soon as I address someone as a friend, I have begun to make someone else my enemy. As soon as I draw a line around those who are mine, I have also drawn a line around those who are strangers to me. All violence is the outcome of the boundary created between those who are 'mine' and those who are outsiders, 'not mine'.

The 'I' is nothing but a name for the sum total of what we call 'our own people'. What we call 'I' is the name for all the accumulations of 'mine'. If all those who are 'mine' are to leave, then I will be no more, then I cannot remain. This 'I' of mine is attached partly to my father, partly to my mother, partly to my friend - to all of these people.

What is even more surprising is that this 'I' is not only attached to those whom we call our own, but it is also attached to those whom we consider outsiders, or 'not mine'. Although this attachment is outside our circle, nonetheless it is there.

Hence, when my enemy dies, we also die a little, since I will not be able to be exactly the same as I was when my enemy was alive. Even my enemy has been contributing something to my life. He as my enemy. He may have been an enemy but he was *'my'* enemy. My 'I' was related to him too: without him I will be incomplete.

'Mine-ness' is nothing but violence. It is a deeper violence; it is not seen. The moment I call someone 'mine', possession has begun. Possessiveness is a form of violence. The husband calls his wife 'mine'; possession has begun. The wife calls the husband 'mine'; possession has begun. But whenever we become a person's owner, right there and then we damn that person's soul. We have just killed that person; we have destroyed that person the moment we claim ownership over him or her.

In fact, by owning a person we treat them not as an individual but as an object. Then the wife becomes 'mine' the same way that a house is mine. Naturally, whenever there is a relationship of 'mine', love is not the outcome. What manifests is only conflict. This is why in this world as long as a husband and wife or a father and son keep claiming their ownership over each other, only conflict can happen between them - never friendship. The assertion of such ownership is the cause of the friendship's destruction. Such an assertion of ownership puts everything awry; everything becomes violent.

Whenever there is an assertion of ownership, only hatred is created; and where there is hatred, violence is bound to follow. That is why all our relationships have become relationships of violence. Our families have come to be nothing but relationships of violence.

Osho – from the book, "Inner War and Peace"

WHY CAN'T MODERN MAN AND WOMAN LOVE?

Love is spontaneous. It cannot be controlled. You cannot 'make' love; you cannot do anything about it. And the more you do, the more you will miss it. You have to allow it to happen. You are not needed for it. Your presence is the hindrance. The more you are absent, the better.

When you are not, love happens. Because of their inability to be absent, modern man and woman have become incapable of love. They are capable of doing things. The whole modern mind is based on doing. Whatsoever can be done, modern man can do more efficiently than any man that has ever existed. Whatsoever can be done, we can do more efficiently. We are the most efficient century; we have turned everything into technology, into a problem of how to do it.

We have developed one dimension and that is the dimension of doing, but in developing this dimension we have lost much. At the loss of being we have learned how to do things, so that which can be done we do better than anyone – better than any society that ever existed on earth.

When the question of love comes, a problem arises because love cannot be done. And not only is this so with love; we have become incapable of all that cannot be done. For example, meditation: we have become incapable of it; it cannot be done. Or play: we have become incapable of it; it cannot be done. Or joy, happiness: we have become incapable of them because they cannot be done. They are not acts; you cannot manipulate them. On the contrary, you have to let yourself go. Then joy happens to you, then happiness comes to you, then love enters you, then love takes possession. And because of this possession we have become afraid.

Modern man, the modern mind, wants to possess everything and not be possessed by anything. Modern man wants to be the master of everything, and you can only be the master of things, not of happenings. You can be the master of a house; you can be the master of a mechanical device. You cannot be the master of anything which is alive. Life cannot be mastered; you cannot possess it. On the contrary, you have to be possessed by it. Only then is there contact with it.

Love is life, and it is greater than you. You cannot possess it. I would like to repeat it: love is greater than you; you cannot possess it. You can only allow yourself to be possessed by it; it cannot be controlled.

The modern ego wants to control everything, and you become scared of whatsoever you cannot control. You become afraid; you close the door. You close that dimension completely because fear enters. You will not be in control. With love you cannot be in control, and the whole trend which has led to this century was one of how to control.

All over the world, and particularly in the West, the trend is for how to control nature, how to control everything, how to control energies. Man must become the master, and you have become the master – of course, only of those things which are possible to possess; and side by side you have been developing an incapacity for those things which cannot be possessed.

You can possess money; you cannot possess love. And because of this we have been turning everything into a thing. You even go on turning persons into things because then you can possess them. If you love a person, you are not the master; no one is the master. Two persons love each other, and no one is the master, neither the lover nor the beloved. Rather, love is the master, and both are possessed by a greater force than themselves, encircled by a greater force, a whirlwind. If they try to possess each other, they will miss. Then they can possess each other. Then the lover will become the husband and the beloved will become the wife. Then they can possess, but a husband is a thing, and a wife is a thing. They are not persons. You can possess them. They are dead entities, legal labels, not alive.

We go on turning persons into things just to possess them, and then we feel frustrated, because we wanted to possess the person and the person cannot be possessed. When you possess a person, he is no more a person; he is a dead thing, and you cannot be fulfilled by a dead thing. Look at this contradiction: you can be fulfilled only by persons, never by things, but your mind desires possessions, so you turn them into things. Then you cannot be fulfilled. Then frustration sets in.

Possessiveness, the attitude to possess, has killed the capacity to love. Don't think in terms of possession. Rather, think in terms of being possessed. That is what surrender means – being possessed: you allow yourself to be possessed by something greater than you. Then you will not be in control. Then a greater force will take you. Then the direction will not be yours. Then you cannot choose the goal. Then the future is unknown; you cannot be secure now.

Moving with a greater force than yourself, you are insecure, afraid. If you are afraid and insecure, it is better not to move with great forces. Just work with lower forces than you; then you can be the master, and you can decide the goal beforehand. Then you will achieve the goal, but you will not get anything out of it. You will have just wasted your life.

The secret of love and the secret of prayer and the secret of anything that can make you fulfilled is surrender, the capacity to be possessed. The problem with love exists because this capacity is not there. There are other reasons also, but this is the base.

There is also too much emphasis on intellect, reason. Man is lopsided. Your head has grown, and your heart has remained absolutely neglected. And love is not a capacity of the intellect. It has a different center; it has a different locus, source. It is in your heart; it is your feeling; it is not reasoning.

But the whole modern education consists of reasoning, logic, intellect, mind. The heart is not even talked about. It is denied, really; it is just a poetic fiction. It is not! It is a reality! Just look at it in this way: If from the very beginning a child is brought up without any training of the mind or the reasoning, without any intellectual training, will he have an intellect? He cannot!

There have been such cases…. Sometimes it has happened that wolves have brought up a human child. Just ten years before, one child was caught in a forest. The wolves had brought him up. He was fourteen years of age. He couldn't even stand on two legs; he would run on all fours. He couldn't speak a single word; he would roar like a wolf. He was in every way a wolf, and fourteen years of age. Those who caught him named him, Ram. The child took six months to learn the name.

Within a year the child died, and the psychologists who worked on him suspected that he died because of too much strain on the intellect. This forcing, this training to get him to stand on two feet, this memory training to get him to remember the name, the effort to make him a human being, killed him. He was robust in health when he was caught, healthier than any human being ever is. He was just like an animal. But this training killed him. Every effort was made so that if you could have asked him, " What is your name?" he would be able to say "Ram." This was his whole intellect. After six months of constant training, punishment, creating a profit motive in him, the only proof that the child could give of his intellect was this much: he would be able to say "Ram."

What happened? If someone from Mars could get hold of this child, he would think that humanity has no mind, no intellect, no reason.

The same has happened to the heart. Without training it is as if it is not. It has been completely neglected, so your whole life energy has been forced towards the head, not towards the heart, and love is a functioning of the heart center.

This is why modern man has become incapable of love: modern man has become incapable of the heart. He calculates, and love is not a calculation. He knows arithmetic and love is not arithmetic. He thinks in terms of logic and love is illogical. He always tries to rationalize everything. Whatsoever he is doing reason must support it, and love is not supported by reason.

Really, when you fall in love you throw your reason completely. That is why we say man 'falls' in love. Falls from where? Falls from the head down into the heart. We use this term of condemnation, 'falling in love', because the head, the reason, cannot look at it without condemning it. It is a fall. Is love really a fall or a rising? Do you become more with it or do you become less? Do you expand or do you shrink?

With love you become more! Your consciousness is more, your feeling is more; your ecstatic sensation is more, your sensitivity is more. You are more alive, but one thing is less: reasoning is less. You cannot reason it out; it is blind. As far as reason is concerned it is blind. The heart has its own reason – that is another thing – and the heart has its own eyes, but that is another thing. The eyes of reason are not there, so reason says it is a fall; you have fallen.

Unless the heart center starts functioning again man will not be capable of love, and the whole misery of modern life is because unless he loves he cannot feel any meaning in his life. Life looks meaningless. Love gives it meaning; love is the only meaning.

Unless you are capable of love you will be meaningless, and you will feel that you are existing without any meaning, futilely, and suicide will become attractive. Then you will like to kill yourself, to finish with yourself, to end, because what is the use of existing? Mere existing cannot be tolerated.

Existence must have a meaning; otherwise, what is the use? Why go on prolonging yourself unnecessarily? Why go on repeating the same pattern every day? Getting out of the bed and doing the same thing, and again falling asleep and the next day the same pattern: why? You have done it so far, and what has happened? And you will do it unless death comes and relieves you of your body. So what is the use?

Love gives meaning. It is not that through love any result comes into being or any goal – no! Through love every moment becomes of value in itself. Then you never ask this. If someone asks what is the meaning of life, know well that love is lacking. Whenever someone asks what is the meaning of life, he is asking because he has not been able to flower in a love experience.

Whenever someone is in love, he never asks what is the meaning of life. He knows the meaning; there is no need to ask. He knows the meaning! The meaning is there: love is the meaning in life.

And through love prayer is possible because prayer is again a love relationship – not between two individuals, but between one individual and Existence itself. Then the whole Existence becomes your beloved or lover. But it is possible only through love experience that you can grow into prayer or into meditation, and the ultimate ecstasy is just like love.

That is why Jesus says that "God is love," not that "God is loving." Christians have been interpreting it in this way – that God is kind, loving. That is not the meaning. Jesus says that God is love. He simply equates God and love. You can say "love" or you can say "God"; they both mean the same. God is not loving; God is love itself. If you can love, you have entered the divine. And when your love grows to such an infinity that it is not concerned with anyone in particular – rather, it has become a diffused phenomenon; when there is no lover for you – rather, the whole Existence, all that is, has become the lover or beloved – then it has become prayer.

And Tantra is a love method. So, the first thing is how to love, and then the second thing is how to grow in love so that love becomes prayer. But one must start from love. And don't be afraid of love because that fear shows you are afraid of the heart.

The head is cunning; the heart is innocent. With the head you feel protected; with the heart you become vulnerable, open. Anything can happen. That is why we have become closed. The fear is there: if you are vulnerable, anything can happen to you; someone can deceive you. With the mind no one can deceive you; you can deceive others. But I tell you be ready to be deceived, but don't close the heart. Be ready to be deceived, but don't close the heart!

That vulnerability to be deceived is of worth because you will not lose anything by it. And if you are ready to be deceived infinitely, only then can you believe in the heart. If you are calculative, cunning, clever, too much clever, then you will miss the heart, and modern man is so educated, so sophisticated, so clever; that is why he has become incapable of love.

Women were not like this, but they are following modern man fast; they are copying modern man fast. Sooner or later, they will become just like man, or they may even overtake him. Now they are also becoming incapable because the same head orientation, the same effort to be cunning and clever, is there now. They may form a 'Women's Liberation Movement' or anything like it, but it is not heart oriented. It is just a copy of the same stupidity that man has been doing with himself. You may go to the other extreme, but if you react, even in your reaction you are following.

A great crisis is there. It is difficult now to prevent women all over the world from copying man and his nonsense because man seems to be so successful. He is successful in a way; he has become the master of things. Now he possesses the whole world. Now he feels he has conquered nature, and 'success succeeds; nothing succeeds like success.'

Now women feel that man has succeeded and has become the master, so they must copy him. But look also at the thing in which man has failed completely: he has lost his heart; he cannot love.

Reason alone is not enough, and reason in control is dangerous. The heart must be higher than reason because reason is just an instrument, and the heart is you. The heart must be allowed to use reason - not *vice versa*. But you have been doing that. The head is allowed to dominate; in its domination, the head has killed the heart.

And thirdly, one thing more has to be remembered as to why modern man has become incapable of love. Love is basically a sort of madness, a sort of deep participation with nature, a sort of dissolving of the ego. It is primal. You are born out of love; your every cell of the body is a love cell. Your very energy, your life energy, is a love energy. You exist in it, but there is no ego in that energy. You cannot feel 'I'. That energy is unconscious, and when you move in love you become unconscious. Only a fragment of your mind is conscious, and in that fragment of the mind exists the ego.

The mind has three layers. First is the unconscious: when you are deeply asleep with no dreams, you are in it. The child in the mother's womb is absolutely unconscious, he is just part of the mother. The child is not aware that 'I am separate'; he is just part of the mother. There is no separation, no defined existence. He is undifferentiated from the mother and from the existence itself. There is no fear because fear comes only when you become aware of yourself. The child is totally at ease; he is unconscious.

And the second layer is of consciousness. It is a very small fragment. One tenth part of the unconscious has become conscious in you through training, education, society, family. It was needed for survival, so a part of you has become conscious. But that part also gets tired very soon; that is why you need sleep. In sleep you become again a child in the womb. You have fallen back; the conscious is no more there. It has become part of the unconscious. That is why sleep is so refreshing. In the morning you feel alive again, fresh, because you have fallen back into the mother's womb.

Sleep refreshes you. Why? Because the conscious mind gets tired. It is just a part, and the Whole is unconscious. It must fall back to the Whole to become revived. It is again resurrected. That is why in the morning you feel good, and morning looks beautiful – not only because morning is beautiful, but because again you have a child's eyes. The afternoon is not so beautiful: the world is the same, but you have lost those innocent eyes again. And the evening becomes ugly because you are tired. You have lived too much in the conscious. This conscious has ego as the center. These are two ordinary states which we know.

The third state is the superconscious. Superconscious means that your whole unconscious has become conscious. In the unconscious there is no ego; you are total. In the superconscious again there is no ego; you are total. But in between the two the conscious mind has a center – the ego. This ego is the problem, this ego creates problems.

You cannot fall in love because then you will have to become unconscious, just as unconscious as you become in sleep. Or, if you want to rise to prayer, you have to become totally conscious like a Buddha or like a Meera. So love becomes impossible, prayer becomes impossible. The ego creates the barrier. You cannot lose yourself, and love is losing, dispersing, dissolving, melting.

If you melt into the unconscious, it is love; if you melt into the superconscious it is prayer – but both are a melting. So what is to be done?

Remember this: you cannot do anything about it. Let it be deeply noted: you cannot do anything about love, about prayer. Your conscious mind is impotent; it cannot do anything. It has to be lost; it has to be put aside. And then remember surrender: whenever you want to move beyond yourself, surrender is the way – either in love or in prayer.

Whenever you long to move beyond, somewhere else where you are not, then surrender, let-go is the path. Allow something to happen to you; don't manipulate. And once you know how to allow, many things will start happening.

You may not be even aware of what is possible for you, of what a great, tremendous energy you have closed within yourself which can explode and then become an ecstasy. Your whole life will be filled with consciousness, light and bliss. But you don't know it.

It is just as if every atom is an atom bomb: if one atom explodes, tremendous energy is released. And every heart is also an atom bomb.

If it explodes in love or prayer, tremendous energy is released. But you have to explode and lose yourself. The seed has to lose itself; only then is the tree born. And if the seed resists and says, 'No, I must survive,' then the seed can survive, but the tree will never be born. And unless the tree is born the seed will feel frustrated, because the tree is the meaning. The seed will feel frustrated! The seed can feel fulfilled only when the tree is there flowering. But then the seed has to lose itself, die.

Modern man has become incapable of love because he has become incapable of death. He cannot die to anything. He clings to life; he cannot die to anything.

In old English, three or four hundred years ago, this was a usual expression. The lover would say to the beloved, "I want to die in you." This was a love expression. It is beautiful: "I want to die in you."

Love is a death, a death of the ego; only then is your real self born. And modern man is very, very afraid of death. In every way, surrender is death, love is death, and life also is a continuous death. If you are afraid, you will miss life itself.

Be ready to die every moment. Die to the past, die to the future, and die in the present moment. Don't cling and don't resist. Don't make any effort for life, and you will have abundant life.

Life will happen to you if you are ready to die. This looks paradoxical, but this is the law. Jesus says that one who is ready to lose will gain, and one who clings will lose everything.

Osho – "Vigyan Bhairav Tantra", Volume 2, Discourse 4

DON'T THROW RESPONSIBILITY ON THE OTHER

Question: *Osho, I know my love stinks, so why do I cling to the smell?*

We live according to the past: our lives are rooted in the dead past; we are conditioned by the past. The past is very powerful, that's why you go on living in a certain pattern; even if it stinks, you will go on repeating it. You don't know what else to do; you have become conditioned to it. It is a mechanical phenomenon. And this is not only so with you, it is so with almost every human being – unless he becomes a Buddha.

To become a Buddha means to get rid of the past and to live in the present. The past is immense, very huge, enormous, of millions of lives. You have lived in a certain way. Now, being here, you may have become aware that your love stinks, but that awareness is also not very deep, it is very superficial. If it becomes really deep, if it penetrates to the very core of your being, you will immediately jump out of it.

It is like if your house is on fire: you will not ask anybody how to get out of it. You will not consult the Encyclopedia Britannica, and you will not wait for some wise man to come and tell you, and you will not consider whether it is appropriate to jump out of the window or not – you won't bother about anything. Even if you are taking a bath naked you will jump naked out of the window; you won't even bother about clothes. When the house is on fire, your life is at risk; now everything else is secondary. If your love stinks, and this has become your experience, then you will come out of it. You will not simply ask a question, you will jump out of it.

But I think that it is just an intellectual idea, because each time you are in love, some misery arises. Each time there is some conflict, some struggle, some fight, some jealousy, some possessiveness. So you have started taking an intellectual standpoint: "My love stinks, so why do I cling to the smell?" Because it is not yet really an existential experience for you.

And it is your own smell. One becomes accustomed to one's own smell. That's why when people aresalone, they don't experience that smell, they experience it only when they are together with somebody.

When you are in love, then you start showing your real face. Love is a mirror. The other starts functioning like a mirror. Every relationship becomes a mirror. Alone, you don't experience your own smell – you cannot; one becomes immune to it. You have lived with it so long, how can you smell it? It is only with the other that you start feeling that he stinks and he starts feeling that you stink. And the fight starts. That is the story of all the couples all over the world.

"Where are you going with that goat, Juan?" asked the policeman.

"I'm taking him home to keep as a pet!" replied Juan.

"In the house?"

"Sure thing."

"But what about the smell?"

"So what? He ain't gonna mind the smell!"

Your own smell is not disturbing to you. In fact, if it suddenly disappears you will feel a little jolted, you will feel a little uprooted, you will not feel your natural self; you will feel something has gone wrong.

If you love and there is no jealousy you will start wondering whether you love or not. What kind of love is this? There seems to be no jealousy! You love a man, and if the man goes with another woman once in a while, you don't make much fuss about it. You take it for granted – it is perfectly good for a change. And if your man is happy, why not let him be happy? You love him. If you really love him, you will respect his happiness too. And he is not going forever.

In fact, if once in a while couples are allowed a little freedom, they will not separate; the divorce rate will drop in the world. Divorce exists only because marriage is too tight. Let marriage be a little more relaxed and divorce will disappear. Divorce is only a by-product of marriage. The tighter the marriage system, the more divorce becomes an absolute need. And if divorce is not allowed, then you have double lives: one to show to the society and one to live.

It is because of marriage that prostitution exists in the world. The whole blame goes to the marriage system. If people are a little more loving and less jealous and if they understand human nature, it is simple.

You eat the same food every day; you get fed up with it and once in a while you would like to go to the hotel. And the hotel food may be worse than what you get in your home, but even that is good – at least that makes your home food look better. And when you come back the next day you feel so relieved that you are back home, and you are so happy to have the same food again!

The more man's mind is understood, the more and more marriage will have to be relaxed. It is perfectly okay to give a few days off in marriage. The woman should be allowed to have her boyfriends and the man should be allowed to have his girlfriends – at least, just as you have Sunday religion, a Sunday marriage! And you will be surprised that your own wife looks far better. Again, a honeymoon starts – a mini-honeymoon. You again start from ABC.

And being with many women and with many men does not destroy marriage – no, not at all. It is a very nonsensical idea that has prevailed over humanity: that it is destructive to marriage and family. It is not so – it is very supportive. It will help the family to be more joyous, less quarrelsome. Otherwise, the woman is constantly spying on the husband and the husband is constantly spying on the woman. And what love can exist between two persons who are constantly at each other's throats?

Yes, your love stinks, as everybody else's love stinks, but you feel it only when you are in relationship. You have not yet felt that it really has something to do with you. Deep down you still feel it must be something wrong with the other. That's how the mind functions: it throws the responsibility on the other. It accepts itself and it is always finding faults in others.

Several people are sitting in the front row of a movie theater. The show has already begun when suddenly there is a terrible smell. One of the spectators turns to the man sitting beside him and asks, "Did you shit in your trousers?"

The man beside him answers, "Yes, why?"

People accept themselves totally! Whatsoever they are doing is right: "Why? What is wrong in it? They are his own trousers, so who are you to interfere? And freedom is everybody's birthright!"

If your love stinks, then try to find out what exactly it is that stinks. It is not love; it is something else. Love itself has a fragrance; it can't stink, it is a lotus flower. Something else must be in it – jealousy, possessiveness. But you have not mentioned jealousy and possessiveness. You are hiding them. Love never stinks, it cannot; that is not the nature of love. Please try to see exactly what it is that creates the trouble. And I am not saying to repress it. All that is needed is a clarity about it – what it is.

If it is jealousy, then I would only suggest one thing: be more watchful of your jealousy. When it arises next time, rather than becoming mad, close your doors, sit silently, sit in meditation, watch your jealousy. See exactly what it is. It will surround you like smoke, dirty smoke. It will suffocate you. You would like to go out and do something. But don't do anything; just be in a state of non-doing, because anything done in a moment of jealousy is going to be destructive. Just watch. And I am not saying repress it, because that is again doing something.

People are either expressive or repressive, and both ways are wrong. If you express, you become destructive to the other person. Whosoever is your victim suffers, and he is going to take revenge. He may not take revenge consciously, but unconsciously it is going to happen.

Just a few months ago, Krishna Bharti fell in love with a woman. Nothing extraordinary about it, but Deeksha got mad! Deeksha could not accept the idea. For centuries we have been told that if a man loves you or a woman loves you and the man or the woman goes to somebody else, that is a rejection of you.

That is utter nonsense. It is not rejection; in fact, it is just the opposite. If a man loves the woman and he enjoys the woman, he starts fantasizing how it will be with other women. It is really the joy that this woman has given him that triggers his fancy. It is not that he is rejecting this woman; it is really an indication that this woman has been such a nourishment that he would like to see and know how other women are. And if a little rope is given, he is not going to go very far, he will come back, because with the other woman it may be novelty, it will be something new, but it can't be that nourishing because there will not be any intimacy. It will have something empty about it. It will be sex without love.

Love needs time to grow, it needs intimacy to grow. It needs a really long time. It is not a seasonal flower that is there within three, four weeks, but then within three, four weeks it is gone too. It is a long, long process of intimacy. Slowly, slowly, two persons melt and merge into each other; then it becomes nourishing. The other woman or the other man cannot be nourishing. It may be just an adventure, a thrill. But then suddenly the feeling will arise – it is bound to arise – that it is good as fun, but it is not nourishing. And the person will be back.

And Krishna Bharti would have been back, but Deeksha went mad. She behaved just like any other woman! But I was waiting...sooner or later she was going to take revenge. Now she is taking revenge. Krishna Bharti fell ill, he was in the hospital, and Deeksha had a little freedom. She fell in love with her own handyman! He really proved handy! Now K.B. is in hell.

There is no need to be so worried about it. I have given K.B. a message: ”Wait, don’t be worried. Just let her take revenge. And it is good that unconscious burden is finished.”

If we understand each other a little more, if we understand human nature a little more, there should be no jealousy. But it is a past heritage of centuries.

So, Amrito, I cannot say you can drop it right now. You will have to meditate over it. Whenever it possesses you, meditate over it. Slowly, slowly, the meditation will create the distance between you and the jealousy. And the greater the distance, the less jealousy will arise. And one day, when there is no jealousy, your love releases such a fragrance that no flower can compete with it. All flowers are poor compared to the flowering of love.

But your love is crippled because of jealousy and possessiveness and anger.

It is not love that stinks, remember, because I have seen people who think it is love that stinks, so they close up, they become closed, they stop loving.

That’s what has happened to millions of monks and nuns down the ages: they became closed to love, they dropped the whole idea of love. Rather than dropping jealousy, which would have been a revolution, rather than dropping possessiveness, which would have been something of immense value, they dropped love. That is easy, that is not much; anybody can do that. To be a monk or a nun is very easy, but to love and not to be jealous, to love and not to be possessive, to love and let the other have the whole freedom is really a great achievement. Only then will you feel love and its fragrance.

A young nurse's first duty on her new job was to bathe the man in room 305. She performed her task and quickly returned to the nursing station.

"How was he?" asked her supervisor, an old, seasoned nurse.

"He was doing fine," she said, "but there was a very strange thing.... He had the word 'little' tattooed on his prick."

The older nurse was very curious and decided to check it out.

She returned forty-five minutes later, hair messed up, clothes askew, and said to the young nurse, "Honey, that tattoo does not say 'little.'

"It says, 'Little Rock, Arkansas, Pride of the South'!"

Osho – "Walking in Zen, Sitting in Zen", Discourse 5

MARRIAGE

Question: *Osho, why can I take almost everything lightly except my husband, Pravasi? Why do I fight him so? Why do I always try to change him?*

Deva Nirdosh, it is the most ancient story. It has nothing to do with you or Pravasi in particular. The institution of marriage is an ugly institution – the ugliest, in fact. All other ugly institutions are based on the institution of marriage.

The day marriage disappears from the world, states will disappear, nations will disappear, because they all need the family as a base. Churches will disappear, religions will disappear. The whole past is rooted in family, and the family is rooted in the invention of marriage.

Marriage is ugly because it destroys the freedom of two persons. Freedom is the ultimate value for me. Anything that destroys freedom is against human nature. And when your freedom is destroyed you are angry, you are in a rage. And on whom are you going to throw all your rage? The wife finds the husband, the husband finds the wife. They are close, available, and bound together in such a way that escape is not easy. The society has made it in every way difficult or almost impossible.

Marriage has an entrance but no exit. Or, even if the exit has become possible in a few countries, it is not really respected; it is condemned, a subtle condemnation. Marriage is praised. The priests go on saying, "Marriages are made in heaven," and they go on saying, "This is something sacred." The whole establishment depends on the sacredness of marriage. But it is not sacred, it is really very ugly. It has destroyed the whole of humanity.

And you cannot take revenge on the priest because he is not directly there; he functions in a very indirect way. You cannot take revenge on the politician; he is very diplomatic. All that you can find is the other person – the wife, the husband – tangibly, physically present, so your anger starts pouring on the other.

Husbands and wives are continuously quarrelling, fighting, as if they were enemies. It is very rare to find a couple which is friendly. They show friendliness when they are with others; when guests come, immediately they start smiling. They wear masks before their children, they avoid clashes. They don't fight on the streets, but they are fighting twenty-four hours a day. Their fight takes so many forms; it is multi-dimensional. It dissipates their energy. And then they have to live together, so somehow they have to make it up.

Sex just becomes a method for making things smooth, for making it up. First fight, then, because you have to live with the other person, use sex to show love and tenderness to the other so that for the time being there is peace. But that peace does not last long; it is just a cold war, not peace. Again the war will erupt. In the morning, again the same story will be repeated.

Unless we become aware that something very stupid has been propounded in the name of marriage, Nirdosh, this is going to continue.

My sannyasins, at least, should become aware: your husband has not done anything wrong to you, nor has your wife done anything wrong to you. If anything is wrong it is the very bondage, the very feeling of bondage that is wrong. Drop that bondage. Give each other more freedom. Respect freedom more than anything else because freedom is the highest value – even higher than love. If your love brings freedom, it is good. If your love does not bring freedom, it is not good – it is not even love either.

Your love brings jealousy, possessiveness; it never brings freedom. It destroys all possibilities of freedom. And it started at the very beginning...

Forget what your rabbi told you! What does he know about romance? Here's the way it really happened:

"Adam, baby," said Eve as she presented him with a bouquet of forget-me-nots she had picked in the Garden of Eden, "do you absolutely and truly love me?"

"Sure," said Adam. "Who else?"

Nirdosh, your story started then!

I have heard that every day when Adam would come back after his day's adventures, in the night Eve would count his ribs! It is a very ancient story. In the very beginning, something went wrong.

You may know, you may not know: Eve was not the first woman. God first created Adam and Lilith. And the first night, the honeymoon night – the first honeymoon – and a quarrel started because there was only one bed. And in those days double beds were not available! This is the story of the beginning: there was just a single bed. So who should sleep on the bed and who should sleep on the floor?

Of course, Adam was as much a male chauvinist pig as anybody! He was muscular, more powerful, so he possessed the bed. But Lilith was not willing. She said, "We are equal, we are made equal." She was the founder of the Lib Movement, the real founder!

They fought so much. I don't know whether clothes were thrown at each other or not, but they must have been thrown if there were clothes! In the middle of the night they knocked on God's door and Lilith said, "This cannot go on. Either I have to be accepted as an equal or I am finished with this man."

So the marriage was not consummated.

And God, being himself a man, of course favored Adam. So he dissolved Lilith and he created Eve, taking out a rib from Adam's body to make sure that Eve was always going to be secondary, just a part of Adam's body, not more than that, so that she could not claim equality. She would have to sleep on the floor!

Now what kind of foolishness is this? Just a double bed was needed!

Nirdosh, you are simply repeating an old story, an old pattern. Get out of this old pattern! Being a sannyasin, that should be the first thing.

There is no need to take your husband Pravasi seriously. Why that poor man? What has he done to you? If you can take everything else lightly, then why take your husband seriously?

Seriousness is a disease. And when you take somebody seriously, sooner or later you will take revenge, because you cannot remain serious for long. One wants to be happy and take things in fun.

But you alone are not at fault. Pravasi must also be making sure that he is being taken seriously. Every husband has been doing that for thousands of years: he should be taken seriously – he is no ordinary person; he is your husband!

In India, husbands have taught the women that, "Your husband is your god." Husbands themselves teaching the wives! And they have forced the poor women to accept them as their gods. But they take revenge – they are bound to take revenge. They cannot accept it. No being can accept such indignity.

But the way of the woman is more subtle. The way of the man is gross: he imposes his superiority by beating the wife. And the wife imposes her superiority by torturing him in very subtle ways – in such subtle ways that he cannot even defend himself.

When somebody is fighting with you, attacking you in a gross way, there is a possibility of defending yourself. You can learn karate – you can give him a few good kicks.

Every woman should learn karate because enough is enough! So when your husband tries to force you, "Take me seriously," you can give him a few good karate kicks! And you should learn karate shouts so that the whole neighborhood knows what is happening!

Life has to be light. Neither the wife has to be taken seriously nor has the husband to be taken seriously. Seriousness is not a good thing. Between two persons, seriousness creates a wall; it destroys intimacy. But if you are bent upon dominating each other, naturally you have to be serious. You cannot dominate playfully. If you become playful and take things in fun, you cannot be dominant, you cannot have any ego trip. Ego functions only in the climate of seriousness.

"Dear," asked the husband, "exactly what is hypnotism?"

"Hypnotism," replied his wife, "is getting a man into your power and then making him do whatever you want him to do."

Snorted the husband, "That's not hypnotism – that's marriage!"

Husbands are trying to force the wives to be just shadows to them. And the wives are trying to force the husbands to be just shadows to them. The whole idea is inhuman, irreligious, insane, neurotic!

If you really want to celebrate life, don't make such demands on life. Take things non-seriously. Remember how long it has been since you laughed with your husband, how long it has been since you danced with your husband informally – not in a formal setting, not at some marriage, or in some Rotarians' meeting or Lions' meeting – not in some formal setting, but just out of sheer joy. How long has it been since you sat silently together listening to music, not arguing, not talking, not nagging, not doing all that nonsense that goes on in the name of marriage?

A wall is created between the wife and the husband. The society perpetuates the wall, and you are so stupid that you go on helping the society to destroy your relationships, to destroy the beauty of your relationships.

Walking down M.G. Road, the middle-aged guy said to his wife, "Hey, did you see that pretty girl smiling at me?"

"That's nothing," said the wife, "the first time I saw you I laughed out loud!"

A Frenchman came home early one day and found his best friend in bed with his wife.

Shaking his head in disbelief, he said, "You know I have to, Pierre – but you?"

The Bravermans married off their last daughter and decided to sell their house and move into a furnished apartment. Mr Braverman showed his wife the apartment he rented.

"I don't like it," said Mrs Braverman.

"Why not?" asked Mr Braverman.

"There are no curtains in the bathroom. Every time I take a bath the neighbors will be able to see me in the nude!"

"Don't worry," said her husband, "when the neighbors see you in the nude, they'll buy the curtains!"

"Ah, yes, my late wife was a most remarkable woman," the mild old Englishman told one of his cronies on a park bench in London. "A very religious woman," he continued. "Never missed a day in church, and at home it was prayers and psalm-singing from morning to night."

"How did she come to die?" the friend inquired.

"I strangled her."

Nirdosh, you say: "Why do I always try to change him?"

Stop! Otherwise, if he strangles you, it will be difficult to save you. Every wife goes on trying to change the husband; that is a subtle strategy to dominate. It is a condemnation: "You are wrong, and you have to be put right." And husbands can't defend themselves because they do a few things which they themselves think are bad, so they can't defend themselves.

For example, they smoke and they themselves say that it is wrong, so the wife goes on nagging, "Stop smoking!" In fact, the more she nags, the more the husband has to smoke because he becomes more nervous. And when he is nervous, there is no other escape than smoking. If he does not smoke, he will strangle the wife! So he strangles a cigarette, or he starts chewing gum; otherwise he will chew the wife! He has to do something just to keep himself engaged so that this moment of anger passes by.

And the wife has a good point there: she is just doing it for your sake – for your health, for you to live a long life. And the husband wants to die as soon as possible!! He goes on smoking more in the hope that smoking really does kill!

He drinks and you are against it – and he is against himself because the whole atmosphere is that he has been told it is wrong and he has accepted the idea. So he cannot say that he is right – he has no guts to say that he is right. He has to accept that the wife is right. And wives don't smoke, they don't drink, they don't gamble, they don't do anything wrong. They are so saintly!

That is one thing good about being saintly: you can torture everybody! In fact, if you cannot torture everybody you will not be a saint at all – the whole joy is lost!

Wives are very holy and very religious for the simple reason that they can torture the husbands, they can torture the children, they can torture everybody. They are so holy! In comparison to them, everybody is a sinner.

My whole approach is human. I don't want you to become sad and serious holy people. We are tired of all these saints!

Please, Nirdosh, don't try to change him. Love means acceptance, accepting the other as he is. These are the ways of hate: trying to change someone is not love. And don't be after him. He has not done anything wrong in getting married to you! Don't make him suffer too much. He has not done anything wrong, so why punish him so much?

Give him freedom. And in giving freedom you will find your freedom too, because we can get freedom only if we give freedom.

And when two persons give freedom to each other, then only can love grow. In absolute freedom, absolute love grows. And when love and freedom are together, their beauty is immense.

My sannyasins have to live freedom, love, meditation, bliss. Drop all these wrong patterns of creating misery for each other.

Osho – "Walking in Zen, Sitting in Zen", Discourse 6

REINCARNATION

The moment the child is born, you think, is the beginning of its life. That is not true. The moment an old man dies, you think, is the end of his life. It is not. Life is far bigger than birth and death.

Birth and death are not two ends of life; many births and many deaths happen within life. Life itself has no beginning, no end: life and eternity are equivalent…

Life begins at the point of your past life's death. When you die, on the one side one chapter of life, which people think was your whole life, is closed. It was only a chapter in a book which has infinite chapters. One chapter closes, but the book is not closed. Just turn the page and another chapter begins.

The person dying starts visualizing his next life. This is a known fact, because it happens before the chapter closes. Buddha has a word for it, he calls it *tanha*. Literally it means desire, but metaphorically it means the whole life of desire. All these things happened: frustrations, fulfillments, disappointments, successes, failures. But all this happened within a certain area you can call desire.

The dying man has to see the whole of it before he moves on further, just to recollect it, because the body is going: this mind is not going to be with him, this brain is not going to be with him. But the desire released from this mind will cling to his soul, and this desire will decide his future life. Whatever has remained unfulfilled, he will move towards that target.

Your life begins far back before your birth, before your mother's impregnation, further back in your past life's end. That end is the beginning of this life. One chapter closes, another chapter opens. Now how this new life will be is 99% determined by the last moment of your death. What you collected, what you have brought with you like a seed - that seed will become a tree, bring fruits, bring flowers, or whatever happens to it. You cannot read it in the seed, but the seed has the whole blueprint.

If a man dies fully alert, seeing the whole terrain that he has passed and seeing the whole stupidity of it, he is born with a sharpness, with intelligence, with courage - automatically. It is not something he does.

Osho – "From Misery to Enlightenment", Discourse 9

PREPARING FOR DEATH

Question: *"How can we prepare ourselves for death?"*

Don't accumulate. Anything whatever. Power, money, prestige, virtue, knowledge, even the so-called spiritual experiences - don't accumulate. If you don't accumulate you are ready to die any moment, because you have nothing to lose.

The fear of death is not really fear of death; the fear of death comes out of the accumulations of life. Then you have too much to lose so you cling to it. That is the meaning of Jesus' saying: "Blessed are the poor in spirit."

I don't mean become a beggar, and I don't mean renounce the world. I mean be in the world but don't be *of* the world. Don't accumulate inside, be poor in spirit. Never possess anything - and then you are ready to die.

Possessiveness is the problem, not life itself. The more you possess, the more you are afraid to lose. If you don't possess anything, if your purity, if your spirit is uncontaminated by anything, if you are simply there alone, you can disappear any moment. Whenever death knocks on the door it will find you ready. You are not losing anything. By going with death you are not a loser. You may be moving into a new experience.

And when I say don't accumulate, I mean it as an absolute imperative. I'm not saying don't accumulate things of this world but go on accumulating virtue, knowledge, and so-called spiritual experiences, visions - no. I am talking in absolute terms: don't accumulate.

There are people, particularly in the East, who teach renunciation. They say, "Don't accumulate anything in this world because it will be taken away from you when death comes."

These people seem to be basically more greedy than the ordinary worldly people. Their logic is: don't accumulate in this world because death will take it away, so accumulate something that death cannot take away from you. Accumulate virtue, *punya*. Accumulate character, morality, knowledge. Accumulate experiences, spiritual experiences,

experiences of kundalini, meditation, this and that. Accumulate something that death cannot take away from you.

But if you accumulate, with that accumulation comes fear. Each accumulation brings fear in the same proportion...then you are afraid.

Don't accumulate and fear disappears.

I don't teach you renunciation in the old sense; my sannyas is an absolutely new concept. It teaches you to be in the world and yet to be not of it. Then you are always ready.

Osho – "The Art of Dying", Discourse 2

SPIRITUAL GLIMPSES vs ACHIEVEMENTS

Whatever you achieve in this life will remain with you, but it has to be an achievement, not just a glimpse. And there is a great difference between an achievement and a glimpse. You can see the Himalayan peaks from thousands of miles away - it is a glimpse; but to reach those peaks will be an achievement.

A glimpse helps you to move onward, towards achievement; but unless something becomes a crystallized experience in your life, it is going to be lost - you will have to start from the very beginning. There will be a little difference, and that will be that in your unconscious a shadow of your past life, a faraway echo - as if you have seen something - will remain. And when you again get the glimpse you may feel that this is not new, I have known it before.

But otherwise, only crystallized achievements go with you, consciously, into the other life; knowingly, not just a dark shadow, a faraway echo in the unconscious, but consciously knowing that these Himalayan peaks exist, and you have been on those peaks. There will be no doubt about it, no wavering about it, no question about it.

You are asking, "Is it possible that we will totally lose these few glimpses of light, beauty, and consciousness that we have got through being sannyasins?"

Such glimpses you have got in many lives before too, and you have lost them. They never became part of your being; they remained only beautiful memories. But the memories are not achievements. It is as if you have seen something in a dream - perhaps it may be true, perhaps it may not be true.

So if you feel that there is something happening now, make every effort that it does not remain only a glimpse but becomes an actual experience, becomes part of your being. Only then can it go with you into another life.

It is possible to take all your experiences with you into another life, and never to begin from scratch but always to begin where you had left off in the past life. But be clear that just a glimpse is very fragile, just a glimpse is very superficial. Howsoever touching it may be in the moment, even tomorrow you may start doubting whether it really happened or you imagined it. And the life after this life is a faraway journey.

Glimpses are simply incentives to move towards crystallization. Make it an experience so deep that it becomes part of you, and there is no way to forget it or to lose it. Don't remain satisfied with glimpses. Enjoy them, but use them only as an indicator towards greater things to happen.

To see something from far away is one thing, and to become that thing is totally another. A glimpse of love is just like a breeze that passes within seconds; a glimpse of silence is just like the fragrance of a rose flower that you felt for a moment, and now you don't know where it has gone.

When I say, "Crystallize your experience," I mean it is not enough to have beautiful glimpses. It is good, but not good enough. You should become the fragrance of the rose itself; the glimpse was only an arrow pointing towards the possibility - it did its work, but you remain there.

In the past life also, many times you have come across many beautiful experiences and right now you don't know even that there have been past lives. Only once in a while you see somebody, and you have a very strange feeling, almost weird, as if you have seen this man before - and certainly not in this life. You come to a place, and suddenly you are startled, as if you had come to this place before too - although certainly not in this life. Everything seems to be known, but has been dormant in your unconscious.

Life has a mechanism that whenever a person dies, unless he is enlightened, he becomes almost unconscious; he goes into a coma before death, actual death, happens. So he knows nothing about the death, and he remains in a state of coma till he is born again. All those nine months in the mother's womb are a state of coma; the child is fast asleep 24 hours a day for nine months.

It rarely happens that somebody dies consciously. It happens only to great meditators, who know well the path death will be coming on because in their meditations they have traveled on the path again and again - it is the same path. As they go deep in their meditation the body is left far away, mind is left far away, the heart is left far away; only a beautiful silence - fully alert and conscious - remains.

The same happens when you die. If you have been meditating, then death is not a new experience. You will be surprised that in your meditation you have been dying every day, and you have been coming back to life every day. Such a person dies very consciously, so he knows what death is - and such a person remains conscious in the mother's womb. He is also born consciously. From his very first moment on the earth, he knows all that has passed before in the past life, and he remembers it.

I have come across many children.... And this happens most particularly in India, because outside India - where Christianity is prominent or Judaism is prominent or Mohammedanism is prominent - they have conditioned the mind that there is only one life. They don't know anything about meditation. They have substituted meditation with prayer, and prayer is praising a fictitious god; it is very childish.

Meditation needs no god - you are enough. You are a reality, and you explore your reality to the deepest core.

In India all the religions are agreed on one point; they differ in their philosophies, they differ on every other thing, but on one thing they are all agreed: that life is a continuity; death comes millions of times. Death is only a change of the body, a change of the house, and this process goes on - unless you become totally enlightened. Then there is no need to enter another womb, because life was just a school, a training; you have completed it. Your enlightenment is the culmination of your education about existence. Now you need not enter into another body. You can enter into the womb of the universe itself - you are prepared for it.

So whenever you are having glimpses, don't be satisfied with them. Your glimpses should create great discontent in you, not content. They should create a longing that what is seen far away you would like to come closer and closer and closer. You don't want just to see it, even from closeness; you want to become it.

You can become love, you can become silence, you can become joy, you can become all these experiences: beauty, light, consciousness.

These are not things that you cannot become; they are your potentials. So take every glimpse to its ultimate end. That's what I call crystallization.

Once it is crystallized, once you have known yourself to be love, yourself to be light, yourself to be consciousness, then there is no problem of forgetting it. Then these experiences will go with you. And in your future life you will be growing further ahead, from consciousness to superconsciousness; you will be going beyond these experiences. But if you remain satisfied with your glimpses, there is every danger they will be erased. Death is such a shock and such a surgery and such a long coma that when you wake up, you will have forgotten all those glimpses.

"Someone stole my bike," complained a priest to his minister friend.

"Bring up the Ten Commandments in your sermon tomorrow, and as soon as you mention, `Thou shalt not steal,' look around in your congregation; you will find the guilty party. Invite him to come forward. Tell him that this is the way to confess, and this is the way to get the forgiveness of God," the minister said confidently.

The next day the priest visited the minister and happily reported that he had found his bike. "Yes", he went on, "when I came to `Thou shalt not commit adultery', I remembered where I had left it."

Osho – "The Golden Future", Discourse 2

MIND IS THE ROOT PROBLEM

The root problem of all problems is mind itself. The first thing to be understood is what this mind is, of what stuff it is made; whether it is an entity or just a process; whether it is substantial, or just dreamlike. And unless you know the nature of the mind, you will not be able to solve any problems of your life. You may try hard, but if you try to solve single, individual problems, you are bound to be a failure – that is absolutely certain, because in fact no individual problem exists. Mind is the problem.

If you solve this problem or that, it won't help because the root remains untouched. It is just like cutting branches of a tree, pruning the leaves, and not uprooting it. New leaves will come, new branches will sprout, even more than before; pruning helps a tree to become thicker. Unless you know how to uproot it, your fight is baseless, it is foolish. You will destroy yourself, not the tree. In fighting you will waste your energy, time, life, and the tree will go on becoming more and more strong, far thicker and dense. And you will be surprised what is happening: you are doing so much hard work, trying to solve this problem and that, and they go on growing, increasing. Even if one problem is solved, suddenly ten problems take its place. Don't try to solve individual, single problems – there are none.

Mind itself is the problem. But mind is hidden underground, that's why I call it the root, it is not apparent. Whenever you come across a problem the problem is above ground, you can see it – that's why you are deceived by it.

Always remember, the visible is never the root; the root always remains invisible, the root is always hidden. Never fight with the visible; otherwise you will fight with shadows. You may waste yourself, but there cannot be any transformation in your life, the same problems will crop up again and again and again.

You can observe your own life and you will see what I mean. I am not talking about any theory about the mind, just the facticity of it. This is the fact: mind has to be solved. People come to me and they ask, "How to attain a peaceful mind?" I say to them, "There exists nothing like that: peaceful mind. Never heard of it."

Mind is never peaceful – no-mind is peace. Mind itself can never be peaceful, silent. The very nature of the mind is to be tense, to be in confusion. Mind can never be clear, it cannot have clarity, because mind is by nature confusion, cloudiness. Clarity is possible without mind, peace is possible without mind, silence is possible without mind.

So never try to attain a silent mind. If you do, from the very beginning you are moving in an impossible dimension. So the first thing is to understand the nature of the mind, only then can something be done.

If you watch, you will never come across any entity like mind. It is not a thing, it is just a process. It is like a crowd. Individual thoughts exist, but they move so fast that you cannot see the gaps in between. The intervals cannot be seen because you are not very aware and alert, you need a deeper insight. When your eyes can look deep, you will suddenly see one thought, another thought, another thought, but no mind!

Thoughts together, millions of thoughts, give you the illusion as if mind exists. It is just like a crowd. Millions of people standing in a crowd: Is there anything like a crowd? Can you find the crowd other than the individuals standing there? But they are standing together, their togetherness gives you the feeling as if something like a crowd exists. Only individuals exist.

This is the first insight into the mind: watch, and you will find thoughts; you will never come across the mind. And if it becomes your own experience, not because I say it. If it becomes your experience, if it becomes a fact of your own knowing, then suddenly many things start changing. Because you have understood such a deep thing about mind, then many things can follow.

Watch the mind and see where it is, what it is. You will feel thoughts floating and there will be intervals. And if you watch long, you will see that intervals are more than the thoughts, because each thought has to be separate from another thought. In fact, each word has to be separate from another word.

The deeper you go, you will find more and more gaps, bigger and bigger gaps. A thought floats, then comes a gap where no thought exists; then another thought comes, another gap follows. If you are unconscious you cannot see the gaps; you jump from one thought to another, you never see the gap. If you become aware you will see more and more gaps.

If you become perfectly aware, then miles of gaps will be revealed to you. And in those gaps, *satoris* happen. In those gaps the Truth knocks at your door. In those gaps, the Guest comes. In those gaps God is realized, or whatsoever way you like to express it. And when awareness is absolute, then there is only a vast gap of nothingness.

It is just like clouds. Clouds move: they can be so thick that you cannot see the sky hidden behind. The vast blueness of the sky is lost, you are covered with clouds. Then you go on watching: one cloud moves and another has not come into the vision yet – and suddenly a peek into the blueness of the vast sky.

The same happens inside: you are the vast blueness of the sky, and thoughts are just like clouds hovering around you, filling you. But the gaps exist, the sky exists. To have a glimpse of the sky is *satori*, and to become the sky is *samadhi*. From *satori* to *samadhi*, the whole process is a deep insight into the mind, nothing else. Mind doesn't exist as an entity, the first thing. Only thoughts exist.

The second thing: the thoughts exist separate from you, they are not one with your nature. They come and go, you remain, you persist. You are like the sky: never comes, never goes, it is always there.

Clouds come and go, they are momentary phenomena, they are not eternal. Even if you try to cling to a thought, you cannot retain it for long; it has to go, it has its own birth and death. Thoughts are not yours, they don't belong to you. They come as visitors, guests, but they are not the host.

Watch deeply, then you will become the host and thoughts will be the guests. And as guests they are beautiful, but if you forget completely that you are the host and they become the hosts, then you are in a mess. This is what hell is. You are the master of the house, the house belongs to you, and guests have become the masters. Receive them, take care of them, but don't get identified with them; otherwise, they will become the masters.

The mind becomes the problem because you have taken thoughts so deeply inside you that you have forgotten completely the distance, that they are visitors, they come and go. Always remember that which abides, that is your nature, your Tao. Always be attentive to that which never comes and never goes, just like the sky. Change the gestalt: don't be focused on the visitors, remain rooted in the host; the visitors will come and go.

Of course, there are bad visitors and good visitors, but you need not be worried about them. A good host treats all the guests in the same way, without making any distinctions. A good host is just a good host: a bad thought comes and he treats the bad thought also in the same way as he treats a good thought. It is not his concern that the thought is good or bad. Because once you make the distinction that this thought is good and that thought is bad, what are you doing? You are bringing the good thought nearer to yourself and pushing the bad thought further away. Sooner or later, with the good thought you will get identified; the good thought will become the host. And any thought when it becomes the host creates misery, because this is not the truth.

The thought is a pretender and you get identified with it. Identification is the disease. Gurdjieff used to say that only one thing is needed: not to be identified with that which comes and goes. The morning comes, the noon comes, the evening comes, and they go; the night comes and again the morning. You abide: not as you, because that too is a thought – as pure consciousness - not your name, because that too is a thought; not your form, because that too is a thought; not your body, because one day you will realize that too is a thought. Just pure consciousness, with no name, no form; just the purity, just the formlessness and namelessness, just the very phenomenon of being aware – only that abides.

If you get identified, you become the mind. If you get identified, you become the body. If you get identified, you become the name and the form – what Hindus call *nama, rupa,* name and form – then the host is lost. Then you forget the eternal and the momentary becomes significant.

The momentary is the world; the eternal is divine. This is the second insight to be attained: that you are the host and thoughts are guests.

The third thing, if you go on watching, will be realized soon. The third thing is that thoughts are foreign, intruders, outsiders. No thought is yours! They always come from without, you are just a passage. A bird comes into the house from one door, and flies out from another: just like that a thought comes into you and goes out of you.

You go on thinking that thoughts are yours. Not only that, you fight for your thoughts, you say, "This is my thought, this is true." You discuss, you debate, you argue about it, you try to prove that, "This is my thought."

No thought is yours, no thought is original – all thoughts are borrowed. And not secondhand, because millions of people have claimed those same thoughts before you. Thought is just as outside as a thing.

Somewhere, the great physicist, Eddington, has said that the deeper science goes into matter, the more it becomes a realization that things are thoughts. That may be so, I am not a physicist, but from the other end I would like to tell you that Eddington may be true that things look more and more like thoughts. If you go deeper; if you go deeper into yourself, thoughts will look more and more like things. In fact, these are two aspects of the same phenomenon: a thing is a thought, a thought is a thing.

When I say a thought is a thing, what do I mean? I mean that you can throw your thought just like a thing. You can hit somebody's head with a thought just like a thing. A thought is a great force, it is a thing. This will be the third insight. It has to be understood and watched within yourself.

Your thoughts are things, so be careful about them. Handle them carefully! If you are not very conscious, you can create misery for yourself and for others – and you have done that. And remember, when you create misery for somebody, unconsciously, at the same time, you are creating misery for yourself – because a thought is a two-edged sword. It cuts you also simultaneously when it cuts somebody else.

Whatsoever Buddha is doing, he is doing without any mind in it. He is spontaneous, it is not activity. He is not thinking about it, it happens. He is not the doer. He moves like an emptiness. He has no mind for it, he was not thinking to do it. But if the existence allows it to happen, he allows it to happen. He has no more the ego to resist; no more the ego to do. That is the meaning of being empty and a no-self: just being a non-being, *anatta,* no-selfness. Then you accumulate nothing; then you are not responsible for anything that goes on around you; then you transcend.

All around there is a noosphere, a thought-sphere, all around. Just as there is air, there is thought all around you, and it goes on entering on its own accord. It stops only when you become more and more aware.

There is something in it: if you become more aware, a thought simply disappears, it melts, because awareness is a greater energy than thought. Awareness is like fire to thought. It is just like you burn a lamp in the house and the darkness cannot enter. You put the light off – from everywhere darkness has entered; without taking a single minute, a single moment, it is there. When the light burns in the house, the darkness cannot enter.

Thoughts are like darkness: they enter only if there is no light within. Awareness is fire: you become more aware, less and less thoughts enter.

If you become really integrated in your awareness, thoughts don't enter you; you have become an impenetrable citadel, nothing can penetrate you. Not that you are closed, remember – you are absolutely open; but just the very energy of awareness becomes your citadel.

And when no thoughts can enter you, they will come and they will bypass you. You will see them coming, and simply, by the time they reach near you they turn. Then you can move anywhere, then you go to the very hell – nothing can affect you. This is what we mean by enlightenment.

Osho – "Tantra the Supreme Understanding", Discourse 2

IGNORANCE vs INTELLECTUAL KNOWLEDGE

Avidya, ignorance of one's own being, is the basic cause of the world. Once *avidya* disappears, the world also disappears – not the world of objects, but the world of desires; not the world that is outside you, but the world that you have been constantly projecting from the inside. The world of your dreams, illusions, projections, immediately disappears the moment ignorance disappears within you.

This has to be understood: ignorance is not simply lack of knowledge, so you can go on gathering knowledge but ignorance will not disappear that way. You can become very knowledgeable, but still you will remain ignorant. In fact, knowledge functions as a protection for ignorance.

Ignorance is not destroyed by knowledge. On the contrary, it is protected by it.

The urge to collect knowledge, accumulate knowledge, is nothing but to hide one's own ignorance. The more you know, the more you think that now you are no longer ignorant. There is a saying in Tibet: "Blessed are they who are ignorant, for they are happy in thinking that they know everything."

Trying to know everything is not going to help; it is missing the whole point. Trying to know one's self is enough. If you can know your own being you have known all because you participate with the Whole, your nature is of the Whole.

You are just like a drop of water. If you know the drop of water totally, you have known all the oceans, past, present and future. In a single drop of water the whole nature of the ocean is present.

A man who is after knowledge continuously forgets himself and goes on accumulating information. He may come to know much, but still he will remain ignorant. So ignorance is not against knowledge; knowledge is not the antidote for ignorance.

Then what is the antidote for ignorance? Yoga says: awareness, not knowledge, but knowing: not focusing yourself outside, but focusing on the very faculty of knowing.

When a child is in the mother's womb, he is completely asleep. The first months in the mother's womb are of deep sleep, what yoga calls *sushupti*, sleep without any dreams. Then, by the end of the sixth or seventh month, the child starts a little dreaming. The sleep is disturbed; it is no more absolute. Something happens outside, a noise, and the child's sleep is disturbed. Vibrations reach him, and in his deep sleep a distraction arrives and he starts dreaming. The first ripples of dream arise.

Dreamless sleep is the first state of consciousness. The second state is: sleep plus dream. In the second state sleep remains, but a new faculty starts functioning: the faculty of dreaming.

Then, when the child is born a third faculty arises, what we ordinarily call the state of waking. It is not really the state of waking, but a new faculty starts functioning and that faculty is of thought. The child starts thinking.

The first state was dreamless sleep: the second state was sleep plus dreaming; the third state is sleep, plus dreaming, plus thinking, but sleep still remains. Sleep has not been completely broken.

You remain asleep in your thinking also. Your thinking is nothing but another way of dreaming; the sleep is not disturbed. These are the ordinary states.

Rarely does a man reach higher than this third stage, of thinking. And that is the goal of yoga: to reach to a state of pure awareness, as pure as the first state is. The first state is of pure sleep, and the last state is of pure awakening, pure awareness. Once your awareness is as pure as your deep sleep, you have become a Buddha, you have attained, you have come home.

Patanjali says: *samadhi*, the ultimate state of awareness, is just like sleep, with one difference: it is as calm and quiet as sleep, as silent, undisturbed as sleep, as integrated and blissful as sleep, with one difference: it is fully alert.

These are the points of evolution. Ordinarily, we remain at the third. Deep down sleep continues, on top of it a layer of dreaming, on top of it another layer of thinking – but the sleep is not broken.

And you can observe it; it is not a theory. You can observe the facticity of it. At any moment you close your eyes, first you will see thoughts, a layer of thinking all around you, thoughts vibrating – one coming, another going – a crowd, a traffic. Remain silent for a few seconds, and suddenly you will see that thinking is no longer there but dreaming has started. You are dreaming that you have become the president of a country, or you have found a brick of gold on the road, or you have found a beautiful woman or a man, and suddenly you start projecting; dreams start functioning. If you continue dreaming for a long time, one moment will come when you will fall asleep – thinking, dreaming, sleep, and from sleep again to dreaming and thinking.

This is how your whole life revolves. Real awareness is not known yet, and that real awareness is what Patanjali says will destroy ignorance – not knowledge, but awareness.

We collect knowledge just to befool ourselves and others. But nobody wants to recognize a simple fact, that they don't know. Everybody tries; whatsoever the question, everybody tries the answer.

You should catch yourself red-handed many times if you try. Somebody asks something, somebody talks about something you don't know, but you start commenting, advising, saying something or other so that you are not caught ignorant, so nobody thinks that you are ignorant. But the first beginning of awareness starts with the recognition that you are ignorant. Ignorance can be destroyed, but not without recognizing it.

Osho – "Yoga: the Alpha & Omega", Volume 10, Discourse 5

SEX, LOVE, SUPERCONSCIOUSNESS

The simple truth is that sex is the starting point of love. Sex is the beginning of the journey to love. The origin of love is sex, passion – and everybody behaves like it is the enemy. Every culture, every religion, every guru, every seer has attacked this source, and the river has remained bottled up.

The hue and cry has always been, "Sex is sin. Sex is irreligious. Sex is poison." But we never seem to realize that ultimately it is the sex energy itself that travels to and reaches the inner ocean of love.

Love is the transformation of sex energy. The flowering of love is from the seed of sex. Only the energy of sex can flower into love. But everyone, including mankind's great thinkers, is against it. This opposition will not allow the seed to sprout, and the palace of love is destroyed at the foundation. The enmity towards sex has destroyed the possibility of love.

Because of basic misconceptions, no one feels the necessity of going through the stages of acknowledging sex and of developing it and of going through the process of transforming it. How can we transform him whose enemy we are, whom we oppose, with whom we are at continuous war?

A quarrel between man and his energy has been forced upon him. Man has been taught to fight against his sex energy, to oppose his sex urges. "The mind is poison, so fight against it," man is told. The mind exists in man, and sex also exists in him; yet man is expected to be free from inner conflicts. A harmonious existence is expected of him. He has to fight and to pacify as well. Such are the teachings of his leaders. On the one hand they drive him mad and on the other they open asylums to treat him. They spread the germs of sickness and then build hospitals to cure the sick.

Another important consideration is that man cannot be separated from sex. Sex is his primary point; he is born of it. God has made the energy of sex the starting point of creation. And great men term as sinful what

God himself does not consider as sin! If God considers sex as sin, then there is no greater sinner than God in this world, no greater sinner in this universe.

At this stage I wish to give you the first principle. If you want to know the elemental truth about love, the first requisite is to accept the sacredness of sex, to accept the divinity of sex in the same way you accept God's existence – with an open heart. And the more fully you accept sex with an open heart and mind, the freer you will be of it.

The measure of your acceptance is the measure of your deliverance. The total acceptance of life, of all that is natural in life, of all that is God-given in life, will lead you to the highest realms of divinity – to heights that are unknown, to heights that are sublime. I call that acceptance, theism, and that faith in the God-given is the door to liberation.

I regard those precepts which keep man from accepting that which is natural in life and in the divine scheme as atheism. "Oppose this; suppress that. The natural is sinful, bad, lustful. Leave this; leave that." All this constitutes atheism, as I understand it.

Those who preach renunciation are atheists.

Accept life in its pure and natural form and thrive on the fullness of it. The fullness itself will elevate you, step by step. And this very same acceptance of sex will uplift you to serene heights you had not imagined possible. If sex is coal, the day is certain to come when it shows itself as diamonds. And that is the first principle.

The second fundamental thing I want to tell you is about something that has, by now, become hardened within us by civilization, culture and religion. And that is the ego, the consciousness that 'I am'. The nature of the sex energy goads it to flow towards love, but the hurdle of 'I' has fenced it in like a wall and so love cannot flow.

The 'I' is very powerful, in bad as well as in good people, in the unholy as well as in the holy. Bad people may assert the 'I' in many ways, but good people also drum the 'I' loudly. They want to go to heaven; they want to be delivered; they have renounced the world; they have built temples; they do not sin; they want to do this; they want to do that. But that 'I', that guiding signal, is ever present.

The stronger a person's ego is, the harder it is for him to unite with anybody. The ego comes in between; the 'I' asserts itself. It is a wall. It proclaims, 'You are you and I am I.' And so even the most intimate experience does not bring people close to each other. The bodies may be near but the people are far apart. So long as there is this 'I' inside, this feeling of otherness cannot be avoided.

One day, Sartre said a wonderful thing: "The other is hell." But he didn't explain any further why the other was hell, or even why the other was the other. The other is the other because I am I, and while I am I, the world around is the other – different and apart, segregated – and there is no rapport. As long as there is this feeling of separation, love cannot be known.

Love is the experience of unity. The demolition of walls, the fusion of two energies is what the experience of love is. Love is the ecstasy when the walls between two people crumble down, when two lives meet, when two lives unite.

When such a harmony exists between two people I call it love. And when it exists between one man and the masses, I call it communion with God. If you can become immersed with me in such an experience so that all barriers melt, so that an osmosis takes place at the spiritual level, then that is love. And if such a unity happens between me and everyone else and I lose my identity in the All, then that attainment, that merging, is with God, with the Almighty, with the Omniscient, with the Universal Consciousness, with the Supreme, or whatsoever you want to call it.

And so I say that love is the first step and that God is the last step – the finest and the final destination.

How is it possible to erase myself? Unless I dissolve myself, how can the other unite with me? The other is created as a reaction to my 'I'. The louder I shout 'I', the more forceful becomes the existence of the other. The other is the echo of 'I'.

And what is 'I'? Have you ever thought calmly about it? Is it in your leg or your hand, in your head or your heart? Or is it just the ego? What and where is your 'I', your ego? The feeling of it is there, yet it is to be found in no particular place.

Sit quietly for a moment and search for that 'I'. You may be surprised, but in spite of an intense search you will not find your 'I' anywhere. When you search deeply inside you will realize there is no 'I' as such; there is no ego. When there is the truth of the self, the 'I' is not there.

Please look inside. Where is your ego? Where is your 'I'? You will not find that 'I' anywhere. It is a manifestation of many energies; that is all. Think about each and every limb, about each and every aspect of yourself, and then eliminate everything, one by one. Ultimately, nothingness will remain. Love is born of that nothingness. That nothingness is God.

Love can only be born out of emptiness. Only a void is capable of merging with another void; only zero can unite totally with another zero. Not two individuals, but two vacuums can meet, because now there is no barrier. All else has walls; a vacuum has none.

So the second thing to remember is that love is born when individuality vanishes, when 'I' and 'the other' are no more. Whatsoever remains then is everything, the limitless – but no 'I'. With that attainment, all barriers crumble and the onrush of the ever-ready Ganges takes place.

Osho – "From Sex to Superconsciousness", Discourse 1

WHEN LOVE ARISES, ALL FEELINGS ERUPT

Feel more, think less, and by and by you will see that the more you can feel, the more relaxed you are. The more you can feel, the more you become aware of the secret of life – that you need not do anything about it, you just have to be available. Just available, I say, and everything comes to you. Once the idea arises to catch hold, to cling, everything disappears.

Love is the very center of all feelings, love is the soul of all feelings. All feelings hang on love. If you don't love, by and by all feelings will disappear. If you love, all feelings will be revived.

And remember, I say *all* feelings: negative, positive, all. When you love, you start hating also – immediately. When you love, you start feeling anger also – immediately. When you love, you feel sad, you feel happy. When you love, all feelings are again back to life.

This is the trouble. That's why no society allows love; because if it were the case that with love only good feelings, feelings that society decides are good, came up, there would be no trouble. But with love, the trouble is that not only heaven starts flowering, but hell also. They are together, they are two aspects of the same coin. They cannot be separated – and there is no need to separate them, because a heaven without a hell would be poorer. A love without anger would be impotent. A love without sadness would be shallow.

Life is a polarity, and through polarities life becomes richer and richer and more and more complex. Life is not like ordinary Aristotelian logic; life is more like Hegelian dialectics: thesis, antithesis. Two polarities meet and fight, and a third phenomenon arises: synthesis. A greater harmony arises out of two polarities; then that greater harmony again becomes thesis, a new antithesis arises, then again a higher rung of the ladder of synthesis is reached.

Man creates fear because of his head. With his heart he is again one with the universe.

Osho – "Just Like That", Discourse 7

LOVE AND LAW vs LOVE AND MEDITATION

A civilized human being is a plastic flower. He has no vitality, no energy - and when there is no energy, there is no delight. One of the greatest English poets, William Blake, has a beautiful line about it, a very deep insight. He says: "Energy is delight." There is no other delight. The very vitality, the very energy of being, is delight, is bliss. Only impotence is misery, weakness is misery.

And duality creates impotence. And whatsoever small energy is left after you are divided in two, that too goes as wastage in the inner conflict. You are continuously fighting inside, continuously suppressing something, continuously trying to force something else. Anger comes, and you would like to be non-angry; greed comes, and you would like to be greed-less; possession comes, and you would like to be non-possessive; violence comes, and you would like to be non-violent; there is cruelty, and you go on imposing compassion; there is much turmoil, and you would like to be serene and silent; something goes on inside, and you go on imposing something else on it, continuous fight dissipates the remaining energy. And this is going to be so, unless you become one again.

There are two ways to become one: either fall back to the animal or rise up to the Buddha.

Of course, falling back is easier. Effort will not be needed; you can simply slip back. It is downhill, no effort, and going up is difficult. Hence millions of people choose the downhill way. What is the downhill way as far as consciousness is concerned? Drugs, alcohol, sex, are the downhill way.

In a deep sexual act you again become an animal, you are no more human. The gap is bridged. In a deep sexual orgasm, the duality disappears; the controller is no more there. In a deep sexual act, your whole starts functioning as a whole. Mind is no longer there, ego is no longer there, the controller and the control are no longer there, because the sexual act is non-voluntary. Your will is not needed, your will is not required. You are no more a will, the will is surrendered. Suddenly you are back to the world, the animal world, the natural world; again you have entered into the Garden of Eden, again you are Adam or Eve - no more a civilized human being.

That's why all societies condemn sex. They are afraid of it. It is a back door to the Garden of Eden. All civilizations are afraid of sex. The fear comes, because once you know an uncontrolled existence then you would not like control at all. You can become a rebel, you can throw all the rules and regulations to the winds, you can throw Confucius to the dust. Again you can become an animal; and civilization is afraid of it.

So, sex is allowed, because if it is not allowed then too it will create trouble. It is such a deep-rooted instinct in the very biology, in the very physiology of you, in the very deeper chemistry, that if it is not allowed, it will create perversion, you may go mad. So society allows it in mild, homeopathic doses. That is the meaning of marriage - marriage is a mild, homeopathic dose controlled in a certain way. You are allowed a little window out of society, but society still manages the outer control. Marriage is love plus law - that 'plus law' is the control around it. If love is allowed without any law, the fear is that man will fall again into an animal world.

And the fear seems to be true; the fear has meaning. Man can fall through love, because man can rise through love. Man can fall through it because the ladder is always the same whether you go up or you go down. Love can rise to such heights that Jesus can say, "Love is God." And love can fall to such depths that society is constantly on watch, the police are always around, the magistrate is sitting there. Then love is not a freedom.

Why, in love, can man fall so deep? Because in love the control is lost, the chasm is bridged, you become one piece again - but you regress to the animal world. Love can also lead you to the Divine, but then love has to be very, very meditative. Then love has to be 'love plus meditation'. That is what Tantra is – 'Love plus meditation'. You move into love, you allow your whole being total freedom, but still, deep at the center, you remain a witness. If the witness is lost, you are going downhill; if the witness remains there, then love, the same ladder, can lead you to the very ultimate heaven.

Osho – "The Grass Grows by Itself", Discourse 6

OSHO IS NOT CELIBATE

I have loved many women, and I am the first enlightened person in the world who is being absolutely truthful to you. You could have never found out whether I am celibate or not. I thought, although I have not said I am celibate, you would consider me a celibate. I have not participated in this lying positively, but negatively I am responsible. And now I am not going to hide anything from you.

Your old religious leaders were captives of your expectations. I am nobody's prisoner. And I feel very light, because I am not burdened. I can say to you everything; there is nothing being withheld. All your Masters were withholding things from you. I do not consider them authentic, open, sincere. Even to their own disciples they were not true.

If enlightenment does not make you transcend hunger, thirst, urination, then why should it make you transcend your sex? Sex is part of your whole being, it is not something separate. Sex is a natural phenomenon.

I think this is very disgusting of these enlightened people – always poking their nose into your affairs, always watching you from the keyhole, what you are doing. And naturally, because they go on watching you from the keyhole, you also go on watching them even more carefully, because you may be following a wrong man. You have to be certain that his is a twenty-four carat enlightenment.

Celibacy is unnatural – at least, up to the age of forty-two. Between fourteen years and forty-two, celibacy is absolutely unnatural, and if you force yourself to remain a celibate, you will become just a pervert.

All other religions have forced you to become perverts. In your monasteries there is masturbation but no meditation. And I want to say the thing as it is: Transcendence simply means slavery is transcended. Now I am not making any love to anybody, for the simple reason that I am no longer healthy, my body is fragile. It is not ready to play tennis! It is nothing spiritual.

But one fact I have proved absolutely and forever – that making love does not destroy enlightenment. On the contrary, it makes it richer, more beautiful – new flowers in it, new colors in it, new fragrances in it, new laughter, new smiles. The whole idea that the enlightened man cannot make love is absolutely wrong.

But you got shocked because of your expectation. You are unenlightened, you don't know enlightenment. First, to become enlightened is so arduous: the camel changing into the lion, the lion changing into the child. And when you have passed this whole long track, you are not courageous enough to do something that may spoil the whole pilgrimage.

But, forgive me, I am a different type of man. When I became enlightened, I wanted to test it in every fire: if it passes through all fire tests, then only is it real. Otherwise, I was hallucinating, I was just imagining that I had become enlightened. And I can say to you now that I have done everything that no enlightened person is expected to do – even things in which I was not interested at all, but just to test that I was not hallucinating.

I have done everything after enlightenment which has been thought would destroy enlightenment. And I tell you now that nothing can destroy enlightenment, because enlightenment is not just an experience, it is a transformation. It is not that it happens once and you see the light, and then the whole of your life you remember with joy that vision, that opening of the window to Existence. It is not like that. Enlightenment transforms you. You are totally a new man.

I have my own individuality. I don't need anybody's respect, because I am so full there is no space for anything else. And it has been a tremendous experience to be so notorious and yet to be loved by millions of people. That gives a great hope, that even an ordinary man can be loved; you need not be extraordinary to be loved.

How much love I have received! I don't think anybody before me has received so much love. And certainly I have received more hostility, anger, condemnation than anybody else. I am richest man in the world – I receive everything!

If you ask me, my enlightenment made me transcend only one thing, and that is the opinion of others. That is their business. They cannot disturb my sleep by their opinions. And I don't have to be concerned about what they are thinking.

Remember perfectly, I am not going to change in any way. If change has to come, it has to come to you and your mind, because it is your disturbance, your shock. It is your problem – take the responsibility for it. See the simple fact that you were carrying some expectations – that means some chains for me. It is time: throw those chains. I am an absolutely free man. There is no bondage for me. I can do anything, you just have to suggest it to me!

Osho – "From the False to the Truth", Discourse 24

FULFILL YOUR DESTINY

Love always looks foolish: foolish to those who are stuck somewhere, foolish to those who have not known anything higher than their body, foolish to those who have not known anything valuable other than money, foolish to those who have not known anything paradoxical, who, in fact, have not known anything mysterious, who have lived with logic, who are Aristotelian.

Those who are just minds – heart is a folly to them because heart has its own reasons which the mind cannot understand. The heart has its own dimension of being, which is completely dark for the mind. Heart is higher and deeper than the mind, beyond the reach of it. It looks foolish.

Love always looks foolish because love is not utilitarian. Mind is utilitarian. It uses everything for something else – that is the meaning of being utilitarian. Mind is purposive, end-oriented. It turns every-thing into a means; and love cannot be turned into a means – that is the problem.

Love in itself is the goal. If you love a person you don't say why you love them. You can't answer the question, Why do you love? You simply shrug your shoulders. If you are really honest you will say, I don't know. If you are dishonest you can find a thousand and one reasons. But no lover worth the name has ever been able to show any reason. He simply says, "It happened. I just fell into love, I don't know why!"

That's why the mind says it is foolish. If you can't answer the why you must be moving in some foolish way: 'Stop! Come back! Be reasonable!' And I must tell you one thing: If you try always to be reasonable you can never be happy because happiness has something unreasonable in it. The very ingredient of being happy is to be unreasonable.

If you can be unreasonably happy, only then can you be happy, otherwise not. If you try to find out the reason, then you will simply be miserable. Misery has reasons, happiness has none.

You can answer: Why are you miserable? But you cannot answer: Why are you happy? Always you are miserable because of you, and always you are happy in spite of you. It has no reason to it. The 'why' cannot be answered. And heart is not arithmetic, it is poetry, paradoxical! It moves from one extreme to another. It comprehends all extremes. It is so vast, it contains all the contradictions in it.

Whatsoever Lao Tzu is saying, he is saying, "Live here and now!" This is folly because a reasonable man always sacrifices today for tomorrow. He says, "I will live tomorrow. When things are put right, when the time is right, and I have leisure, enough money, a big palace to live in, then I will live. Right now how can I live?"

Every parent is teaching to every child: 'Sacrifice the present for the future. Sacrifice this moment for the next. Sacrifice yourself for something else.' This is reasonableness – to postpone life.

Heart says: 'Live now!' That's what Lao Tzu says: "Live now!" In fact, there is no other way of living. Either you live now, or you just pretend to live. You never live, you just postpone. You only die, you never live. Because to live there is no other time than the present. Existence is always in the present. But the reason always thinks and plans for the future.

Of course, if somebody says, 'Live now,' you will say, 'How is it possible? I have to make arrangements first. I have to plan. When the right time comes I will live.' It never comes. Millions and millions of people have died; it never came for them, it will never come to you.

All great wisdom resembles folly. Only fools look reasonable in this world. Only fools are rational. All wise people look a little eccentric. They don't belong to the crowd. They don't belong to the notions of the crowd. They live their being. They look like idiots.

This word 'idiot' is beautiful. It comes from a Greek word *idioti,* and *idioti* in Greek means 'private'. This is something! An idiot is somebody who is living his private life! Not a life of the crowd. Not part of a collective mass. He who is living his own life in his own way is an idiot.

All greatness is so beyond the mediocre mind! And mind is mediocre! Remember it: mind itself is mediocre. The mind can never be great;

there have never been great minds. If you have heard about great minds you have heard wrongly. If you ask all the great minds they will say that whatsoever they have attained has come from beyond the mind, not from the mind; something that filters through the mind but is not part of the mind.

Ask Madame Curie how she solved her problem and became a Nobel laureate. She tried for years, for three years almost, to solve a single mathematical problem upon which her whole research depended. She failed and failed and failed. Frustrated one night, she dropped the whole project, went to sleep; and in the night, in a dream, the problem was solved. She got up, wrote it down at the desk, went back to sleep.

In the morning she completely forgot about it, and when she came to work at the desk she was surprised – there was the answer, miraculously there! For three years she had been working at it – where had it come from? And there was nobody else, she was alone in the room, and nobody else could have solved it even if there had been somebody there. Nobody, no servant, could have done that trick, she herself had been working on it for three years.

Then she remembered a dream. In the dream she had seen the whole answer written. Then she remembered that she had got up in the night; and then she looked at the handwriting – it was her own.

Now, the Nobel Prize should not go to the mind – but it has gone to the mind. Now Madame Curie is a great mind – and the answer has come from beyond the mind. Always it has been so. Always it will be so. Mind is mediocre. It is good at small things, petty things of the market – you can run a small business, you can earn a little money, you can have a bank balance, there it is okay. But not beyond that.

Bodhidharma reached China. The whole country was waiting for him. The king himself had come to the border of the country to receive him. A million people had gathered, because a great Master was coming. And when the Master appeared, people started giggling. It was impossible to believe their own eyes. Even the emperor felt very uneasy because this man Bodhidharma had one shoe on one foot and the other he was carrying on his head. What manner of man was this?

The king said, "Excuse me, sir, but what are you doing? We had come to receive a sane man. Are you insane?"

Bodhidharma laughed and said: "So you have failed in the examination. If you can understand this only then can you understand other things that I have to say. If you cannot tolerate such a small contradiction: it's not much, just carrying a shoe on the head. If you cannot tolerate and understand this much it will be useless for me to stay here."

He turned back. He left the town, went into the forest. He said, "There is no need to stay, nobody will be able to understand me; now I will wait. Those who can understand me, they should come to me." He never entered into the capital again.

Contradictions are very difficult for the mind. Mind lives in a routine. The shoe must be on the foot, that's the accepted thing. It should not be carried on the head. Such an innocent thing – he was not doing any harm to anybody. But no, impossible. We have a leveling of everything.

Life is a circle. A child is a fool, innocently foolish, and that is the beauty of a child. All children are beautiful. You cannot come across an ugly child. But then where does all that beauty disappear to? Behind the labels, all that beauty disappears. Then masks are there, not faces. Behind the dishonesties, the reality disappears. But each child is beautiful, beautiful and foolish! And innocent!

Then you learn much, and you lose much in your learning. Then you move into the world. You become knowledgeable, you become worldly wise, but then you are losing your innocence. Then layers and layers of worldly knowledge, of the so-called worldly wisdom, gather around you. You are encaged.

If you can understand Lao Tzu you suddenly drop out of this imprisonment which you yourself are carrying around you. Nobody is insisting, nobody is forcing it on you; you simply drop all the identities and all the deadness that has accumulated around you. This is renunciation. If you ask me, this is sannyas. You simply drop all that you have gathered, you simply become completely unburdened, and again become a child. Of course the whole world will say you have become a fool, because the world now cannot account for you.

Many times people ask me why in the name of Lao Tzu there has not been a great organized religion. It was not possible. The man is impossible. The man is so wisely foolish that it is difficult to create an establishment around him. He remains a lonely rebel, beautiful in his aloneness, but incomprehensible, very far away, distant, like Everest – you can look at it, but to create a mass organization around him, and to lead the masses towards the Everest is not possible.

What is love in fact? What happens? What is this phenomenon, love? First thing: With love you function as a heart and you don't function as a mind. You don't function as reason, you function as feeling. You don't think, you feel.

This is the first thing to be understood about love; that you become a feeling phenomenon not a thinking entity. Your center of being falls from the head to the heart. You become headless. You don't identify with the head, you become identified with the heart – and the heart is absolutely foolish; foolish in the eyes of the world, wise in its own ways. You start feeling. It has become very difficult because whenever you feel, you in fact only think that you feel. It is not direct.

Sometimes people come to me and they say that they have fallen in love, and I ask, "Are you certain?"

They say, "We think that we have fallen in love."

Even feeling has to pass through thinking first, then it comes to you. You heart has to beg the mind to be allowed a little freedom. This is absurd. Because thinking is a device. It is useful, but it is not your whole being. It is like a radar: it helps you to look around, to have a little peep into the future so that you can move well, but it is not you.

And howsoever you train your mind you will never be happy with it because happiness is not a quality which is felt by the mind.

It is just as if you are trying to smell something through the eyes. The eyes are not meant to smell, they are meant to see. Or it is as if you are trying to see something through the ears; those ears are not meant to see, they are meant to hear.

Mind is a bio-computer. The very mechanism exists there to help you to move safely in an unknown world, in a strange world. It is just a safety guard. It is not meant that you should be happy through it – and that is what you have been trying to do! And that is how you have created hell around you: you are trying to be happy through the mind, which is not possible!

Mind people are the most unhappy in the world, and this is as it should be. Mind is to look around as a watchdog, to feel the way. Whenever it is needed it should be used. Whenever it is not needed it should be put aside. But you have become so dependent on the slave that the slave has become the master. And the master has become completely lost. You are not even able to feel where the master is.

Lao Tzu says: "Drop down towards the heart. Love things, don't think things. Love people, don't think people. Feel more, think less, and you will be more and more happy."

The trees are more happy than man, the birds are more happy than man, the animals are more happy than man – this is unbelievable! What has happened to man? He has got hooked into the mechanism of mind.

It is good that the mind is there. It is beautiful if you can use it. But you should not be a head, rather you should be a head master. You should use it as one uses a mechanism – just as you drive a car. Don't become identified with the car. Be the driver, remain the driver. And when you don't want to drive, don't allow the car to force you. If you need it, you use it. If you don't need it, you don't use it. Head is a subtle mechanism around you. You are just like a driver, hidden behind the mechanism.

Drop the identity with the mind, then only will you know what love is – because once you drop the identity with the mind suddenly you fall towards the heart. The heart is the driver.

But how is it to be done? You start slowly to move in that direction. Sit by the side of a rock, close your eyes and feel the rock. Don't think, and don't say it is beautiful – these are all mind trips. Just lie down on the rock, spread your hands and body on the rock as if you are on the breast of your mother. Feel the rock, close your eyes, touch the rock with your tongue, kiss the rock, and let it give you a feeling.

Go and embrace a tree. Just put your head on a tree and rest there, and feel how the energy of the tree starts flowing in you, and how it rejuvenates you, how it makes you absolutely fresh and clean, how suddenly deep down in you some flowers start opening and flowering. Listen to the sound of a bird, just listen, because the bird is not saying anything, he is simply singing. Listen to the poetry of the waters. Just listen to the poetry of the trees and their color, and feel.

In the beginning it will be hard; again and again you will start thinking. Remember, drop thinking, again feel. By and by you will come to have the knack of it. Once you have the knack of feeling you will laugh! How you were missing! Behind the mechanism you were hiding. The driver was lost and the car had become the totality. Now the driver is separate, now you can come. You can put the car off, or you can put the car on, it is for you to decide. Mind is a mechanism, it can be put off and on.

When I talk to you I have to put it on, when you are gone I take the key out of it. It is non-functioning. It stops. Your car is continuously on, your motors are continuously functioning. They create such noise within you: the inner chatter.

The first step towards love is to feel more. And the second step towards love is: Be more.

Don't pay much attention to that which you do; pay attention to that which you are. You always think in terms of doing: you are an engineer, you are a doctor, you have done this and that. Forget all this doing! Just try to be more. Have the feeling of being; just sitting, feel you are. 'Isness', being, should be the mantra. Just feel you are, and let this feeling get deeply rooted within you. Never get identified with what you have done. That is nothing. That is just dirt. Get clean out of it and just feel who you are.

In the East the greatest mantra is, 'Who am I?' Not that you start thinking about yourself, because that is how it is happening in the West. Coming to know that in the East the teaching has been: Know who you are, there are many people who sit silently and repeat inside: 'Who am I? Who am I?' If you do this then you are making a fool of yourself. It is stupid. Don't say, 'Who am I?' otherwise you are thinking again. Just feel, be. Just close your eyes and grope in the dark for the being. Grope! The new generation has a beautiful word for it; that is 'to groove'. Groove for it, focus on it. In darkness, try to grope. There is nothing like it. Once you can groove on it, once you can focus on it, it is the most groovy thing possible.

First drop thinking and come nearer and closer to feeling; and then drop doing and come closer and nearer to being. If these two things can be done you will be able to gain the first glimpse of what love is. And then your life will be filled more and more by love and love's light. Then you can enter into a relationship which will not be sexual. Sex may be part of it, but if it is part of love sex itself becomes beautiful. And if love is part of prayer then love becomes religious and sacred. And if prayer is part of meditation it becomes the ultimate, beyond which there is no goal, the last fulfillment.

Why does Lao Tzu say, "Never too much" - the disease I call overdoing? Because mind is fed by overdoing, and heart is always fed by balance. A loving person is always balanced, he is always in the middle; never too much to the left, never too much to the right. Even if sometimes he has to lean towards the right he leans only to gain balance. That's all. Otherwise he remains exactly in the middle: still, tranquil, silent. He is always in equilibrium.

Mind is always after the extreme. It exists because of the extreme. Mind is the extremist. It is always overdoing – either on the left or on the right, but it is always overdoing. Whenever you are overdoing a thing you are becoming a slave to the mind. Whenever you are balanced, non-extremist, you are going deeper than the mind, you are moving in the heart.

I say: 'Renounce *in* the world. Don't renounce the world, renounce *in* the world.' Be in the world but don't be of it. Be in the world but don't allow the world to be in you, then an equilibrium is attained.

That's why my *sannyas* looks contradictory, paradoxical, because I am giving *sannyas* to people who are going to live in the world. I am not telling anybody to move to the monasteries. I am insisting: 'Remain in the market.' If the market and the meditation can both go together there will be an equilibrium attained.

Even too much of God is bad. Too much of meditation is a disease. Too much of anything is wrong. It has happened in the East, we have done too much meditation. In Zen monasteries they are doing eight hours, ten hours, per day. It seems they are born here only to meditate, nothing else. Their whole life seems to be just sitting. They don't enrich life. They don't enrich themselves by life experiences. They don't move in the world – they are afraid, fear-ridden. And all their meditation is nothing but deep suppression. Meditate, but go to the market, because there is the test whether you have been meditating rightly or not.

Whenever you love you don't want to be first in the world. That's why I said: When love goes wrong, politics is born. Politics is the effort to be first in the world – to be the president, to be the prime minister, to be the richest person in the world, to be the most famous in the world, to be first in the world.

Have you watched? If you love somebody you would like him or her to be the first in the world, not yourself. Suddenly a change of inner being happens. If you love somebody you would like him or her to be the first. And if you love the whole world – then you would like to be the last. That's what Jesus says: "Those who are first in this world will be the last in the kingdom of my God." And *vice versa*.

Lao Tzu says, "Never be the first in the world." The very ambition of being first shows that you missed life. You are not blessed. You are not exalted. You are not fulfilled. Ambition is insanity. Ambition shows that you are not at ease with yourself, that you are not at home. Ambition shows that now you want that others should know you are very great. That is just to hide your smallness. You would like the whole world to know that 'I am the greatest man in the world'.

This is just the opposite of what you feel inside – you feel inferior. Only an inferior mind is ambitious. A superior mind need not be ambitious; there is no point in being ambitious. He is so fulfilled, if you put him last he will be happy there. He knows how to be happy! So wherever he is he is happy. If you throw him in hell he will be happy there.

I have heard: There was an English thinker, Edmund Burke. He used to go to church on Sundays. He was not a believer but he liked the preacher and the way he talked about things. Somebody asked him: "You are not a believer and you are not a religious man, so why do you go every Sunday, and so regularly?"

He said: "Once in a while I like to see a person who really believes. Just to see a person who has faith is beautiful in itself. I don't have any faith, but this preacher is a man of faith. He may be wrong – I know that he is wrong, but that doesn't matter. He is beautiful in his faith. It seems that he has attained. Maybe he is in a delusion, but that is not the point. I am continuously trying to achieve something and he has attained. So just to look at him, I go there."

One day he asked the priest – because the priest had preached that evening that people who are good, virtuous, and believe in God will go to heaven. After the sermon Burke asked the priest: "What about people who are good and virtuous but don't believe in God? Where will they go? Will they go to heaven? If you say 'Yes,' then to believe in God is not necessary. Then the belief, the whole hypothesis is useless! If a person can go to heaven just by being virtuous then what is the point of belief? And if you say that people who are virtuous and good and don't believe in God will have to go to hell, then what is the point of being virtuous and good? Just believing in God will do."

This Burke was a logician, and the priest was puzzled. He said: "Give me a few days, I will have to enquire. I don't know exactly what happens." He tried for seven days to think from every nook and comer, but he couldn't get it, because the puzzle was there. If he says 'Yes,' then there is a problem. If he says, 'No,' then too there is a problem.

On the seventh day he came to the church one hour before his sermon; he went to the terrace, was brooding there, closed his eyes – the whole of the previous night he could not sleep because he was thinking and thinking and thinking – and again he fell into sleep, and he had a dream.

In dream he saw himself going in a train somewhere. He asked: "Where is this train going?" And people said: "We are going to heaven." He said: "This is good. This is the right thing. I will ask where those people are who are virtuous, for example Socrates – good, virtuous, but he never believed in God; where are they?"

So he went into heaven. But he didn't like the look of the place. It looked a little ruinous, no happiness, a little boring, no excitement – of course, silent – but it looked dead. He could not believe that this was heaven.

Then he asked, "When does the train leave for hell?" The train was ready, so he entered. He went to hell. He could not believe his eyes again because things were really beautiful. Beautiful trees, greenery, flowers, birds singing, and everybody was happy. He said, "There is something wrong! This seems to be like heaven."

He went into the town. He asked people: "Is Socrates here?" They said, "Yes, he is working in the fields." So he went to Socrates and he said: "Are you here? You, good and virtuous, but you didn't believe in God? So you have been thrown in hell?"

Socrates said: "I don't know about hell at all, but since we came here we have turned it into heaven."

Shocked, the priest's eyes opened.

Edmund Burke was waiting downstairs. The priest came there and he said: "I don't know now exactly, but a dream I had I will tell you. In the dream I came to realize that people who are good and virtuous, wherever they go – that place becomes heaven. People who are not virtuous and good, even if they believe in God, wherever they go – that place becomes a hell. This is how it has been revealed to me in my dream."

The world has become a hell because nobody trusts himself. Nobody is fulfilled. Nobody is happy with himself. Everybody is ambitious. Ambition creates hell. If you ask me who is the non-religious person I will say: the ambitious mind. If you ask me who is the religious person I will say: the non-ambitious mind. A non-ambitious mind is religion incarnated. He has the quality, because he is so fulfilled. Around him you will find an aura of fulfillment. He is not competing with anybody else. There is no need. He feels enough! More than enough. He feels grateful. Whatsoever he has got is ecstatic. More is not possible. And he is not competing with anybody else because there is no need.

The inner riches are such – there is no need to compete. That is the meaning of inner treasures. If you go for outer treasures you will be in competition. If you go for inner treasures there is no competition, no need for it. There is an infinite sky; you can have the whole sky for yourself, there is nobody else to compete with you.

That's the difference between religion and politics. Politics attracts inferior people, people who are filled with inferiority complexes. To be religious is to drop the inferiority complex. That's why I go on insisting that you are not to achieve anything. It is already there within you.

You are not to become gods, you are gods! And you are not to postpone it for tomorrow. There is no need. You can enjoy it right now. The question is not to achieve something, the question is to delight in it. It is already there! You lack nothing! If you want to be happy you can be happy this very moment! Not for a single moment has it to be delayed, there is no need because all that is needed for being happy is there.

You have just to become alert, aware. You have just to open your eyes and find that everything is there: all guests have come, the food is ready, the celebration is on! You have just to open your eyes and participate.

I don't say, 'Become gods,' because that is politics, then you are running to achieve something; you become ambitious. I say, 'You are gods. Realize it; it is not to be attained. You have just to pay a little attention to it. You have become oblivious of the fact that you are gods.' And then who bothers to be the first in the world? You are already the first.

Everybody is the first in the world, that is the meaning of it. Nobody is comparable to you, has never been, will never be; you are incomparable, unique. You are already the first.

Unless you attain to love you will always be afraid. A deep turmoil and fear will be there in your being. You will go on trembling, because unless you attain to love you cannot know that you are deathless. Fear will be there.

One who loves deeply becomes deathless. One who loves deeply goes beyond death. One who knows love knows also that death does not exist. Because in deep love you come to know death. You die! And you resurrect.

The cross and resurrection both happen in love; that's why people are afraid of love. They come to me and they say, 'We would like to love but we are afraid.' Man is afraid of woman, women are afraid of men. Even if you are in love you are not wholeheartedly in it. You move with very, very safe secured steps. And you move always to that point from where withdrawal is easy. You never move to that point where withdrawal will be impossible. You never move to that depth from where return is not possible. You stretch out your hand, but you are always ready to take it back any moment if danger comes. That's why your love remains superficial.

Love is a death, death of the ego. And when you die only then you know that you cannot die, that something in you transcends death.

Remember you are here to be only you and nobody else. Don't allow anybody else to manipulate you, and don't try to manipulate anybody else. You are not here to fulfill anybody else's expectations, nor is anybody else here to fulfill your expectations. Each individual is unique, sacred, divine. And each individual has his own destiny, and he has to fulfill his own destiny. His own destiny fulfilled, he fulfills the Whole. Unfulfilled, he remains like a wound in the heart of the Whole.

There is only one sin if you ask me, and that sin is: not to fulfill your destiny. And there is only one virtue: to become that which you are meant to be, non-competitively.

Just think if the whole world disappears and you are alone on the earth – what will you do? Just think – what will you do if the whole of humanity disappears, leaving only you on the earth. What will you do? Just close your eyes sometimes and see what you will do.

If it comes to you that you will dance, then that is your destiny. Dance! Or if you think that you will just relax under a tree and go to sleep – go under a tree and go to sleep! That is your destiny. Just think of yourself alone – and you are alone really – and then you will feel fulfilled. Small things fulfill if they are in tune with your being. Even great things cannot fulfill if they are not in tune with you.

So these are the two paths: if you follow your own inner being, the still small voice within, you will be fulfilled. If you don't follow it, you are doomed. And if you feel that you are already doomed, don't be miserable – there is always enough time to drop out. Even in the last moment one can drop out.

In a single moment one's destiny can be fulfilled. But don't go on playing roles which others have imposed on you. Others are trying to say, 'Be this; be that.' Just be yourself. That's why when many people come to me and they say, "Why don't you ask your sannyasins to be a little more disciplined?" I say, "I cannot. If the discipline comes from their own understanding, it is okay. If it is not coming, that too is okay. Who am I to force any discipline on you?" I am here to make you free.

If out of freedom a discipline is born, and you become mature, understanding, responsible, it is good. If not, that too is good. But I am not here to impose any discipline on you. An imposed discipline is a slavery, and when it comes from your innermost core it is freedom, freedom fulfilled, freedom come to its ultimate blossoming.

Osho – "Tao, The Three Treasures", Volume 4, Discourse 1

AWAKENING KUNDALINI

The space where the life force is stored is like a *kunda*, a pool near the sex center; that is why the energy is known as kundalini, as if it is a *kunda* or pool of water.

Another reason it is called kundalini is that it looks like a snake coiled and sleeping. If you have seen a sleeping serpent you know how it lies in coils with its hood on top. But if you disturb the sleeping serpent it will wake up, uncoil and raise its hood up. This energy is called kundalini also because the pool of life-force, or the seed of life, is precisely located near the sex center and it is from here that life expands in all directions.

It will be good to remember that the small pleasure that we derive from sex is not the pleasure of sex; it really comes from the vibrations arising in the pool of vital energy along with sex. The sleeping serpent is slightly moved by the sex act and we consider it to be the whole pleasure of life. We are not at all aware of what happens when the whole serpent is awakened and it travels across our entire being and reaches the ultimate center in the brain. We are completely unaware of it. We live on the first step of the ladder of life. There are other steps, greater steps, that lead to God.

The small distance of two to three feet that is there in our body is in another sense a very big distance; it is the distance between nature and God, between matter and soul, between sleep and wakefulness, between death and immortality. That distance is very long, but there is also a small distance inside our being which we can traverse in meditation.

If you have to awaken the energy that is lying asleep in you, you should know well that it is not less dangerous than trying to disturb and awaken a sleeping serpent. In fact, disturbing a sleeping serpent is not that dangerous. But playing with the kundalini power, which I am talking about, is dangerous indeed; there is nothing more dangerous than this. No danger can be greater than this. But what is the danger?

This is a kind of death. If the energy within is awakened, you will die as you are right now and a totally new individual will be born, an individual that you never were before awakening. And it is this fear that prevents people from becoming religious. It is the same fear which, if it grips a seed, prevents it from becoming a tree.

Now the greatest danger facing a seed is that it will be buried in the soil, it will be treated with water and manure and then it will die as a seed. It is again the same danger that faces an egg when it grows and breaks its shell. Then it has to die as an egg so that it becomes a bird.

In the same way we are in the preceding state of something yet to be born. We are like an egg which is going to become a bird. But we take the egg to be everything and nestle down in it.

When this energy will rise, you will be no more; there is no way for you to survive. And if you get frightened, your fate will be what Kabir describes in a beautiful couplet. Kabir has said a beautiful thing. He says, "He alone found it who sought it by diving deep in the sea. But I proved myself a fool as I kept sitting on the seashore, although I had been there seeking."

Whoever has found it has done so by seeking it in the depths. What is essential is a readiness to be drowned, a readiness to disappear. If it has to be said in one word – though it is not a happy word – it is 'death', readiness for death. And he who will be afraid of being drowned will of course survive, but he will only survive as an egg; he will never become a bird on the wing. He who will fear being drowned will of course survive, but he will only survive as a seed; he will never become a tree under whose shade thousands of travelers may relax.

But is it worthwhile to survive as a seed? It would be worse than death really.

So, there is great danger. The danger is that the person that I was till yesterday will not survive; when the energy will be awakened it will totally transform me. New centers will be awakened, a new individuality will emerge, new experiences will happen, everything will be new. If you are prepared for the new, then you must gather courage to part with the old.

Where is this energy coming from? This energy too, is your own energy that was lying asleep in you. But even this energy is not enough for meditation. Even when you run for your life, being pursued by a gunman, you are not running with your entire might. In meditation you will need to stake much more than this. You will have to stake your utmost. And the moment you touch the point where your entire energy is pressed into action, you will find that you are connected with some other energy, that some hidden energy within you has started waking up. For sure you will experience the awakening of this extraordinary energy. It is like you have suddenly contacted some electric current. You will feel that some energy within you, lying low at the sex center, has started rising upward. This energy is hot like a flaming fire, and at the same time it is cool like the morning breeze. It is like a harsh prick of thorns and at the same time it is as soft as a flower. And many things will happen when that energy will be rising upward.

Please don't withhold yourself at any point when the energy is moving upward. Let go of yourself completely, like a man leaves himself in the hands of the river and just floats with its current. In short, 'let go' is the key.

Now the second thing. First you have to stake your all; and when as a result of this total staking, then you have to leave yourself fully in the hands of that 'something'. This is the second thing. Let go of yourself; just float as one floats on the surface of the water, just floating. You should be ready to go wheresoever the current of the river takes you. It is true that to a certain extent we have to provoke it, but when the energy is awakened, we have just to leave ourselves in its hands, we have to let go of ourselves. Higher forces have taken over, we need not worry anymore. We have to just float.

And third, with the upward rise of this energy many things will happen. Please see that you don't get scared when they happen, because new experiences are frightening. When a child is born, when he comes out of his mother's cozy womb, he gets frightened. Psychologists call it a trauma, a traumatic experience, an experience which a child will never forget, which will haunt him for the whole of his life.

The child's fear of the new begins with his birth, because he had lived in complete security in the mother's womb for nine months. He had no worries whatsoever; he did not have to breathe or eat or cry or do anything for himself; the mother did everything. The child was in a state of absolute rest and comfort. Coming out of the mother's womb he encounters a new and strange world altogether. This is the first shock of life, and it is here, at the very doorstep of life that fear grips him.

That is why everybody fears the new; they cling to the old and fear the new. It is the first experience of our life that the new puts us in great trouble. Mother's womb was a much better place than this world. That is why most of our contrivances that we use in daily living are fashioned after the mother's womb.

So, the first experience after coming from mother's womb is one of fear of the new. The experience of the awakening of the kundalini, the primordial energy, is a new experience greater than the child's, because while the childbirth happens only at the level of the body, the awakening of the kundalini happens at the level of the soul.

It is therefore a totally new birth.

It is for this reason that we call him a *brahmin* who goes through this experience. *Brahmin* is he who is twice born. He is also called *dwij* – one who is twice born.

So, when that energy awakens, a second birth happens. In this birth you are both – you are the mother and you are the child. You alone are both together.

Osho – "In Search of the Miraculous"

SEVEN BODIES OF MEN AND WOMEN

The individual can be divided into seven bodies. The first body is the physical body which we all know. The second is the etheric body, and the third – which is beyond this second – is the astral body. The fourth – which is beyond this – is the mental or psychic body; and the fifth – which is beyond this again – is the spiritual body. The sixth is beyond the fifth, and it is called the cosmic body. Then the seventh and the last is the *nirvana sharir*, or the nirvanic body, the bodiless body.

In the first seven years of life, the *sthul sharir*, the physical body, alone is formed. The other bodies are in seed form. They have a potential for growth but they lie dormant in the beginning of life. So the first seven years are years of limitation. There is no growth of intellect, emotion or desire during these years. Only the physical body develops within this period.

Some people never grow beyond seven years; they stagnate at this stage and are no more than animals. Animals develop only in the physical body; the other bodies remain untouched within them.

In the next seven years – that is from seven years to fourteen years – the *bhawa sharir*, the etheric body, develops. These seven years are years of emotional growth of the individual. This is why sexual maturity, which is the most intense form of emotion, is reached at the age of fourteen. Now some people stagnate at this stage. Their physical bodies grow but they are stuck with the first two bodies.

In the third seven-year period, between the ages of fourteen and twenty-one, the *sukshma sharir*, the astral body, develops. In the second body emotion is developed. In the third body reasoning, thinking and intellect are developed.

After the development of the second body a person reaches adulthood. But this is the adulthood of sex. Nature's work is complete with this development, and this is why nature gives its full cooperation up to this stage. But at this stage man is not man in the full sense of the word.

The third body, where reason, intellect and the thinking power develop, is an outcome of education, civilization and culture. This is why the right to vote is granted to a person when he is 21 years of age. Though this is prevalent all over the world, some countries are debating whether to allow an 18-year-old the right to vote. This is natural, because as man is becoming more and more evolved the usual span of seven years for the growth of each body is becoming less and less.

All over the world girls reach puberty at the age of 13 to 14 years. Since the last 30 years the age for this is becoming less and less. Even a girl of 11 reaches puberty. The lowering of the voting age to 18 is an indication that man now completes the work of 21 years in 18 years. Normally, however, 21 years are required for the growth of the third body, and the majority of people do not develop further than this. Their growth stops short with the development of the third body, and there is no further development for the rest of their lives.

What I call the 'psyche' is the fourth body – the *manas sharir*. This body has its own wonderful experiences. Now a person whose intellect is not developed may not be able to take interest in or enjoy mathematics, for instance. Mathematics has its own charm, and only Einstein can be absorbed in it as a musician is in music or a painter is in colors. For Einstein mathematics was not work but play, but the intellect must reach this peak of development in order to turn mathematics into play.

With each body that develops infinite possibilities open before us. One whose etheric body does not develop, who stagnates after the first seven years of development, does not have any interest in life beyond eating and drinking. So the cultures of those civilizations where the majority of people have developed only up to the first body revolve entirely around their taste buds.

The civilization where the majority of people have got stuck at the second body will be sex centered. Their personalities, their literature, their music, their films and books, their poetry and paintings, even their houses and vehicles, will all be sex centered: all these things will be completely filled with sex, with sexuality.

In the civilization in which the third body develops fully, people will be intellectual and contemplative. Whenever the development of the third body becomes very important in a society or in a nation, many intellectual revolutions take place.

In Bihar, the majority of people were of this caliber at the time of Buddha and Mahavira. This is why eight persons of the stature of Buddha and Mahavira were born in the small province of Bihar. Besides, there were thousands of others at the time who were endowed with genius. Such was the condition of Greece at the time of Socrates and Plato; such also was the condition of China at the time of Lao Tzu and Confucius. What is even more wonderful to note is the fact that all these luminous beings existed within a period of 500 years. Within those 500 years the development of the third body in man reached its peak.

Generally man halts at the third body. The majority of people do not develop after 21 years.

There are unusual experiences of the fourth body. Hypnotism, telepathy, clairvoyance, are all the potential of the fourth body. Persons can have contact with one another without hindrances from time or place; they can read the thoughts of another without asking or project thoughts into another. Without any external help one can instill a seed of thought into another. A person can travel outside of his body; he can do astral projection and know himself apart from the physical body.

There are great possibilities in the fourth body, but we do not normally develop this body as there are many hazards as well as much deception. As things begin to get more and more subtle, the possibilities of deception increase. Now it is difficult to find out whether a man has actually stepped out of his body or not. He can dream that he stepped out of his body and he can actually do so too, and in both the cases there is no other witness than himself. So there is every possibility of deception.

The world that starts from the fourth body is subjective, whereas the world before that is objective. If I have a rupee in my hand, I can see it, you can see it, 50 others can also see it. This is a common reality in which we can all take part, and it can be investigated whether the rupee is or is not. But in the realm of my thoughts you cannot be a partner, nor can I be a partner in the realm of your thoughts. From here the personal world begins with all its hazards; none of our external rules of validity can be used here.

So the real world of deception starts from the fourth body. All the deceptions of the preceding three can be seen through. The greatest danger is that it is not necessarily the case that the deceiver is aware of the fact that he is deceiving. He can deceive, unknowingly, himself as well as others. Things are so subtle, so rare and personal on this plane that one has no means to test the validity of his experiences. So he cannot tell whether he is imagining things or whether they are really happening to him. So we have always tried to save humanity from this fourth body, and those who made use of this body were always condemned and slandered.

Hundreds of women were branded as witches and burnt in Europe because they used the faculties of the fourth body. Hundreds who practiced Tantra were killed in India because of the fourth body. They knew some secrets that seemed dangerous to human beings. They knew what was taking place in your mind; they knew where things were placed in your house without ever having stepped into it. So the realm of the fourth body was looked upon as 'black art' all over the world, as one never knew what might happen.

We have always tried our best to stop progress from going any further than the third body, because the fourth has always seemed very dangerous. There are hazards, but together with these there are wonderful gains.

The fourth body exists, but it is very subtle; it cannot come within our grasp. Only the physical body can be grasped. Yet there are corresponding points between the first body and the fourth body. If we were to place seven sheets of paper one on top of the other, prick a hole through them with a pin so that all the papers are pierced, then even if the hole disappears from the first sheet it will still carry a mark that corresponds to the holes in the rest of the sheets. Then although the first paper does not have the hole, it has the point which will correspond directly with the pinholes on the other sheets when it is placed upon them.

So chakras, kundalini, *et cetera,* do not belong to the first body as such, but there are corresponding points in the first body. So a physiologist is not wrong if he denies them. The chakras and the kundalini are in other bodies, but points corresponding to them can be found on the physical body.

So kundalini is the happening of the fourth body and it is psychic. And when I say that this is psychic, happening is of two kinds – one true and one false – then you will understand what I mean. It will be false when it is a product of your imagination, because imagination is also a characteristic of the fourth body.

Animals do not have the power of imagination, so they have very little memory of the past and no idea of future. Animals are free from anxiety, as anxiety is always of the future. Animals see many deaths taking place, but they never imagine that they can die also; therefore, they have no fear of death.

Among men also there are many who are not bothered by the fear of death. Such a man always associates death with others and not with himself. The reason is that the power of imagination in the fourth body has not developed fully enough to see into the future. This means that imagination can also be true or false.

True imagination means that we are capable of seeing further ahead, that we can visualize that which has not yet come to pass. But to imagine that something will happen that cannot be, which does not exist, is false imagination. When imagination is used in its right perspective it becomes science. Science is primarily only imagination.

Since thousands of years man has dreamed of flying. The men who had dreamed in this way must have been very imaginative. If man had never dreamed about flying, it would have been impossible for the Wright brothers to make the first airplane. They made man's desire to fly something concrete. This desire took some time to shape; then experiments were carried out, and finally man succeeded in flying. Also, for thousands of years man has wanted to reach the moon. First it was only in his imagination; slowly, slowly it gained ground, and now it has been fulfilled.

Now, these imaginations were authentic: that is, they were not on a false path. These imaginations were on the path of a reality which could be discovered at a later date.

So a scientist also imagines, and so does a person who is mad. If I say that science is imagination and madness is also imagination, don't think they are one and the same thing. A madman imagines things which do not exist and which have no relationship with the physical world. The scientist also imagines: he imagines things which are directly related with the physical world. And if it does not seem so at first there is a complete possibility of their being so in the future. Among the possibilities of the fourth body there is always a chance of going wrong. Then the false world begins. This is why it is best if we do not harbor any expectations before entering this body. This fourth body is the psychic body.

Now, for instance, if I want to go down to the ground floor of this house I will have to look for a lift or a staircase in order to do so. But if I want to go down in my thoughts there is no need for a lift or a staircase. I can sit right here and go down. The hazard of imagination and thoughts is that one has to do nothing except imagine or think, and so anyone can do it. Moreover, if anyone enters this realm with preconceived ideas and expectations, then he immediately goes down only into these, because then the mind will be only too willing to cooperate. It will say, 'You want to awaken the kundalini? All right! It is rising...it has risen!' Then you will begin to imagine kundalini rising, and the mind will encourage you in this false feeling until ultimately you will feel that it is fully awakened and that the chakras are fully activated.

But there is a way of testing the validity of it, and that is that with the opening of each chakra there will be a distinct change in your personality. This change you cannot imagine or preconceive, because this change takes place in the world of matter.

So, for instance, when the kundalini awakens you cannot take intoxicants; it is impossible. The mental body gets influenced by alcohol very quickly as it is very delicate. This is why – and you will be surprised to know this – when a woman consumes alcohol she becomes more dangerous than a man who does so. This is because her mental body is even more delicate, and it gets affected so quickly that things get out of her control. This is why women have protected themselves from this hazard by certain rules in society.

This is one place where women did not seek equality with men, although unfortunately of late she is trying to. The day she asserts her equality in this area and tries to outdo men in it she will cause such harm to herself as has never been caused by any action by men.

In the fourth body the awakening of the kundalini cannot be proved by your telling about the experience, because, as I said before, you can falsely imagine the awakening and experiencing of the kundalini also. It can only be judged by your physical traits: whether any radical transformation has taken place in your personality. No sooner does the energy awaken than there will be immediate signs of change in you.

This is why I always say that behavior is the outer criterion and not the inner cause. It is a criterion of what has happened within. With each attempt some things inevitably begin to happen. When the energy awakens it becomes impossible for the meditator to take any intoxicants. If he does indulge in drugs and alcohol, then know that his experiences are all imaginary, because it is absolutely impossible.

After the awakening of the kundalini the tendency for violence disappears completely. Not only does the meditator not commit violence, but he has no feeling of violence within himself. The urge to commit violence, the urge to harm others, can only exist when the vital energy is dormant. The moment it awakens the other ceases to be the other and so you cannot wish to harm him. Then you will not have to repress violence within yourself because then you cannot be violent. If you find that you have to repress the feeling of violence, then know that the kundalini has not awakened.

So there will be a radical change in your behavior with the awakening, and all the religious vows like those of the *mahavrata* – nonviolence, not-stealing, non-possession, celibacy and full awareness - will become natural and easy for you. Then know that your experience is authentic. It is psychic, however, but authentic all the same. Now you can proceed further. You can proceed ahead if your path is authentic, but not otherwise.

You cannot stay forever in the fourth body because it is not the goal. There are yet other bodies that have to be crossed. We find, as I said, that very few are able to develop the fourth body.

That is why there are miracle performers in the world today. If the fourth body in everyone were developed, miracles would vanish from the earth at once. If there were a society of people whose development had stagnated after the fourteenth year of age, then the one who had developed a little further, who could add or subtract, would be thought to be performing miracles.

A thousand years ago, when a person declared the date of the eclipse of the sun, it was considered a miracle that only the very wise could perform. Today we know that even a machine can give us this information. It is a matter of calculation and does not require an astronomer or a prophet or a very learned person. A computer can give the information not of a single eclipse but of millions of eclipses. It can even forecast the day when the sun will get cold – because these are all calculations. The machine can calculate from the data provided that the total energy of the sun divided by quantity of energy the sun emits per day gives the number of years the sun will last.

But all this does not look like a miracle to us now, because now we are all developed up to the third body. A thousand years ago it was a great miracle if a man prophesied that next year, in this month, on this night, there would be an eclipse of the moon. He would be considered superhuman.

The 'miracles' that take place nowadays – the magic charms, the ash dropping from picture frames – are all ordinary happenings of the fourth body. But since we do not know, it is a miracle for us.

It is just as if you are standing under a tree and I am sitting on the tree, and we two are talking. Now I see a cart coming from far away and I tell you that in an hour's time a cart will come and halt under the tree. You will say, "Are you a prophet? You talk in riddles. There is no cart anywhere around. I do not believe what you say." But in an hour's time the cart rolls up to the tree, and then of necessity you have to touch my feet and say, "Beloved Master, my respects. You are a prophet."

The difference was only this, that I was sitting on a little higher level than you – on the tree – from where the cart became visible an hour before it did for you. I was not talking of the future, I was talking very much in the present. But there is a distance of one hour between your present tense and mine because I am at a higher level. For you it will become the present after one hour, but for me it is present now.

The deeper a man stands within his inner being, the greater a miracle he becomes for those who are still on the surface layers. Then all his doings will become miraculous for us because we have no way to gauge these happenings as we do not know the laws of the fourth body.

This is how magic and miracles take place: they are a slight growth of the fourth body. So if we want miracles to end in this world, it will not happen by preaching to the masses. Just as we have given man the education of the third body and made him understand languages and mathematics, we must now give him training for the fourth body. Each man has to be qualified accordingly, because only then will miracles cease; otherwise, someone or other will always take advantage of this. The fourth body develops until the twenty-eighth year – that is, for seven years more. But very few people are able to develop it.

The *atma sharir* – the fifth body, which is called the spiritual body – is of great value. If growth in life continues in the proper manner, then by the age of 35 this body should be fully developed. But this is a faraway idea because even the fourth body is only developed in a very few people. This is why the soul and such things are only a topic of discussion for us; there is no content behind the word.

Only if the kundalini awakens in the fourth body is entrance possible in the fifth; otherwise we cannot enter. We are not aware of the fourth body, so the fifth also remains unknown. Very few people have discovered the fifth body; they are those whom we call spiritualists. These people take this to be the journey's end and declare, "To attain the *atman* is to attain all." But the journey is not yet over.

However, these people who stop at the fifth body, deny God. Just as the materialist says, "The body is everything; when the body dies, everything dies," so the spiritualist declares, "There is nothing beyond the *atman*: the *atman* is everything; it is the highest state of being."

But this is only the fifth body.

The sixth body is the *brahma sharir* – the cosmic body. When a person evolves beyond his *atman*, when he is willing to lose it, he enters the sixth body.

If mankind develops scientifically, the natural development of the sixth body would take place at the age of 42, and that of the *nirvana sharir* – the seventh body – at the age of 49.

The seventh body is the nirvanic body which is nobody – which is a state of bodilessness, an incorporeal state. This is the ultimate state where only the void remains – not even the *brahman*, the cosmic reality, but only the emptiness. Nothing has remained; everything has disappeared.

So when anyone asked Buddha, "What happens there?" he replied, "The flame dies out."

"Then what happens?" he would be asked again.

"When the flame is lost, you do not ask, 'Where has it gone? Where is the flame now?' It is lost and that is all."

The word *nirvana* implies the extinction of the flame. Therefore, Buddha said, "*Nirvana* takes place."

The state of *moksha* is experienced in the fifth body. The limitations of the first four bodies are transcended and the soul becomes totally free.

So liberation is the experience of the fifth body.

Heaven and hell pertain to the fourth body, and he who stops here will experience them. For those who stop at the first, second or third body, life between birth and death becomes everything; there is no life beyond death for them. If a person goes beyond into the fourth body, after this life he experiences heaven and hell where there are infinite possibilities of happiness and misery.

If he reaches up to the fifth body there is the door of liberation. And if he reaches up to the sixth there is the possibility of the state of God-realization.

Then there is no question of liberation or no liberation; he becomes one with that which is. The declaration of *"aham brahmasmi"* — "I am God" - is of this plane.

But there is yet one step more, which is the last jump – where there is no *aham* and no *Brahman*, where I and thou are totally nonexistent, where there is simply nothing – where there is total and absolute void.

That is *nirvana.*

These are the seven bodies which are developed within a period of 49 years. This is why the midpoint of 50 years was known as the point of revolution.

For the first 25 years there was one system of life. Within this period efforts were made to develop the first four bodies; then one's education was supposed to be complete. Then one was supposed to search for his fifth, sixth and seventh bodies throughout the remainder of his life, and in the remaining 25 years he was expected to attain to the seventh body. Therefore, the age of 50 was looked upon as a crucial year. At this time a man should turn his gaze towards the forest – that now he should turn his eyes away from people, society and the marketplace.

The age of 75 was yet another point of revolution – when a man was to become initiated into *sannyas*. To turn toward the forest means to remove oneself from crowds and people. *Sannyas* means, now the time has come to look beyond the ego, to transcend the ego. In the forest the 'I' will necessarily be with him though he has renounced all else, but at the age of 75 this 'I' too has to be renounced. However, the condition was that in one's life as a householder, one had to pass through and develop all the seven bodies so that the rest of the journey would become spontaneous and joyful.

If this is not done it is very difficult, because with every seven-year cycle a particular state of development is connected. If the physical body of a child does not grow fully in the first seven years of his life, he will always be sickly. At the most we can see to it that he does not remain ill – but healthy he will never be because his basic foundation for health that should have been formed in the first seven years has been shaken. That which should have become strong and firm was disturbed, and that was the time for its development. It is just like laying the foundations for a house: if the foundations are weak it will be difficult – no, impossible – to repair it once the roof is reached. At the foundation stage only could it have been well laid. So in the first seven years, if proper conditions are available for the first body, the body develops properly.

Now if the second body and the emotions do not develop fully over the next seven years, a number of sex perversions result. Then it is very difficult to remedy these later.

So the period of development for a particular body is most crucial. On each step of life, each body has its predetermined period of development. There may be a slight difference here and there, but that is beside the point. If a child does not develop sexually within 14 years his whole life becomes a long ordeal.

If the intellect does not develop by the time he is 21, there is very little chance of its developing at a later period. But so far we are in agreement: we take care of the first body, then we take care to send the child to school to develop his intellect also. But we forget that the rest of the bodies also have their apportioned time which if lost puts us in great difficulties.

A man takes 50 years to develop the body he should have developed in 21 years. It is obvious that he does not have as much strength at 50 as he had at 21, so he has to put in a lot of effort. Then what would have been easier to accomplish at the age of 21 becomes long and arduous.

There is yet another difficulty which he encounters: at the age of 21 he was right at the door but he missed it. Now, over the following 30 years, he has been to so many places that he has lost sight of the right opening. His wandering now makes it impossible for him to locate the place where he stood at 21 and which then needed only a slight push to open.

Therefore, a well-organized situation is required for children until they reach the age of 25. It should be so well planned that it takes them to the fourth body level.

After the fourth body the rest is easy. The foundation will then be well laid; now only the fruits remain to grow. The tree is formed up to the fourth body; then fruits begin to appear from the fifth which culminate in the seventh. We may have to make a little allowance here and there, but we should be very mindful of the foundations. In this respect a few more things should be kept in mind...

There is a difference between man and woman throughout the first four bodies.

For instance, if the individual is a man, his physical body is a male body. But his second body – the etheric body, which is behind the physical body – is female, because no negative or positive pole can exist by itself. A male body and a female body, in the terms of electricity, are positive and negative bodies.

The woman's physical body is negative; therefore, she is never aggressive in the matter of sex. She can bear the violence of man in this respect, but cannot be violent herself. She can do nothing to a man without his consent. Man's first body is positive – aggressive. He can, therefore, do something aggressive to a woman without her consent; he has an aggressive first body.

But by negative is not meant zero or absent. **In terms of electricity, negative means receptivity, reservoir.** In the woman's body, energy lies in reserve; much energy lies in reserve. But it is not active: it is inactive. She can only wait; that is why she can only produce children.

Man has a positive body, but wherever there is a positive body there must be a negative body behind it or else it cannot last. Both are present together; then the circle is complete. So the second body of a man is female, whereas the second body of a female is male.

This is why – and this is an interesting fact – man looks and is, as far as his physical body goes, very strong. But behind this outward strength stands a weak female body. This is why he manages to show his strength only for a few moments at a time. In the long run he loses at the hands of the female, because the body behind her weak female body is a strong positive body. This is why a woman's power of resistance, her capacity to endure, is greater than a man's. If a man and a woman suffer from the same illness the woman can endure it longer than the man.

Women produce children. If men had to produce children they would realize the ordeal that has to be passed through. Then perhaps there would be no need for family planning – because man cannot bear so much pain for so long a time. For a moment or two he can freak out in anger, beat a pillow perhaps, but he cannot carry a child in his abdomen for nine months, nor bring him up patiently for years afterwards. If it cries all night long he might strangle it. He will not be able to tolerate the disturbance. He has extraordinary strength, but behind him is a frail, delicate etheric body. Because of this he cannot bear pain or discomfort.

This is why women fall sick less than men, their lifespan is longer than that of men. For this reason we should keep a difference of five years between a boy and a girl at the time of marriage, or else the world would be filled with widows. If the boy is 20 we should choose a girl of 24 or 25 for him. Man's lifespan is four or five years less, so this difference would equalize things and both synchronize each other.

116 males are born to every 100 females. The difference in number at time of birth is 16, but later on the number becomes equal. 16 males die by the time they reach the age of 14, and so the number becomes almost equal. More boys die earlier than girls. This is because the latter have a great power of resistance that comes to them through the second male body.

Now the third body of the male – that is the astral body – will again be male, and the fourth or the psychic body will again be female. Just the reverse will be the case in the female.

This division of male and female exists only up to the fourth body; the fifth body is beyond sex. Therefore, as soon as the *atman* is attained there is no male and no female – but not until then.

There is another thing that comes to mind in this connection. Since every male has a female body within him and every female has a male body within her, if by coincidence a woman gets a husband who is identical with the male body within her, or if a man marries a woman who is identical with the female body within him, then only is a marriage successful; otherwise not. This is why 99% of marriages are failures because the intrinsic rule of success is not known yet.

As long as we are unable to ascertain the right alliance between the respective energy bodies of two persons, marriages are bound to remain a failure no matter what steps we take in other directions. Successful marriages can only be possible if absolutely clear scientific details concerning these various inner bodies are achieved.

If by coincidence the right connections are made, then both the man and woman are satisfied; otherwise, dissatisfaction remains and a thousand perversions result from this. The man then goes to a prostitute or seeks the woman next door. His distress grows day by day, and this misery is bound to increase with the growth of man's intellect.

Now in places like America, where education has made great strides and where the third body has developed completely, marriages break.

They are bound to, because the third body rebels at a wrong partnership. So divorce results, because it is not possible to drag such marriages along.

The correct form of education is that which develops the first four bodies. Right education is that which takes you up to the fourth body. There the work of education is complete.

No education can help you enter the fifth; you have to go there by yourself. Right education can easily take you up to the fourth body. After this the growth of the fifth body, which is very valuable and personal, begins. Kundalini is the potential of the fourth body; this is why kundalini is a psychic phenomenon.

Osho – "In Search of the Miraculous"

MYSTERIES OF THE SEVEN BODIES

To say that there are obstacles in the path of spiritual growth means there are obstacles within the seeker himself. The path too lies within and it is not very difficult to understand one's own hindrances. It will have to be explained at length what obstacles are and how they can be removed.

Yesterday I told you about the seven bodies. We shall talk in greater detail about these and it will become clear to you. As there are seven bodies, so there are also seven chakras, energy centers, and each chakra is connected in a special way with its corresponding body.

The chakra of the physical body is the *muladhar*. This is the first chakra and it has an integral connection with the physical body. The *muladhar* chakra has two possibilities. Its first potentiality is a natural one that is given to us with birth; its other possibility is obtainable by meditation.

The basic natural possibility of this chakra is the sex urge of the physical body. The very first question that arises in the mind of the seeker is what to do in regard to this central principle. Now there is another possibility of this chakra, and that is *brahmacharya*, celibacy, which is attainable through meditation. Sex is the natural possibility and *brahmacharya* is its transformation.

The more the mind is focused upon and gripped by sexual desire, the more difficult it will be to reach its ultimate potential of *brahmacharya*. Now this means that we can utilize the situation given to us by nature in two ways. We can live in the condition that nature has placed us in – but then the process of spiritual growth cannot begin – or we transform this state. The only danger in the path of transformation is that there is the possibility that we may begin to fight with our natural center.

What is the real danger in the path of a seeker?

The first obstacle is that if the meditator indulges only in nature's order of things he cannot rise to the ultimate possibility of his physical body and he stagnates at the starting point. On the one hand there is a need; on the other hand there is a suppression which causes the meditator to fight the sex urge. Suppression is an obstacle on the path of meditation. This is the obstacle of the first chakra. Transformation cannot come about with suppression.

If suppression is an obstruction, what is the solution? Understanding will then solve the matter. Transformation takes place within as you begin to understand sex.

There is a reason for this. All elements of nature lie blind and unconscious within us. If we become conscious of them, transformation begins.

Awareness is the alchemy; awareness is the alchemy of changing them, of transforming them. If a person becomes awake toward his sexual desires with his total feelings and his total understanding, then *brahmacharya* will begin to take birth within him in place of sex.

Unless a person reaches *brahmacharya* in his first body it is difficult to work on the potentiality of other centers.

The second body, as I said, is the emotional or the etheric body. The second body is connected to the second chakra – the *swadhishthan* chakra. This too has two possibilities. Basically, its natural potential is fear, hate, anger, and violence. All these are conditions obtained from the natural potential of the *swadhishthan* chakra.

If a person stagnates at the second body, then the directly opposite conditions of transformation – love, compassion, fearlessness, friendliness – do not take place.

The obstacle on the meditator's path in the second chakra is hate, anger and violence, and the question is of their transformation. Here too the same mistake is made. One person can give vent to his anger; another can suppress his anger. One can just be fearful; another can suppress his fear and make a show of courage. But neither of these will lead to transformation.

When there is fear it has to be accepted; there is no use hiding or suppressing it. If there is violence within there is no use in covering it with the mantle of nonviolence. Shouting slogans of nonviolence will bring no change in the state of violence within. It remains violence. It is a condition given to us by nature in the second body. It has its uses just as there is meaning to sex. Through sex alone other physical bodies can be given birth. Before one physical body falls, nature has made provisions for the birth of another.

Fear, violence, anger, are all necessary on the second plane; otherwise man could not survive, could not protect himself. Fear protects him, anger involves him in struggle against others and violence helps him to save himself from the violence of others. All these are qualities of the second body and are necessary for survival, but generally we stop here and do not go any further.

If a person understands the nature of fear he attains fearlessness, and if he understands the nature of violence he attains nonviolence. Similarly, by understanding anger we develop the quality of forgiveness. In fact, anger is one side of the coin, forgiveness is the other. They each hide behind the other – but the coin has to be turned over. If we come to know one side of the coin perfectly we naturally become curious to know what is on the other side – and so the coin turns. If we hide the coin and pretend we have no fear, no violence within, we will never be able to know fearlessness and nonviolence.

He who accepts the presence of fear within himself and who has investigated it fully will soon reach a place where he will want to find out what is behind fear. His curiosity will encourage him to see the other side of the coin. The moment he turns it over he becomes fearless. Similarly, violence will turn into compassion. These are the potentials of the second body.

Thus, the meditator has to bring about a transformation in the qualities given to him by nature. And for this it is not necessary to go around asking others; one has to keep seeking and asking within oneself.

We all know that anger and fear are impediments - because how can a coward seek truth? He will go begging for truth; he will wish that someone should give it to him without his having to go into unknown lands.

The third is the astral body. This also has two dimensions. Primarily, the third body revolves around doubt and thinking. If these are transformed doubt becomes trust and thinking becomes *vivek*, awareness.

If doubts are repressed you never attain to *shraddha*, trust, though we are advised to suppress doubts and to believe what we hear. He who represses his doubts never attains to trust, because doubt remains present within though repressed. It will creep within like a cancer and eat up your vitality.

Beliefs are implanted for fear of skepticism. We will have to understand the quality of doubt, we will have to live it and go along with it. Then one day we will reach a point where we will begin to have doubt about doubt itself.

The moment we begin to doubt doubt itself, trust begins.

We cannot reach to the clarity of discrimination without going through the process of thinking. There are people who do not think and people who encourage them not to think. They say, "Do not think; leave all thoughts." He who stops thinking lands himself in ignorance and blind faith. This is not clarity. The power of discrimination is gained only after passing through the most subtle processes of thinking.

What is the meaning of *vivek*, discrimination? Doubt is always present in thoughts. It is always indecisive. Therefore, those who think a great deal never come to a decision. It is only when they step out of the wheel of thoughts that they can decide.

Decision comes from a state of clarity which is beyond thoughts. Thoughts have no connection with decision.

He who is always engrossed in thoughts never reaches a decision. That is why it invariably happens that those whose life is less dominated by thoughts are very resolute, whereas those who think a great deal lack determination. There is danger from both.

Those who do not think go ahead and do whatever they are determined to do, for the simple reason that they have no thought process to create doubt within. The dogmatists and the fanatics of the world are very active and energetic people; for them there is no question of doubting – they never think! If they feel that heaven is attained by killing 1,000 people, they will rest only after killing 1,000 people and not before.

They never stop to think what they are doing so there is never any indecision on their part.

A man who thinks, on the contrary, will keep on thinking instead of making any decision. If we close our doors for fear of thoughts we will be left with blind faith only. This is very dangerous and is a great obstacle in the path of the meditator.

What is needed is an open-eyed discretion and thoughts that are clear, resolute, and which allow us to make decisions. This is the meaning of *vivek*: clarity, awareness. It means that the power of thinking is complete. It means we have passed through thoughts in such detail that all the doubts are cleared. Now only pure decision is left in its essence.

The chakra pertaining to the third body is *manipur*. Doubt and trust are its two forms. When doubt is transformed trust is the result. But, remember, trust is not opposed or contrary to doubt. Trust is the purest and most ultimate development of it. It is the ultimate extreme of doubt, where even doubt becomes lost because here doubt begins to doubt even itself and in this way commits suicide. Then trust is born.

The fourth plane is the mental body or the psyche, and the fourth chakra, the *anahat*, is connected with the fourth body. The natural qualities of this plane are imagination and dreaming. This is what the mind is always doing: imagining and dreaming. It dreams in the night and in the daytime it daydreams.

If imagination is fully developed, that is to say if it is developed to its fullest extent, in a complete way, it becomes determination, will. If dreaming develops fully it is transformed into vision – psychic vision.

If a man's ability to dream is fully developed he has only to close his eyes and he can see things. He can then see even through a wall. At first he only dreams of seeing beyond the wall; later he actually sees beyond it. Now he can only guess what you are thinking, but after the transformation he sees what you think. Vision means seeing and hearing things without the use of the usual sense organs. The limitations of time and space are no more for a person who develops vision.

In dreams you travel far. If you are in Bombay you reach Calcutta.

In vision also you can travel distances, but there will be a difference: in dreams you imagine you have gone, whereas in vision you actually go. The fourth, psychic body can actually be present there.

As we have no idea of the ultimate possibility of this fourth body, we have discarded the ancient concept of dreams in today's world. The ancient experience was that in dream one of the bodies of man comes out of him and goes on a journey.

There was a man, Swedenborg, whom people knew as a dreamer. He used to talk of heaven and hell and that they can only exist in dreams. But one afternoon, as he slept, he began to shout, "Help! Help! My house is on fire." People came running, but there was no fire there. They awoke him to assure him that it was only a dream and there was no danger of fire.

He insisted, however, that his house was on fire. His house was 300 miles away and it had caught fire at that time. On the second or third day news came of this disaster. His house was burnt to ashes, and it was actually burning when he cried out in his sleep. Now this is no longer a dream but a vision. The distance of 300 miles was no longer there. This man witnessed what was happening 300 miles away.

Now scientists also agree that there are great psychic possibilities of the fourth body. Thirty years ago a man set out to explore the North Pole. He was equipped with all that was necessary for wireless communication. One more arrangement was also made which has not made known up until now. A psychic person whose fourth body faculties were functioning was also made to receive the transmission from the explorer. The most surprising thing was that when there was bad weather the wireless failed, but this psychic person received the news without any difficulty. When the diaries were compared later on it was found that 80 to 95% of the time the signals received by the psychic person were correct, whereas the news relayed by the radio was not available more than 72% of the time, because there were many breakdowns.

Now Russia and America are both very eager, and a great deal of work is going on in the field of telepathy, clairvoyance, thought projection and thought reading. All these are the possibilities of the fourth body. To dream is its natural quality; to see the truth, to see the real, is its ultimate possibility. *Anahat* is the chakra of this fourth body.

The fifth chakra is the *vishuddhi* chakra. It is located in the throat. The fifth body is the spiritual body. The *vishuddhi* chakra is connected to the spiritual body.

The first four bodies and their chakras were split into two. The duality ends with the fifth body.

As I said before, the difference between male and female lasts until the fourth body; after that it ends. If we observe very closely, all duality belongs to the male and the female. Where the distance between male and female is no more, at that very point all duality ceases. The fifth body is non-dual. It does not have two possibilities but only one.

This is why there is not much effort for the meditator to make: because here there is nothing contrary to develop; here one has only to enter. By the time we reach the fourth body we develop so much capability and strength that it is very easy to enter the fifth body.

In that case, how can we tell the difference between a person who has entered the fifth body and one who has not? The difference will be that he who has entered the fifth body is completely rid of all unconsciousness. He will not actually sleep at night. That is, he sleeps but his body alone sleeps; someone within is forever awake.

If he turns in sleep he knows it; if he does not he knows it. If he has covered himself with a blanket he knows it; if he has not then also he knows it. His awareness does not slacken in sleep; he is awake all the 24 hours. For the one who has not entered the fifth body, his state is just the opposite. In sleep he is asleep, and in the waking hours also one layer of him will be asleep.

People appear to be working. When you come home every evening the car turns left into your gate; you apply the brake when you reach the porch. Do not be under the illusion that you are doing all this consciously. It happens unconsciously by sheer force of habit. It is only in certain moments, moments of great danger, that we really come into alertness.

You get angry, then you say, "I do not know how I got angry; I did not want to." You say, "Forgive me! I did not want to be rude, it was a slip of the tongue." You have used an obscenity and it is you who deny the intention of its use. The criminal always says, "I did not want to kill. It happened in spite of me." This proves that we are going about like an automaton. We say what we do not want to say; we do what we do not want to do.

In the evening we vow to be up at four in the morning. When it is four o'clock and the alarm goes off we turn over saying there is no need to be up so early. Then you get up at six and are filled with remorse for having overslept. Then you again swear to keep the same vow as yesterday. It is strange that a man decides on one thing in the evening and goes back on it in the morning! Then what he decides at four in the morning changes again before it is six, and what he decides at six changes long before it is evening, and in between he changes a thousand times.

These decisions, these thoughts, come to us in our sleepy state. They are like dreams: they expand and burst like bubbles. There is no wakeful person behind them, no one who is alert and conscious.

So sleep is the innate condition before the beginning of the spiritual plane. Man is a somnambulist before he enters the fifth body, and there the quality is wakefulness. Therefore, after the growth of the fourth body we can call the individual a buddha, an awakened one. Now such a man is awake.

Buddha is not the name of Guatama Siddharth, but a name given him after his attainment of the fifth plane. Gautama the Buddha means Gautama who has awakened. His name remained Gautama, but that was the name of the sleeping person, so gradually it dropped and only Buddha remained.

This difference comes with the attainment of the fifth body. Before we enter into it, whatever we do is an unconscious action which cannot be trusted.

One moment a man vows to love and cherish his loved one the whole life and the next moment he is quite capable of strangling her. The alliance which he promised for a lifetime does not last long. This poor man is not to be blamed. What is the value of promises given in sleep? In a dream I may promise, "This is a lifelong relationship." What value is this promise? In the morning I will deny it because it was only a dream.

A sleeping man cannot be trusted. This world of ours is entirely a world of sleeping people; hence, so much confusion, so many conflicts, so many quarrels, so much chaos. It is all the making of sleeping men.

There is another important difference between a sleeping man and an awakened man which we should bear in mind: a sleeping man does not know who he is, so he is always striving to show others that he is this or he is that. This is his lifelong endeavor. He tries in a thousand ways to prove himself. Sometimes he climbs the ladder of politics and declares, "I am so and so". Sometimes he builds a house and displays his wealth, or he climbs a mountain and displays his strength. He tries in all ways to prove himself. And in all these efforts he is in fact unknowingly trying to find out for himself who he is. He knows not who he is. Before crossing the fourth plane we cannot find the answer.

The fifth body is called the spiritual body because there you get the answer to the quest for 'Who am I?' The call of the 'I' stops once and for all on this plane; the claim to be someone special vanishes immediately. If you say to such a person, "You are so and so," he will laugh. All claims from his side will now stop, because now he knows. There is no longer any need to prove himself, because who he is now is a proven fact.

The conflicts and problems of the individual end on the fifth plane. But this plane has its own hazards. You have come to know yourself, and this knowing is so blissful and fulfilling that you may want to terminate your journey here. You may not feel like continuing on. The hazards that were up to now were all of pain and agony; now the hazards that begin are of bliss.

The fifth plane is so blissful that you will not have the heart to leave it and proceed further. Therefore, the individual who enters this plane has to be very alert about clinging to bliss so that it does not hinder him from going further. Here bliss is supreme and at the peak of its glory; it is in its profoundest depths. A great transformation comes about within one who has known himself, but this is not all; there is further to go also.

It is a fact that distress and suffering do not obstruct our way as much as joy. Bliss is very obstructive. It was difficult enough to leave the crowd and confusion of the marketplace, but it is a thousand times more difficult to leave the soft music of the veena in the temple. This is why many meditators stop at *atma gyan*, self-realization, and do not go up to *brahma gyan*, experience of the Brahman, the cosmic reality.

We shall have to be alert about this bliss. Our effort here should be not to get lost in this bliss. Bliss draws us towards itself; it drowns us; we get immersed in it completely. Do not become immersed in bliss. Know that this too is an experience. Happiness was an experience, misery was an experience.

Bliss too is an experience. Stand outside of it, be a witness.

As long as there is experience there is an obstacle: the ultimate end has not been reached. At the ultimate state all experiences end. Joy and sorrow come to an end, so also does bliss.

Our language, however, does not go beyond this point. This is why we have described God as *sat-chit-ananda* – truth-consciousness-bliss. This is not the form of the supreme self, but this is the ultimate that words can express.

Bliss is the ultimate expression of man. In fact, words cannot go beyond the fifth plane. But about the fifth plane we can say, "There is bliss there; there is perfect awakening; there is realization of the self there." All this can be described.

Therefore, there will be no mystery about those who stop at the fifth plane. Their talk will sound very scientific because the realm of mystery lies beyond this plane. Things are very clear up to the fifth plane. I believe that science will sooner or later absorb those religions that go up to the fifth body, because science will be able to reach up to the *atman*.

When a seeker sets out on this path his search is mainly for bliss and not truth. Frustrated by suffering and restlessness he sets out in search of bliss. So one who seeks bliss will definitely stop at the fifth plane; therefore, I must tell you to seek not bliss but truth. Then you will not remain long here.

Then a question arises: 'There is *ananda*: this is well and good. I know myself: this too is well and good. But these are only the leaves and the flowers. Where are the roots? I know myself, I am blissful – it is good. But from where do I arise? Where are my roots? From where have I come? Where are the depths of my existence? From which ocean has this wave that I am arisen?'

If your quest is for Truth you will go ahead of the fifth body. From the very beginning, therefore, your quest should be for Truth and not bliss; otherwise your journey up to the fifth plane will be easy but you will stop there. If the quest is for Truth, there is no question of stopping there.

So the greatest obstacle on the fifth plane is the unequaled joy we experience – and more so because we come from a world where there is nothing but pain, suffering, anxiety and tension. Then, when we reach this temple of bliss, there is an overwhelming desire to dance with ecstasy, to be drowned, to be lost in this bliss. This is not the place to be lost. That place will come, and then you will not have to lose yourself; you will simply be lost.

There is a great difference between losing yourself and being lost. In other words, you will reach a place where even if you wish you cannot save yourself. You will see yourself becoming lost; there is no remedy. Yet here also in the fifth body you can lose yourself. Your effort, your endeavor, still works here – and even though the ego is intrinsically dead on the fifth plane, 'I-am-ness' still persists.

It is necessary, therefore, to understand the difference between ego and I-am-ness. The ego, the feeling of 'I', will die, but the feeling of 'am' will not die.

There are two things in 'I am': the 'I' is the ego and the 'am' is *asmita* – the feeling of being. So the 'I' will die on the fifth plane, but the being, the 'am', will remain: 'I-am-ness' will remain.

Standing on this plane, a meditator will declare, "There are infinite souls and each soul is different and apart from the other." On this plane the meditator will experience the existence of infinite souls, because he still has the feeling of 'am', the feeling of being which makes him feel apart from others. If the quest for Truth grips the mind, the obstacle of bliss can be crossed – because incessant bliss becomes tedious.

A single strain of a melody can become irksome. Bertrand Russell once said jokingly, "I am not attracted to salvation, because I hear there is nothing but bliss there. Bliss alone would be very monotonous – bliss

and bliss and nothing else. If there is not a single trace of unhappiness
– no anxiety, no tension in it – how long can one bear such bliss?"

To be lost in bliss is the hazard of the fifth plane. It is very difficult to
overcome. Sometimes it takes many births to do so. The first four steps
are not so hard to cross, but the fifth is very difficult. Many births may
be needed to be bored of bliss, to be bored of the self, to be bored of the
atman.

So the quest up to the fifth body is to be rid of pain, hatred, violence
and desires. After the fifth the search is in order to be rid of the self.
There are two things: the first is freedom from something; this is one
thing and it is completed at the fifth plane. The second thing is freedom
from the self, and so a completely new world starts from here.

The sixth is the *brahma sharira,* the cosmic body, and the chakra the
agya chakra. Here there is no duality. The experience of bliss becomes
intense on the fifth plane, and the experience of existence, of being, on
the sixth.

Asmita will now be lost – 'I am'. The 'I' in this is lost at the fifth plane
and the 'am' will go as soon as you transcend the fifth. The isness will
be felt; *tathata*, suchness, will be felt. Nowhere will there be the feeling
of 'I' or of 'am'; only that which is remains.

So here will be the perception of reality, of being – the perception of
consciousness. But here the consciousness is free of me; it is no longer
my consciousness. It is only consciousness – no longer *my* existence,
but only Existence.

Some meditators stop after reaching the *Brahma sharira*, the cosmic
body, because the state of 'I am the Brahman' has come: of '*Aham
Brahmasmi,*' when I am not and only the Brahman is.

Now what more is there to seek? What is to be sought? Nothing remains
to be sought. Now everything is attained. The Brahman means the total.
One who stands at this point says, "The Brahman is the ultimate truth,
the Brahman is the cosmic reality. There is nothing beyond."

It is possible to stop here, and seekers do stop at this stage for millions
of births, because there seems to be nothing ahead. So the *Brahma
gyani*, the one who has attained realization of the Brahman, will get

stuck here; he will go no further. This is so difficult to cross because there is nothing to cross to. Everything has been covered.

Does not one need a space to cross into? If I want to go outside of this room there must be someplace else to go. But the room has now become so enormous, so beginningless and endless, so infinite, so boundless, that there is nowhere to go.

So where will we go to search? Nothing remains to be found; everything has been covered. So the journey may halt at this stage for infinite births. So the Brahman is the ultimate obstacle – the last barrier in the ultimate quest of the seeker. Now only the being remains, but non-being has yet to be realized. The being, the isness, is known, but the non-being has yet to be realized – that which is not still remains to be known.

Therefore, the seventh plane is the *nirvana kaya, nirvanic* body, and its chakra is the *sahasrar*. Nothing can be said in connection with this chakra. We can only continue talking at the most up to the sixth – and that too with great difficulty. Most of it will turn out to be wrong.

Until the fifth body the search progresses within a very scientific method; everything can be explained. On the sixth plane the horizon begins to fade; everything seems meaningless. Hints can still be given but ultimately the pointing finger breaks and the hints too are no more because one's own being is eliminated. So the Brahman, the absolute being, is known from the sixth body and the sixth chakra.

Therefore, those who seek the Brahman will meditate on the *agya* chakra which is between the eyes. This chakra is connected to the cosmic body. Those who work completely on this chakra will begin to call the vast infinite expanse that they witness, 'the third eye'. This is the third eye from where they can now view the cosmic, the infinite.

One more journey yet remains – the journey to non-being, non-existence. Existence is only half the story: there is also non-existence.

Light is, but on the other side there is darkness. Life is one part, but there is also death. Therefore, it is necessary also to know the remaining non-existence, the void, because the ultimate truth can only be known when both are known – existence and non-existence.

Being is known in its entirety and non-being is known in its entirety: then the knowing is complete. Existence is known in entirety and non-existence is known in its entirety: then we know the Whole; otherwise our experience is incomplete. There is an imperfection in *brahma gyan*, which is that it has not been able to know the non-being.

Therefore, the *brahma gyani* denies that there is such a thing as non-existence and calls it an illusion. He says that it does not exist. He says that to be is the truth and not to be is a falsity. There simply is no such thing, so the question of knowing it does not arise.

Nirvana kaya means the *shunya kaya*, the void from where we jump from the being into the non-being. In the cosmic body something yet remains unknown. That too has to be known - what it is not to be, what it is to be completely erased. Therefore, the seventh plane in a sense is an ultimate death.

Nirvana, as I told you previously, means the extinction of the flame. That which was 'I' is extinct; that which was 'am' is extinct. But now we have again come into being by being one with the all. Now we are the Brahman, and this too will have to be left. He who is ready to take the last jump knows the existence and also the non-existence.

So these are the seven bodies and the seven chakras, and within them lie all the means as well as the barriers.

There are no barriers outside. Therefore, there is not much reason to inquire outside. If you have gone to ask someone or to understand from someone, then do not beg. To understand is one thing, to beg is another. Your search should always continue. Whatever you have heard and understood should also be made your search. Do not make it your belief or else it will be begging.

What I told you should become your quest. It should accelerate your search; it should stimulate and motivate your curiosity. It should put you into greater difficulty, make you more restless and raise new questions in you, new dimensions, so that you will set out on a new path of discovery. Then you have not taken alms from me, then you have understood what I said. And if this helps you to understand yourself, then this is not begging.

So go forth to know and understand; go forth to search. You are not the only one seeking. Many others are also. Many have searched, many have attained. Try to know, to grasp, what has happened to such people and also what has not happened; try and understand all this. But while understanding this, do not stop trying to understand your own self.

Do not think that understanding others has become your realization. Do not put faith in their experiences; do not believe them blindly. Rather, turn everything into questioning. Turn them into questions and not answers; then your journey will continue. Then it will not be begging: it will be your quest.

It is your search that will take you to the last. As you penetrate within yourself you will find the two sides of each chakra. As I told you, one is given to you by nature and one you have to discover.

Anger is given to you; forgiveness you have to find. Sex is given to you; *brahmacharya* you have to develop. Dreams you have; vision has to evolve. Your search for the opposite will continue up to the fourth chakra.

From the fifth will start your search for the indivisible, for the non-dual. Try to continue your search for that which is different from what has come to you in the fifth body. When you attain bliss try to find out what there is beyond bliss. On the sixth plane you attain the Brahman, but keep inquiring, "What is there beyond the Brahman?"

Then one day you will step into the seventh body, where being and non-being, light and darkness, life and death, occur together. That is the attainment of the ultimate; there are no means of communicating this state.

This is why our scriptures end with the fifth body, or at the most they go up to the sixth body. Those with a completely scientific turn of mind do not talk about what is after the fifth body. The cosmic reality, which is boundless and unlimited, begins from there, but mystics like the Sufis talk of the planes beyond the fifth. It is very difficult to talk of these planes because one has to contradict oneself again and again.

The greater the crowd, the harder and more condensed is your ego. Therefore, it has long been a practice to get out of the crowd and try to drop the ego in solitude. But man is strange: if he stays under a tree for long he will begin to talk to it and address it as 'you'. If he stays near the ocean he will do the same. The 'I' in us will go to any length to keep itself alive. It will create the other no matter where you go, and it will establish sentimental relationship even with inanimate objects and will begin to look upon them as individuals.

When a person approaches the last stage he makes God the other so that he can save his 'I'. Therefore, the devotee always says, "How can we be one with God? He is he and we are we. We are at his feet, and he is God." The devotee is saying nothing but this, that if you want to be one with him you will have to lose your ego. So he keeps God at a distance and he begins to rationalize. He says, "How can we be one with him? He is great, he is absolute. We are wretched outcastes so how can we be one with him?" The devotee is saving the 'thou' in order to save his 'I'.

Therefore, the bhakta, the devotee, never rises above the fourth plane. He does not even go up to the fifth plane: he gets stuck at the fourth. Instead of imagination, on the fourth plane visions come to him. He discovers all the best possibilities of the fourth body. So many happenings take place in a devotee's life that are miraculous, but the bhakta remains on the fourth plane all the same.

The *atma sadhak* – one who is searching for the self – the *hatha yogi* – the yogi who goes through austerities – and many others who undergo similar practices, reach the fifth plane at the most. Such a *sadhak's* intrinsic desire is to attain bliss, to attain liberation and freedom from suffering. Behind all of these desires stands the 'I': he says, "I want liberation" – not liberation from the 'I', but liberation *of* the 'I'. He says, "I want to be free. I want beatitude." His 'I' stands condensed, so he only reaches to the fifth plane.

The *raja yogi* reaches up to the sixth plane. He says, "What is there in the 'I'? I am nothing; He alone is – not 'I', but He, the Brahman, is everything." He is ready to lose the ego but he is not prepared to lose his being. He says, "I shall remain as part of the Brahman; I am one with him. I am the Brahman. I shall let myself go, but my inner being within me will remain merged in him." Such a seeker can go up to the sixth body.

A meditator like Buddha reaches the seventh plane because he is ready to give up all – even the Brahman. He is ready to lose himself and lose everything. He says, "Let what is remain. On my part I do not desire anything to remain: I am ready to lose my all." He who is prepared to lose everything is entitled to gain all.

The nirvanic body is attained only when we are prepared to be nothing. Then there is a readiness to know even death. For knowing life many are ready. Therefore, he who wants to know life will stop at the sixth plane. But he who is ready to investigate death also will be able to know the seventh plane.

Mysticism starts with the sixth plane. Therefore, where there is no mysticism in a religion, know that it has finished on the fifth body. But mysticism also is not the final stage. The ultimate is the void, nothingness. The religion that ends with mysticism ends with the sixth body. The void is the ultimate, nihilism is the ultimate, because after it there is nothing more to be said.

So the search for *adwaita,* the non-dual, starts with the fifth body. All search for the opposites ends with the fourth body. All barriers are within us and they are useful, because these very obstacles when transformed become your means to go ahead.

A rock is lying on the road. As long as you do not understand it will remain an obstacle for you. The day you understand it will become a ladder for you. The rock is lying on the road. As long as you did not understand you shouted, "The rock is in my way. How can I go ahead?" When you have understood you will climb over the rock and go ahead, thanking the rock with the words, "You have blessed me very much, because after climbing over you I have found myself on a higher plane. Now I am proceeding along on a higher level. You were a means and I took you to be a barrier," you will say.

The road is blocked by this boulder. What will happen? Cross over it and know. In this way, overcome anger; cross over it and reach forgiveness which is on a different level. Cross over sex and attain *brahmacharya* which is an entirely different plane. Then you will thank sex and anger for being the stepping stones.

Every rock on the path can be a barrier as well as a medium. It depends entirely on what you do with it. One thing is certain: do not fight with the rock, because then you will only break your head and the rock will not be helpful. If you fight with the rock, the rock will bar your way, because wherever we fight we stop. We have to stop near the person or thing we fight with; we cannot possibly fight from a distance.

That is why if someone fights sex he has to be involved with sex just as much as another who indulges in it. In fact, many times he is closer to sex, because the one who indulges in it can get out of it someday, can transcend it. But the one who fights cannot get out of it; he keeps going around and around.

So the seeker has to beware of the tendency to fight. He should try his utmost to understand, and by trying to understand is meant: understanding that which is given to him by nature. Through that which has been given to you, you will attain that which is yet to be attained. This is the starting point. If you run away from that which is the very beginning it is impossible to reach the goal.

If you run away from sex in fright, how will you ever reach *brahmacharya?* Sex was the opening given by nature and *brahmacharya* is the quest that has to be undertaken through this very opening. If you see in this perspective there is no need to beg from anywhere; understanding is what is required.

All of existence is there for the purpose of understanding. Learn from anybody, hear everyone, and, finally, understand your own self within.

Question: "Do those who reach the fifth and following bodies again assume physical forms after death?

Yes, it is true. One who attains the fifth or the sixth body before death is reborn in the highest celestial realm, and there he lives on the plane of the devas. He can stay in this realm as long as he likes, but to attain nirvana he has to come back to the human form.

After attaining the fifth there is no birth in the physical body, but there are other bodies. In fact, what we call devas or gods signifies the kind of body that is obtained. This type of body is obtained after reaching the fifth body.

After the sixth body, even these will not be there. Then we shall obtain the form of what we call *ishwar,* the supreme being.

But all these are still bodies. What type is a secondary matter. After the seventh there are no bodies. From the fifth onwards the bodies become more and more subtle until they reach the bodiless state after the seventh.

Osho – "In Search of the Miraculous"

BARDO AND OTHER MYSTERIES

There is a Tibetan book called "The Tibetan Book of the Dead, The Bardo". Everyone in Tibet who attained the fourth body has worked on one project: how a person can best be assisted after death.

Suppose you are dead: I love you, but I cannot help you after death. But in Tibet there is a full arrangement to guide and assist a man and to encourage him to take a special birth and enter a special womb.

Science will still take time to discover this, but it will discover it, there is no difficulty. And the Tibetans have found ways and means to test the validity of these happenings also. In Tibet, when the Dalai Lama dies, he tells beforehand where he will take birth next and how the others should recognize him. He leaves symbols behind for his recognition. Then after he dies the search starts all over the country. The child that tells the secret of the symbol is taken to be the incarnation of the dead lama, because he alone knows the secret.

The present Dalai Lama was discovered in this manner. The Dalai Lama preceding him had left a symbol. A special saying was proclaimed in every village, and the child who could explain it was understood to be the one in whom the former lama's soul had taken entry. The search took long, but finally the child was discovered who could explain the code. It was a very secret formula, and only the authentic Dalai Lama could know its meaning.

So the curiosity of a man of the fourth plane is entirely different. Infinite is the universe and infinite are its mysteries and secrets. Do not think that we have discovered all that is to be discovered by present-day scientific research. A thousand new sciences will come to light because there are thousands of different directions and dimensions. And when new sciences develop, people will call us nonscientific people, because we will not have known what they will know. But we should not call the ancient people nonscientific; it is only that their curiosity was of a different nature. The possible dimensions for inquiry are so diverse and so many.

You will be shocked to know the number of herbal remedies prescribed in the Ayurvedic and Yunanic branches of medicine. How could these people, without the aid of research in laboratories, discover the proper cures for every illness? There is every possibility that this was brought about by the use of the fourth body.

There is a well-known story about Vaidya Lukman which tells that he would go up to each plant and ask what were its uses. Now, this story has become meaningless in the world of today. It seems to be a failure of logic to expect plants to talk. It is also a fact that until the last 50 years plants were not supposed to have life. But now science admits there is life in plants.

30 years ago we did not believe that plants also breathe; now we admit that they do. 15 years ago we did not believe that plants could feel, but in the last 15 years we have had to admit that they do. When you approach a plant in anger, its psychic state changes, and when you approach it in love, then again it changes. So it will not be out of place if we discover in the next 50 years that we can talk to plants also, but this will be a gradual development. However, Lukman proved it long ago. But this mode of conversation could not have been the same as ours. To become one with plants is a quality of the fourth body. Then they can be questioned.

I believe this story because there is no mention of any laboratory huge enough in those days where Lukman could have carried out his research on the millions of varieties of herbs he brought into use. It is improbable, because each herb would require a lifetime to reveal its secret if done scientifically, whereas this man talked of unlimited herbs. Now science admits the efficiency of many of these herbal cures in illness and they are still used.

All of the research of the past is the research of the men of the fourth plane.

Now we treat thousands of illnesses, which is very unscientific. The man of the fourth plane will say, "There are no illnesses at all. Why are you treating them?" Now science understands this and allopathy is using new methods of treatment. In some hospitals in America they are working on new methods.

Suppose there are ten patients suffering from the same ailment. Five are given water injections and the other five are given the regular medicinal treatment. Then the findings show that the patients of each group respond to their treatment equally. This proves that those treated with water were not really ill but had an illusion of illness. If these people were given the regular treatment for this illness it would have poisoned their systems and brought about contrary results. They required no treatment.

Many illnesses are born out of unnecessary treatment and then they are difficult to cure. If you have no real illness, only a phantom illness, the medicine for that illness will have to act in some way even though the necessary conditions of the illness are not within you. It will create poisons within for which you will have to undergo new treatments. The phantom illness will go on giving way to some actual malady.

According to science, 90% of illnesses are psycho-somatic. 50 years ago modern science refused to believe this, but now allopathy admits it as 50% are psycho-somatic. I say they will have to admit to another 40%, because that is the reality.

There is now no one to define what the man on the fourth plane knew; no one has tried to interpret him. There is no man who can put his knowledge in the right perspective in today's scientific terms; this is the only difficulty. Once this can be done there will be no problem. But the language of parables is very different. People with parapsychic faculties predict things much earlier and science understands them much later. But then predictions are all in a symbolic language. It is only when science proves the same facts that they are put down in the normal day-to-day language.

A very strange fact came to light. A man in Arabia has in his possession a map of the world which is 700 years old. This is an aerial view of the world which could not possibly have been conceived of on land. There are only two solutions: either there were airplanes 700 years ago – and this does not seem possible – or some person lifted himself that high in his fourth body and then drew the map. One thing is certain: there were no airplanes then. But this aerial map of the world was made 700 years ago. What does this mean?

If we were to study Charak and Sushrut, two ancient masters of the science of herbs, we would be shocked to know that they have described everything about the human body which scientists came to know by dissection. There could be only two means of knowing: One possibility is that surgery had become so subtle that there could be no evidence of surgery being carried out, because no surgical instruments or books on surgery have been discovered. But there are descriptions of very minute parts of the human body – parts so minute that science could discover them only much later, parts which only 25 years ago scientists refused to accept as being present. But these have been described by these ancient physicians.

There is a second possible way by which they could have known: a person in a state of vision may have entered the human body and seen these things.

Today we know that x-rays can enter the human body. If a man said that he could photograph our bones a hundred years ago we would not have believed him. Today we have to believe because it is so.

But do you know? The eyes of a man in the fourth body can see even more deeply than an x-ray, and that a picture of your body can be made which is more complete than that which is made as a result of dissection.

Surgery developed in the West because there they bury their dead. In a place like India where the body is burned this was not possible. And you will be surprised to know that this research came about with the help of thieves, so they would steal the dead bodies and sell them to the physicians for research and studying.

The custom of cremation was also the idea of psychic persons, because they believed that the soul had difficulty in taking a new birth if the body of the previous life still remained. It then hovered around the old body. If the body is burned to ashes the soul will be rid of this encumbrance – because once it sees the body turning to ashes, in the next body it will perhaps realize that what it considered to be its own was after all only a destructible thing.

So what we have come to know by countless dissections, books 3,000 years old reveal without any dissection. This only proves that there is another method by which things can be known besides scientific experimentation.

Osho – "In Search of the Miraculous"

FIVE MEDICINES FOR FIVE BODIES

Patanjali takes the whole complexity of the human being into account. That has to be understood. Never before and never after has such a comprehensive system ever been evolved.

Man is not a simple being. Man is a very complex organism. A rock is simple because the rock has only one layer, the layer of the body. It is what Patanjali calls *anamayakos*: the most gross, only one layer. You go into the rock; you will find layers of rock but nothing else.

Look at a tree and you will also find something else other than the body. The tree is not just the body. Something of the subtle has happened to it. It is not so dead as a rock; it is more alive – a subtle body has come into existence. If you treat a tree like a rock, you mistreat it. Then you have not taken into account the subtle evolution that has happened between the rock and the tree. The tree is highly evolved. It is more complex. Then, take an animal – still more complex. Another layer of subtle body has evolved.

Man has five bodies, five seeds, so if you really want to understand man and his mind – and there is no way of going beyond if you don't understand the whole complexity – then we have to be very patient and careful. If you miss one step, you will not be able to reach to your innermost core of being.

The body that you can see in the mirror is the outermost shell of your being. Many have mistaken it as if this is all. In psychology, there is a movement called behaviorism, which thinks that man is nothing but the body. Always beware of people who talk of 'nothing buts'. Man is always more than any 'nothing but' can imply.

Behaviorists, Pavlov, B. F. Skinner and company, think that man is the body – not that you have a body, not that you are in the body, but simply that you are the body. Then man is reduced to the lowest denominator. And of course, they can prove it. They can prove it because that is the most gross part of man and is easily available to scientific experimentation. The subtle layers of man's being are not so easily available. Or, to say it in other words: scientific instrumentation is not yet so sophisticated. It cannot touch the subtler layers of man.

Freud, Adler, go a little deeper into man. Then man is not just the body. They touch something of the second body, what Patanjali calls *pranamayakos*: the vital body, the energy body. But only a very fragmentary part is touched by Freud and Adler; one part by Freud and another part by Adler.

Freud reduces man to just sexuality. That is also there in man, but that is not the whole story. Adler reduces man to just ambition, will to power. That too is there in man. Man is very big, very complex. Man is an orchestra; many instruments are involved in it.

But this has always happened. This is a calamity, but this has always happened: when once somebody finds something, he tries to make a total philosophy out of his finding. That's a great temptation.

Freud stumbled upon sex, and that too, not the whole of sex. He stumbled only upon the repressed sexuality. He came across repressed people. Christian repression has made many blocks in man where energy has become coiled up within itself, has become stagnant, is no longer flowing. He came against those rock-like blocks in the stream of human energy, and he thought – and the ego always thinks that way – that he had found the ultimate truth.

Adler, working in a different way, stumbled upon another block of man: the will to power. And then he made a whole philosophy out of it. Man has been taken in fragments. Yoga is the only philosophy in existence which takes the whole of man into account.

Jung went still a little further, deeper. One fragment of the third body of man, *manomayakos* – he caught hold of it and he created a whole philosophy out of it.

To comprehend the whole body – even that has not been possible because the body itself is very complex: millions of cells in a great harmony, functioning in a miraculous way.

When you were born in your mother's womb, you were just a small cell. Out of that one cell, another cell arises. The cell grows and divides in two, then the two cells grow and divide into four. Out of one division –

and division goes on – you have millions of cells. And they all function in a deep cooperation, as if somebody is holding them. It is not a chaos; you are a cosmos. And then, some cells become your eyes, some cells become your ears, some cells become your genital organs, some cells become your skin, some cells your bones, some cells your brain, some cells your nails and your hair; and they all are coming out of one cell. They are all alike. They have no qualitative difference, but they function so differently. The eye can see; the ear cannot see. The ear can hear, but cannot smell. So those cells not only function in harmony, but they become experts. They gain to a certain specialization.

A few cells turn into the eyes. What has happened? What type of training is going on? Why do certain cells become eyes, and certain other cells become ears, and still certain others become your nose, and they are all alike? There must be a great training inside, some unknown power training them for a specific purpose. And remember, when those cells are getting ready to see, they have not yet seen anything. When the child is in the womb, he remains completely blind. He has not seen any light; the eyes are closed. A miracle: no training to see and the eyes are ready, no possibility to see and the eyes are ready.

The child does not breathe with his own lungs, he has not known what breathing is, but the lungs are ready. They are ready before the child is going to enter into the world and breathe. The eyes are ready before the child is going to enter into the world and see. Everything is ready. When the child is born he is a perfect human being of tremendous complexity, specialization, subtlety. And there has been no training, no rehearsal. The child has never taken a single breath, but immediately out of the mother's womb, he cries and takes his first breath. The mechanism is ready before any training has been given. Some tremendous power, some power which comprehends all the possibilities of the future, some power which is preparing the child to be able to face all possibilities of life for the future, is working deep within. Even the body is not completely understood, not yet. Our whole understanding is fragmentary.

The science of man does not exist yet. Patanjali's yoga is the closest effort ever made. He divides the body into five layers, or into five bodies. You don't have one body, you have five bodies; and behind the five bodies, your being.

The same as has happened in psychology has happened in medicine. Allopathy believes only in the physical body, the gross body. It is parallel to behaviorism. Allopathy is the grossest medicine. That's why it has become scientific, because scientific instrumentation is only capable yet of very gross things. Go deeper…

Acupuncture, the Chinese medicine, enters one layer more. It works on the vital body, the *pranamayakos*. If something goes wrong in the physical body, acupuncture does not touch the physical body at all. It tries to work on the vital body. It tries to work on the bioenergy, the bio-plasma. It settles something there, and immediately the gross body starts functioning well.

If something goes wrong in the vital body, allopathy functions on the body, the gross body. Of course, for allopathy, it is an uphill task. For acupuncture, it is a downhill task. It is easier because the vital body is a little higher than the physical body. If the vital body is set right, the physical body simply follows it because the blueprint exists in the vital body. The physical body is just an implementation of the vital.

Now acupuncture is gaining respect, by and by, because a certain very sensitive photography, Kirlian photography, in Soviet Russia, has come across the 700 vital points in the human body as they have always been predicted by acupuncturists for at least 5,000 years. They had no instruments to know where the vital points in the body were. But by and by, just through trial and error, through centuries, they discovered 700 points.

Now Kirlian has also discovered the same 700 points with scientific instrumentation. And Kirlian photography has proved one thing: that to try to change the vital through the physical is absurd. It is trying to change the master by changing the servant. It is almost impossible because the master won't listen to the servant. If you want to change the servant, change the master. Immediately, the servant follows. Rather than going and changing each soldier, it is better to change the general. The body has millions of soldier cells, simply working under some order, under some commandment. Change the commander, and the whole body pattern changes.

Homeopathy goes still a little deeper. It works on the *manomayakos*, the mental body. The founder of homeopathy, Hahnemann, discovered one of the greatest things ever discovered, and that was: the smaller the quantity of the medicine, the deeper it goes. He called the method of making homeopathic medicine "potentizing". They go on reducing the quantity of the medicine.

He would work in this way: he would take a certain amount of medicine and would mix it with ten times the amount of milk sugar or with water. One quantity of medicine, nine quantities of water; he would mix them. Then he would again take one quantity of this new solution, and would again mix it with nine times more water, or milk sugar. In this way he would go on: again from the new solution he would take one quantity and would mix it with nine times more water. This he would do, and the potency would increase.

By and by, the medicine reaches to the atomic level. It becomes so subtle that you cannot believe that it can work; it has almost disappeared. It has almost disappeared, but then it enters the most deep core of *manomaya*: it enters into your mind body. It goes deeper than acupuncture. It is almost as if you have reached the atomic, or even the sub-atomic level. Then it does not touch your body. Then it does not touch your vital body; it simply enters. It is so subtle and so small that it comes across no barriers. It can simply slip into the *manomayakos*, into the mental body, and from there it starts working. You have found an even bigger authority than the *pranamaya*.

Ayurved, the Indian medicine, is a synthesis of all three. It is one of the most synthetic of medicines.

Hypnotherapy goes still deeper. It touches the *vigyanmayakos*, the fourth body, the body of consciousness. It does not use medicine. It does not use anything. It simply uses suggestion, that's all. It simply puts a suggestion in your mind. Call it animal magnetism, mesmerism, hypnosis, or whatsoever you like – but it works through the power of thought, not the power of matter.

Even homeopathy is still the power of matter in a very subtle quantity. Hypnotherapy gets rid of matter altogether, because howsoever subtle, it is matter. 10,000 potency, but still it is a potency of matter. It simply jumps to the thought energy, *vigyanmayakos*: the consciousness body. If your consciousness just accepts a certain idea, it starts functioning.

Hypnotherapy has a great future. It is going to become the future medicine, because if by just changing your thought pattern your mind can be changed, through the mind your vital body and through the vital body your gross body, then why bother with poisons, why bother with gross medicines? Why not work it through thought power?

Have you watched any hypnotist working on a medium? If you have not watched, it is worth watching. It will give you a certain insight. You may have heard, or you may have seen – in India it happens; you must have seen firewalkers. It is nothing but hypnotherapy. The idea that they are possessed by a certain god or a goddess and no fire can burn them, just this idea is enough. This idea controls and transforms the ordinary functioning of their bodies. They are prepared: for twenty-four hours they fast. When you are fasting and your whole body is clean, and there is no excreta in it, the bridge between you and the gross drops.

For twenty-four hours, they live in a temple or in a mosque, singing, dancing, getting in tune with God. Then comes the moment when they walk on the fire. They come dancing, possessed. They come with full trust that the fire is not going to burn, that's all; there is nothing else. How to create the trust is the question. Then they dance on the fire, and the fire does not burn.

It has happened many times that somebody who was just a spectator became so possessed. Twenty persons walking on fire are not burned, and somebody would immediately become so confident: "If these people are walking, then why not I?" And he has jumped in and the fire has not burned. In that sudden moment, a trust arose. Sometimes it has happened that people who were prepared, were burned. Sometimes an unprepared spectator walked on fire and was not burned. What happened? The people who were prepared must have carried a doubt. They must have been thinking whether it was going to happen or not. A subtle doubt must have remained in the *vigyan mayakos*, in their consciousness. It was not total trust. So they came, but with doubt. Because of that doubt, the body could not receive the message from the higher soul. The doubt came in between, and the body continued to function in the ordinary way; it got burned.

That's why all religions insist for trust. Trust is hypnotherapy. Without trust, you cannot enter into the subtle parts of your being, because a small doubt, and you are thrown back to the gross.

Science works with doubt. Doubt is a method in science because science works with the gross. Whether you doubt or not, an allopath is not worried. He does not ask you to trust in his medicine; he simply gives you medicine. But a homeopath will ask whether you believe, because without your belief it will be more difficult for a homeopath to work upon you. And a hypnotherapist will ask for total surrender. Otherwise, nothing can be done.

Religion is surrender. Religion is a hypnotherapy. But there is still one more body. That is the *anandmayakos*, the bliss body. Hypnotherapy goes up to the fourth. Meditation goes up to the fifth.

'Meditation' – the very word is beautiful because the root is the same as 'medicine'. Both come from the same root. Medicine and meditation are off-shoots of one word: that which heals, that which makes you healthy and whole is medicine; and on the deepest level, that is meditation.

Meditation does not even give you suggestions because suggestions are to be given from the outside. Somebody else has to give you suggestions. Suggestion means that you are dependent upon somebody. They cannot make you perfectly conscious because the other will be needed, and a shadow will be cast on your being.

Meditation makes you perfectly conscious, without any shadow – absolute light with no darkness. Now even suggestion is thought to be a gross thing. Somebody suggests – that means something comes from the outside, and in the ultimate analysis that which comes from the outside is material. Not only matter, but that which comes from the outside is material. Even a thought is a subtle form of matter. Even hypnotherapy is materialistic.

Meditation drops all props, all supports. That's why to understand meditation is the most difficult thing in the world, because nothing is left – just a pure understanding, a witnessing.

In you two things are happening. One is a cyclone of thoughts, emotions, desires: a great whirlwind around you, constantly changing, constantly transforming itself, constantly on the move. It is a process.

Behind this process is your witnessing soul – eternal, permanent, not changing at all. It has never changed. It is like the eternal sky: clouds come and go, gather, disperse; the sky remains untouched, uninfluenced, unimpressed. It remains pure and virgin. That is the Lord, the eternal within you.

Mind goes on changing. Just a moment before you had one mind, a moment afterwards you have another mind. Just a few minutes before you were angry, and now you are laughing. Just a moment before you were happy, and now you are sad. Modifications, changes, continuous waves up and down; like a yo-yo you go on.

But something in you is eternal: that which goes on witnessing the play, the game. The witnesser is the Lord. If you start witnessing, by and by, you will come closer and closer to the Lord.

Start witnessing objects. You see a tree. You see the tree, but you are not aware that you are seeing it; then you are not a witness. You see the tree, and at the same time you see that you are seeing; then you are a witness. Consciousness has to become double-arrowed: one arrow going to the tree, another arrow going to your subjectivity.

It is difficult, because when you become aware of yourself you forget the tree, and when you become aware of the tree you forget yourself. But by and by, one learns to balance, just as one learns to balance on a tight-rope. Difficult in the beginning, dangerous, risky, but by and by, one learns the balance.

Just go on trying. Wherever you have an opportunity to be a witness, don't miss it, because there is nothing more valuable than witnessing.

Doing an act: walking or eating or taking a bath, become a witness also. Let the shower fall on you, but inside you remain alert and see what is happening – the coolness of the water, the tingling sensation all over the body, a certain silence surrounding you, a certain wellbeing arising in you – but go on becoming a witness.

You are feeling happy; just feeling happy is not enough – be a witness; just go on watching. "I'm feeling happy. I'm feeling sad. I'm feeling hungry" – go on watching.

By and buy, you will see that happiness is separate from you, unhappiness also. All that you can witness is separate from you. This is the method of *viveka,* discrimination. All that is separate from you can be witnessed, and all that can be witnessed is separate from you.

You cannot witness the witnesser; that is the Lord. You cannot go behind the Lord. You are the Lord. You are the ultimate core of Existence.

The mind itself can be seen. It can become an object. It can be perceived, so it is not the perceiver. Ordinarily, we think that it is the mind which is seeing the flower. No, you can go beyond the mind and you can see the mind, just as the mind is seeing the flower. The deeper you go, the more you will find that the observer itself becomes the observed.

That's why Krishnamurti goes on saying again and again, "The observer is the observed; the perceiver is the perceived." When you go deep, first you see the trees, and the rose and the stars, and you think the mind is witnessing. Then close your eyes. Now, see the impressions in the mind: of roses, stars, trees. Now who is the perceiver?

The perceiver has gone a little deeper. Mind itself has become an object. These five *koshas*, these five seeds, are five stations where the perceiver again and again becomes the perceived.

When you move from the gross body, the food body, the *anamayakos,* to the vital body, you immediately see that from the vital body the gross body can be seen as an object. It is outside the vital body. Just as the house is outside you, when you stand in the vital body, your own body is just like a wall around you.

Again you move from the vital body to *manomayakos,* the mental body; the same happens. Now, even the vital body is outside you, like a fence around you; and this way it goes on. It goes on to the ultimate point where only the witnesser remains. Then you don't see yourself as, "I am blissful"; you see yourself as a witness of bliss.

The last body is the bliss body. It is the most difficult to separate from because it is very close to the Lord. It almost surrounds the lord like a climate. But that too has to be known. Even at that last point when you are ecstatically blissful, then too you have to do the ultimate effort, the last effort of discrimination: seeing that the bliss is separate from you.

Then is liberation, *kaivalya.* Then you are left alone – just the witnesser – and everything has been reduced to objects: the body, the mind, the energy. Even the bliss, even the ecstasy, even meditation itself is no more there.

When meditation becomes perfect, it is no more a meditation. When the meditator has really achieved the goal, he does not meditate. He cannot meditate because that too is now an activity like walking, eating. He has become separate from everything.

That is the difference between *dhyan* and *samadhi,* between meditation and *samadhi.* Meditation is of the fifth body, the bliss body. It is still a therapy, a medicine. You are still a little ill; ill because you are identifying yourself with something which you are not.

All illness is identification, and absolute health is through non-identification. *Samadhi* is when even meditation has been left behind.

Patanjali is saying, step by step, that it is impossible for the mind to do two things: to be perceived and to be the perceiver. Either it can be the perceiver or it can be the perceived.

So when you can witness your mind, that proves absolutely that the mind is not the perceiver. You are the perceiver. You are not the body; you are not even the mind. The whole emphasis is: how to help you to discriminate from that which you are not.

One has to understand something absolutely inside, behind which there is nothing. Otherwise there is a confusion of memories; otherwise, a chaos. Body, mind, and the witnesser: the witnesser is absolute.

Yoga believes that the witness is a self-illuminating phenomenon. It is just like a light. You have a small candle in your room – the candle illuminates the room, the furniture, the walls, the painting on the wall. Who illuminates the candle?

You don't need another candle to find this candle; the candle is self-illuminating.

It illuminates other things, and simultaneously it illuminates itself. Innermost consciousness is self-illuminating.

It is of the nature of light.

The sun illuminates everything in the solar system – at the same time it illuminates itself.

The witnesser witnesses everything that goes on around in the five seeds and in the world, and at the same time it illuminates itself.

Osho – "Yoga: the Alpha and Omega", Volume 10, Discourse 7

All the past buddhas came from royal families and Gautama Siddartha was no exception. He enjoyed money, enjoyed sex, lived in the most luxurious way possible; and still he found a deep emptiness inside himself. Gautama renounced the world, became a beggar, and finally renounced the world of a seeker and woke up spiritually. Today he is simply called "Buddha".

But all human beings are not born in royal families. They don't have the chance to experience money, sex, and all the pleasures of the outside world. Because the royal kings were frustrated - the money was not fulfilling, the sex was superficial, all the pleasures were repetitive and became routine - they were utterly bored. They renounced the world.

Because of their renunciation of the world - going into the forest and mountains - a fallacy arose that unless you renounce the world and worldly pleasures, you cannot become awakened, you cannot become enlightened. Gautama's individual experience was made into a universal principle. It is a human tendency. It sill persists.

For example, only psychological sick people went to Sigmund Freud. Obviously, he who is healthy mentally has no need to go to Sigmund Freud. Freud came across only sick people, and he extended the principle to the whole of humanity, as if everyone is sick. He only knew the dreams of sick people, and he thought all dreams are repressive. In his experience that was so, but his experience is not universal.

It happens with you, too, a very basic human fallacy: you come across a Mohammedan, and he cheats you, or a Hindu and he deceives you - and immediately you jump to the conclusion that no Hindu is worth believing, that no Mohammedan should ever be trusted. A single instance becomes to you a universal principle. It is not. In fact, all the past buddhas support my thesis. Of course, they were not aware of it.

What I am saying is, unless you are deeply acquainted with the outside world, unless you have been a Zorba* in totality and intensity, there is no possibility for you to become a buddha.

First you have to live in the world to be capable of renouncing it. How can you renounce something which you don't have? You have to become so frustrated, so nauseated with the outside pleasures that they become almost pain, anxiety and anguish. Only then can you turn inward.

But all these buddhas of the past have fallen into the same human fallacy: they project their own experience. They thought perhaps a starving person, a person who has never known any pleasure in his life, will also understand them. And the result has been a tremendous calamity.

The poor in the East have remained poor, thinking, 'What is the point of achieving wealth, what is the point of attaining luxury?' because they have seen all those great, enlightened people renouncing luxury, so perhaps they are in a better position: they are poor already.

Buddha became a beggar by renouncing his kingdom. But do you think he is the same kind of beggar, can be put in the same category as any other beggar who has never know anything of delicious food, of a beautiful woman, of a palace, of all the joys that are possible?

On the surface they may look the same: both have a begging bowl. But they are not the same - they belong to totally different categories. I would like you to belong to the category of Buddha. But first he was a Zorba, and only then he became a buddha. The other has never experienced outside reality. He can only repress his sex; he is not frustrated with it.

Buddha has no need to repress – he has lived it, over-lived it; otherwise, in 29 years one does not renounce the world.

Note: Zorba is a character in the book "Zorba the Greek" by Nikos Kazantzaki. Zorba passionately enjoys life's sensual pleasures and helps a young intellectual break out of a boring controlled life.

The story is that when he was born all the astrologers of his father's kingdom were called, because Buddha was the only son and he was born in the king's old age. The king wanted to know exactly what Buddha's life was going to be; all the astrologers were puzzled, and nobody was ready to say anything.

The king was in much difficulty: "Why don't you say something? Even if it is bad news, at least don't keep me in confusion. Say it."

Then the youngest of them spoke. He said, "The problem we are all facing is that he does not have a fixed destiny. There is an alternative destiny – and that is a very rare case such as we have never come across.

"It is expected that we should tell you what is going to happen to him. But he has an alternative destiny – two destinies: either he will become a world conqueror, a *chakravartin,* or he will become a renouncer of the world. They are extreme polarities, and we have not been able to find which one is weightier; they are of equal weight. So we cannot say anything definitively.

"All that we can say is that these are the two alternatives: either he will become the greatest emperor the world has known, or he will become one of the greatest enlightened persons the world has known. In any case he will be one of the greatest persons. But whether he will be a beggar or an emperor is beyond our understanding and our science."

The king was also puzzled; this was his only son. He had conquered new lands, he had made a very big kingdom – and the only successor has an alternative destiny. He asked the astrologers, "Help me. Advise me what should be done so that he never renounces the world, but conquers the world. That has been my dream my whole life. He is going to be the fulfillment of my dream. He is my child – he has brought my dream in his heart. Just tell me how to prevent him from renouncing the world."

They all suggested with ordinary logic - and ordinary logic destroyed the whole thing. They said, "Surround him with as much luxury and comfort as possible so he never feels the miseries of life. Gather around him the most beautiful girls so he never feels any sexual deprivation. Make beautiful palaces for him in different places of your kingdom for different seasons, so that he never feels that it is too hot or too cold or too much rain.

"He should never see a leaf which is becoming pale, old, ready to die. In the night, all the flowers which are going to die soon should be removed. No old man, old woman should be allowed to enter into his palaces. And whenever he passes on the roads, arrangements should be made that he never comes across a dead body or a sannyasin."

All these preparations were done, and the old king managed everything that the astrologer had said. But the ordinary logic is not the only logic. There is a transcendental logic which they were not aware of.

I would not have suggested this. I would have told him, "Let him live like an ordinary human being. Let him strive for comfort; don't give it to him. Let him strive to find a beautiful woman – don't just gather women like cattle around him. Let him know the pains of desire and longing and passion." Perhaps he would never have renounced the world, because he would never have come to know the world in its reality so soon.

Those 29 years were almost equal perhaps to 200 or 300 years. Even in 300 years you may not be able to attain all the luxury that was showered on him. And that was the reason that he renounced the world – seeing that it is all superficial and routine.

Seeing one dead man.... In 29 years he had not seen even a dead leaf. If he had seen from his very childhood that people die, he would have become accustomed to it. But for 29 years he had never thought about death. The very idea was not a question to him. But how long can you prevent?

One day he happened to see a dead man, and the whole palace of playing cards that his father had made, collapsed. He asked his charioteer, "What has happened to this man?"

The charioteer said, "Master, I am not supposed to tell you; but I cannot lie to you either. This man is dead."

And immediately the question was asked which ordinarily you don't ask. Immediately he asked, "Is this the destiny of every man? Am I also going to die one day?"

And just when the charioteer was saying, "There is no way to avoid death: even to you it will happen," a sannyasin passed by.

Gautam had never seen an orange-robed sannyasin, and he asked, "What type of man is this? What has happened to him?"

And the charioteer said, "He has also become aware of death, old age, and he has renounced the world. He is going in search of that which never dies."

They were going to participate in a youth festival. Gautam Buddha said to his charioteer, "Turn the chariot back. For me now there is no youth festival. I am old, I am dead. Just take me back home." And that very night he escaped from the kingdom. The charioteer – an old man, a very faithful servant of the king – tried to persuade him.

Buddha said, "There is no way. If you cannot prevent old age, don't try to persuade me. If you cannot prevent death, don't try to persuade me. I am going in search of that which never dies."

So it is a double fallacy. Buddha renounced and he found the truth; and he also must have thought that it was because of renunciation that he had found the truth. That was not the case. It was because of his luxurious life that the search began – because luxury had failed, money had deceived, palaces became empty, the kingdom became meaningless, conquering the whole world became pointless.

If you are going to die, what is the point of bothering with killing millions of people when in the end your hands are empty? So he himself thought that renouncing the kingdom had been helpful in finding the truth. But he forgot one thing: that everybody does not have a kingdom.

And Buddha's fallacy became a universal fallacy. Others who didn't have kingdoms started moving into mountains, into forests, into isolation. A poor man can become respectable by becoming a beggar in the name of religion, but he will never become enlightened.

Hence my emphasis is: before you enter into the inner world, be finished with the outer. Live it so totally – your life torch should burn from both the ends together. The more totally you live, the quicker you will understand that there is not much.

It is only the unlived part of life that seems to be attractive. If you have lived totally then nothing seems to be attractive. And only in that state can you move inwards without hesitation and without any split.

I am not saying renounce the outside. There is no need. Renunciation is out of fear. And naturally, 25 centuries have passed since Gautama Buddha. In these 25 centuries not only scientific technology has progressed; spiritual consciousness and the methods that can lead you to enlightenment have also been refined.

I would like my people to live at ease, with all that is available on the outside. Don't be in a hurry, because anything left unlived will pull you back again. Finish it. And then there is no need to escape from your house or from your bank account, because they are no longer a burden on you. They don't mean anything. Perhaps they have a certain utility, but nothing is wrong with them.

Even a Gautama Buddha needs food, but somebody else earns it. He needs clothes, and somebody else earns them for him. You earn your own food. It is better to earn your own clothes, your own shelter.

What is the point to be understood? – there is nothing in them that binds you. What binds you is the lust for the unlived life. So live life totally and let this lust disappear. Then you can live in a palace with the same ease as you can live in a poor man's hut. But if a palace is available, then why unnecessarily torture yourself in a poor man's hut? Just, the palace should not be your prison.

And because all these great enlightened people consistently renounced the world, it created an atmosphere in the whole of the East that poverty is something spiritual. It is sheer nonsense. Poverty is not spiritual; it is ugly. It is one of the wounds that has to be healed. If poverty were spiritual, then there would have been millions of Gautama Buddhas in the East. But we have never heard about beggars becoming buddhas.

My approach is a discontinuity with the past. I teach you first to live as a Zorba, and only on that foundation will be raised the temple of your buddhahood. And in this way we are joining the outer and the inner in a single unity. The outer is also yours as much as the inner. There is no question of denying anything; there is no question of being against anything.

So I say to you: pleasure may be the lowest step, but it is part of the same ladder. The highest step may be enlightenment, may be blissfulness, but it is the same ladder. And if you renounce the first rung of the ladder, you will never reach to the last rung.

Just think – you are standing upon the first rung of the ladder. There are two ways of renouncing it: one is getting down, the other is moving to the second rung. Both have renounced the first rung of the ladder.

Gautama Buddha moves to the second, and you are moving below the first. You see that he has left the first rung, but you have not understood that he has left the first rung for the second. He will leave the second rung for the third, and he will go on leaving the third and the fourth for the final.

But you have become afraid of the first, because you have seen buddhas leaving the first, so you never step on the first. You remain below the first. These people have reached to the highest fulfillment of bliss, and you remain hungry, thirsty even for the shallowest pleasure that the first rung can make available to you.

And secondly, the buddhas of the past were not concerned with any social revolution. Their whole concern was with their own achievement, with their own spiritual attainment. In a certain way they were very self-centered. And because of their self-centeredness, the East has not known any revolution at all.

All the geniuses became so self-centered, who was going to give the masses the idea of a revolution? At the most they can teach charity to the poor, but they cannot conceive of a world without poverty.

I conceive of a world without poverty, without classes, without nations, without religions, without any kind of discrimination. I conceive of a world which is one, a humanity which is one, a humanity which shares everything – outer and inner – a deep spiritual brotherhood.

So my function is not simply finished with my own enlightenment. In fact, my work began after my enlightenment. Gautama Buddha's work came to an end when he became enlightened; I started my work after my enlightenment. As far as I am concerned, I don't need to live a single moment more, because life, either outer or inner, cannot give me anything more than I have already achieved.

But to me it seems to be selfish. I would like millions of people to be aflame with the same light, with the same vision, with the same dream. I would like a new man to be born, a new humanity, where ugly discriminations disappear, where there are no wars, no atomic or nuclear weapons, no nations, no races; where man can share all the bounties of existence and all the experiences of his inner being. I want this whole humanity to be one ocean of consciousness.

Whatever the buddhas in the past did was good, but not enough. They created for themselves the highest peak of consciousness. I would like to create that highest peak for everyone – at least for those who are in search of it.

And I cannot say, "Renounce the outer" – because the outer is as essential as the inner. Just don't cling to it. How can you renounce the outer? You can renounce the palace, but how are you going renounce your breathing? Each moment the outer breath comes in. How can you renounce food? – it comes from the outside. How can you renounce water? – it comes from the outside.

Looked at with clarity, there is no division between the outer and the inner, but a constant harmony – just like the incoming breath and outgoing breath. I am giving you a new conception, a new vision, a new dream.

Osho – "The Rebellious Life"

The being doesn't come and go. It the subtle body that comes and goes; it is the gross body, the physical body, that comes and goes. We receive the physical body from our parents, we receive the subtle body from our past life, and the being is ever-present.

Without the subtle body one cannot receive a physical body. Once the subtle body disperses, it is impossible to attain a physical body. That's why the moment the subtle body disperses, two things happen. On the one hand, as the subtle body disperses, the journey into physical bodies comes to an end. And on the other hand, the boundary that existed between the Whole and you disappears.

The dispersal of the subtle body is the whole spiritual discipline. The connecting bridge that joins you with the physical body on one side and the Whole, falls. Breaking down this bridge is what spiritual discipline is all about.

But it is necessary to understand all that constitutes this subtle body. Our desires, our passions, our ambitions, our wishes, our expectations; the actions that we have committed, the actions that we did not commit but only thought about committing; our thoughts, our deeds; whatever we have been; all that we have ever thought of, dreamt of, done; all that we have ever experienced, felt - all of these together with their electrical imprints make up our subtle body.

It is the dispersal of this subtle body that brings two outcomes. The first is that the journey to the womb comes to an end. When Buddha attained enlightenment he said, "Oh mind, I declare that you, who until now built so many houses called 'the body' for me, can now go to rest. Now you don't need to build any more houses for me. I thank you, and I let you go. There is no longer any work left for you to do, because there is no longer any desire left in me. Oh mind, builder of many, many houses for me, now you no longer need to build any."

Just before Buddha was about to die, people asked him, "Now, as your being will merge with the Whole, where will you be?"

Buddha said, "If I can be somewhere, how can I merge with the Whole? Because one who is somewhere cannot be everywhere." He said, "Don't even ask this question. Now I will not be anywhere, because I will be everywhere." But still the devotees kept asking, "Please tell us where you will be from now on."

This is like asking a dewdrop where will it be after becoming one with the ocean. The drop will say, "I will become that very same ocean." But the other drop will say, "That's alright, but still...where exactly will you be? Maybe someday we can come and visit you!"

So the drop that is about to become one with the ocean says, "Just merge into the ocean and our meeting will happen." But actually the meeting will be with the ocean, not with the drop.

If one wishes to meet Buddha, Khrishna, Mahavira, Jesus or Mohammed, he cannot meet them in their drop form. No matter how many statues you make and keep of them, you will never be able to meet that drop anymore. That drop is now one with the ocean.

The outer form of the drop comes from our parents. The inner arrangement of the drop comes from our previous lives. And the life energy, which is our being, is received from the Whole. But until we have thoroughly recognized these two layers of the drop, we will not be able to know that which is beyond the two.

Osho – From the book "Inner War and Peace"

ALL IS ILLUSION EXCEPT THE WITNESS

All is illusion except the witness. All is dream except the witness. Only the knower is true, is real. Whatsoever you see is illusory; the seer is not illusory.

In the night you see one type of dream, in the day you see another type of dream. In the night the dreams of the day are forgotten, in the day the dreams of the night are forgotten. Sometimes you dream with open eyes and sometimes you dream with closed eyes, but one thing remains eternally there, never changing, and that is your consciousness.

In the night you see dreams; in the day you see things, the world. Everything changes: night into day, day into night, dreams into thoughts, thoughts into dreams; only one thing remains eternally there – your witnessing. That which is eternal is true. That which is changing is illusory.

Remember, by 'illusion' I don't mean that it is not. By 'illusion' I only mean that it is not eternally true. And what is the meaning of something being temporarily true, only for the moment? Before the moment it was untrue, after the moment it again becomes untrue.

That's why in the East we have not been chasing life. Before birth it was not there, after death it will not be there again, so this momentary phenomenon is not of much value. There is no need to get obsessed by it; one can pass through it unconcerned, untouched by it.

The emphasis of the West is on that which is seen, and the emphasis of the East is on that which is the seer. Either you focus on the object or you focus on yourself. When you focus on the object your approach is scientific, objective. When you focus on the subject your approach is religious. This subject is eternally true.

The Bible says, "In the beginning was the word." The East cannot say that. The East says, "In the beginning there was the witness, in the middle there is the witness, in the end there will be the witness; one thing remains eternally the substratum of all." Even if the word had been there in the beginning, somebody must have heard it – the seer, the witness, otherwise it could not have been. So the one who heard it precedes the word; the word cannot be in the beginning.

Just go on looking more and more for the witness and go on getting more and more involved into the witness and one day the gestalt changes. Your focus goes through a transformation.

For example, right now you are listening to me. You can listen in two ways, because each thing can be done in two ways: Eastern and Western. You are listening to me; your emphasis can be on what I am saying, on the speaker – then it is a Western approach. The Eastern approach is that your emphasis be on the listener, the watcher, the observer, the witness. You are not too concerned with what is being said or what is being heard, but with who this witness is who is hearing this.

You are seeing me. Who is this seer who is seeing? That transform-ation, that change of gestalt, will bring you to the world of non-illusion; otherwise everything is illusory.

The outside is unreal. It is not that something is real and something is unreal; the outside is unreal and the inside is real. With the outside, mind grows; with the inside, meditation.

To work with the outside, your mind becomes more and more efficient. In the West the mind has become tremendously clever. When you start looking at the inside, at the looker, then meditation grows. Then you don't become a great thinker or a great philosopher, but you experience Truth - you become a great mystic, you become a Buddha, a Lieh Tzu, a Jesus.

But the whole emphasis – always remember – is on the mirror that reflects. Don't become too attached to that which is reflected. You look in the mirror; your image looks so real, but it is unreal. Don't get too obsessed with the image. The image is unreal in the mirror and the person who is standing before the mirror is also unreal.

Only one thing is real: the consciousness that knows 'I am standing before the mirror', the consciousness which knows that the mirror is reflecting the one who is standing. That transcendental consciousness is reality, and through that descends the benediction, *'sat-chit-anand'*; through that one becomes true, conscious and blissful.

Why do we call the world illusory? Let me remind you again: by 'illusory' we don't mean unreal, we mean temporarily real, only for the time being real.

Why do we call the outer world unreal? Because it brings only misery and it gives you only projections, ambitions, desires; it never allows you to be really happy, authentically happy. It gives you hope but never fulfills it. It leads you on many journeys but the goal never arrives, hence it is called *'maya'*, illusion. It deceives you, it is a mirage – it appears to be there, but when you reach there you don't find anything; and by the time you reach there, your desires are being projected further ahead. It is like the horizon: you go towards it, it goes on receding. You never arrive – you cannot arrive, by its very nature it is not possible, it only appears – it is not there.

Just the opposite is the case when you enter your inner world of consciousness: the closer you come, the more real it becomes; the closer you come, the more blissful, the more cheerful, the more joyful you become. The closer you come, the more authentic and true you become; and the moment you stand at the very center, you are truth itself. In that moment the Upanishadic seer declared: "I am God, I am *Brahma*". In that moment of inner centering, Mansur el-Hallaj declared: *"Ana el haqq:* I am the Truth"*. In that moment, Jesus says: "I and my God are not two, but one".

If you move towards the object, you are moving away from yourself; and the further away you go from yourself, the further away you are going from Truth, because Truth is centered in you.

Everything is illusion, except you. When I say 'you', I don't mean the 'you' that you know; I mean the 'you' that is yet undiscovered by you. The 'you' that you know belongs to the outside world, it is as much unreal as the outside world. The 'you' that you know is nothing but an accumulation of all the illusions, all the dreams and desires. The 'you' I am talking about has nothing to do with you as such; it is the eternal 'you', the eternal 'thou'. It is not yours, it is not mine, it is nobody else's. It is everybody's; it is the very center of all.

When your 'I' drops then the real I arises. When your self disappears, the real self arrives.

People come to me and they say, "We feel it is very difficult to surrender because surrendering means we will be losing ourselves." They are true and they are not really true. They are true because their self, the self that they have known up to now, is going to be dropped. But they are not really true because once this false self is dropped, the real self arises. It is there, it is hidden behind the cloud of the false self.

You - as you really are in your center - are the reality. Everything else is illusory. To know this reality one has to come to a moment of total inactivity because whenever you are acting, you are outside yourself. That's why Lieh Tzu, Chuang Tzu, Lao Tzu, emphasized passivity so much. When you are active, you are relating with the outside world.

What is activity? Activity means relating with the outside. When you are passive, you are not relating at all. You are simply there, unrelated; there is no bridge between you and the outside – all bridges have disappeared. In this total silence, in this total unrelatedness, you become aware of who you are. Otherwise the activity keeps you so occupied that there is no space for the self to assert, to manifest, itself. It goes on waiting. It goes on waiting and you go on remaining occupied with trivia, with mundane things.

One has to learn to do nothing.

Osho – "Yoga: the Alpha and Omega", Volume 10

CHOICELESS AWARENESS IS WITNESSING

Choice is bondage, choicelessness freedom. The moment you choose something, you have fallen in the trap of the world. If you can resist the temptation to choose, if you can remain choicelessly aware, the trap disappears on its own accord, because when you don't choose you don't help the trap to be there – the trap is also created by your choice. So this word "choice" has to be understood very deeply, because only through that understanding can choicelessness flower in you.

Why can't you remain without choosing? Why does it happen the moment you see a person or a thing, immediately a subtle wave of choice has entered in you, even if you are not aware that you have chosen?

A woman passes by and you say she is beautiful. You are not saying anything about your choice, but the choice has entered: for to say of a person that she is beautiful means, "I would like to choose her." In fact, deep down you have chosen; you are already in the trap. The seed has fallen to the soil; soon there will be sprouts, there will be a plant and a tree.

The moment you say, "This car is beautiful," choice has entered. You may not be aware at all that you have chosen, that you would like to possess this car, but in the mind a fantasy has entered, a desire has arisen. When you say something is beautiful, you mean that you would like to have it. When you say something is ugly, you mean that you would not like to have it.

Choice is subtle and one has to be very minutely aware about it. Whenever you say something remember this: that saying is not only saying, not a mere saying - something has happened in the unconscious.

Don't make the distinction: this is beautiful and that is ugly, this is good and that is bad. Don't make the distinctions. Remain aloof. Things are neither bad nor good. The quality of goodness and badness is introduced by you. Things are neither beautiful nor ugly; they are simply there as they are – the quality of being beautiful and ugly is introduced by you, it is your interpretation.

You simply see the whole trick: it is your own creation. What do you mean that something is ugly? If man is not on the earth will there be ugliness and beauty? Trees will be there, of course, and they will bloom, of course; rains will come, and summer and seasons will follow one another – but there will be nothing like beautiful and ugly; it will disappear with man and his mind. The sun will rise and in the night the sky will be filled with stars – but nothing will be beautiful and nothing will be ugly. It was just man creating noise. Now he is no more there; the interpretations have disappeared; what will be good and what will be bad?

In Nature nothing is good and nothing is bad.

Hindus in the East have made a criterion of Truth: they say Truth is that which lasts forever, forever, forever; and untruth is that which lasts only for a moment. No other distinction is there. The momentary is the untrue and the everlasting is the Truth. And life is everlasting; existence is everlasting.

Mind is momentary – so whatsoever mind gives to life remains momentary; it is a color that the mind gives to the life, it is an interpretation. By the time the interpretation is complete, the mind has changed. You cannot maintain the interpretation because mind cannot be maintained for two consecutive moments in the same situation in the same state. Mind goes on changing, mind is a flux. It has already changed – by the time you realize that this man is beautiful, the mind has already changed. Now you will be falling in love with something which is there no more, even in your mind.

Tantra says: understand the mechanism of the mind and cut the root. Don't choose, because when you choose you get identified. Whatsoever you choose you become, in a certain way, one with it. If you love a car, you become one with that car in a certain way. You come closer and closer, and if the car is stolen, something of your being is stolen. If something goes wrong with the car, something goes wrong with you.

If you fall in love with a house you become one with the house. Love means identification, coming so close, as if you put two wax candles closer, closer, closer, and put them very close – they become one. The heat, the burning of the flame...by and by they become one. This is identification. Two flames coming closer and closer and closer, they become one. And when you are identified with something you have lost your soul. This is the meaning of losing your soul in the world: you have become identified with millions of things, and with everything a part of you has become a thing.

Choice brings identification. Identification brings a hypnotic state of sleep. Gurdjieff has only one thing to teach to his disciples and that is not to be identified. His whole school, all his techniques, methods, situations, are based on one single base, and that base is: not to be identified.

You are crying; when you are crying, you have become one with the crying. There is nobody to watch it, there is nobody to see it, be alert and aware of it – you are lost in crying. You have become the tears and the red, swollen eyes and your heart is in a crisis.

Teachers like Gurdjieff, when they say not to be identified, they say, "Cry, nothing is wrong in it, but stand by the side and look at it – don't be identified."

And it is a wonderful experience if you can stand by the side. Cry, let the body cry, let the tears flow, don't suppress it because suppression helps nobody; but stand by the side and watch. This can be done because your inner being is a witness, it is never a doer.

Whenever you think it is a doer there is an identification. It is never a doer. You can walk the whole earth – your inner being never walks a single step. You can dream millions of dreams – your inner being never dreams a single dream. All movements are on the surface. Deep in the depth of your being there is no movement. All movements are on the periphery, just like a wheel moves, but at the center nothing moves.

At that center everything remains as it is, and on the center the wheel moves. Remember the center!

Watch your behavior, your actions, your identifications, and a distance is created; by and by a distance comes into existence – the watcher and the doer become two. You can see yourself laughing, you can see yourself crying, you can see yourself walking, eating, making love; you can act many things, whatsoever is going on around – and you remain the seer. You don't jump and become one with whatsoever you are seeing.

The innermost being is just like a mirror. Whatsoever comes before it, it mirrors, it simply becomes a witness. Disease comes or health, hunger or satiety, summer or winter, childhood or old age, birth or death — whatsoever happens, happens before the mirror, it never happens to the mirror.

This is non-identification, this is cutting the root, the very root — to become a mirror. And to me this is sannyas: to become like a mirror. Don't become like a very sensitive photo plate — that is identification. Whatsoever comes before the lens of the camera, the photo plate immediately takes it in, becomes one with it.

Become like a mirror. Things come and pass and the mirror remains vacant, empty, void. The mirror has no self to be identified with. It simply reflects. It does not react, it simply responds. It doesn't say, "This is beautiful, that is ugly." An ugly woman stands before it, the mirror is as happy as when a beautiful woman stands before it. It makes no difference. It reflects whatsoever is the case but it doesn't interpret. It doesn't say, "Go away, you disturb me very much," or "Come a little closer, you are so beautiful." The mirror says nothing. The mirror simply watches without any distinction, friend or foe. The mirror has no distinctions to make. And when somebody passes, goes away from the mirror, the mirror doesn't cling to it. The mirror has no past. It is not that you have passed and the mirror will cling a little to your phantom. It is not that the mirror will cling to your shadow a little while. It is not that the mirror will try to retain the reflection that has happened in it. No. You have passed, the reflection has gone; not even for a single second the mirror retains it.

This is the mind of a buddha: You come before it, he is filled with you; you go away, you have gone. Not even a memory flashes. A mirror has no past, neither has a buddha. A mirror has no future, neither has a buddha. The mirror doesn't wait: "Now who is coming before me; now who am I going to reflect? I would like this person to come and not like that person." The mirror has no choice, he remains choiceless.

Try to understand this metaphor of the mirror because this is the real situation of the inner consciousness. Don't get identified by things that are happening around you. You remain centered and rooted in your being. Things are happening and they will continue to happen, but if you can be centered in your mirror-like consciousness, nothing will be the same – the whole has changed. You remain virgin, innocent, pure. Nothing can become an impurity to you, absolutely nothing because nothing is retained. You reflect, for a moment somebody is there and then everything is gone. Your emptiness is untouched.

Even while a mirror is reflecting somebody, there is nothing happening to the mirror. The mirror is not changing in any way; the mirror remains the same. This is cutting the very root.

Identification is the root and everything else is nothing but leaves. Being identified with greed, being identified with anger, being identified with sex, is the root. And remember, it is the same whether you are identified with greed, or sex, or even meditation - love, *moksha*, God – it makes no difference, it is the same identification.

Being identified is the root, and all else is just like leaves. Don't cut the leaves, leave them, nothing is wrong in them. That's why Tantra does not believe in improving your character. It may give you a good shape – if you prune a tree you can make any shape out of it – but the tree remains the same. Character is just an outer shape – but you remain the same, no transmutation happens. Tantra goes deeper and says, "Cut the root!"

All practice is of the mind. Whatsoever you do is of the mind. Only witnessing is not of the mind, remember this. So, even while you are doing meditation, remain a witness, continuously see what is happening.

A teacher is one who teaches you something; a Master is one who helps you to unlearn all that you have already learned. A Master is to help you unlearn. A Master is to give you the taste of the non-practiced. It is already there; through your learning you have lost it. Through your unlearning you will regain it.

Truth is not a discovery, it is a rediscovery. It was already there in the first place. When you came into this world it was with you, when you were born into this life it was with you, because you are it! It cannot be otherwise. It is not something external, it is intrinsic in you, it is your very being.

Meditation is witnessing. All techniques can be helpful but they are not exactly meditation, they are just a groping in the dark. Suddenly one day, doing something, you will become a witness.

Go slowly; take proportions only which you can digest and absorb. Even as I am here, I will be saying many things because you are many, and I will be talking many dimensions because you are many. But you absorb only that which is a nourishment to you; you digest. Whatsoever you find nourishing, you digest it; chew it well, digest it; let it become your blood and bones, the very marrow of your bones – but follow your inclination.

Osho – "Tantra the Supreme Understanding", Discourse 8

THE ALCHEMY OF AWARENESS

If I was going to teach you, I would not tell you whom to love, how to love. That is all nonsense. Love is your intrinsic quality. You are born with it, just as hate is also there. I will teach you, be aware. Before anything happens to you – love or hate, anger, passion, compassion, anything – be aware.

Let everything arise out of your awareness. And the miracle of awareness is that without your saying anything, without doing anything, it simply dissolves all that is ugly in you into all that is beautiful.

Awareness is a transforming force.

For example, if you are aware of anger, it will disappear. If you are aware of love, it will become stronger. If there is hate and you become aware of it, it will disappear, dissipate. Soon you will find that that cloud of hatred has disappeared and instead a totally opposite quality – a mixture of compassion, kindness, lovingness – has been left behind like an aroma.

To me this is the criterion: Whatsoever deepens with your awareness is virtue. Whatsoever disappears with your awareness is sin. To me this is the definition.

I don't label any act as sin, virtue, right, wrong – acts don't have that quality. It is your awareness. Just try it and you will be simply amazed that there are things in you which cannot stand in front of awareness, they simply disappear. Awareness functions almost like magic.

You will have to experiment with it. You will have to see, with the different things in you, what remains and what disappears. And it is only you who can find what is right for you and what is wrong for you. Then keep the thread of awareness running through all your actions, and in your life you will not find any hate, any anger, any jealousy. Not that you have dropped them, not that you have repressed them, not that you have somehow got rid of them, not that you have practiced doing something against them. No, you have not done anything, you have not even touched them.

This is the beauty of awareness: it never represses anything; but there are things which simply melt in the light of awareness and change. And there are things which become more solid, more integrated, more profound, more strong: love, compassion, kindness, friendliness, understanding.

All the religions up to date have been focusing people's minds on actions; and labeling – this is bad, this is good, this you have to do, this you have not to do. I want to change the whole emphasis. Actions have nothing to do with right and wrong. It is you, your alertness, which is decisive. Any action with awareness may become beautiful; the same action without awareness may be ugly. With your awareness, the same action in one situation may disappear, and in another situation may become solid, stronger.

So it is not something like a fixed quality of any act, of any emotion; it all depends on a thousand and one things. But your awareness takes note of everything, you need not be worried. It is just like light in which everything becomes clear to you, you can see it.

Osho – "From Misery to Enlightenment", Discourse 13

THE WARRIOR AND THE KING PATHS

There are two paths. One is the path of the warrior, the soldier; another is the path of the king, the royal path. Yoga is the first, Tantra is the second.

A soldier has to fight inch by inch; a soldier has to be aggressive; a soldier has to be violent; the enemy has to be destroyed, or conquered. Yoga tries to create a conflict within you. It gives you a clear-cut distinction between what is wrong and what is right, what is good and what is bad, what belongs to God and what belongs to the devil. And almost all the religions, except Tantra, follow the path of Yoga. They divide reality and they create an inner conflict; through conflict they proceed.

For example: you have hate in you; the path of the warrior is to destroy hate within. You have anger and greed and sex, and millions of things. The path of the warrior is to destroy all that is wrong, negative, and develop all that is positive and right. Hate has to be destroyed and love evolved. Anger has to be completely destroyed and compassion created. Sex has to go and give place to *brahmacharya,* to pure celibacy.

Yoga immediately cuts you with a sword in two parts: the right and wrong. The right has to win over the wrong. What will you do? Anger is there – what does yoga suggest to do? It suggests: create the habit of compassion, create the opposite; make it so habitual that you start functioning like a robot – hence it is called the way of the soldier.

All over the world, throughout history, the soldier has been trained in a robot-like existence; he has to create habits. Habits function without consciousness, they don't need any awareness, they can move without you.

If you have habits – and everybody has habits – you can watch this. A man takes out his packet of cigarettes from the pocket, watch him – he may not be at all aware what he is doing. Just robot-like he reaches to the pocket. If there is some inner restlessness, immediately his hand goes to the pocket; he brings out the cigarette, starts smoking. He may throw the remaining part, the last part of the cigarette; he may have moved through all the gestures without even being aware of what he was doing.

A robot-like existence we teach to the soldier. The soldier has to do and follow, he has not to be aware. When he is commanded to turn to the right, he has to turn; he has not to think it, about whether to turn or not – because if he starts thinking then it is impossible, then the wars cannot continue in the world. Thinking is not needed, nor is awareness needed. He should simply be this much aware – that he can understand the order, that's all. The minimum of awareness: here the order is given, and there, immediately, like a mechanism, he starts following. It is not that he turns to the left when he is ordered to turn left – he listens and turns. He is not turning; he has cultivated the habit. It is just like putting off or on the light: the light is not going to think about it, whether to be on or off – you push the button and the light is on. You say, "Left turn!" and the button is pushed and the man moves left.

William James has reported that once he was sitting in a coffeehouse and an old soldier – retired almost for 20 years – was passing with a bucket of eggs. Suddenly William James played a joke. He loudly called "Attention!" and the poor old man stood to attention. The eggs fell from his hands, they were destroyed. He was very angry; he came running and said, "What type of joke is this?"

But William James said, "You need not follow it. Everybody is free to call 'Attention!' You are not forced to follow it. Who told you to follow it? You should have gone on your way."

The man said, "That is not possible – it is automatic. Of course 20 years have passed since I have been in the military, but the habit is deep-rooted." Many years of training – a conditioned reflex is created.

This word "conditioned reflex" is good. It is coined by a Russian psychologist, Pavlov. It says you simply reflect; somebody throws something in your eye – you don't think to blink it or close it, the eye simply closes. A fly comes flying and you close the eye: you need not think, there is no need, it is a conditioned reflex – it simply happens. It is in your body-habit, it is in your blood, in your bones. It simply happens – nothing has to be done about it.

The soldier is trained to be in a completely robot-like way. He has to exist in conditioned reflexes. The same is done by Yoga. You get angry. Yoga says, "Don't get angry, rather cultivate the opposite: compassion". By and by, your energy will start moving in the habit of compassion. If you persevere for a long time, anger will disappear completely, you will feel compassion. But you will be dead, not alive. You will be a robot, not a human being. You will have compassion, not because you have compassion, but only because you have cultivated a habit.

You can cultivate a bad habit, you can cultivate a good habit. Somebody can cultivate smoking, somebody can cultivate no-smoking; somebody can cultivate non-vegetarian styles of food, somebody can cultivate vegetarian style – but both are cultivating, and in the final judgment both are the same because both live through habits.

This point has to be pondered over very deeply because it is very easy to cultivate a good habit and it is very difficult to become good. And the substitute of a good habit is cheap, it can be done very easily.

Now, particularly in Russia, they are developing a therapy: conditioned reflex therapy. They say people cannot leave their habits. Somebody has been smoking for 20 years – how can you expect him to leave it? You may try to explain to him that it is bad, the doctors may say he may be even in a dangerous situation, cancer may be developing; but 20 years of long habit – now it is engrained, now it has moved into the deepest core of his body, now it is in his metabolism. Even if he wants, even if he desires, even if he desires sincerely, it is difficult – because it is not a question of sincere desire: 20 years of continuous practice – it is almost impossible. So what to do?

In Russia they say there is no need to do anything, and no need to explain to him. They have developed a therapy: the man starts smoking and they give him an electric shock. The shock, the pain of it, and the smoking, become joined together, become associated. For seven days he is hospitalized and whenever he starts smoking, immediately, automatically, he gets an electric shock. After seven days the habit is broken. Even if you persuade him to smoke he will be trembling. The moment he will take the cigarette in the hand the whole body will tremble because of the idea of the shock. They say now he will never smoke; they have broken the habit by a very sharp shock treatment.

But now he cannot become a buddha just by shock treatment because he does not have an old habit. All the habits can be changed through shock treatment. Will he become a buddha, enlightened, because he has no bad habits anymore? No. He will not be even a human being now – he will be a mechanism. He will be afraid of things, he will not be able to do them because you have given him new habits of fear.

That is the whole meaning of hell: all the religions have used it as a shock treatment. Hell is nowhere, nor is there any heaven. Both are tricks, old psychotherapeutic concepts. They have painted hell so horrible that a child can become afraid from the very childhood onwards. The mentioning of the name of hell and fear arises and he trembles. This is just a trick to prevent bad habits. And heaven is also a trick to help good habits. So much pleasure, happiness, beauty, eternal life is promised in heaven if you follow good patterns. Whatsoever the society says is good you have to follow. Heaven is to help you towards positivity, and hell is to prevent you from going into the negative direction.

Tantra is the only religion which has not used any such conditioned reflexes, because Tantra says you have to flower into a perfectly awakened being, not a robot-like mechanism. So if you understand Tantra, habit is bad; there are no bad habits, there are no good habits – habit is bad. And one should be awake so there are no habits. You simply live moment to moment with full awareness, not by habits.

If you can live without habits that is the royal path.

Why is it royal? – because a soldier has to follow, a king need not. The king is above, he gives orders, he receives no orders from anybody. A king never goes to fight, only soldiers go. A king is not a fighter. A king lives the most relaxed of all lives. This is just a metaphor: a soldier has to follow, a king simply lives loose and natural; there is nobody above him.

Tantra says there is nobody above you whom you have to follow, through whom you have to get your pattern of life, through whom you have to become imitators – there is nobody. You live a loose and natural and flowing life – the only thing is: just be aware.

Through fighting you can cultivate good habits, but they will be habits, not natural. People say a habit is a second nature. Maybe, but remember the word 'second'. It is not natural; it may look almost natural, but it is not.

What will be the difference between real compassion and a compassion cultivated? A real compassion is a response – the situation and the response. A real compassion is always fresh; something has happened and your heart flows towards it. A child has fallen and you run and help the child to stand back up, but this is a response. A false compassion, a cultivated compassion, is a reaction.

These two words are very, very meaningful: 'response' and 'reaction'. Response is alive to the situation; reaction is just an engrained habit. Because in the past you have been training yourself to help somebody if he has fallen, you simply go and help, but there is no heart in it.

When the situation creates the action and you respond with full awareness, only then something of beauty happens to you. If you react because of the ideology, old habit patterns, you will not gain anything out of it. At the most you can gain a little ego, which is not a gain at all. You may start bragging that you have saved a man who was drowning in the river. You may go to the marketplace and shout loudly, "Look, I have saved another human life!" You may gain a little more ego, you have done something good, but it is not a gain. You have lost a great opportunity of being spontaneous, of being spontaneous in compassion. If you had responded to the situation, then something would have flowered in you, a blossoming; you would have felt a certain silence, a stillness, a blessing.

You should live moment to moment, enjoying moment to moment – spontaneity should be the way. And why bother about tomorrow? – this moment is enough. Live it! Live it in totality. Respond, but don't react. 'No habits' should be the formula.

Now we will try to understand the sutra: "To transcend duality is the kingly view." To transcend, not to win – to transcend. This word is very beautiful. What does it mean, to "transcend"?

It is just as if a small child is playing with his toys. You tell him to put them away and he becomes angry. Even when he goes to sleep he goes with his toys, and the mother has to remove them when he has fallen asleep. In the morning the first thing that he demands to know is where his toys are and who has taken them away. Even in the dream he dreams about the toys.

Then suddenly one day he forgets about the toys. For a few days they remain in the corner of his room, and then they are removed or thrown away; never again does he ask for them. What has happened?

He has transcended, he has become mature. It is not a fight and a victory; it is not that he was fighting against the desire to have toys. No, suddenly one day he sees this is childish and he is no more a child; suddenly one day he realizes that toys are toys, they are not real life and he is ready for the real life. His back is turned towards the toys. Never again in dreams will they come; never again will he think about them. And if he sees some other child playing with toys, he will laugh; he will laugh knowingly, a knowing laugh, a wise laugh.

He will say, "He's a child, still childish, playing with toys." He has transcended. Transcendence is a very spontaneous phenomenon. It is not to be cultivated. You simply become more mature. You simply see the whole absurdity of a certain thing and you transcend.

You appear imperfect not because you are imperfect but because you are a growing perfection. This looks absurd, illogical, because we think perfection cannot grow, because we mean by perfection that which has come to its last growth – but that perfection will be dead. If it cannot grow then that perfection will be dead.

God goes on growing. God is not perfect in that way, that he has no growth. He is perfect because he lacks nothing, but he goes from one perfection to another, the growth continues. God is evolution; not from imperfection to perfection but from perfection to more perfection, to still more perfection. When perfection is without any future, it is dead. When perfection has a future to it, still an opening, a growth, still a movement, then it looks like imperfection.

And I would like to tell you: be imperfect and growing, because that is what life is. And don't try to be perfect, otherwise you will stop growing. Then you will be like a Buddha statue, stone, but dead. Because of this phenomenon – that perfection goes on growing – you feel it is imperfect. Let it be as it is. Allow it to be as it is. This is the royal way.

Distractions are there, when you will lose your consciousness again and again. You meditate, you sit for meditation, a thought comes – and immediately you have forgotten yourself; you follow the thought, you have got involved in it. Tantra says only one thing has to be conquered, and that is distractions.

What will you do? Only one thing: when a thought comes, remain a witness.

Look at it, observe it, allow it to pass your being, but don't get attached to it in any way, for or against. It may be a bad thought, a thought to kill somebody – don't push it, don't say, "This is a bad thought." The moment you say something about the thought, you have become attached, you are distracted. Now this thought will lead you to many things, from one thought to another. A good thought comes, a compassionate thought: don't say, "Aha, so beautiful! I am a great saint. Such beautiful thoughts are coming to me that I would like to give salvation to the whole world. I would like to liberate everybody."

Don't say that. Good or bad, you remain a witness.

Still, in the beginning, many times you will be distracted. Then what to do? If you are distracted, be distracted. Don't be worried too much about it, otherwise that worry will become an obsession. Be distracted! For a few minutes you will be distracted, then suddenly you will remember, "I am distracted." Then it is okay, come back. Don't feel depressed. Don't say, "It was bad that I was distracted" – again you are creating a dualism: bad and good. Distracted, okay – accept it, come back. Even with distraction you don't create a conflict.

That's what Krishnamurti goes on saying. He uses a very paradoxical concept for it. He says if you are inattentive, be attentively inattentive. That's okay! Suddenly you find you have been inattentive, give attention to it and come back home. Krishnamurti has not been understood and the reason is that he follows the royal path. If he had been a yogi he would have been understood very easily. That's why he goes on saying there is no method – on the royal path there is no method. He goes on saying that there is no technique – on the royal path there is none. He goes on saying no scripture will help you – on the royal path there is no scripture.

Distracted? The moment you remember, the moment this attention comes to you that "I have been distracted," come back. That's all. Don't create any conflict. Don't say, "This was bad"; don't feel depressed, frustrated that you have been again distracted. Nothing is wrong in distraction – enjoy it also. If you can enjoy the distraction, less and less it will happen to you. And a day comes when there is no distraction – but this is not a victory. You have not pushed the distracting trends of your mind deep into the unconscious. No. You allowed it also. It too is good. This is the mind of Tantra, that everything is good and holy. Even if there is distraction, somehow it is needed. You may not be aware why it is needed; somehow it is needed.

If you can feel good about everything that happens, then only are you following the royal path. If you start fighting with anything whatsoever, you have fallen from the royal path and you have become an ordinary soldier, a warrior. Nothing is to be practiced because practice creates habits. One has to become more aware, not more practiced. The beautiful happens through the spontaneous, not through the practiced.

To a few people it may be absolutely natural to move in the mountains; they have to be in the mountains. The thing to be remembered as a criterion is being loose and natural. If you are natural in the market, beautiful – the market is also divine. If you feel loose and natural in the Himalayas, beautiful – nothing is wrong in it. Remember only one thing: Be loose and natural. Don't strain, and don't try to create a tension within your being.

Remaining loose and natural, soon you will come to the orgasmic peak with the existence, and you will attain that which cannot be attained. Why? Why say it cannot be attained? – because it cannot be made a goal. It cannot be attained by a goal-oriented mind. It cannot be attained by an achieving mind.

Many people here are of the same trend of the achieving mind. They are uptight because they have made a goal of that which cannot be made a goal. It *happens* to you. You can only be passive, loose and natural, and wait for the right time, because everything has its own season. It will happen in its own season. What is the hurry? If you are in a hurry then you will become uptight, then you will be constantly expecting.

You cannot make a target of it: 'I am going to attain it'. You cannot reach it like an arrow, no. The mind which is arrowed towards a goal is a tense mind. Suddenly it comes, when you are ready – not even the footsteps are heard. Suddenly it comes. You do not even become aware that it is coming. It has bloomed. Suddenly you see the blooming – you are filled with the fragrance.

Osho – "Tantra the Supreme Understanding", Discourse 7

THE RELIGIOUS EGO AND THE WORLDLY EGO

Life is simple; there is nothing sacred and nothing secular. My whole effort here is to help you to dissolve the distinction between the sacred and the secular. The secular should become the sacred and the sacred should become the secular. That's why I insist that you should remain part of the market world and meditate. Meditation should not be a thing apart from life; it should be amidst life, it should be a part of life an organic part, nothing separate. The temple should exist exactly in the middle of the market, and all distinctions between the sacred and the secular should be dissolved.

Life is one.

But again the priest comes in. He wants to make distinctions, he wants to tell you that your life is ugly, that your life is mundane, that you are a worldly being. He is spiritual, he is something superior beyond you, beyond your reach. He is holy, you are unholy; he is a saint and you are a sinner. These distinctions have to be created. These are ego distinctions: somebody is rich, somebody is poor; then the ego can exist. Somebody is holy and somebody is not holy; again the ego can exist. The ego can exist only through distinctions of inferiority and superiority: 'This world is inferior.'

A man who lives an ordinary life, loves his wife, children, goes to work, is an ordinary human being condemned by the priests, by the so-called *mahatmas*. They exploit this same ordinary man, they live on him, they are suckers – but they are holy, they are spiritual. Their hands are never muddied because they don't work, they don't move into life. They remain far away: they are 'holy'. And the man who lives is 'unholy'.

If you look deeply you will find that the very word 'sacred' is based on ego distinctions. What is sacred and what is not sacred? If God is everywhere, then everything is sacred. If God is in the rock and in the tree and in the man and in the woman, then everything is sacred. God is everywhere, in everything; God is the only reality – then how can anything be undivine? Even the devil has to be divine. And that is the beauty of the word 'devil': it comes from the same root as 'divine'. The devil has to be divine otherwise he cannot be.

So I want to dissolve all distinctions, because through distinctions ego exists. So I don't say what is sacred and what is ordinary. To me the ordinary is extraordinary, the mundane is sacred, the day-to-day life is holy life – hence I use the word 'esoteric' as a ridiculous word. It hurts many people because there are many people who think that if religion is obvious then where will they find their ego-trip? If everything is unhidden from the very beginning, then their ego has no challenge.

Ego is challenged only by the difficult. This is my observation: that if you find 100 persons interested in religious enquiry, 99 will be there only because God is almost impossible. That gives the thrill, that makes them feel good – that they are going to attain the impossible. Others are only working for the possible and they are working for the impossible. They feel very good; their ego is strengthened.

Here with me, God is the only possibility; nothing else is possible. And God is not impossible. He is just in front of you, he is not hidden. He is holding your hand; he is sitting by your side. He is in your child in your wife, in your husband. He is in your friend, and he is in your foe. He surrounds you from everywhere: you exist in the ocean of God.

Osho - "Tao the Pathless Path", Volume 1, Discourse 14

MELT INTO THE WITNESS

The observer and the observed are two aspects of the witness. When they disappear into each other, when they melt into each other, when they are one, the witness for the first time arises in its totality.

But this question arises in many people; the reason is that they think the witness is the observer. In their minds, the observer and the witness are synonymous. It is fallacious; the observer is not the witness, but only a part of it. And whenever the part thinks of itself as the whole, error arises.

The observer means the subjective, and the observed means the objective. The observer means that which is outside the observed, and the observer also means that which is inside. The inside and the outside can't be separate; they are together, they can only be together. When this togetherness, or rather oneness, is experienced, the witness arises.

You cannot practice the witness. If you practice the witness you will be practicing only the observer, and the observer is not the witness. Then what has to be done? Melting has to be done, merging has to be done. Seeing a rose flower, forget completely that there is an object seen and a subject as a seer. Let the beauty of the moment, the benediction of the moment, overwhelm you both, so the rose and you are no more separate, but you become one rhythm, one song, one ecstasy.

Loving, experiencing music, looking at the sunset, let it happen again and again. The more it happens the better, because it is not an art but a knack. You have to get the knack of it; once you have got it, you can trigger it anywhere, any moment.

It is not a question of what you do, it is a question of how you do it. And ultimately it is a question whether you do it or you allow it to happen. If you allow it to happen, then whenever there is a creative meeting you will suddenly become a witness. The observer and the observed become one in it - in fact it happens only when they become one.

Modern physics has discovered one of the greatest things ever discovered, and that is: matter is energy. That is the greatest contribution of Albert Einstein to humanity: $e = mc^2$, matter is energy. Matter only appears; otherwise, there is no such thing as matter, nothing is solid. Even the solid rock is a pulsating energy, even the solid rock is as much energy as the roaring ocean. The waves that are arising in the solid rock cannot be seen because they are very subtle, but the rock is waving, pulsating, breathing; it is alive.

Your body is energy, your mind is energy, your soul is energy. Then what is the difference between these three? The difference is only of a different rhythm, different wavelengths, that's all. The body is gross - energy functioning in a gross way, in a visible way.

Mind is a little more subtle, but still not too subtle, because you can close your eyes and you can see the thoughts moving; they can be seen. They are not as visible as your body; your body is visible to everybody else, it is publicly visible. Your thoughts are privately visible. Nobody else can see your thoughts; only you can see them - or people who have worked very deeply into seeing thoughts. But ordinarily they are not visible to others.

And the third, the ultimate layer inside you, is that of consciousness. It is not even visible to you. It cannot be reduced into an object, it remains subject.

There is no relationship of consciousness and energy. Consciousness *is* energy, purest energy; mind is not so pure, body is still less pure. Body is much too mixed, and mind is also not totally pure. Consciousness is total pure energy. But you can know this consciousness only if you make a cosmos out of the three, and not a chaos.

Consciousness is the highest form of energy. And when all these three energies function together, the fourth arrives. The fourth is always present when these three function together. When these three function in an organic unity, the fourth is always there; the fourth is nothing but that organic unity. In the East, we have called that fourth simply "the fourth", *turiya*; we have not given it any name. The three have names, the fourth is nameless.

To know the fourth is to know God. Let us say it in this way: God is when you are an organic orgasmic unity. God is not when you are a chaos, a disunity, a conflict. When you are a house divided against yourself there is no God. When you are tremendously happy with yourself, happy as you are, blissful as you are, grateful as you are, and all your energies are dancing together, when you are an orchestra of all your energies, God is. That feeling of total unity is what God is.

God is not a person somewhere. God is the experience of the three falling in such unity that the fourth arises. And the fourth is more than the sum total of the parts.

Drop old ideas of meditations, that just sitting underneath a tree with a yoga posture is meditation. That is only one of the ways, and may be suitable for a few people but is not suitable for all. For a small child it is not meditation, it is torture. For a young man who is alive, vibrant, it is repression, it is not meditation. Maybe for an old man who has lived, whose energies are declining, it may be meditation.

My effort is to make meditation available to each and everybody; whosoever wants to meditate, meditation should be made available according to his type. If he needs rest, then rest should be his meditation. Then 'sitting silently doing nothing, and the spring comes and the grass grows by itself' - that will be his meditation.

We have to find as many dimensions to meditation as there are people in the world. And the pattern has not to be very rigid, because no two individuals are alike. The pattern has to be very liquid so that it can fit with the individual.

In the past, the practice was that the individual had to fit with the pattern. I bring a revolution. The individual has not to fit with the pattern, the pattern has to fit with the individual. My respect for the individual is absolute. I am not much concerned with means; means can be changed, arranged in different ways.

But the basic fundamental is, whatsoever the meditation, it has to fill this requirement: that the body, mind, consciousness, all three should function in unity. Then suddenly one day the fourth has arrived: the witnessing. Or if you want to, call it God; call it God or Nirvana or Tao or whatsoever you will.

Osho – "The Book of Wisdom", Volume 2, Discourse 7

AUTHENTIC RELIGION IS EDUCATION

Zen has no teaching, what to say about special or not special. It has a method of awakening you, but it has no doctrine, no theology. It does not teach you anything, it simply wakes you up and leaves you liberated. It does not program you for anything. Its function is finished the moment you are aware. Your very awareness will become your discipline, your compassion, your love. Your actions will be transformed by your awareness, not by rehearsals, not by repressing the opposite.

What are teachings? What are doctrines? Ways of repressing: to teach you that you are a Christian, and you should love even your enemy. Now in the first place if you are really a man of love, how can you find an enemy? And if you have an enemy, then it is going to be absolutely difficult to love him. It is difficult to love even the friend. And if you want to know the ultimate fact, it is even difficult to love yourself, because you don't know what you are. You don't know what love is. So what will you do? You will simply impose, you will become a hypocrite.

Every Christian, every Mohammedan, every Hindu, every Buddhist is nothing but a hypocrite. He has to cover up all jealousy, hate, cruelty, greed - and cover them up with beautiful disciplines, practiced well. But howsoever you practice them, what you are doing is simply repressing. So what you have repressed remains in you, and will come out at any moment.

All discipline is limited. You cannot condition a man absolutely. You can cover him up with a thin layer, but just scratch the layer and immediately all discipline is forgotten. All Christianity is forgotten, all Buddhism is forgotten; immediately your animal comes out. Hence, masters like Joshu have improved immensely on Gautam Buddha. Although they are disciples of Gautam Buddha, he has shown the way...but the way is always capable of being refined, more refined.

Joshu has made a great contribution. He has no teaching, no 'special teaching.' He simply wakes you up and then it is up to you how to live.

If your wakefulness does not prevent you from being greedy and ambitious, hateful, jealous, revengeful, then nothing can transform you. The ultimate principle of transformation has been given to you. You are awake, alert, responsible - now you are free. You can do whatever comes spontaneously to you. There is no abiding teaching, no abiding theology. You are your own decision, your own discipline. That is the beauty of Zen that no other religion has.

Zen is the only way of life which has nothing to teach you. It does exactly what the English word 'education' means in its original roots. To educate means to bring out what is inside you. It is almost like drawing water from a well.

All our educational systems are doing just the opposite. They should not be called educational institutions. But such is the blindness, and such is the unintelligence, the retardedness, of the people who decide the fate of millions - the politicians, the priests. They can't see a simple thing, that your educational institutions are feeding things from outside into your mind. They are programming your mind, they are not doing education. They are not drawing your life to the circumference; they are not drawing your innermost awareness into your life.

I have been fighting with the Indian government for my whole life but they cannot understand the simple fact that this is an educational institution and what you call educational institutions are not; they are programming schools. But it is almost one man against the whole world. They go on denying that this place is a place of education. They don't understand the meaning of the word at all.

Zen is not a teaching but it is an education. It draws out whatever you have in your innermost core - the joy, the bliss, all the flowers that are possible; compassion and love, all the songs that are hidden in you, all the dances, all creativity.

You are part of a creative universe; you must have some part to play in the whole creativity that is going on everywhere. But your so-called educational systems, rather than bringing anything out from you, do just the opposite: they force things upon you. Your religions do the same, your society, culture, everybody is doing the same. Nobody is careful of the delicate seed. They go on throwing all kinds of rubbish and the seed is covered, is never given the right soil, is never given the right climate. Its season never comes. It never becomes a sprout, green and living and radiant. It never becomes foliage; it never brings roses, which you all are carrying.

I am calling those roses hidden in you "the buddha." Everybody is carrying a buddha within him, just it has to be carried out. Devices have to be made so that you can carry your center out to the circumference. This is the only education in the world. Everything else is a teaching, not education; and teaching is always in the favor of the vested interests.

Teaching can never be revolutionary. The teacher is the servant of the vested interests. Only a sannyasin can be a revolutionary because he has no vested interest, no obligation to any investment. He has liberated himself from all connections, all dominating forces. He stands alone. He is capable of giving a lion's roar, which may trigger the same roar in you also. Only very few sannyasins in the world have been authentic rebels. Joshu is a great rebel, a whole rebellion.

In awareness, there is no teaching, no special teaching; one just goes on acting spontaneously. Whatever situation arises, one is a mirror, and goes on reflecting whoever comes before the mirror. Awareness is just a mirror, and your response is not a repetition from an old teaching. Your response is fresh, of this moment. Even you were not aware that you would respond in this way, because you are not repeating a memorized answer; you are simply responding with full awareness. Seeing the situation, whatever is needed in this moment comes out of you from the very center - not from the memory but from your very being.

A man of awareness acts in the moment according to his own awareness, not according to some principle. But all the religions are full of principles, and those principles have destroyed humanity, its awareness, its responsibility.

I have told you…. When God made the world he went around asking different people - the Babylonians, the Egyptians - "Do you want a commandment?"

The Babylonians said, "First we would like to know what the commandment is. Without knowing, we don't want one." He said, "You should not commit adultery."

The Babylonians said, "Then what shall we do? Keep your commandment."

He said to the Egyptians, "You should not steal." And they said, "Life will not be so juicy. We are not interested in such commandments; stealing is a game."

Then he met Moses, and you can see immediately the response of Moses: He did not ask, "What is the commandment?" He immediately asked, "How much?" God said, "It is absolutely free." Moses did not even ask what the commandments were. He simply said, "Then I will have ten, if they are free."

Now, those ten commandments are not just in the Jewish tradition. Similar commandments are in every tradition: you should do this, you should not do this. Times change, life goes on changing, but those commandments remain heavy on the heart.

For example, Mohammed gave the commandment to the Mohammedans: "You should not take interest on money." Now, all business depends on interest. If Mohammedans are poor - and they are poor everywhere around the world - the simple reason is that they are still following a strange idea that you should not give or take interest on money. Now, no bank can give you money without interest. Even the richest people go on borrowing money from banks because they can use it to earn much more than the interest. But the Mohammedans are carrying a heavy principle on their hearts, that it will be a betrayal to the religion if you take or give interest. So obviously they are poor. In India the poorest jobs are being done by the Mohammedans. It is just an example.

Zen emphasizes the fact that man's consciousness in its ultimate form is enough to decide how to respond in any particular situation. So the only important thing is to become as conscious as possible.

Osho – "Joshu, The Lion's Roar", Discourse 8

THE EVOLUTION OF ZEN

What is Zen? Zen is a very extraordinary growth. Rarely does such a possibility become an actuality because many hazards are involved. Many times before the possibility has existed - a certain spiritual happening could have grown and become like Zen, but it was never realized to its totality. Only once in the whole history of human consciousness has a thing like Zen come into being. It is very rare.

Zen was born in India, grew in China, and blossomed in Japan. The whole situation is rare. Why did it happen that it was born in India, but could not grow here and had to seek a different soil? It became a great tree in China, but could not blossom there; it had to again seek a new climate, a different climate - and in Japan it blossomed like a cherry tree, in thousands of flowers. It is not coincidental, it is not accidental; it has deep inner history. I would like to reveal it to you.

India is an introvert country, Japan is extrovert, and China is just in the middle of these two extremes. India and Japan are absolute opposites. So how come the seed was born in India and blossomed in Japan? They are opposites; they have no similarities; they are contradictory. And why did China come just in the middle, to give soil to it?

A seed is introversion. Try to understand the phenomenon of the seed, what a seed is. A seed is in-going; a seed has really turned upon itself. A seed is an introvert phenomenon, it is centripetal - the energy is moving inwards. That's why it is a seed, covered and closed from the outer world completely. In fact a seed is the loneliest, most isolated thing in the world. It has no roots in the soil, no branches in the sky; it has no connection with the earth, no connection with the sky. In fact it has no relationships around it. A seed is an absolute island, isolated, caved in. It does not relate. It has a hard shell around it, there are no windows, no doors; it cannot go out and nothing can come in.

Seed is natural to India. The genius of Indian can produce seeds of tremendous potentiality, but cannot give them soil. India is an introverted consciousness. India says the outer doesn't exist and even if it exists it is of the same stuff that dreams are made of. The whole genius of India has been trying to discover how to escape from the outer, how to move to the inner cave of the heart, how to be centered in oneself, and how to come to realize that the whole world that exists outside consciousness is just a dream - at the most beautiful, at the worst a nightmare. Whether beautiful or ugly, in reality, it is a dream, and one should not bother much about it. One should awake, and forget the whole dream of the outer world.

The whole effort of Buddha, Mahavir, Tilopa, Gorakh, Kabir, their whole effort through the centuries, has been how to escape from the wheel of life and death: how to enclose yourself, how to completely cut yourself from all relationships, how to be unrelated, detached, how to move in and to forget the outer. That's why Zen was born in India.

Zen means *dhyan*. Zen is a Japanese change of the word *dhyan*. *Dhyan* is the whole effort of Indian consciousness. *Dhyan* means to be so alone, so into your own being that not even a single thought exists. In fact, in English, there is no direct translation. Contemplation is not the word. Contemplation means thinking, reflection. Even meditation is not the word because meditation involves an object to meditate upon; it means something is there. You can meditate on Christ, or you can meditate on the cross. But *dhyan* means to be so alone that there is nothing to meditate upon. No object, just simple subjectivity exists without clouds, a pure sky.

When the word reached China it became *ch'an*. When *ch'an* reached Japan, it became Zen. It comes from the same Sanskrit root, *dhyan*. India can give birth to *dhyan*. For millennia the whole Indian consciousness has been traveling on the path of *dhyan* - how to drop all thinking and how to be rooted in pure consciousness.

With Buddha the seed came into existence. Many times before also, before Gautam Buddha, the seed came into existence, but it couldn't find the right soil so it disappeared. And if the seed is given to the Indian consciousness it will disappear, because the Indian consciousness will move more and more inwards, and the seed will become smaller and smaller and smaller, until a moment comes when it becomes invisible. A centripetal force makes things smaller, smaller, smaller - atomic - until suddenly they disappear.

Many times before Gautam Buddha the seed was born - to become a *dhyani*, to become a great meditator. In fact he is one of the last of a long series. He himself remembers 24 Buddhas before him. Then there were 24 Jaina *Teerthankaras* and they all were meditators. They did nothing else, they simply meditated, meditated, meditated, and came to a point where only they were, and everything else disappeared, evaporated. The seed was born with Parasnath, with Mahavir, Neminath, and others, but then it remained with the Indian consciousness.

The Indian consciousness can give birth to a seed, but cannot become the right soil for it. It goes on working in the same direction and the seed becomes smaller and smaller, molecular, atomic and disappears. That's how it happened with the Upanishads; that's how it happened with the Vedas; that's how it happened with Mahavir and all others.

With Buddha it was also going to happen. Bodhidharma saved him. If the seed had been left with the Indian consciousness, it would have dissolved. It would never have sprouted, because a different type of soil is needed for sprouting - a very balanced soil. Introversion is a very deep imbalance, it is an extreme.

Bodhidharma escaped with the seed to China. He did one of the greatest things in the history of consciousness: he found the right soil for the seed that Buddha had given to the world. Buddha himself is reported to have said, "My religion will not exist for more than 500 years; then it will disappear." He was aware that it always happened that way. The Indian consciousness goes on grinding it into smaller and smaller and smaller pieces; then a moment comes when it becomes so small that it becomes invisible. It is simply no longer part of this world; it disappears into the sky.

Bodhidharma's experiment was great. He looked all around the world and observed deeply for a place where this seed could grow. China is a very balanced country, not like India, not like Japan. The golden mean is the path there. Confucian ideology is to remain always in the middle: neither be introvert, nor be extrovert; neither think too much of this world, nor too much of that world - just remain in the middle. China has not given birth to a religion, just morality. No religion has been born there.

The Chinese consciousness cannot give birth to a religion. It cannot create a seed. All the religions that exist in China have been imported, they have all come from the outside; Buddhism, Hinduism,

Mohammedanism, Christianity - they have all come from the outside. China is a good soil but it cannot originate any religion, because to originate a religion one has to move into the inner world.

To give birth to a religion one has to be like a feminine body, a womb. The feminine consciousness is extremely introvert. A woman lives in herself; she has a very small world around her, the most minimum possible. That is why you cannot interest a woman in things of great vastness. No. You cannot talk about Vietnam to her, she doesn't bother. Vietnam is too far away, too outer. She is concerned with her family, her husband, the child, the dog, the furniture, the radio set, the TV. A very small world is around her, just the minimum. Because she doesn't have a very big world around it is very difficult for man and woman to talk intelligently - they live in different worlds.

Women live in a different world. A woman is centripetal, introvert. All women are Indian - wherever they are it makes no difference. Man is centrifugal, he goes out. The moment he can find an excuse he will escape from the home. He comes to the home only when he cannot go anywhere else; when all the clubs and hotels are closed, then, what to do? He comes back home. Nowhere to go, he comes home.

A woman is always home-centered, home-based. She goes out only when it is absolutely necessary, when she cannot do otherwise. When it has become an absolute necessity she goes out. Otherwise she is home based.

Man is a vagabond, a wanderer. The whole of family life is created by women, not by men. In fact, civilization exists because of woman, not because of man. If he is allowed he will be a wanderer, no home, no civilization. Man is outgoing, woman is ingoing; man is extrovert, woman is introvert. Man is always interested in something other than himself, that's why he looks healthier. Because when you are too concerned with yourself, you become ill. Man is more happy looking.

You will always find women sad and too concerned with themselves. A little headache and they are very concerned, because they live inside - the headache becomes something big, out of proportion. But a man can forget the headache; he has too many other headaches. He creates so many headaches around himself that there is no possibility of coming upon his own headache and making something out of it. It is always so little he can forget about it. A woman is always concerned - something is happening in the leg, something in the hand, something in the back, something in the stomach, always something because her own consciousness is focused inwards.

A man is less pathological, more healthy, more outgoing, more concerned about what is happening to others. That's why, in all religions, you will find that if there are five persons present, four will be women, and one a man. And that one man may have only come because of some woman - the wife was going to the temple so he had to go with her. Or, she was going to listen to a talk on religion, so he came with her. In all churches this will be the proportion, in all churches, temples, wherever you go. Even with Buddha this was the proportion, with Mahavir this was the proportion. With Buddha there were 50,000 sannyasins – 40,000 women and 10,000 men. Why?

Physically man can be healthier; spiritually woman can be healthier, because their concerns are different. When you are concerned with others you can forget your body, you can be more physically healthy, but religiously you cannot grow so easily. Religious growth needs an inner concern. A woman can grow very, very easily into religion, that path is easy for her, but to grow in politics is difficult. And for a man to grow in religion is difficult. Introversion has its benefits, extroversion has its benefits - and both have their dangers.

India is introvert, a feminine country; it is like a womb, very receptive. But if a child remains in the womb forever and forever and forever, the womb will become the grave. The child has to move out from the mother's womb otherwise the mother will kill the child inside. He has to escape, to find the world outside, a greater world. The womb may be very comfortable - it is! The womb is just a heaven. But even the child has to leave that heaven and come outside the mother. Beyond a certain time the mother can become very dangerous. The womb can kill, because it will then become an imprisonment - good for a time, when the seed is growing, but then the seed has to be transplanted to the outside world.

Bodhidharma looked around, watched the whole world, and found that China had the best soil; it was just a middle ground, not extreme. The climate was not extreme, so the tree could grow easily. And it had very balanced people. Balance is the right soil for something to grow: too cold is bad, too hot is bad. In a balanced climate, neither too cold nor too hot, the tree can grow.

Bodhidharma escaped with the seed, escaped with all that India had produced. Nobody was aware of what he was doing, but it was a great experiment. And he proved right. In China, the tree grew, grew to vast proportions. But although the tree became vaster and vaster, no flowers grew. Flowers did not come, because flowers need an extrovert country. Just as a seed is introvert, so a flower is extrovert.

The seed is moving inwards; the flower is moving outwards. The flower opens to the outer world and releases its fragrance to this outside world. Then the fragrance moves on the wings of the wind to the farthest possible corner of the world. To all directions, the flower releases the energy contained in the seed. It is a door. Flowers would like to become butterflies and escape from the tree. In fact, that is what they are doing, in a very subtle way. They are releasing the essence of the tree, the very meaning, the significance of the tree to the world. They are great sharers. A seed is a great miser, confined to itself, and a flower is a great spendthrift.

Japan was needed. Japan is an extrovert country. The very style of life and consciousness is extrovert.

In India nobody bothers about the outside world very much: about clothes, houses, the way one lives. Nobody bothers. That is why India has remained so poor. If you are not worried about the outside world, how can you become rich? If there is no concern to improve the outside world you will remain poor. And India is always very serious, always getting ready to escape from life, with Buddha's talking about how to become perfect drop-outs from existence itself - not only from society, ultimate drop-outs from existence itself. The existence is too boring. For the Indian eye life is just a grey color - nothing interesting in it, everything just boring, a burden. One has to carry it somehow, because of past *karmas*. Even if an Indian falls in love he says it is because of past *karmas*, one has to pass through it. Even love is like a burden one has to drag.

Japan is totally different. With the Japanese consciousness it is as if the inner doesn't exist, only the outer is meaningful. Look at Japanese dresses. All the colors of flowers and rainbows - as if the outer is very meaningful. Look at an Indian when he is eating, and look at the Japanese. Look at an Indian when he takes his tea - and the Japanese. Japanese create a celebration out of simple things. Taking tea, he makes it a celebration. It becomes an art. The outside is very important; clothes are very important, relationships are very important. Japan is very concerned with the outer. Japan was the right country. And the whole tree of Zen was transplanted in Japan, and there it blossomed, in thousands of colors. It flowered.

This is how it has to happen again. I am again talking about Zen. It has to come back to India because the tree has flowered, and the flowers have fallen and Japan cannot create the seed.

Japan cannot create the seed: it is not an introvert country. So everything has become an outer ritual now. Zen is dead in Japan. It did flower in the past, but now, if by reading in books you go to Japan in search of Zen, you will come back empty-handed. Now Zen is here; in Japan it has disappeared. The country could help it to flower, but now the flowers have disappeared, fallen to the earth, and nothing is there any more.

Hence I am talking so much about Zen here – because, again, only India can create the seed. The whole world exists in a deep unity, in a harmony. In India the seed can again be given birth. But now many things have changed around the world. China is no longer a possibility, because it has itself become an extrovert country. It has become communistic: matter is more important than the spirit. And now it is closed for new waves of consciousness.

To me, if any country can in the future become again the soil, it is England. You will be surprised, because you may think it is America. No. Now the most balanced country in the world is England, just as in the ancient days it was China. The seed has to be taken to England and planted there; it will not flower there, but it will become a big tree. English consciousness - conservative, always following the middle way, the liberal mind, never moving to the extremes, just remaining in the middle - will be helpful.

And from England it can go to America, and it will have flowering there, because America is the most extrovert country right now.

A man of awareness simply slips from one moment to another, just like a dewdrop slipping from the blade of grass, not carrying anything. A man of awareness has no cargo, he moves unburdened. Then everything is new, and then no problems are created.

Live life in its totality, and don't be afraid of the total life. Don't be a coward, and don't try to escape to the mountains and the monasteries. I have given you *sannyas* to live in the world as totally as possible. Just by living totally in the world you will transcend it. Suddenly you will come to know that you are in the world, but not of it. I bring you a totally new concept of *sannyas*.

The old *sannyas* said: Escape, renounce! But I tell you that those who escape are not total, not whole. I tell you that those who escape are crippled. It is not for you. You live life in its totality; you live it, as wholly as possible. And the more whole you are, the more holy you will become.

The quality of sacredness comes when one lives courageously without fear, without hope, without desire. One simply slips from one moment to another, completely fresh and new. This is what *sannyas* is to mean to you. *Sannyas* is living life in its totality, moment to moment; allowing it to happen without any conditions on your part. And then, if you allow this much, life allows you a transcendence. Remaining in the valley, you become the peak, and only then it is beautiful. If you go to the peak, the valley is lost - and the valley has its own beauties. If you remain in the valley, the peak is lost - and the peak has its own beauties.

And I would like you to become a man of valley and peak, both together. Remaining in the valley, be a peak - and then you will be able to understand what Zen is.

Osho – "The Grass Grows by Itself", Discourse 1

INTELLIGENCE AND INTELLECT

Intellect is something pseudo, something false. It is a substitute for intelligence. Intelligence is a totally different phenomena, the real thing. Intelligence needs tremendous courage. Intelligence needs an adventurous life. Intelligence needs you to always go into the unknown, into the uncharted sea. Then intelligence grows, it becomes sharpened. It grows only when it encounters the unknown every moment.

People are afraid of the unknown. People feel insecure with the unknown. They don't want to go beyond the familiar, hence they have created a false plastic substitute for intelligence. They call it intellect. Intellect is only a mental game. It cannot be creative.

Intellect is imaginative but not creative. Intelligence is creative. Intelligence creates because intelligence makes you capable of participating with God. God is the source of all creativity. You can be creative only when you are in rapport with God, when you are rooted in the very Existence, when you are part of Divine Energy.

You cannot be creative on your own. You can be creative only as a medium of God. When the poet creates, he is only a medium, a hollow bamboo on the lips of God. And suddenly, the hollow bamboo is no more a hollow bamboo. It becomes a flute. The emptiness of the bamboo becomes full of song, dance, celebration. Creativity means you have to disappear, you have to allow God to be, you have to get out of the way. Creativity means bringing the new into existence, making a way for the unknown to penetrate the known, making a way for the sky to come to the earth.

Osho – "The Dhammapada", Volume 4, Discourse 2

MATURITY AND AGING

There is a great difference between maturity and aging, a vast difference, and people always remain confused about it. People think to age is to become mature, but aging belongs to the body. Everybody is aging, everybody will become old, but not necessarily mature.

Maturity is an inner growth.

Aging is nothing that you do, aging is something that happens physically. Every child born, when time passes, becomes old. Maturity is something that you bring to your life. It comes out of awareness. When a person ages with full awareness he becomes mature. Aging plus awareness, experiencing plus awareness, is maturity.

You can experience a thing in two ways: You can simply experience it as if you are hypnotized, unaware, not attentive to what is happening; the thing happened but you were not there. It didn't happen in your presence, you were absent. You just passed by. It never struck any note in you. It never left any mark on you. You never learned anything from it. It may even have become a part of your memory because in a way you were present, but it never became your wisdom. You never grew through it. Then you are aging. But if you bring the quality of awareness to an experience the same experience becomes maturity.

There are two ways to live: one, to live in a deep sleep. Then you age, every moment you become old, every moment you go on dying, that's all; your whole life consists of a long slow death. But if you bring awareness to your experiences – whatsoever you do, whatsoever happens to you, you are alert, watchful, mindful, you are savoring the experience from all the corners, you are trying to understand the meaning of it, you are trying to penetrate the very depth of it, what has happened to you, you are trying to live it intensely and totally – then, it is not just a surface phenomenon. Deep down within you something is changing with it. You are becoming more alert.

If this is a mistake, this experience – you will never commit it again. A mature person never commits the same mistake again. But an old person goes on committing the same mistakes again and again. He lives in a circle. He never learns anything. You will be angry today, you were angry yesterday, and the day before yesterday, and tomorrow also you are going to be angry, and the day after tomorrow also. Again and again you get angry, again and again you repent, again and again you take a deep decision that you are not going to do it again, but that decision makes no change. Whenever you are disturbed the rage takes over, you are possessed. The same mistake is committed. You are aging.

If you live an experience of anger totally, never again will you be angry. One experience will be enough to teach that it is foolish, that it is absurd, that it is simply stupid – not that it is a sin, it is simply stupid. You are harming yourself, and harming others, for nothing. The thing is not worth it. Then you are getting mature. Tomorrow the situation will be repeated, but anger will not be repeated.

And a man who is gaining in maturity never decided that he will not be angry again; no, that is the sign of a man who is not getting mature. A man of maturity never decides for the future. The maturity itself takes care. You live today. That very living will decide how the tomorrow is going to be – it will come out of it.

If the anger was painful, poisonous, you suffered hell through it, what is the point of deciding, or taking a vow and going to the temple and saying before the Master, "Now I take a vow that I will never be angry again"? All this is childish. There is no point!

If you have known that anger is poisonous – finished! That way is closed. That door no more exists for you. The situation will be repeated tomorrow but you will not be possessed by the situation. You have learnt something – that understanding will be there. You may even laugh, you may even enjoy the whole thing of how people get so foolish. Your understanding is growing through every experience.

You can live life as if you are in a hypnosis – that's how 99% of people live – or you can live with intensity, awareness. If you live with awareness you mature, otherwise you simply become old. And to become old is not to become wise. If you have been a fool when you were young and now you have become old, you will be just an old fool, that's all, nothing. Just becoming old, you cannot become wise. You may be even more foolish, because you may have attained to mechanical habits, robot-like.

Life can be lived in two ways. If you live unconsciously you simply die; if you live consciously you attain to more and more life. Death will come, but it never comes to a mature man, it comes only to a man who has been aging and getting old. A mature one never dies, because he will learn even through death. Even death is going to be an experience to be intensely lived, and watched, allowed.

A mature man never dies. In fact before a mature man, on the rock of maturity, death struggles and shatters itself, commits suicide. Death dies, but never a mature man – that is the message of all the awakened ones: that you are deathless. They have known it, they have lived their death. They have watched, and they have found that it can surround you but you remain aloof, you remain far away. Death happens near you but it never happens to you.

Deathless is your being, blissful is your being, divine is your being, but those experiences you cannot cram in the mind and in the memory. You have to pass through life and attain them. Much suffering is there, much pain is there. And because of pain and suffering people like to live stupidly.

It has to be understood why so many people insist that they should live in a hypnosis; why Buddhas and Christs go on telling people to be awake, and nobody listens. There must be some deep involvement in hypnosis, there must be some deep investment. What is the investment? Why don't you attain to awareness? If it leads to the infinite bliss, then why not be aware? Why do you insist on being sleepy?

There is some investment – and this is the investment: if you become aware, there is suffering. If you become aware, you become aware of pain, and the pain is so much that you would like to take a tranquilizer and be asleep.

This sleepiness in life works as a protection against pain. But this is the trouble: if you are asleep against pain, you are asleep against pleasure also.

Think of it as if there are two faucets: on one is written "pain" and on another is written "pleasure". You would like to close the faucet on which pain is written, and you would like to open the faucet on which pleasure is written.

But this is the game: if you close the faucet "pain", the "pleasure" immediately closes, because behind both there is only one faucet on which "awareness" is written. Either both remain open or both remain closed, because both are two faces of the same phenomenon, two aspects.

And this is the whole contradiction of mind: mind wants to be more and more happy; happiness is possible if you are aware. And then mind wants to be less and less in pain, but less and less pain is possible only if you are unaware.

Now you are in a dilemma. If you want no pain – immediately pleasure disappears from your life, happiness disappears. If you want happiness, you open the faucet – immediately there is pain also flowing.

If you have to be aware, you have to be aware of both. Life is pain, pleasure. Life is happiness, unhappiness. Life is day and night. Life is life and death. You have to be aware of both.

So remember it. If you are afraid of pain you will remain in hypnosis, you will age, become old and die. You missed an opportunity. If you want to be aware, then you have to be aware of both pain and pleasure. They are not separate phenomena. And a man who becomes aware becomes very happy, but also becomes capable of deep unhappiness, of which you are not capable.

You cannot be so sensitive to pain, you are so fast asleep. You move like a drunkard – the drunkard falls on the street, hits his leg, his head in the gutter – nothing happens. If he was aware there would have been pain.

A Buddha suffers infinitely, Buddha enjoys infinitely. Always remember, whenever you reach to a high peak, simultaneously near the high peak a deep valley is being created. If you want to reach to the heavens, your roots will have to go to the very hell.

Because you are afraid of pain you cannot become aware – and then you cannot learn anything. It is just like – you are afraid so much of enemies that you have closed the doors of your house. Now even the friend cannot enter, even the lover is left out. The lover goes on knocking on the door but you are afraid: maybe it is the enemy. So you are closed – that's how I see you all: closed, afraid of the enemy, and the friend cannot enter. So the friend you have turned into an enemy. Now nobody can enter, you are so afraid.

Open the door. When the fresh air enters the house there is every possibility of dangers also entering. When the friend comes, the enemy comes also, because day and night enter together, pain and pleasure enter together, life and death enter together.

So don't be afraid of pain otherwise you will live in anesthesia. Afraid of pain, you take anesthetics. The surgeon gives an anesthetic before he operates on you, because there is going to be much pain, you will not be able to tolerate it. Your consciousness has to be dimmed, darkened. Then he can cut your whole body and you will not suffer.

Because of the fear of pain you have forced yourself to live in a dim consciousness, in a very dimmed existence almost not alive. This is the fear – you have to drop that fear, you have to face pain, you have to move through suffering, only then the possibility opens for the friend to enter.

And when you know both you immediately become the third. When you know both, pain and pleasure, the duality, the day and night, suddenly you have become transcendental. Maturity is awareness. Aging is just wasting yourself.

Osho – "Tao the Three Treasures", Volume 4, Discourse 6

MEDIOCRACY AND THE NATURAL PERSON

Mediocrity is the general state of humanity as it is. It is a retarded intelligence. Nobody wants you to be intelligent, because the more intelligent you are, the more it is difficult to exploit you, to enslave you.

Every vested interest wants you to be mediocre. A mediocre person is just like a tree whose roots have been continuously cut so it cannot grow. The mediocre person never comes to know fruition, flowering, fragrance. He lives just like a vegetable. But this is the common state. And to keep the mediocre, mediocre, a strange thing has to be put in his mind: that he is extraordinary.

George Gurdjieff used to tell a story.... There was a shepherd who was a magician, and he had many sheep. To take care of them and not to let them wander into the forest and be eaten by wild animals, he managed a strategy. He hypnotized all the sheep and told them, "You are not sheep, you are lions." Since that day, the sheep started behaving like lions.

The mediocre person will rebel against mediocrity because it is ugly to be mediocre. But the society in many ways gives him the feeling of being extraordinary. Hence, it is very difficult to find a man who does not, deep down, believe that he is special – the only begotten son of God.

He may not say so, because he knows what happens if you say that you are the only begotten son of God. Then crucifixion is certain. And resurrection, nobody knows whether it happened or not. So he keeps it inside. This helps him to remain mediocre.

If he understands he is mediocre, that very understanding will destroy his mediocrity. To understand you are mediocre is a great jump into intelligence.

The ordinary person I talk about is the natural person. Nature does not produce special people. It produces unique people, but not special. Everybody is unique in his own way.

The big pine tree and the small rosebush – who is higher? Neither the pine tree ever boasts that she is higher, nor the rosebush ever boasts that "You may be higher, but where are the roses? The real height is in the roses and the fragrance, in the flowering. Height itself is not enough to be higher." But the rosebush and the pine remain together without any quarrel, competition, for the simple reason that both understand they are part of the same nature.

When I say ordinariness, I am saying drop the idea of being extraordinary, which is keeping you mediocre. To be ordinary is the most extraordinary thing in the world. Just watch yourself. It hurts very much, it is painful to accept that you are not extraordinary.

Watch when you accept the idea that you are ordinary: a great burden is relieved. Suddenly you are in the open space, natural, just the way you are. The ordinary person has a uniqueness and a simplicity, humbleness. Out of his simplicity, humbleness, uniqueness, he has really become extraordinary, but he has no idea of it.

So it is a paradox: the people who think they are extraordinary are simply retarded, mediocre. And the people who are humble and just accept that they are ordinary people like everybody else – you will see a light in their eyes. You will see a grace in their actions.

Osho – "From Bondage to Freedom", Discourse 3

SELF-ACTUALIZATION IS A BASIC NEED

First, try to understand what is meant by self-actualization. A. H. Maslow has used this term self-actualization. Man is born as potentiality. He is not really actual – just potential. Man is born as a possibility, not as an actuality. He may become something; he may attain actualization of his potentiality or he may not attain. The opportunity may be used or it may not be used. And nature is not forcing you to become actual. You are free.

Self-actualization means a person has become what he was to become. He was born as a seed and now he has flowered. He has come to the complete growth, an inner growth, to the inner end. The moment you feel that all your potentialities have become actual, you will feel the peak of life, of love, of existence itself.

Abraham Maslow, who has used this term "self-actualization," has also coined another term: "peak experience". When one attains to oneself, he reaches a peak – a peak of bliss. Then there is no hankering after anything. He is totally content with himself. Now nothing is lacking; there is no desire, no demand, no movement. Whatsoever he is, he is totally content with himself. Self-actualization becomes a peak experience, and only a self-actualized person can attain peak experiences. Then whatsoever he touches, whatsoever he is doing or not doing – even just existing – is a peak experience for him; just to be is blissful. Then bliss is not concerned with anything outside, it is just a by-product of the inner growth.

A buddha is a self-actualized person. That is why we picture Buddha, Mahavir and others – why we have made sculptures, pictures, depict-ions of them – sitting on a fully blossomed lotus. That fully blossomed lotus is the peak of flowering inside. Inside they have flowered and have become fully blossomed. That inner flowering gives a radiance, a constant showering of bliss from them. All those who come even within their shadows, all those who come near them feel a silent milieu around them.

Self-actualization is the basic need. And when I say basic, I mean that if all your needs are fulfilled, all except self-realization, self-actualization, you will feel unfulfilled. In fact, if self-actualization happens and nothing else is fulfilled, still you will feel a deep, total fulfillment. That is why Buddha was a beggar, but yet an emperor.

Really, a self-actualized person will become desireless, remember this. Ordinarily we say that if you become desireless, you will know yourself. The contrary is more true: if you know yourself, you will become desireless. And the emphasis of Tantra is not on being desireless, but on becoming self-actualized. Then desirelessness follows.

What to do about self-actualization? Two things have to be understood. One: self-actualization doesn't mean that if you become a great painter or a great musician or a great poet you will be self-actualized. Of course, a part of you will be actualized, and even that gives much contentment. If you have a potentiality of being a good musician, and if you fulfill it and you become a musician, a part of you will be fulfilled – but not the total. The remaining humanity within you will remain unfulfilled. You will be lopsided. One part will have grown, and the remaining will have stayed just like a stone hanging around your neck.

Look at a poet. When he is in his poetic mood he looks like a buddha; he forgets himself completely. The ordinary man in the poetic mood is as if he is no more there. So when a poet is in his mood, he has a peak – a partial peak. And sometimes poets have glimpses which are only possible with enlightened, buddha-like minds. A poet can speak like a buddha.

For example, Khalil Gibran speaks like a buddha but he is not a buddha. He is a poet, a great poet. So if you see Khalil Gibran through his poetry, he looks like Buddha, Christ or Krishna. But if you go and meet the man Khalil Gibran, he is just ordinary. He talks about love so beautifully – even a buddha may not talk so beautifully. But a buddha knows love with his total being. Khalil Gibran knows love in his poetic flight. When he is on his poetic flight, he has glimpses of love – beautiful glimpses. He expresses them with rare insight. But if you go and see the real Khalil Gibran, the man, you will feel a disparity. The poet and the man are far apart. The poet seems to be something which happens to this man sometimes, but this man is not the poet.

That is why poets feel that when they are creating poetry someone else is creating; they are not creating. They feel as if they have become instruments of some other energy, some other force. They are no more. This feeling comes because, really, their totality is not actualized – only a part of it is, a fragment. You have not touched the sky. Only one of your fingers has touched the sky, and you remain rooted on the earth. Sometimes you jump, and for a moment you are not on the earth; you have deceived gravity. But the next moment you are on the earth again.

Because of this, poets, musicians, great artists, creative people are more tense – because they have two types of being. Ordinary man is not so tense because he always lives in one: he lives on the earth. But poets, musicians, great artists jump; they go beyond gravity. In certain moments they are not on this earth, they are not part of humanity. They become part of the buddha world – the land of the buddhas. Then again they are back here. They have two points of existence; their personalities are split.

So every creative artist, every great artist is in a certain way insane. The tension is so much! The rift, the gap between these two types of existences is so great – unbridgeable. Sometimes he is just an ordinary man; sometimes he becomes buddha-like. Between these two points he is divided, but he has glimpses.

When I say self-actualization, I do not mean that you should become a great poet or you should become a great musician. I mean that you should become a total man. I do not say a great man because a great man is always partial. Greatness in anything is always partial. One moves and moves and moves in one direction, and in all other dimensions, all other directions, one remains the same – one becomes lopsided.

When I say become a total man, I do not mean become a great man. I mean create a balance, be centered, be fulfilled as a man – not as a musician, not as a poet, not as an artist, but fulfilled as a man. What does it mean to be fulfilled as a man?

A great poet is a great poet because of great poetry. A great musician is great because of great music. A great man is a great man because of certain things he has done – he may be a great hero. A great man in any direction is partial. Greatness is partial, fragmentary. That is why great men have to face more anguish than ordinary men.

What is a total man? What is meant by being a whole man, a total man? It means, firstly, be centered: do not exist without a center. This moment you are something, the next moment something else. People come to me and I generally ask them, "Where do you feel your center – in the heart, in the mind, in the navel, where? In the sex center? Where? Where do you feel your center?"

Generally they say, "Sometimes I feel it in the head, sometimes in the heart, sometimes I do not feel it at all." So I tell them to close their eyes before me and feel it just now. In the majority of cases this happens: they say, "Just now, for a moment, I feel that I am centered in the head." But the next moment they are not there. They say, "I am in the heart." And the next moment the center has slipped, it is somewhere else, at the sex center or somewhere else.

A total man is centered. Whatsoever he is doing, he remains in the center. If his mind is functioning, he is thinking, thinking goes on in the head but he remains centered in the navel. The center is never missed. He uses the head, but he never moves to the head. He uses the heart, but he never moves to the heart. All these things become instruments, and he remains centered.

Secondly, he is balanced. Of course, when one is centered one is balanced. His life is a deep balance. He is never one-sided, he is never at any extreme – he remains in the middle. Buddha has called this the middle path. He remains always in the middle. A man who is not centered will always move to the extreme. When he eats he will eat much, he will overeat, or he can fast, but right eating is impossible for him. Fasting is easy, overeating is okay. He can be in the world, committed, involved, or he can renounce the world – but he can never be balanced. He can never remain in the middle, because if you are not centered you do not know what middle means.

A person who is centered is always in the middle in everything, never at any extreme. Buddha says his eating is right eating; it is neither overeating, nor fasting. His labor is right labor – never too much, never too little. Whatsoever he is, he is always balanced.

First thing: a self-actualized person will be centered. Second thing: he will be balanced.

Thirdly: if these two things happen – centering, balance – many things will follow. He will always be at ease. Whatsoever the situation, the at-easeness will not be lost. I say whatsoever the situation, the at-easeness will not be lost, because one who is at the center is always at ease. Even if death comes, he will be at ease. He will receive death as one receives any other guest. If misery comes, he will receive it. Whatsoever happens, it cannot dislodge him from his center. That at-easeness is also a by-product of being centered.

For such a man, nothing is trivial, nothing is great; everything becomes sacred, beautiful, holy – everything! Whatsoever he is doing, whatsoever, it is of ultimate concern. Nothing is trivial. He will not say, "This is trivial, this is great." Really, nothing is great, nor is anything small and trivial. The touch of the man is significant. A self-actualized person, a balanced, centered person, changes everything. The very touch makes it great.

If you observe a buddha, you will see that he walks and he loves walking. If you go to Bodhgaya where Buddha attained enlightenment, to the bank of the Niranjana – to the place where he was sitting under the Bodhi tree – you will see that the place of his steps has been marked. He would meditate for one hour, then he would walk around. In Buddhist terminology this is called *chakraman*. He would sit under the Bodhi tree, then he would walk. But he would walk with a serene attitude, as if in meditation.

Someone asked Buddha, "Why do you do this? Sometimes you sit with closed eyes and meditate, then you walk." Buddha said, "Sitting in order to be silent is easy, so I walk. But I carry the same silence within. I sit, but inside I am the same – silent. I walk, but inside I am the same - silent." The inner quality is the same.

When he meets an emperor and when he meets a beggar, a buddha is the same, he has the same inner quality. When meeting a beggar he is not different, when meeting an emperor he is not different; he is the same. The beggar is not a nobody and the emperor is not a somebody. And really, while meeting a buddha, emperors have felt like beggars and beggars have felt like emperors. The touch, the man, the quality remains the same. He was the same in life and death.

So thirdly, the self-actualized man is at ease. Life and death are the same; bliss and misery are the same. Nothing disturbs him, nothing dislocates him from his home, from his centeredness. To such a man you cannot add anything. You cannot take anything out of him, you cannot add anything to him – he is fulfilled. His every breath is a fulfilled breath, silent, blissful. He has attained. He has attained to existence, to being; he has flowered as a total man.

This is not a partial flowering. Buddha is not a great poet. Of course, whatsoever he says is poetry. He is not a poet at all, but even when he moves, walks, it is poetry. He is not a painter, but whenever he speaks, whatsoever he says becomes a painting. He is not a musician, but his whole being is music par excellence. The man as a totality has attained. So now, whatsoever he is doing or not doing...when he is sitting in silence, not doing anything, even in silence his presence works, creates; it becomes creative.

Tantra is concerned not with any partial growth, it is concerned with you as a total being. So three things are basic: you must be centered, rooted, and balanced; that is, always in the middle – of course, without any effort. If there is effort you are not balanced. And you must be at ease – at ease in the universe, at home in the existence, and then many things follow. This is a basic need, because unless this need is fulfilled you are a man only in name. You are a man as a possibility, you are not actually a man. You can be, you have the potentiality, but the potentiality has to be made actual.

Osho – "Vigyan Bhairav Tantra", Volume 1, Discourse 10

THE PSYCHOLOGY OF THE BUDDHAS

The present psychology is not yet comprehensive enough; it touches only the periphery of human individuality. It remains confined to the mind. It is not right to call it "psychology". Psychology means "the science of the soul", and the present psychology is not only not the science of the soul, it denies even the existence of the soul. The moment you deny the soul, consciousness, something which is beyond the mind but within you - this denial is not an ordinary denial because it destroys the whole dignity of man. It takes away his very center. He becomes center-less, soul-less, just a robot.

The right name for modern psychology is "robotology", because it studies only the mechanical behavior of man and the mechanics of mind. Its studies cannot go very deep for the simple reason that if mind is all, and there is nothing more to life than mind, you cannot ever become one, undivided.

To be divided is the nature of the mind; to be always balanced between opposites: love and hate, courage and fear, yes and no, atheism and theism. Mind does not feel at ease unless it has divided a thing in two. It cannot conceive of light unless it is contrasted with darkness; it cannot conceive of life unless it is defined by death.

And because psychology remains within the boundaries of the mind it cannot help man to grow to his potential heights. Psychology will discourage you: spiritual search is nothing but a mirage; the seeking of Truth is hallucinatory.

It is not a coincidence that we are the most intelligent generation, because 10,000 years of growth is within us. So on the one hand it is the most intelligent generation that has ever existed, and on the other hand, because of psychology spreading these poisonous ideas - that there is no consciousness, no soul, no life beyond death, and man is just matter, that mind is also nothing but a certain combination of material elements - this has created a very strange situation. Intelligence is pulling man towards more growth and the people who deal with growth are pulling man backwards, telling him," There is no beyond, just be normal – that is more than you can dream of."

"Just to be normal" is the goal of psychology. A great goal, just to be normal! People have lived for thousands of years without any psychology – and normally. In fact, as you go backwards you will not find so many murders, you will not find so many suicides, you will not find so many rapes, you will not find so many sexual perversions. As you go back, they start becoming less. Primitive man was more innocent than you are. He was not as intelligent as you are, but he was more innocent. You inherit his innocence, but you are keeping it repressed.

The combination of intelligence and innocence is meditation.

The moment innocence and intelligence start growing within you.... It is not that you become capable of solving all the problems of the mind, but a totally new thing happens: you start going beyond mind. The problems of the mind are left far behind, as if they never belonged to you. In fact they never belonged to you. And once you know how to slip out of your mind, a totally different psychology will be founded on the art of slipping out of the mind.

A person who can get out of his mind helps the mind to cool down. The mind is getting no more energy – it cools, calms down on its own accord. That's why I have said meditation is a medicine too – and both words come from the same root. Once your intelligence and your innocence are available to you, just like two wings, the whole sky is yours. There are no more boundaries for you.

I have called the psychology that is based on meditation, "The Psychology of the Buddhas". Modern psychology is the psychology of people who are asleep. It has to be understood...

The people who came to Sigmund Freud, the founder of modern psychology, were all sick people, obviously; otherwise, why should they come to the psychoanalyst? They were seriously sick, their minds were falling apart. Sigmund Freud came in contact only with sick people. That gave him the impression that man himself is sick. In a way he is logical because everybody he examined, everybody he analyzed, everybody he treated was sick. And these were high-class people, bourgeois – professors, scientists, very rich people – because a psychoanalyst's time is the costliest thing in the world today. All these people were basically living an insane life, but because everybody else is also living the same insane life, you don't become aware of it.

If Sigmund Freud denied that there is any possibility of a soul in man he cannot be blamed. He never came across a Gautam Buddha, he never came across a man who had gone beyond mind. The trouble was, these people who have gone beyond mind have no reason to go to Sigmund Freud. And Sigmund Freud is afraid to go to such people because they are against the very foundation upon which he has raised a whole empire – certainly there was a great vested interest.

If just a simple method of meditation can help a person...not only to be normal, because to be normal can never be accepted as the goal. That means you remain a mediocre person for your whole life; you never go beyond the boundaries of the society. In everything you remain half-hearted, there is no intensity, there is no totality. A normal person is wishy-washy, just in a limbo, neither here nor there, hanging in between.

It is unfortunate that the great psychologists of the West had no opportunity to know the mystic and to become acquainted with his world, which is absolutely extraordinary. He lives 24 hours among you, but not with you; his kingdom is far away. He has tasted love, of which you have been only dreaming. He has experienced Truth, of which you have been only thinking and philosophizing. He has encountered existence directly without any mediation of a priest, a prophet, a savior. He has seen existence in its freshness. He is not a Christian, he is not a Hindu – because these are so old, so full of dust and borrowed, they cannot give you a transformation.

Remember one thing: unless the Truth is your own experience, whatever you believe about Truth is only a belief. And all beliefs are lies, and all believers are blind.

The Psychology of the Buddhas means that we accept man as a three-storied building: There are a few who remain only on the ground floor, only in their bodies; all their interests are centered in the body – this is the lowest life for someone to choose, as if you are living on the porch when the whole building is yours.

The second level of life is that of a well-understood mind. But who is going to understand the mind? You can see the difficulty of the psychologist: he studies the mind, but if you ask who is studying the mind…

Mind cannot study itself. There must be something beyond: a witness, a watcher who studies the mind. The scientist is studying only from the outside. He is studying the behavior of other people and from their behavior he is deducting principles upon which human behavior is based. But his observation is of the behavior, not of the real being inside. He can be deceived. You can be sad but you can smile, you can hold back the tears. Or if you are a little artful, you can manage to bring crocodile tears. Your behavior is not reliable. We don't know what is happening inside you, whether your behavior is an expression of your inside or it is a camouflage, hiding you in beautiful garbage.

Buddha accepts three steps: the body, the mind, the consciousness. Even the consciousness is only a step. These three steps lead to the temple of the divine, of the immortal, of beauty, of celestial music. You start touching heights, Himalayan heights where you can find virgin snow which has never melted. In your inner being also you are carrying greater peaks than Everest, with eternal beauty.

The Psychology of the Buddhas is comprehensive of the whole individuality of man, and it does not end there. By studying, by experiencing the body, the mind, the consciousness, and the beyond, Buddha is preparing you to dissolve into the universal.

Just like a dewdrop slipping from a lotus leaf into the lake. On a beautiful morning the sun is rising and the whole sky is so colorful. Just a cool breeze is there, but it is enough for the rose petals, for other flowers, for the lotus. In the early morning sun the dewdrops on the lotus petals look like pearls – or it will be better to say that pearls look like the dewdrops. They are slipping slowly, slowly towards the vast ocean, in which they will be lost and yet not lost. As dewdrops they will be lost, but they will emerge as the whole ocean.

Unless psychology can bring human beings to this oceanic experience it is immature; it has just started its ABC's. And in the West it is going around in a circle – because you do not accept higher realities, where can you go? You are stuck with the mind: analyze it, analyze its dreams, analyze its repressions.

But it should be taken as a very significant question that there is not a single man in the whole world who is completely analyzed. This is a failure of the whole system of psychoanalysis: 12 years, 15 years people have been in psychoanalysis and they have not moved anywhere. Yes, they have learned psychological jargon, it has become more difficult to talk with them! But they are the same persons with all the weaknesses, with all the frailties. 12 or 15 years of psychoanalysis has not been able to a make even a single dent in their personality. It is a rich man's game. Just as poor people have their games, rich people have their own games. Psychology is still a game, guesswork, with no foundation in reality.

The mystics in the East have never bothered too much about the mind; they have only developed methods to bypass the mind. Those methods are the techniques of meditation – they are just to bypass the mind. Once you have bypassed the mind, once you can have a bird's-eye view of your own mind, things start settling. It is your energy that disturbs the mind, that gives it the power to be violent, to be sad, to be angry, to be hateful, to be jealous. Now you are no longer giving it any energy. It won't take a long time. The mind withers almost like a cloud – it was there and it is no more.

The moment mind disperses, your meditation has come to maturity. Now your meditation will be the medium, not the mind. The mind will be used as a mechanism by your meditative forces, but mind is put aside; it is no longer the master. And it is one of the strangest stories that for 10,000 years in the East we have worked on meditation and we have been absolutely successful, not only in becoming meditative, but also in dissolving all the problems of the mind.

There is only one way to solve the mind and its problems, and that is to get out of it. But modern psychology has no idea of where to go, so they go on around and around but they remain just ordinary beings.

In my way of looking at things, mind itself is sick. Unless you get out of it, you cannot help the poor mind to become healthy. You are too much identified. Not being identified with the mind is the shortest way to your own being. And your being is always healthy, it does not know what sickness is. It cannot know, it is not in its nature. Just as mind cannot know peace, your being cannot know tensions, anxieties, anguish.

The question is not of curing the mind, the question is shifting your whole energy, your whole focus, from mind to being. Meditation helps you to shift. This great shift of your attention, of your awareness, is what I call the Psychology of the Buddhas.

And any other psychology is going to be wrong, because only a man of eyes knows what light is. There may be millions of people who are blind – there are millions, but it is not a question of democracy. They cannot vote, they cannot assert a single word about light. That one man is right and those millions of people are wrong. The question is not of numbers. The only question that is significant is the transformation of your being from mind to no-mind.

Modern psychology thinks it is the science of the mind. The Psychology of the Buddhas will be the science of no-mind.

Osho – "Sermons in Stones", Question 1

PSYCHOLOGY OF THE NO-MIND

All the psychologies are of the mind. The Psychology of the Buddhas will be of the no-mind. It is going to be diametrically opposite to the ordinary psychologies in every aspect, in every direction, because it is a totally new dimension – never touched before, never even thought about before. It is easy to study the mind. It is very difficult, almost impossible, to study the no-mind.

The no-mind reminds me of a modern painting...

One modern painter was exhibiting his works of art. A man was standing before a painting for almost half an hour. The painter was moving around the exhibition, explaining to people when they had any questions about a painting.

This man was absolutely absorbed by the painting, and the painter came many times, but felt it was not right to disturb him. But finally he had to, because the painting was nothing but an empty canvas. He asked the man, "Are you interested in the painting?"

The man said, "I am certainly interested, because I am wondering, where is the painting? It is an empty canvas, but if it is being exhibited there must be a painting, somewhere, in some way. Are you the painter?"

The man said, "Yes, I am the painter and I am here to explain it to you: this is a painting of a cow eating grass." There was no cow and there was no grass.

The man said, "But I don't see the cow."

The painter said, "She has eaten and gone home."

The man said, "But I don't even see the grass!"

The painter said, "The cow has eaten the grass and gone home, so there is no cow and no grass. That's why I have left the canvas empty."

The study of no-mind is just the study of an empty canvas. The thoughts are gone, the emotions are gone, the sentiments are gone, the moods are gone. Nothing is left except a pure, empty space.

So we have to study this empty space in a different way than we study the ordinary mind – because the ordinary mind has contents, and this empty space has no content. It has a certain quality, but it has no content. It has a certain fragrance, but it has no content. There is nothing objective; it is pure subjectivity.

All scientific studies are objective; they need something to study. In this empty space there is no object; you don't have anything to study. So a new dimension has to be explored with totally different approaches.

So first, let me say a few things about ordinary psychology – what it has discovered, where it is – because that will help you to understand the emptiness, the spaciousness of the no-mind.

Sigmund Freud was the first man in the West who came to discover the unconscious mind. In the East it has been known for centuries, so it was not a discovery. Sigmund Freud was just not aware that it had been discovered long before. He is not really the founder. It was discovered so long ago that we don't even know the name of the person who discovered the unconscious mind.

Freud came to the unconscious mind via dreams. He found that people say things when they are awake which are not true: they say things which they are supposed to say, they behave the way they are expected to behave. They are not sincere, they are not authentic. Their whole conscious mind is hypocritical – because for centuries they have been told how to be, what to say, what to do, what is respectable. Their conscious mind has been conditioned by the centuries. Listening to them you cannot discover the real content of their being. You can simply reach to the surface of their mask, but not to their original face. Because the person says one thing but does another, he's continuously lying – and each lie needs more lies to protect it. That gave Freud some idea that it would be better, perhaps.... Man cannot deceive in his dreams because he has no control over dreams, and the conditioning of the society has not reached to his dreams.

You may see a beautiful woman, and you may behave like a perfect gentleman with her, but that is not your truth. In a dream you can rape the woman, you can make love to the woman. You will not bother that she is not your wife, because dreams don't believe in your social codes and mores and behavior patterns. Dreams don't know that marriages exist. Dreams are not aware that the woman is not yours, she is somebody else's wife. In a dream you simply do what you feel like doing; you are true. That's why Freud started studying the dreams of people. And he was surprised that dreams contain tremendous treasures to help to understand the real man, to take away his mask and to see something real.

But there is a difficulty with dreams: they are pictorial. The conscious mind is linguistic. The conscious mind is educated, cultured, civilized; the unconscious mind, in sleep, is primitive. Civilization has not touched it at all. And who cares what you dream? You may murder somebody, you cannot be caught for the crime.

Only in one society, a small aboriginal commune in Thailand of which Sigmund Freud was not aware; otherwise his theories about dreams would have been different. For centuries that tribe has accepted dreams as part of reality. If you misbehave in your dream, in the morning you have to go the person you misbehaved with, and you have to make an apology. You have to bring fruits and sweets to offer him, and say to him how nasty you have been in your dream: "Please forgive me. Until you forgive me, I will not be able to feel right again." Naturally, he is forgiven, because the person has not been harmed, he knows nothing about your dream.

But that is the only society in the whole world which takes dreams seriously, as being almost parallel to reality. And everything that happens in the dream has to be told to the elders of the society the first thing in the morning, whatever it is. You may have raped a woman – you have to say it. You have to say who is the woman, and you have to apologize to the woman, to her husband, to the family.

Strangely enough, this is the only tribe in the whole world which dreams very rarely – because they don't repress their dreams. On the contrary, they express them and they settle them, so nothing remains hanging. They have done whatever they could do; they have offered an apology, they have presented some gift, whatsoever they could manage, and they have been forgiven. The dream thing is settled – that dream is finished. So it is very rare in that community for people to dream, very rarely will a person dream.

But in Western society where Sigmund Freud was working, out of eight hours of sleeping, you are dreaming six hours. Only for two hours here and there are you not dreaming. Six hours is a lot of time – and dreams have their own chronology, so in six hours you can dream of sixty years. In six hours you can manage to dream as much as you want. Dreaming does not follow the same time scale, so sometimes it may happen that you have just fallen asleep for a few seconds, and you are awakened by some noise or something. And you wonder that only a few seconds have passed on your watch but you had such a long dream – in a few seconds such a long dream is not possible. It is possible because the dream does not follow the same time scale. So in six hours you are going through so much garbage, and that garbage is accumulated by our repressions.

That aboriginal community in Thailand has no repression. Even the dream has to be given expression, so you are free of it. It is psychologically healthy. Nobody has ever gone mad in that community. Nobody has ever murdered anybody in that community. Nobody has ever committed suicide in that community. And the last and the most emphatic thing to remember is that that is the only community in the whole of history which has never fought a war. It does not know that wars exist.

Perhaps wars have something to do with your repressions. After each ten, twenty years the whole humanity is so full of repressions that a great explosion into a war is an absolute necessity; otherwise you all will go mad.

War is a civilized way to go mad and yet retain the idea that you are sane.

Listening to people's dreams, Freud came to see that people are living an absolutely false life. And this false life is created by your religions, by your moralities, by your educational system. They have not given you any method of transformation – they have simply given you a false face to cover your original face.

In dreams people are doing all kinds of things. They are embarrassed when they are awake, even to accept what they did in their dreams. So Freud discovered a layer within and below the conscious mind – he called it the unconscious mind, because you are not aware of it. And his whole life's work was concerned with how to sort out dreams and how to make those dreams conscious.

It is one of the great findings of Freud that once a dream becomes conscious it loses its grip on you; hence psychoanalysis became of great importance. Nothing else has to be done; the dream just has to be brought fully to the conscious mind. You have to accept in all its minute details, that it is your dream, that you are carrying such thoughts within you. You should not deny it. If you deny it, it will remain within you. If you accept it, it evaporates.

The idea is that if all the dreams evaporate, your unconscious becomes clean, without garbage; and that gives you a tremendous feeling of well-being. You are not carrying something against yourself. You are not creating a division between your conscious mind and the unconscious mind; you are no longer split. When there is no dream left – which Sigmund Freud did not succeed in doing.... He helped people to lessen the quantity of dreams, but he was not able, even with a single patient, to make him completely free of dreams. So there is not a single person in the whole world who is fully psychoanalyzed. There are people who have been in psychoanalysis for 15 years or 20 years, and still they go on digging and more and more rubbish goes on coming.

This was the reason why Carl Gustav Jung got an idea that perhaps below the unconscious mind there is another mind which goes on supplying more and more dreams. You go on analyzing, dispersing, but something keeps welling up and the unconscious is never clear, never clean; hence he came to the idea of the collective unconscious.

The idea of the collective unconscious is very important. It means that there is a point in your mind where you are connected with all the minds around you. This mind is collective, it is not just your own. And there is constant traffic within the collective mind, so you may get rid of dreams in your unconscious mind, but the collective mind goes on supplying more and more junk. And the collective mind is like a continent. Everybody else is involved in it; not only the present people, but centuries that have passed and the people who have lived – all have left impressions on the collective unconscious.

There is a possibility Jung never explored – that perhaps the collective unconscious has something to do with Charles Darwin's theory of evolution. Perhaps you are carrying the collective unconscious mind of many lives...since the first life was born in the ocean as a fish and then developed through many forms up to the ape, and from ape to man. All those memories are there. Somebody has to work with the collective mind through Charles Darwin's approach, and that will also give a tremendous insight into Eastern religions and their idea of rebirth: that you had many births before, and not necessarily only human. You have been in other forms of life.

Gautam Buddha says in one of his lives he was an elephant, and he relates many stories of his past lives in which he was different animals. Perhaps all three – Carl Gustav Jung, Charles Darwin, and the Eastern idea of rebirth – are significant as far as the collective mind, the collective unconscious, is concerned. And it is so full: from so many dimensions so many rivers are filling it; it is oceanic. And unless it is cleaned, you can never have a clean unconscious mind because this collective mind will go on supplying new stuff. Jung stopped at the collective unconscious.

The East has not stopped there. The East has these ideas – the unconscious mind, the collective unconscious mind – and it has one more mind, the deepest, the very base: it can be called the cosmic collective unconscious. It is not only concerned with life, it is concerned with Existence itself. There, the whole Existence is supporting you. The whole Existence is giving energy to the collective unconscious, which is a smaller thing; and the collective unconscious is giving to the unconscious, which is smaller still. But this is all in darkness.

Western psychology has gone only into the darker part of the mind, and in that too it has not reached yet to the cosmic unconscious. This is going below, into the basement.

The Eastern psychology has a similar pattern above the conscious mind. Just as there is an unconscious mind below the conscious mind, above the conscious mind there is a superconscious mind. Western psychology has not even dreamed about it.

Above the superconscious mind there is the collective superconscious mind, and above that there is the cosmic superconscious mind. It seems very logical, and very mathematical that if there is a basement, a foundation in the dark, then there must be something above.

Things are always balanced in nature.

If a tree has roots and you only study the roots and forget the tree, you will be utterly wrong. The roots go downwards, deeper and deeper in the darkness; the tree goes upwards. It is strange that the roots go downwards and the tree goes upwards – in different directions. At a certain point where the roots and the tree join there is a meeting point, and a departure point too. You have to learn about the tree, its foliage, its flowers, its fruits; otherwise just studying the roots will be incomplete. Unless you know the tree too, you will not understand the meaning of the roots. The meaning of the roots is in the flowers, it is not there in the roots themselves.

Just as through dreams Freud reached to the unconscious mind, through meditation man can reach to the superconscious mind. And as meditation deepens he can reach to the collective superconscious mind – which joins us again, but on a conscious level. At the highest point of meditation you reach to the cosmic superconscious. That joins you with the whole cosmos. But as you are going higher you are losing your ego. With the cosmic superconscious mind you are, but you are no more an ego. Nothing separates you from the Whole.

This is the point where Al-Hillaj-Mansoor said, *"Ana'l haq*: I am God, myself"*. Or the Upanishads say, *"Aham brahmasmi*: I am the Whole. I am the Ultimate. I am the Absolute." The emphasis is not on the "I", the emphasis is on the Absolute, the Ultimate. The "I" has to be used only because of the language.

These are the seven stages of the mind: three below the conscious mind and three above the conscious mind. Only one thing remains which is beyond all these, and that is the state of no-mind. That comes only when you become an observer of the superconscious, of the collective superconscious, of the cosmic superconscious.

You are simply a witness.

Things are becoming more and more beautiful, more and more majestic, miraculous – there is every danger you may be lost. You may become too attached to the beauties that you are coming across. Here again, I remind you that the Master is a need: to push you, to tell you that this is nothing, there is something more ahead.

When you become a witness of the cosmic superconscious mind, mind disappears with all its seven forms. The whole tree disappears as if it had never existed, and there is pure space. This pure space is not empty. It is full, overfull with all the potentialities. It is the very source of all creation. Everything has come out of it and one day will go back into it. Buddha has called it "nothingness".

That word "nothingness" gives a certain negative color. It is better to call it pure space, which is natural. It does not give you any idea of the negative or of the positive, just spaciousness.

A story…. A Sufi mystic used to see a woodcutter going to the forest every day. The woodcutter was old, very old, but there was no other way: he had no son, no family, all had died. He had survived longer than he needed to. Just for his needs he had to continue to cut wood and sell it. He always came to the mystic to touch his feet and go into the forest, and in the evening he would return with the load. It was really heavy for him, and every day it was becoming more and more difficult.

One day the mystic said, "Wait! You have become too old, and now this work is not for you. I will show you a simpler way. Today don't cut the wood, just go a little farther, and soon you will come to a mine of copper. Collect some copper, and that will give you enough money to live at least for seven days; you need not come again for seven days. So once a week you can come and collect copper."

The man went, found the mine, and thanked the mystic. He was immensely happy because the burden was too much, and he was becoming so ancient, weak, old, and he could not see well.

After a few days the mystic said, "You are a strange man! I was thinking that finding the copper mine you would think – you would become curious to go a little farther. Perhaps there is something more. But it seems you have lost all curiosity, all adventurousness. So I have to say to you again, go a little further and you will find a silver mine. You can collect silver, and that will be enough for a whole month. No need to come every week, you are getting too old, once a month you can come."

The man went ahead, found the silver, thanked the mystic and said, "Your compassion and grace is so great, I cannot repay it in any way. I am a poor old man."

The mystic said, "Don't be worried about it. Just remain curious about finding something more." The old man said, "What? Is there more, too? But this is enough – once a month." The mystic said, "No. If you go ahead you will find a gold mine. That will suffice for the whole year."

Next day the man came, and he went and found the gold. But the mystic said, "My life is going to come to an end. I will not always be here to tell you to go ahead. So I should rather tell you now not to stop at the gold, because just a little further there is a diamond mine. And that will suffice not only for you, but for a few of your relatives and friends. You can feed the whole neighborhood. But don't stop there." The woodcutter said, "But what can be worth more than diamonds?"

The mystic said, "Can't you see me sitting here? There must be something more than diamonds; otherwise I would not be sitting here, I would be simply carrying diamonds to the market. Don't you want to reach where I have reached? It is beyond the diamonds, just a little further."

The poor woodcutter could not understand – what can be more than diamonds? But he went a little further, and he was surprised: he found the same mystic sitting under a tree!

The mystic said, "So you have come! Now there is no need to go back. You can also sit under the tree." In Eastern mythology there is a tree called *kalpavriksha*. If you sit under that tree, whatever you desire is fulfilled immediately. It is a symbol. It is a symbol of the contented mind that really never desires anything, so there is no question of discontent.

The old man sat with the Master and was surprised that he had no desire, that he did not want anything: diamonds, gold, silver, nothing – that all was fulfilled, that suddenly he had come to a place where nothing was needed.

The mystic said, "How does it feel?" The woodcutter said, "But you are a tricky man! Why did you not say it in the beginning? Why did you make me go from one place to another, from one mine to another?"

The mystic said, "If I had told you in the beginning you would not have believed me. It was to create trust. Because I proved trustworthy about the copper, the silver, the gold, the diamonds – that's why you have been able to follow my instruction to go further. Otherwise, everybody argues, 'What can there be beyond diamonds?'

"You trusted: 'If the man is right up to diamonds, there must be something more. And if he is saying so, I am going.' This is the same tree I have always been sitting under. I could have told you anytime but you would not have listened."

This is to remind you that man has to move through meditation from consciousness to superconsciousness, from superconsciousness to collective superconsciousness, from collective superconsciousness to cosmic superconsciousness.

And then only can the Master persuade him to take a jump. And the Master has been right up to now – your distrust has melted away. And if he says, "Walk on," you will take the risk. The trust is now deep enough that you can jump into pure space; that is no-mind. And to attain to no-mind is to attain all. There is nothing more than that, because it is peace, it is silence, it is blissfulness. It is godliness, it is immortality, it is eternity.

No-mind is all that is possible.

Osho – "Light on the Path", Discourse 17

EAST vs WEST RELIGIOUS PSYCHOLOGY

The concept of sin creates a very different consciousness around it. This concept is lacking in the Eastern mind. Rather, it is substituted for by the concept of ignorance. In Eastern consciousness the root of all evil is ignorance, not sin. Evil is there because you are ignorant. So the problem is not of guilt but of discipline. You have to be more aware, more knowing. In the East, knowledge is transformation – and meditation is the instrument for that transformation.

With Christianity, sin became the center. And it is not only your sin. It is the original sin of humanity. You are burdened with a concept of sin. This creates guilt, tension. That is why Christianity could not really develop meditative techniques. It only developed prayer. What can you do to fight sin? You can be moral and prayerful!

There is nothing like the Ten Commandments in the East. An overly moral concept is not there. So the problems in the East are different from the West. With people who come from the West, guilt is the problem. Deep down they feel guilty. Even those who have revolted feel guilty. It is a psychological problem, concerned more with the mind and less with the being.

First, their guilt has to be released. That is why the West had to develop psychoanalysis and confession. They were not developed in the East because they were never needed. In the West you have to confess. Only then can you get free from the guilt that is deep inside. Or you have to go through psychoanalysis so that the guilt is thrown out. But it is never thrown out permanently, because the concept of sin remains. The guilt will accumulate again. So psychoanalysis and confession can only be a temporary help. You have to confess again and again. They are only temporary helps against something that has been accepted. The root of the disease – the concept of sin – has been accepted.

In the East it is not a question of psychology, it is a question of being. It is not a question of mental health. Rather, it is a question of spiritual growth. You have to grow spiritually, to be more aware of things. You do not have to change your behavior, but to change your consciousness. Then the behavior follows.

Christianity is more concerned with your behavior. But behavior is just peripheral. The question is not what you do; the question is what you are. If you go on changing what you are doing, you are not really changing anything. You remain the same. You can be a saint outwardly and still be the same being inside. The problem of those coming from the West is because of the guilt they have about their behavior. I have to struggle with them just to make them aware of their deeper problem – which is of the being, not of the psyche.

Buddhism and Jainism have also created guilt. Not the same kind of guilt, but guilt in a different way. Jainas in particular have created a very deep feeling of inferiority. Guilt in the Christian sense is not there because there is no question of sin, but there is a deep feeling that unless one goes beyond certain things, one is inferior. This deep inferiority works in the same way as guilt.

Jainas have not created any meditative techniques either. They have only created different formulas: Do that. Do that. Don't do this. The whole concept is centered around behavior. A Jaina monk is ideal as far as his behavior is concerned, but as far as his inner being is concerned he is very poor. He goes on behaving just like a puppet. That is why Jainism has become a dead thing.

Buddhism is not dead in the same way because a different emphasis is there. The ethical part of Buddhism is just a consequence of the meditative part. If behavior has to be changed, it is just as a help to meditation. In itself, it is meaningless. In Christianity and Jainism it is meaningful in itself. If you are doing good, then you are good. For Buddhism this is not the case. You have to be transformed inwardly. Doing good can help, it can become a part, but meditation is the center.

So of the three, only Buddhists have developed deep meditation. Everything else in Buddhism is just a help – not significant. You can even discard it. If you can meditate without any other help, then you can discard the rest.

Osho – "The Psychology of the Esoteric", Discourse 1

The ancient methods of meditation were all developed in the East. They never considered the Western man, the Western man was excluded. I am creating techniques which are not only for the Eastern man, but which are simply for every man – Eastern or Western.

There is a difference between the Eastern tradition and the Western tradition – and it is the tradition that creates the mind. For example, the Eastern mind is very patient – thousands of years of teaching to remain patient, whatever the conditions may be. The Western mind is very impatient. The same methods of technique cannot be applicable to both.

The Eastern mind has been conditioned to keep a certain equilibrium in success or in failure, in richness or in poverty, in sickness or in health, in life or in death. The Western mind has no idea of such equilibrium; it gets too disturbed. With success it gets disturbed; it starts feeling at the top of the world, starts feeling a certain superiority complex. In failure it goes to the other extreme; it falls into the seventh hell. It is miserable, in deep anguish, and it feels a tremendous inferiority complex.

The Western mind is torn apart and life consists of both: there are moments which are beautiful, and there are moments which are ugly. There are moments when you are in love, there are moments when you are in anger, in hatred. The Western mind simply goes with the situation. It is always in a turmoil.

The Eastern mind has learned…it is a conditioning, it is not a revolution. It is only a training, a discipline, it is a practice. Underneath it is the same, but a thick conditioning makes it keep a certain balance. The Eastern mind is very slow because there is no point in being speedy; life takes its own course and everything is determined by fate, so what you get, you don't get by your speed, your hurry. What you get, you get because it is already destined, so there is no question of being in a hurry. Whenever something is going to happen, it is going to happen – neither one second before nor one second after it. This has created a very slow flow in the East. It seems almost as if the river is not flowing; it is so slow that you cannot detect the flow. Moreover, the Eastern conditioning is that you have already lived millions of lives, and there are millions ahead to be lived, so the life span is not only seventy years; the life span is vast and enormous. There is no hurry; there is so much time available: why should you be in a hurry? If it does not happen in this life, it may happen in some other life.

The Western mind is very speedy, fast, because the conditioning is for only one life – 70 years – and so much to do. One third of your life goes into sleep, one third of your life goes into education, training – what is left? Much of it goes into earning your livelihood. If you count everything, you will be surprised: out of 70 years you cannot even have 7 years left for something that you want to do.

Naturally there is hurry, a mad rush, so mad that one forgets where one is going. All that you remember is whether you are going with speed or not. The means becomes the end in the same way, in different directions.

The Eastern mind has cultivated itself differently than the Western mind. Those 112 methods of meditation developed in the East have never taken account of the Western man; they were not developed for the Western man. The Western man was not yet available. The time that *Vigyan Bhairva Tantra* was written – in which those 112 techniques have come to perfection – is about five to ten thousand years before us. At that time there was no Western man, no Western society, no Western culture. The West was still barbarous, primitive, not worth taking into account. The East was the whole world, at the pinnacle of its growth, richness, civilization.

My methods of meditation have been developed out of an absolute necessity. I want the distinction between the West and the East to be dissolved.

After Shiva's *Vigyan Bhairva Tantra*, in these five or ten thousand years, nobody has developed a single method. But I have been watching the differences between East and West: the same method cannot be applied immediately to both. First, the Eastern and the Western mind have to be brought into a similar state. My techniques of Dynamic Meditation, Kundalini Meditation, and others, are all cathartic; their basis is catharsis. You have to throw out all the junk that your mind is full of. Unless you are unloaded you cannot sit silently.

It is just as if you tell a child to sit silently in the corner of the room. It is very difficult, he is so full of energy. You are repressing a volcano! The best way is, first tell him, "Go run outside around the house ten times; then come and sit down in the corner." Then it is possible, you have made it possible. He himself wants to sit down now, to relax. He is tired, he is exhausted; now, sitting there, he is not repressing his energy; he has expressed his energy by running around the house ten times. Now he is more at ease. The cathartic methods are simply to throw all your impatience, your speediness, your hurry, your repressions.

One more factor has to be remembered, that these are absolutely necessary for the Western man before he can do something like *vipassana* – just sitting silently doing nothing and the grass grows by itself. But you have to be sitting silently, doing nothing – that is a basic condition for the grass to grow by itself. If you cannot sit silently doing nothing, you are going to disturb the grass.

So these methods are absolutely necessary for the Western mind. But a new factor has also entered: they have become necessary for the Eastern mind too. The mind for which Shiva wrote those 112 methods of meditation no longer exists – even in the East now. The Western influence has been tremendous. Things have changed.

In Shiva's time there was no Western civilization. The East was at its peak of glory; it was called "A Golden Bird." It had all the luxuries and comforts: it was really affluent. Now the situation is reversed: the East has been in slavery for 2,000 years, exploited by almost everyone in the world, invaded by a dozen countries, continuously looted, raped, burned. It is now a beggar.

300 years of British rule in India have destroyed India's own educational system – which was a totally different thing. They forced the Eastern mind to be educated according to Western standards. They have almost turned the Eastern intelligentsia into a second-grade Western intelligentsia. They have given their disease of speediness, of hurry, of impatience, of continuous anguish, anxiety, to the East.

Osho – "The Light on the Path"

BELIEF vs EXISTENTIAL KNOWING

Zen is more like poetry, like music, like dance. It is not a philosophy; hence, no conceptual thinking can comprehend it. Mind is absolutely impotent as far as Zen is concerned. You have to go beyond mind to have some taste of Zen. Going beyond the mind simply means dropping all thoughts, creating a vacuum, a nothingness. But that nothingness is not empty; it is just like the sky: it is full of nothingness. And when your eyes are without any dust and your mind is without any thoughts, you see clearly, straight into reality.

It is not a question of belief. You don't have to believe what you will be seeing, you have simply to clean your inner eye, your vision, and the reality will appear on its own accord, not according to anybody's belief. Hence, those who have beliefs never attain to reality.

I am making a statement against all religions. They are all based on belief: believe first, then you will know. But once you believe you have closed the doors of inquiry, once you believe you have accepted your ignorance, your blindness. You have accepted that somebody else has known: "What is the need for me to know? I have just to believe in Jesus Christ or Krishna or Buddha."

But when Buddha drinks the water, your thirst is not quenched; and when Jesus eats, your hunger does not disappear. Even these ordinary things, mundane, you have to experience individually - what to say about the ultimate experience? And Zen is the name of the ultimate experience.

You cannot depend on anybody. You cannot believe anybody's experience. You have to drop all beliefs, all thoughts, all philosophies, all religions, and you have to go utterly innocent inside your own being. From there the door opens and life takes a new color, a new radiance, a new joy. Your words are no more empty, they contain overflowing significance. Your gestures become meaningful for the first time. Your actions have a poetry of their own. Your very movement is a dance because you have known the innermost blissfulness. It starts overflowing you in your actions, in your words, in your silences. It starts overflowing and reaching to others. You become almost a fountain, showering all around. Or you can say you become a beautiful lotus spreading, radiating its perfume all over the space; whether anybody is there or not is not the point. Even in the faraway forest the rose will spread its joy, its fragrance. Perhaps a passer-by may be enriched by it, but it is not the point whether anybody gets it or not.

When Truth is realized, the overflowing of it is intrinsic.

When you have a headache, how do you know? There must be a watcher behind the head who knows the headache. The headache itself cannot know; there must be a witness, a watcher, who knows the headache, who knows the stomachache, who feels emotions and can watch those emotions. When you are full of anger, if you sit down and watch, you can watch the anger clouds all around you, dark. When you are in love, you can watch a certain perfume, a certain beauty, a certain blissfulness all around you.

Every moment in ordinary life you are coming across the witness but you have never recognized it, you have just not taken note of it. At this very moment I am speaking to you, you are hearing me. Just look a little more back - there is a witness who knows that you are hearing. That witness is your eternity. Your inner center - which is the connecting link with the universal heart from where you get your life, your love, your joy - is to be found in witnessing.

The Master is a witness. Becoming intimate with him, the fire of witnessing simply jumps in a single, instantaneous moment. Where there was all dark suddenly becomes light; where there was all misery suddenly becomes a tremendous joy overflowing you, and a great longing arises in you.

We are all drunk, almost living in sleepiness. Our actions go wrong; our intentions go wrong; our life becomes a misery, a pain, an anguish. But the ultimate reason and cause is that we are not aware of our being.

Just a single thing contains all the essence of all the religions: awareness of oneself. And then you cannot do anything wrong.

Osho – "The Language of Existence", Discourse 7

THE BUSINESSMAN TYPE

Jesus said, "A man had guest-friends, and when he had prepared the dinner, he sent his servant to invite the guests. The servant went to the first and said to him: 'My master invites thee.' The man replied, 'I have a claim against some merchants. They will come to me in the evening. I will go and give them my orders. I pray to be excused from dinner.'

"He went to another and said to him, 'My master has invited thee.' The man replied, 'I have bought a house and they request me for a day. I will have no time.'

"He came to another and said to him, 'My master invites thee.' The man replied, 'My friend is to be married and I am to arrange a dinner. I shall not be able to come. I pray to be excused from the dinner.'

"He went to another and said to him, 'My master invites thee.' The man replied, 'I have bought a farm. I go to collect the rent. I shall not be able to come. I pray to be excused.'

"The servant came and said to his master, 'Those whom thou hast invited to the dinner have excused themselves.'

"The master said to his servant, 'Go out to the roads. Bring those whom thou shall find so that they may dine. Tradesmen and merchants shall not enter the places of my father.'"

Jesus talks in parables. The parables are very simple but very significant. They are not literal, so we will have to understand the symbolic meaning of them.

These sayings today are concerned with a particular type, not exactly tradesmen and businessmen, but the type. You may not be a businessman but you may be the type; you may be a businessman and you may not be the type.

So remember, there is a particular type and that particular type constitutes almost 99% of people: businessmen and traders are all over.

They may be doing something else, but their mind is that of a businessman. So the first thing to be understood: Who is a businessman, who is a trader?

A businessman is one who is busy about nonsignificant things, who is busy about the trivial, who is busy about the outside, who is busy about things, commodities, but not about himself. He has completely forgotten himself, he is lost in the world. He thinks of money, possessions, but never of consciousness, because consciousness is not a commodity; it can neither be sold nor purchased, it is useless.

A businessman is one who is a utilitarian: poetry is meaningless, religion is meaningless, God is meaningless, because they cannot be converted into salable objects; you cannot earn money through them.

And money is the most significant thing for this type. He can sell himself, he can lose himself, he can destroy his whole life, just to accumulate money. This is the first characteristic of the type.

I have heard that two businessmen met in a market. It was the peak of the season, of the year. And one said to the other, "Have you heard that Sheik Fakhruddin, the clothier, died this morning?"

The other said, "What? In the middle of the season?"

Neither is life meaningful, nor death, only the season. His measurement is money, he measures a man with money; how much you have got, not who you are - that is meaningless. If you have money you are significant, if you don't have money you are nobody. If he pays respect to you, he pays respect to your possessions, never to you. If you lose your possessions he will not even look at you.

Once it happened: A rich man became poor. He was in misery and he was saying to his wife, "I believed that I had so many friends. 50% of them have already left me, and the other 50% do not yet know that I have become poor."

All of them are going to leave, they were never with you. You cannot have a friendship with a businessman. No, he is only friendly with the money that you have. The moment money is not there, the friendship disappears - it was never with you.

You cannot relate to a businessman, that is impossible: you cannot be a wife, you cannot be a husband, you cannot be a son, you cannot be a father to a businessman, because he relates only to money. Everything else is beside the point, his target is money. If your son starts earning money, the son is valuable; if your father is rich, then he is your father; if he is poor, you would not like people to know that he is your father.

This actually happens every day in life: you will recognize a father who is rich; if he is a poor man or a beggar, you will not recognize him - you recognize only the money. The businessman - the type - cannot love, because love is the most anti-money phenomenon in the world.

Love is concerned with being. Love is a sharing, it is a giving away - not only what you possess, but what you are. A businessman can never be a lover, and a businessman always thinks that lovers are a little crazy, they have gone nuts, they are not in their senses, they are doing nonsense. "Why are you wasting your time? Time is money!" - that's what a businessman says.

His whole concern is about things, not about persons. Love is concerned with persons, the money-oriented mind is concerned with things. And this type of man is continuously busy; he is never at rest, he cannot be, because there is always more and more to be accumulated. There is no end to it.

A man of love can rest. There is a fulfillment when you can rest. But a man after money can never rest because there is no end to it. And there is never fulfillment because money cannot fulfill the soul; the soul remains empty, the inner remains a void. You go on throwing things into it but they never touch your inner emptiness. The more you accumulate, the more you become aware that you are empty, your hands are empty; money is with you but you have lost yourself. Your whole effort is not to look at this fact, because this is very painful.

The businessman runs after money more and more. He wants to completely forget himself in the money; money becomes an intoxicant. He is always busy, a businessman is always busy about nothing. I say about nothing, because in the end it proves nothing. All that you possess proves to be as if you were making drawings on water: they disappear; death comes and your whole effort is nullified.

Death negates the businessman. I would like to tell you that only the businessman dies, nobody else - but he constitutes 99% of people. Only the businessman dies because only he accumulates things, and death can snatch things away.

Death cannot take your love, death cannot take your prayer, death cannot take your meditation, death cannot take away your God. But a businessman only becomes interested in God if there is some business to be done.

Once it happened: The weather was bad and stormy, and an airplane was lost. The fog was so dense that everybody became afraid and fearful. A minister was aboard; except for him, everybody was weeping, crying, perspiring. The moment was dangerous - any moment, death. Even the pilot was perspiring and nervous. The minister told everybody to kneel down and pray. They all, except the businessman, a small man, kneeled and started praying.

The minister asked the businessman, "Why are you not praying?"

The man said, "Forgive me, Father, because I don't know how to pray. I have never prayed." And there was no time to teach the man: any moment the plane would be falling, any moment it would crash.

So the minister said, "Okay, there is no time left now. So just behave as if you are in a church."

The businessman walked down the aisle and collected money from people.

The type - even at the moment of death he knows only one way to behave in a church: to collect money. At the last moment money still remains the focus. This is the first thing to be understood, then you will be able to understand these sentences.

Second thing: in this parable Jesus says God's invitation is always there. Many times he comes and knocks, or his messenger comes and knocks, at your door. He invites you to come for a dinner, but you are always busy and you cannot go. You want to be excused.

Think about yourself: if a messenger comes and invites you, are you ready to go? You have so many things to do and finish first - and you will never be able to finish them, because there is no end to them. The invitation is rejected. You say, "I would have come, I would have liked to come..." but these are all false things.

Why can't you accept the invitation? Because more important things are to be done: there is some marriage and you have to go because it is a business relationship; or you have purchased land and you have to go and collect the rent; or something else. God is always the last item on the list of a businessman. And he never comes to the last item - before that, death comes.

God is the most useless phenomenon. People come to me and they ask, "Why meditate? What will we achieve out of it?" They are asking, "What profit? What are we going to achieve out of it?" And if I say, "Nothing," they simply cannot understand. Why are people coming to me? To learn nothing? To attain nothing?

The businessman needs something visible, tangible. If he meditates and money starts falling on him, then it is worthwhile; if he meditates and he becomes successful in the world, then it is worthwhile; if he meditates and the illness disappears from the body, then it is worthwhile.

But if you say, "Nothing", or "God" - which means the same, just the words differ, because God is nothing - if you use your measurements that you use in this world, what is God? You cannot categorize him. Where will you put him? In what category? How will you label him? And how will you decide the price? He is nothing, he does not belong to this world. In what way can you use him? You cannot use him because God is not a utility, he is an ecstasy.

An ecstasy cannot be used. You can enjoy it but you cannot use it. What is the difference between enjoying and using?

You look at a tree, at the green, the sun rising - you enjoy it but you cannot sell it. You look at a flower, you enjoy it. But the businessman will pluck the flower and go and sell it in the market. You cannot pluck God and go and sell him in the market. You have tried; that's why temples, mosques, *gurudwaras*, churches exist. This is how the businessman has behaved with God: he has tried to sell him also and earn something out of it. It is a great business.

And the priest is the businessman turned into a religious man - he is not religious at all. That's why he is always against Jesus, Buddha, Nanak, Kabir; he is against all of them because these people are dangerous, they destroy the whole business.

A businessman is not interested in God, in poetry, in prayer, in love, in beauty, in goodness; he is not interested in ecstasy. Just to enjoy means nothing to him. He says, "What is the profit out of it?"

A businessman postpones rest for the future: "Work here, now. Have a bank balance, then retire, then rest and enjoy!" But that never comes, it cannot come. A businessman can never retire - that is not in the type, that is not the quality of the type. He may retire from one business, but immediately, or even before it, he will manage another, because he cannot rest. He always thinks in the future, he postpones his enjoyment.

Remember, a man who is religious enjoys here and now. The heaven of a religious man is not somewhere in the sky, in the future. No! That is how a businessman looks at heaven.

The heaven of a religious man is here and now, right this moment. He enjoys it, he does not postpone it, because nobody knows about the future. There is no future, to be exact, only the present exists. The future is a fallacy; it is just somehow to console yourself that someday you will be able to enjoy. And your whole life you are training yourself not to enjoy, and postponing - even if you enter heaven.

Drop the businessman's mind! Otherwise, you have missed many buddhas before, you may miss again and again. And it becomes a routine for you to miss, it becomes habitual.

Jesus is right: "Tradesmen and merchants shall not enter the places of my father." That kingdom is not for them, because they are not interested in that kingdom at all; their interest is in the kingdom of this world. Their eyes are focused downwards, they look downwards, they look at the material, at the world. Because of the way their look is focused they cannot look above. Then the invitation goes flat - they hear, but they excuse themselves.

You have chosen the nonessential and you have rejected the essential. You have chosen the worthless, you have chosen that which intrinsically is going to die and you have rejected the immortal. You have chosen the body and rejected the internal, the inner, the consciousness. And whatsoever you choose, you move in that direction.

Be mindful about it. Look at the situation, and don't start thinking about others: "That man is a businessman." Look at yourself, because out of 100 persons, 99% are businessmen; there is every possibility that you will be a businessman. Don't think that you are the exception, because that exception is always totally different. That exception has already entered, he is already dining with God.

Osho – "Seeds of Revolution" or "The Mustard Seed", Discourse 19

Jesus says, "A man can serve only one master." You have misunderstood Jesus. When he says that, he is not saying that you cannot serve two enlightened Masters. He is not comparing two enlightened Masters; he is not saying you can serve only Jesus or Buddha or Krishna – he is not saying that. Christians have interpreted it in that way – that you can serve only one Master, and if you believe in Jesus you have to believe in Jesus absolutely, you have to believe that Jesus is the only door, the only begotten son. Others may be good, saintly people, but not real enlightened Masters.

This is absolutely a misinterpretation of Jesus' saying. When Jesus says you can serve only one master, *look at the context!* He was talking about either serving money or serving God. That was the context. Either you can serve the world, the worldly desires – greed, ambition, politics – or you can serve God – meditation, desirelessness, peace, silence. You cannot serve two Masters. That was his reference. You cannot serve mammon and God both together.

A person cannot be religious and political together, not even a person like Mahatma Gandhi. Nobody can be religious and political together. If you are really political, religion will be a pretension; if you are really religious you will not bother about politics. Who bothers? Or at the most, politics will be a pretension. But a person cannot be both together because politics needs ambition, desire, competition, jealousy. All the poisons are needed. Religion says drop all the poisons, purification is needed.

When Jesus says you cannot serve two Masters he means you cannot serve the outer and inner together. He is not comparing Buddha and Krishna and himself. Beware of interpretation. Whenever you are reading words of Jesus, Buddha, Lao Tzu, be very careful. Your mind can play tricks with you. Your mind can color them with your own prejudice.

I understand why this problem arises. This problem arises because our minds are very narrow, monogamous: you can love only one woman, you can love only one man. Even mothers think that they cannot love all their children in the same way. If you insist, they will say that one is a favorite. This is because of the narrowness of the mind, because you think love has to be directed. Love need not have any direction, love need not be a relationship, love can be just a state of your being. In fact, a man is satisfied only when he becomes love, not loving – when he becomes love.

The greatest, the deepest longing inside your heart is not to become more loving; the deepest desire is to become love.

What is the difference?

When you are loving, you will be loving to somebody – and when you are loving to somebody, others will be in the shadow. When you focus your mind on one thing, everything else goes out of focus. When you are looking exclusively at one thing, everything else is excluded, bracketed out. Love can be a concentration, then it is monogamous.

Love can be meditative, then it is not monogamous. And when love is not monogamous, then it is religious, spiritual.

Osho – "Tao the Pathless Path", Volume 2, Discourse 10

Once Lao Tzu was made a magistrate. Knowing that he was one of the wisest men in the country, the Chinese emperor appointed him a magistrate. He wanted to escape, he wanted to be forgotten, but the emperor was very insistent. He said, "No. You are the wisest man, you should be my greatest magistrate."

He said, "Okay."

The first case came to court: a thief had been caught red-handed. And Lao Tzu gave him six months jail and also gave six months jail to the rich man from whom he had stolen.

The rich man said, "Are you in your senses? Six months jail for me too? For what?"

Lao Tzu said, "In fact I am being very lenient with you – you should get one year's jail. You have accumulated the whole wealth of the town – you are the original criminal. This man comes only second. If you had not accumulated all the wealth there would have been no need for him to steal. You have created the need to steal. In fact, you are the culprit!"

The rich man went to the emperor. He said, "What nonsense is this? Have you ever heard of this before? Is there any precedent?"

And the king was also worried because if this rich man was a criminal, then what about the emperor? He immediately relieved Lao Tzu from his duties. He said, "You may be a wise man, but you are not needed. You are not able to be a judge. A judge has to follow the rules."

Lao Tzu said, "I am following the ultimate law."

The king said, "There is no question of ultimate law. The law that I have decided, that has to be followed."

Lao Tzu said, "Your law is all nonsense. I follow the Tao. You are also one of the criminals."

Question: *Do you use your mind when you speak in discourse?*

What discourse? You call this discourse? And what mind? One can easily see that whatsoever I utter is absolutely mindless. I am a madman. What mind?

One madman came to the house of another madman and knocked at the door. The man opened the window from above and shouted down, "I'm not at home!"

The madman below looked up and said, "Well, then I'm glad I didn't come!"

Question: *Osho, will you please tell a few jokes about the Portuguese? We poor Portuguese sannyasins feel completely ignored by you.*

From today it will not be so.

A bunch of Portuguese rogues enter a bank.

"Hands up, everybody!" shouts Joachim, the chief. "This is a holdup! Manuel, lock everybody in the toilets. Antonio, bring the manager here!"

The manager is brought trembling to Joachim who asks him for the key of the safe.

"Please, for God's sake, don't kill me! I have left the key at home!" cries the manager.

"Don't worry, man," replies Joachim. "It's only the rehearsal today – tomorrow is the real thing!"

A Portuguese enters a hospital and says, "Doctor, I want to have my testicles removed."

Shocked, the doctor asks, "Have you really given this decision your full consideration?"

"Yes, doctor, I've really decided. I want my testicles removed."

So the doctor operates on him. Weeks later, fully recovered, Manuel visits his friend, who asks him, "So, Manuel, did you follow my advice? Have you had your tonsils removed?"

"Oh, my God!" cries Manuel. "Was it 'tonsils'?"

A Portuguese was on his first flight – Rio to Lisbon.

As the plane was ready to take off, the voice of the pilot came through the speakers: "Ladies and gentlemen, welcome aboard our Jumbo Boeing 747. Our plane is equipped with the most modern and sophisticated equipment for your comfort and security. We have 380 passengers aboard, a crew of 25 people and 30 tons of cargo. We have 2 super-equipped kitchens that can provide 500 meals, 2 bars, 12 toilets, a gambling hall, 2 cinemas with 200 seats, a TV for each passenger, and on the upper floor a disco with an orchestra of 20 musicians.

"Now, please, fasten your belts, extinguish your cigarettes and say your prayers – we are trying to take off with all this junk!"

Osho – "Walking in Zen, Sitting in Zen", Discourse 13

SIMPLE, TRUE, HONEST BUSINESS

My father had a small clothes shop. Once in a while I used to sit there just to watch people, and to see what was going on, and sometimes it was really interesting. I was puzzled, because my father was so simple, so true and honest. He would simply tell people the price of an item like this: "This is my cost price. Now it is up to you how much profit you want to give us. I leave it to you. I cannot reduce the cost price of course, but you can decide how much you want to pay." He would tell his customers, "Twenty rupees is the cost price, you can give me one or two rupees more. Two rupees means ten percent profit, and that's enough for me."

Osho – "Glimpses of a Golden Childhood"

FOLLOW THE LAW BUT LIVE LOVE

Whenever you hear truth, suddenly something in you immediately perceives it. It is not a question of time. Others who cannot perceive it will think that you have been hypnotized: ague, reason, think about it, brood, then believe. But whenever you hear truth, the very quality of it is such that immediately it fills your gap, because your own truth has been called.

Whenever you hear a truth, it is not coming from the outside. The outside is just an opportunity for the inside to open. Immediately, you know that this is true. Not that you can argue about it, not that you can prove it, not that you are convinced by it, no. You are transformed by it, not convinced. It is a conversion, not a conviction.

Love is the higher law; law is the lower love. Law is followed by moralists; love is followed by people who are religious.

Religion is not law, it is love.

Law has a discipline to it; it is a forced thing. It makes you robot-like. You move like a train moves on the track. Law moves in a fixed, routine way. It is mechanical.

Love has no outer discipline to it. Love is freedom. You move like a river, not like a railway train. You move like a river. By your own movement, you create the path. The path is not fixed. Anytime, the river can change it. Love is like a river, a freedom.

Love is a great responsibility because you are free and there is no outer discipline to keep you under control. There is only an inner feeling. Only that inner feeling gives you a discipline.

With law, you are always following a dead routine. It becomes part of your mechanical mind. You need not be responsible. You need not even bother about it; it becomes automatic. Law has to be practiced.

Love has to be lived not practiced. Love is as if you are moving in a wilderness. By your walking you create the path; the path is not already there waiting for you. It is a tremendous responsibility.

Religion has nothing to do with law; it has something to do with grace and love. Religion has nothing to do with the rules that we have invented. Those rules are social things. They are needed. They are just like rules of traffic: "Keep to the left". It has no ultimacy about it. If you keep to the right you are not committing a sin, but you will create trouble for yourself and others, because others are keeping to the left. If the whole country decides, "Keep to the right" then there is no problem: you keep to the right.

Love is ultimate. It has no utility about it. Love means sharing. Love means giving without any thought of return, of reward. Whatsoever you have, give to those who don't have it. Share your being, distribute yourself.

When a poor man hears, "Go and distribute all that you have", he may not feel sorrowful because he has nothing to give. He can say, "Yes, I am already poor and I have nothing to give."

But a rich man has much. The more you have, the more miserly you become. The more you have, the more you cling to it and protect it. The more you have, the more afraid; the more you have, the less willing to share it. A poor man can share easily. The problem arises with a rich man.

Ordinarily we would think it should be otherwise, just the reverse: a rich man has so much that he can share. But he cannot share, because he has so much and he is afraid. If he shares he will be losing. A poor man has nothing to lose.

That's why poor people are more loving than rich people. They can afford love because they have nothing to lose. If you go into the villages of India, people are very poor but very loving. They don't have much - in fact they don't have anything - but they will always be ready to share. They will invite you to eat with them. They may not have enough for two, but they will always be willing to share it.

A rich man is bound to become sorrowful. He has so much. How can he just go and sell everything and distribute it? His whole identity is with riches: he is somebody because of all that he has.

Remember, having becomes a substitute for being. If you have much, you think you are much. And once having is thought to be like your being it becomes difficult to share, because the less you have, the less will become your being. One clings because riches give you a feeling that you are full. If riches are gone, you will be empty.

Only in deep emptiness does God descend. Only in emptiness the door opens. You are so full of worldly things that there is no space for the divine to enter in you. Jesus is simply saying, "Create a space. Create love."

Love and space always go together. Whenever you have too many things around you, love is suffocated and dies. It is very rare to find a man who is rich *and* loving - very rare.

People know it well. If you are a son of a rich man you know. If you are a wife of a rich man you know. If you are a husband of a rich woman you know that rich people are not loving. They are always afraid. Love seems dangerous because when you love you have to share. That is the fear.

The more you possess, the less you can love. And love is the door. Or, the less you can love, the more you start possessing things. Things become a substitute. Let us try to understand it...

A child is born. If the mother loves him, psychoanalysts have been studying, much research has been done - if the mother loves him, the child never drinks too much milk; never, because he knows, it is a tacit understanding, that the mother is always available and she's always ready to share. So what is the fear?

If the mother loves the child, the child will drink only as much milk as is needed. If the child is loved, you will never see a big belly in the child. The child will be proportionate. In fact the mother will be constantly worried that the child is not eating or drinking or taking as much food as needed. But the child has understood that whenever the need arises, the mother is there. He can rely on love.

But if the mother does not love the child, then he is afraid for the future. Love is not there, the tacit understanding is not there, so whenever he gets the opportunity he will eat as much as he can, he will drink as much milk as he can. Now he is already becoming a miser; he has already started accumulating things in the body. He's afraid. Who knows about tomorrow? This mother is not reliable; he has to accumulate for emergencies. So he will accumulate fat, eat more.

People who have not been loved in their childhood continue to eat more. No dieting can help unless love arises. They will eat; eating has become a substitute for love. If somebody loves them, they will immediately see that their overeating has stopped.

Love and food both come from the mother's breast. The first experience of love is from the mother's breast and the first experience of food is also from the mother's breast. So love and food become associated. If there is less love, it has to be substituted for by more food.

If love is enough, you can afford not to eat much. There is no need. Have you watched it? Whenever you fall in deep love, hunger disappears. You don't feel hungry. Love fulfills so deeply that you feel full. Then one starts eating less and less.

Nobody is so poor that he has nothing. And nobody is so rich that he has everything. Even the poorest has his own clinging, and the richest yet has his own ambitions. Even a beggar is rich because he has something which he clings to. It may be just a begging bowl, but it doesn't matter whether it's a kingdom or a begging bowl.

The question is not of the objects you possess; the question is whether you are possessive. You can have a kingdom non-possessively, and you can be a beggar and very possessive.

So when Jesus says that a rich man cannot enter into the kingdom of God, he's talking about the man who is possessive, who is miserly, the man who is closed and cannot share, the man who cannot participate in life - who remains afraid and becomes an island unto himself, who separates himself from the whole and becomes a closed thing, who remains in a cocoon. This man is what Jesus means by a rich man.

Jesus brings to the world the law of grace. Once you understand your helplessness - and once you cry, and once you raise your eyes towards the sky and ask for his help - then that which is impossible with man becomes possible with God.

Jesus says: "Ask, and it shall be given. Knock, and the doors shall be opened unto you." But because of your ego, you have not even knocked. Because of the ego, you have not even asked. That's why things are impossible. If you are helpless and a prayer arises in your helplessness, immediately the impossible becomes possible. But the ego has to be dropped. Only then, grace functions.

Grace functions only when the ego is not there. When you are empty, suddenly you are no more a part of the world of gravitation. You have become part of the world of grace.

There are only two types of people in the world. One, those who go on protecting their ego. They are protecting their own death, they are protecting all that is foolish and stupid, they are protecting their ignorance. Then they go on being miserable and they ask how to be happy.

Then there is the other type, very rare people, who see the whole thing, the whole stupidity of it, that 'I' is the only problem. Not that God is not there, not that bliss is not possible. Things which are impossible for man are possible for God, but then you have to disappear completely. You have to give way; you have to bow down, surrender.

In that surrender, what Jesus calls poverty - the inner poverty of the spirit - arises. What Buddha calls emptiness: in that emptiness, you are open. The breeze of God can flow through you, and birds of God can sing within you, and the rivers of God can dance within you. But then you not there.

You are the only problem. There is no other problem. All other problems are by-products of the basic problem. The basic problem is the ego.

'Jesus on the cross' is a symbol that the ego has to be crucified. The third day after Jesus died on the cross, he was resurrected - a totally different being: luminous, not made of matter, but made of spirit; not born out of the earth, but out of heaven. A totally different type of being. But that happened only when Jesus died. Before that, he was son of man. After that, he was son of God. And everybody has to pass that cross. Everybody has to pass through the death which brings resurrection.

Love is the essential religion. Law is to live with man; love is to live with God. Follow the law because you are part of the society. Follow love, because you are even more a part of God.

Society is temporary. God is eternal. Society is just made by man; it is just a human creation. Be part of it: follow the law. That is necessary, but not enough. Needed, but it can't be a fulfillment.

Follow the law but live love. That is the only way to follow Jesus. If you are too possessive, miserly, afraid, you will not be able to step into the world of love. But I tell you, unless you step into that world, you have not lived at all.

There is no life except love, and there is no God except love. Love is the *sumum bonum*.

Osho – "Come Follow Yourself", Volume 2, Discourse 1

MEDITATION HARMONIZES MIND AND HEART

The first thing to be understood is that there is no way, either of head or of heart. Every way leads you away, away from the Truth that you are.

It would have been so easy if there were a Truth somewhere. Howsoever difficult the way, people would have reached. The more difficult, the more far away the Truth was, the more challenging to the ego. If man's ego challenges him to reach the highest peak in the Himalayas, Everest, where nothing is to be found; if man's ego gives him incentive to waste billions of dollars to reach the moon, risking lives. But man has reached the moon. And the first man who walked on the moon must have looked silly to himself – there was nothing for which so much endeavor, technology, preparation was needed.

Remember, the ego wants challenges. It lives through challenge. Why have so few people been able to have a glimpse of the Truth? Because it is not a challenge; it is not there. It is here within you. It does not need any way, you are already it.

Will it ever be possible for the head and heart to be married, or are they going to remain forever divorced? It all depends on you, because both are mechanisms.

You are neither the head nor the heart.

You can move through the head, you can move through the heart. Of course you will reach different places because the directions of the head and the heart are diametrically opposite.

The head will go round and round thinking, brooding, philosophizing; it knows only words, logic, argument. But it is very infertile; you cannot get anything out of the head as far as Truth is concerned, because Truth needs no logic, no argument, no philosophical research. Truth is so simple; the head makes it so complex.

Down the centuries philosophers have been seeking and searching for the Truth through the head. None of them has found anything, but they have created great systems of thought. I have looked into all those systems: there is no conclusion.

The heart is also a mechanism – different from the head. You can call the head the logical instrument; you can call the heart the emotional instrument. Out of the head all the philosophies, all the theologies are created; out of the heart, come all kinds of devotion, prayer, sentimentality. But the heart also goes round and round in emotions.

The word 'emotion' is good. Watch: it consists of 'motion', movement. So the heart moves, but the heart is blind. It moves fast, quick, because there is no reason to wait. It does not have to think, so it jumps into anything. But Truth is not to be found by any emotionality.

Emotion is as much a barrier as logic.

The logic is the male in you and the heart is the female in you. But Truth has nothing to do with male and female. Truth is your consciousness. You can watch the head thinking, you can watch the heart throbbing with emotion. They can be in a certain relationship.

Ordinarily, the society has arranged that the head should be the master and the heart should be the servant, because society is the creation of man's mind, psychology, and the heart is feminine. Just as man has kept the woman a slave, the head has kept the heart a slave. We can reverse the situation: the heart can become the master, the head can become the servant.

If we have to choose between the two, if we are forced to choose between the two, then it is better that the heart becomes the master and the head becomes the servant.

There are things which the heart is incapable of. Exactly the same is true about the head. The head cannot love, it cannot feel, it is insensitive. The heart cannot be rational, reasonable. For the whole past they have been in conflict. That conflict only represents the conflict and struggle between men and women.

If you are talking to your wife, you must know it is impossible to talk, it is impossible to argue, it is impossible to come to a fair decision, because the woman functions through the heart. She jumps from one thing to another without bothering whether there is any relationship between the two. She cannot argue, but she can cry. She cannot be rational, but she can scream. She cannot be cooperative in coming to a conclusion.

The heart cannot understand the language of the head. The difference is not much as far as physiology is concerned: the heart and the head are just a few inches apart from each other. But as far as their existential qualities are concerned, they are poles apart.

My way has been described as that of the heart, but it is not true. The heart will give you all kinds of imaginings, hallucinations, illusions, sweet dreams – but it cannot give you the Truth.

The Truth is behind both; it is in your consciousness, which is neither head nor heart. Just because the consciousness is separate from both, it can use both in harmony.

The head is dangerous in certain fields, because it has eyes but it has no legs – it is crippled. The heart can function in certain dimensions. It has no eyes but it has legs; it is blind but it can move tremendously, with great speed – of course, not knowing where it is going.

It is not just a coincidence that in all the languages of the world love is called blind. It is not love that is blind, it is the heart that has no eyes.

As your meditation becomes deeper, as your identification with the head and the heart starts falling, you find yourself becoming a triangle. And your reality is in the third force in you: the consciousness. Consciousness can manage very easily, because the heart and the head both belong to it.

You know the story of a blind beggar and a crippled beggar. They both lived outside the village in the forest. Of course, they were competitors to each other, enemies. Begging is a business. But one day the forest was on fire. The cripple had no way to escape, because he could not move on his own. He had eyes to see which way they could get out of the fire, but what use is that if you don't have legs? The blind man had legs, could move fast and get out of the fire, but how was he going to find the place where the fire had not reached yet?

Both were going to die in the forest, burned alive. It was such an emergency that they forgot their competition. In such emergencies only a Jew can remain a businessman, and certainly those two beggars were not Jews. In fact, to be a beggar and a Jew is a contradiction in terms.

They immediately dropped their antagonism – that was the only way to survive. The blind man took the cripple on his shoulders, they found the way out of the fire. One was seeing, and the other was moving accordingly.

Something like this has to happen within you – of course, in reverse order. The head has the eyes, the heart has the guts to move into anything. You have to make a synthesis between the two. And the synthesis, I have to emphasize, should be that the heart remains the master, and the head becomes the servant.

You have as a servant a great asset – your reasoning. You cannot be befooled, you cannot be cheated and exploited. The heart has all feminine qualities: love, beauty, grace. The head is barbarous. The heart is far more civilized, far more innocent.

A conscious man uses his head as a servant and his heart as the master - just the opposite of the story I told you. And this is so simple for the man of consciousness to do. Once you are unidentified with head or heart, and you are simply a witness of both, you can see which qualities should be higher, which qualities should be the goal. And the head as a servant can bring those qualities, but it needs to be commanded and ordered.

Right now, and for centuries, just the opposite has been happening: the servant has become the master. And the master is so polite, such a gentleman, that he has not fought back, he has accepted the slavery voluntarily. The madness on the earth is the result.

We have to change the very alchemy of man. We have to rearrange the whole inside of man. And the most basic revolution in man will come when the heart decides the values. It cannot decide for war, it cannot go for nuclear weapons; it cannot be death-oriented. The heart is life's juice.

Once the head is in the service of the heart, it has to do what the heart decides. And the head is immensely capable of doing anything, just right guidance is needed; otherwise, it is going to go berserk, it is going to be mad. For the head there are no values. For the head there is no meaning in anything. For the head there is no love, no beauty, no grace, only reasoning. But this miracle is possible only by disidentifying yourself from both.

Watch the thoughts, because in your watching them, they disappear. Then watch your emotions, sentimentalities; by your watching, they also disappear. Then your heart is as innocent as that of a child, and your head is as great a genius as Albert Einstein, Bertrand Russell, Aristotle.

But the trouble is far bigger than you can conceive. It is a male-dominated society; man has been creating all the rules of the game, the woman has just been following. And the conditioning has gone so deep, because it has been going on for millions of years.

If in the individual the revolution happens and the heart is enthroned, given its right place as the master, and the head given the right place as a great servant, this will affect your whole social structure.

You can see it happening in my commune. The woman is the master; she is no longer the mistress, and the man is no longer the master. People go on asking me why, for all significant posts, I have chosen women? For the simple reason that the woman will not create the third world war.

It has been a historical fact that each war is created by the man, but the woman suffers most. Strange - the man is the criminal and the consequence happens to the woman! The woman loses her husband, the woman loses her children. The woman loses her dignity, because whenever a country is invaded, the soldiers are so much repressed – just like the monks. Sexually they had no opportunity while the war was going on. When the opportunity arises – they invade a city and conquer it – their first attack is on the woman. And the war has nothing to do with the woman, she is simply outside of the game – it is a male game, just like boxing – but she has to be raped. Those soldiers are hankering not to be victorious for their nation's glory – that is a faraway thing – they are hankering to get the women of the enemies as quickly as possible.

I am putting women in all significant, powerful positions. It is symbolic. Man has a tremendous capacity to do things, but he should not be the guide anymore. He is hung up in his head. He can also become the master if he puts his heart above his head.

That's why I said that all of my sannyasins are women – even those who biologically, physiologically, are men. The moment they become sannyasins they have accepted a new structure: they have put something above their head – their heart. This is what I mean: that even men around me start learning feminine qualities. And feminine qualities are the only qualities worth having.

So there is a possibility, but the possibility has a basic condition to be fulfilled: you become more conscious, a witness, a watcher of all that goes on inside you.

The watcher becomes immediately free from identification. Because he can see the emotions, it is an absolute certainty that "I am not the emotions." He can see the thoughts; the simple conclusion is, "I am not my thought process."

"Then who am I?" – a pure watcher, a witness.

And you reach to the ultimate possibility of intelligence in you: you become a conscious man. Amongst the whole world sleeping, you become awake, and once you are awake there is no problem. Your very awakening will start shifting things to their right places.

The head has to be dethroned, and the heart has to be crowned again. This change amongst many people will bring a new society, a New Man in the world. It will change so many things, you cannot conceive.

Science will have a totally different flavor. It will not serve death anymore, it will not make weapons that are going to kill the whole of life on the earth. It will make life richer, discover energies which can make man more fulfilled, which can make man live in comfort, in luxury, because the values will have completely changed. It will still be mind functioning, but under the direction of the heart.

My way is the way of meditation.

I have to use language, unfortunately, that's why I say my way is the way of meditation: neither of head nor of heart, but of a growing consciousness which is above both mind and heart. This is the key to open the doors for a New Man to arrive on the earth.

Osho – "From the False to the Truth", Discourse 31

RELATIONSHIPS MIRROR THE MIND

Once it happened: Aesop, the greatest master of storytelling, was going out of Athens. He met a man who was coming from Argos. They talked. The man from Argos asked Aesop, "You are coming from Athens. Please tell me something about the people there: what manner of men they are, what they are like." Aesop asked the man, "First you tell me what type of people are there in Argos." The man said, "Very disgusting, nauseating, violent, quarrelsome." And all these qualities flashed on the face of the man.

Aesop said, "I am sorry. You will find the people of Athens just the same."

Later on, he met another man who was also from Argos, and he also asked the same question: "You are coming from Athens and you have lived your whole life there - what manner of men are they there? What are they like?" And Aesop again asked, "First tell me what manner of men are there in Argos." And the man became aflame with nostalgia, a very loving memory of the people of Argos. His face shone and he said, "Very pleasant, friendly, kind, and good neighbors."

Aesop said, "I am happy to tell you that you will find the people of Athens just the same."

The story is tremendously beautiful. It tells a very basic truth about man: wherever you go, you will always find yourself; wherever you look, you will always encounter yourself. The whole world is nothing but a mirror, and all relationships are mirrors. Again and again you encounter yourself - and again and again you misunderstand. You never realize the point, that it is your own face that you have looked at, that it is your own mood that you have come across.

Why have I started with this story of Aesop? For a very basic reason. You can recognize Jesus only if you have recognized something of the beyond within yourself; otherwise not. You can recognize Buddha only if a part of you has become like Buddha; otherwise you cannot recognize. You cannot recognize that which has not happened to you.

If you are dark, only darkness can be recognized. If you are light, then you become capable of recognizing light. Your eyes can see light because they are part of the sun, because something within you has become of the nature of light. A deep transformation has happened within you. Only then is it possible to recognize a Jesus, a Buddha, a Krishna, a Mohammed. Otherwise you will misunderstand them; you will think that you have understood them. It will be nothing but your own reflection, it will be nothing but your own echoes. It is your own voice that you have heard coming from them; it is your own face that you have looked at in their mirror.

So before you can understand Jesus, you have to understand yourself. Before you can have the vision that Jesus has something, at least something of the same vision has to be allowed within you.

Osho – "Come Follow Yourself", Volume 3, Discourse 3

CREATIVITY AND EDUCATION

All children are creative. All children, wherever they are born, are creative. But we don't allow their creativity, we crush and kill their creativity, we jump upon them. We start teaching them the right way to do things.

Remember, a creative person always goes on trying the wrong ways. If you always follow the right way to do a thing you will never be creative – because the right way means the way discovered by others. And the right way means that of course you will be able to make something, you will become a producer, a manufacturer, you will be a technician, but you will not be a creator.

What is the difference between a producer and a creator? A producer knows the right way of doing a thing, the most economical way of doing a thing; with the least effort he can create more results. He is a producer. A creator fools around. He does not know what is the right way to do a thing so he goes on seeking and searching again and again in different directions. Many times he moves in a wrong direction, but wherever he moves, he learns. He becomes more and more rich. He does something which nobody has ever done before. If he had followed the right way to do things he would not have been able to do it.

Listen to this small story....

A Sunday school teacher asked her students to draw a picture of the Holy Family.

After the pictures were brought to her, she saw that some of the youngsters had drawn the conventional pictures – the Holy Family in the manger, the Holy Family riding on the mule, and the like.

But she called up one little boy to ask him to explain his drawing, which showed an airplane with four heads sticking out of the plane windows.

She said, 'I can understand why you drew three of the heads to show Joseph, Mary, and Jesus. But who is the fourth head?'

'Oh,' answered the boy, 'that's Pontius the Pilot!'

Now this is beautiful. This is what creativity is. He has discovered something.

But only children can do that. You will be afraid to do it. You will look foolish. A creator has to be able to look foolish. A creator has to risk his so-called respectability. That's why you always see that poets, painters, dancers, musicians, are not very respectable people. And when they become respectable, when a Nobel Prize is given to them, they are no longer creative. From that moment creativity disappears.

Only those who are ready to put their prestige, their pride, their respectability, again and again at stake, and can go on into something which nobody thinks is worth going into. Creators are always thought to be mad people. The world recognizes them, but very late. It goes on thinking that something is wrong. Creators are eccentric people.

Somewhere between the age of 7 and 14 a great change happens in a child. You have two minds, two hemispheres. The left hemisphere of the mind is uncreative. It is technically very capable but as far as creativity is concerned it is absolutely impotent. It can only do a thing once it has learned it, and it can do it very efficiently, perfectly; it is mechanical. This left hemisphere is the hemisphere of reasoning, logic, mathematics. It is the hemisphere of calculation, cleverness, of discipline, order.

The right hemisphere is just the opposite of it. It is the hemisphere of chaos, not of order; it is the hemisphere of poetry, not of prose, it is the hemisphere of love, not of logic. It has a great feeling for beauty, it has a great insight into originality – but it is not efficient, it cannot be efficient. The creator cannot be efficient, he has to go on experimenting.

The creator cannot settle anywhere. The creator is a vagabond; he carries his tent on his shoulders. Yes, he can stay for an overnight stay, but by the morning he is gone again – that's why I call him a vagabond. He is never a householder. He cannot settle. Settling means death to him. He is always ready to take a risk. Risk is his love affair.

But this is the right-side hemisphere. The right-side hemisphere is functioning when the child is born; the left-side hemisphere is not functioning. Then we start teaching the child – unknowingly, unscientifically. Down the ages we have learned the trick of how to shift the energy from the right hemisphere to the left hemisphere; how to put a stop to the right hemisphere and how to start the left hemisphere.

That's what our whole schooling is. From kindergarten to university that's what our whole training and so-called education is. It is an effort to destroy the right hemisphere and to help the left hemisphere. Somewhere between the ages of 7 and 14 we succeed and the child is killed, the child is destroyed.

Then the child is wild no more – he becomes a citizen. Then he learns the ways of discipline, language, logic, prose. He starts competing in the school, becomes an egoist, starts learning all the neurotic things that are prevalent in the society, becomes more interested in power, money, starts thinking how to become more educated so that he can become more powerful, how to have more money, how to have a big house, and all that. He shifts.

Then the right hemisphere functions less and less – or functions only when you are in dream, fast asleep. Or sometimes when you have taken a drug.

The great appeal of drugs in the West is only because the West has succeeded in destroying the right hemisphere completely because of compulsory education. The West has become too educated – that means it has gone to the very excess, to one side. It has become extreme. Unless you introduce some ways which can help the right hemisphere to be revived again in the universities and colleges and the schools, drugs are not going to go. There is no possibility of prohibiting drugs by law alone. There is no way to enforce it unless the inner balance is put right again.

The appeal of the drug is that it immediately shifts gear – from the left hemisphere your energy moves to the right hemisphere. That's all the drug can do. Alcohol has been doing it for centuries but now far better drugs are available – LSD, marijuana, psilocybin - and even better drugs will be available in the future.

And the criminal is not the drug-taker, the criminal is the politician and the educationalist. It is they who are guilty. They have forced the human mind into one extreme – into such an extreme that now there is a need to revolt. And the need is so great! Poetry has completely disappeared from people's life, beauty has disappeared, love has disappeared... money, power, pull, they have become the only gods.

How can humanity go on living without love and without poetry and without joy and without celebration? Not for long.

And the new generation all over the world is doing a great service by showing the stupidity of your so-called education. It is not a coincidence that drug-takers almost always become dropouts. They disappear from the universities, colleges. It is not a coincidence – this is part of the same revolt.

And once a man has learned the joys of drugs it becomes very difficult for him to drop them. Drugs can be dropped only if better ways can be found which can release your poetry. Meditation is a better way – less destructive, less harmful, than any kind of chemical. In fact, it is not harmful at all, it is beneficial. Meditation also does the same thing: it shifts your mind from the left hemisphere to the right hemisphere. It releases your inner capacity of creativity.

A great calamity that is going to be in the world through drugs can be avoided by only one thing – that is, meditation. There is no other way. If meditation becomes more and more prevalent and enters peoples' lives more and more, drugs will disappear. And education must start to be not so absolutely against the right hemisphere and its functioning.

If the children are taught that both are their minds, and if they are taught how to use both, and if they are taught when to use which.... There are situations when only the left-side brain is needed, when you need to calculate – in the marketplace, in the everyday business of life. And there are times when you need the right hemisphere.

And remember always, the right hemisphere is the end and the left hemisphere is the means. The left hemisphere has to serve the right hemisphere, the right hemisphere is the master – because you earn money only because you want to enjoy your life and celebrate your life. You want a certain bank balance only so that you can love. You work only so that you can play – play remains the goal. You work only so that you can relax. Relaxation remains the goal, work is not the goal.

This kind of education has to be totally transformed. More joy has to be brought to the schoolroom, more chaos has to be brought to the university – more dance, more song, more poetry, more creativity, more intelligence. Such dependence on memory has to be dropped.

To me a religious person is one who is a creative person. Everybody is born creative but very few people remain creative.

It is for you to come out of the trap. You can. Of course, you will need great courage because when you start undoing what the society has done to you, you will lose respect. You will not be thought to be respectable. You will start becoming bizarre; you will look bizarre to people. You will look like a freak. People will think, 'Something has gone wrong with the poor man.' This is the greatest courage – to go into a life where people start thinking you are bizarre.

Difficulties will be there. But naturally you have to risk. If you want to be creative you will have to risk all. But it is worth it. A little creativity is more worthwhile than this whole world and its kingdom. The joy that comes by creating something new, whatsoever it is – a small song, a small painting, anything…

When you create something new you participate with the creator because God is the creator. When you create, you are in tune with God. When you create really, God creates through you – that's why great joy arises. When you repeat, you repeat alone. God is not there. You are a desert, you are a machine. When you create, God simply enters your heart. You become a hollow bamboo and he starts playing on you and you become a flute. Great song is possible.

Everybody is carrying that song and unless that song is sung, you will never feel fulfilled. My sannyas is nothing but an initiation into creativity, initiation into danger, initiation into a new kind of life.

Osho – "Sufis: People of the Path", Volume 1, Discourse 8

NO EXPERIENCE IS SPIRITUAL

All experience is an error. The error arises because you don't discriminate, you don't know who is who.

Patanjali says all experience is an error – error in your vision. You become identified with the object, and the subject starts thinking as if it is the object. You feel hunger, but you are not hungry – the body is hungry. You feel pain, but you are not in pain – the body is in pain; you are only alert.

Next time something happens to you – and every moment something or other is happening – just watch. Just try to keep hold of this remembrance that "I am the witness," and see how much things change.

Once you can realize you are the witness, many things simply disappear, start disappearing. And one day comes which is the final day, the day of enlightenment, when all experience falls flat. Suddenly you are beyond experience: you are not in the body, you are not in the mind; you are beyond both. Suddenly you start floating like a cloud, above all, beyond all. That state of no-experience is the state of *kaivalya*.

Now one thing more about it. There are people who think that spirituality is also an experience. They don't know. There are people who come to me, and they say, "We would like to have some spiritual experience." They don't know what they are saying. Experience as such is of the world. There is no spiritual experience – there cannot be. To call an experience "spiritual" is to falsify it.

The spiritual is only a realization of pure awareness, *purusha*.

Osho – "Yoga the Alpha and the Omega", Volume 8, Discourse 7

CREATIVE POWER

There is the famous statement of an English philosopher: "Power corrupts, absolute power corrupts absolutely." I do not agree with him. My analysis is totally different. Everybody is full of violence, greed, anger, passion – but has no power; so he remains a saint. To be violent you need to be powerful. To fulfill your greed you need to be powerful. To satisfy your passions you need to be powerful.

So when power happens into your hands, all your sleeping dogs start barking. Power becomes a nourishment to you, an opportunity. It is not that power corrupts, you are corrupted. Power only brings your corruption into the open. You wanted to kill somebody, but you had not the power to kill; but if you have the power, you will kill.

It is not power that corrupts you, corruption you carry within yourself; power simply gives you the opportunity to do whatever you want to do.

Power in the hands of a man like Gautam Buddha will not corrupt; on the contrary, it will help humanity to raise its consciousness. Power in the hands of Genghis Khan destroys people, rapes women, burns people alive. Whole villages are burnt, people are not allowed to get out. It is not power…this man Genghis Khan must have been carrying all these desires in him.

It is almost like when rain comes, different plants start growing; but different plants have different flowers. Whatever is hidden in your seeds, whatever is your potentiality, power gives you a chance – because most human beings are living so unconsciously that when they come to power all their unconscious instincts have a chance to be fulfilled. Then they don't care whether it kills people, whether it poisons people.

You are asking me about the misuse of power. Power is misused because you have desires which are ugly, which are an inheritance from the animals.

In a better world the first things should be…. We waste almost one third of life in educating our children. In that one third of life, time should be given to cleanse their unconscious; so by the time they graduate from their university, and they have some power somewhere – somebody will become a police commissioner, somebody will become a governor, somebody will become a prime minister – if they do not have anything in their unconscious that is poisonous, destructive, then power cannot be misused. Who is going to misuse it? Power is neutral….

These people are not corrupted by power. These people are corrupted; power simply brings their corruption into action. Power in itself is neutral. In a good man's hand it will be a blessing. In an unconscious man's hand it is going to be a curse.

But for thousands of years we have condemned power, without thinking that power has not to be condemned; people have to be cleaned of all the ugly instincts that are hiding within them, because everybody is going to have some kind of power or other.

It does not have to be great power. You may be just sitting in a railway station selling tickets, but that too gives you power. You are standing at the window, and the man does not even look at you. He goes on turning his file – and you can see that he is not concerned with the file, he simply wants to show you your place. Even the peon sitting outside the collector's office behaves as if he is the president of the country. So it is not a question of where you are; wherever you are, you will have some kind of power.

If mankind comes to understand the deep psychological roots and changes man's unconscious so that there are no seeds, power can go on raining but there will be no flowers of corruption. Otherwise power is going to be misused always. And you cannot take power from people's hands; somebody must be a mother, somebody must be a father, somebody must be a teacher.

The only way is, to cleanse people's unconscious with meditation, fill their inner being with light. It is only meditation that gives you a clean heart which cannot be corrupted. Then power can never be misused, then power can be a blessing – it is going to be creative. Then you are going to do something to make life more lovable, more livable; to make existence a little more beautiful. But that great day has not yet arrived, and to make an effort for that great day to arrive, all the power-addicted people are going to be against you.

It has been again and again asked of me, "Why is the whole world against you?" They are all power-addicted people, and I am trying to make man a pool of serenity: peace and silence and love and ecstasy."

Osho – "The Razor's Edge", Discourse 6

MORALITY IS PSEUDO-RELIGION

Tzu-Hsia asked the Master Lieh-Tzu, "What sort of man is Yen-Hui?"

"For kindness he is a better man than I am."

"What about Tzu-Kung?"

"For eloquence he is a better man than I am."

"Tzu-Lu?"

"For courage he is a better man than I am."

"Tzu-Chang?"

"For dignity he is a better man than I am."

Tzu-Hsia rose from his mat and asked, "Then why do these four serve you?"

"Sit down. I will tell you. Yen-Hui can be kind but cannot check the impulse when it will do no good. Tzu-Kung can be eloquent but cannot hold his tongue. Tzu-Lu can be brave but cannot be cautious. Tzu-Chang can be dignified but cannot unbend in company. Even if I could have the virtues of the four men all together, I should be unwilling to exchange them for my own. That is why they serve me without misgiving."

OSHO

The greatest enemy of religion is not materialism but morality. Why? Because morality tries to impose spirituality; it is a conditioning and religion can flower only from the within, it cannot be imposed from the without. Hence morality creates an illusion of false religion. Morality is a pretender, morality is a pseudo-religion. It gives you respectability but it does not give you understanding. It gives you a great ego trip but it cannot give you humility. It makes you feel superior but it doesn't help inner growth. And the man who feels superior cannot grow. He is stuck with the ego.

Morality is a sort of decoration of the ego. Yes, through morality you can cultivate great virtues, but you will never be virtuous. Through morality you can become very talented in certain directions but those talents will remain unconscious. Morality cannot bring awareness because morality is not based on enlightenment. The essential has to come from the inner, the essential has to grow like a tree, the essential is alive. The non-essential is imposed from the outside.

There are two kinds of unity in life. One unity is mechanical – for example, a car. A car has a certain unity, a functional unity, but it is assembled, it comes out of an assembly line. You cannot assemble a tree, you cannot assemble a baby. They also have a sort of unity – but it is totally different. Their unity is organic. A car is mechanical, a baby is organic. A machine is mechanical, a tree is organic. You cannot put a tree together, it grows. It grows out of its own inner center. At the most you can help or hinder – but you cannot put a tree together. You can put a car together, you can assemble a car – hence a car has no soul, no self, no center. It is a superficial unity. And the car cannot grow, it cannot give birth to new baby cars. The tree grows and can give birth to millions of trees. And the tree has a center, it is run by its innermost center. When fall comes and the old leaves drop, who brings the new leaves? From where do they come? They evolve from the innermost core of the tree. If a mechanical part of the car is missing you will have to replace it. The car cannot evolve it itself. It depends on you; it has no soul, it has no inner discipline of its own. If you cut off a branch of a tree another branch is supplied by the center, but if you destroy a machine nothing will come from the center; there is none, there is no center.

Morality is mechanical, religion is organic. This is the first basic thing to be understood. Morality is put together from the outside; religion grows from the innermost core of your being.

Morality comes out of conditioning, religion comes out of meditation.

Morality is enforced by others, religion you have to seek and search for yourself. Morality is a social device, religion is an adventure. Morality is dominated by the politician and the priest, religion is a rebellion. Very rarely is a person religious – and whenever there is a religious person there is a great revolution around him.

Moral people are ordinary people, as ordinary as the immoral – sometimes even more ordinary than the immoral. The immoral may sometimes have courage but the moral has no courage. The immoral may sometimes have intelligence but the moral has no intelligence. The immoral may sometimes be original but the moral is always repetitive.

Morality is the greatest enemy of religion because it is a pseudo-coin. It pretends and it can deceive people. It has deceived down the ages; millions and millions of people are and have been deceived by morality. And they think that when they have morality they have religion.

The second thing: morality is always relative. You can have more intelligence than somebody else, or somebody else can have more virtue than you. Somebody can be more courageous than you or more cowardly than you. Somebody can be more sharing, more loving, or you can be more loving than somebody else. Morality is comparative.

Nobody can be more religious than you or less religious than you – religion is non-comparative. When religion is there it is simply there.

Can you say Buddha was more religious than Jesus? Can you say Mahavira was more religious than Mohammed? Can you say Lao Tzu was more religious than Krishna? It would be absurd, the very statement would be absurd – because religion is not quantity, it is quality of being. You cannot have more or less. There are no degrees.

You can be more honest than somebody else, you can be more of a thief than somebody else – there are possibilities – but how can you be more religious or less religious than somebody else? Religion means awakening. Religion means you have come home. How can you be less at home or more at home than somebody else?

When a man has become aware, his awareness is always total and complete, utterly complete. It does not come in parts, it comes as a whole – hence it is holy. Religion comes as a whole, morality comes in all shapes and sizes. You can have a family size or a medium size morality, like toothpaste. Morality comes in all shapes and sizes, religion is just complete. Either it is or it is not.

Sometimes people come to me and they ask, "Who is more enlightened – Buddha or Mahavira?" The question is absurd. Who is more enlightened? Enlightenment means that you have gone beyond relativity; more and less cannot exist now. Who is more enlightened? Enlightenment means that you have disappeared – and so have all relative concepts. You are simply there, a pure 'isness'. Whenever anybody becomes a pure isness, a pure existence, a primordial innocence, there is no comparison. To go beyond comparison is to become enlightened. So you cannot ask the question, "Who is more enlightened?" The very question is meaningless. Religion either is or is not. This is the second thing to be remembered .

The third thing: when religion comes, you are naturally moral but the vice versa is not the case – you may be moral but you may not be religious. When you are religious you are naturally moral; morality comes like a shadow.

A disciple came to Lieh Tzu and asked Lieh Tzu, "What should I do, Master, to become enlightened?" And Lieh Tzu said, "You stand in the sun, walk, and watch your shadow."

The man went out, stood in the sun, walked and watched his shadow, came back, bowed down, thanked the Master, and said, "You have shown me the way."

The other disciples were very much puzzled. What had transpired between the Master and this new man? They asked Lieh Tzu and he laughed. He said, "It is so simple. I told him to go into the sun and walk and watch his shadow. And he understood the point. If the body walks, the shadow follows; the shadow cannot walk on its own. And even if you can arrange for the shadow to walk on its own, the body will not follow, there is no necessity."

Morality is like the shadow, religion is the real figure. When religion is there, morality comes on its own – it has to come, there is no other possibility. But if morality is there, there is no necessity for religion to be there. You can become a moral person without becoming religious at all. You can have good qualities. You can be honest, sincere, true, non-violent, but that doesn't make you religious. If you are religious all moral qualities simply follow you.

When you are moral you have to manage those good qualities continuously; they have to be maintained, otherwise they will disappear. A moral man has to manage his honesty continuously because every moment there is a fear that he may function dishonestly. The dishonesty has not disappeared, it has been repressed. It is there, it is waiting in the basement of his being for its opportunity, and once the opportunity is there it will assert itself with vengeance. It is there and the moral person knows it well. He may be trying to be loving but he knows that the hatred is there boiling within him. He may be smiling but he knows that his eyes are full of tears. He may not be showing his anger but he knows that his heart is burning, and he wants to kill. He may be praying but really he wants to curse. He knows it. There is no way not to know.

You can deceive others but how can you deceive yourself? Even if you try to deceive yourself, reality will assert itself again and again and you will have to encounter it again and again. And you know that although you can pretend that you are a very good man, deep down you know how bad you are. That hangs like a stone around your neck, like a rock and keeps you pulled down.

The moral person is dual: he is one thing on the outside and just the contrary on the inside. There is a continuous struggle in his being. He is split. The moral person is a schizophrenic. The whole earth has become schizophrenic because of moral teachings. Teach a person to be moral and sooner or later you will send him to the psychiatrist's couch. You have created madness in him.

The person is feeling angry and you say, "Don't be angry, anger is bad" – because Moses says so, or Mohammed says so, or Mahavira says so. "Anger is bad. Don't be angry." Anger is coming up naturally but you teach against it – because great is the stake. If he becomes angry he will lose his respect. He can be respected only if he is not angry, so he has to pretend in order to get respectability.

Look at people. They have lost their original faces. They are carrying masks, they are hiding behind masks. You can never be certain who is hiding behind the masks. You love a person but by and by you will find it is not the same person you fell in love with.

Have you not observed it again and again? When you fall in love with a person, after a few months – or even after a few days if you are a great observer - you will find that the person is something else. The woman is not the same woman, the man is not the same man that you fell in love with. You fell in love with the mask and now, by and by, the reality becomes clear. When you live with a person he cannot wear the mask for twenty-four hours. It is heavy and he wants to rest. And sometimes he is on a holiday; even saints have their holidays.

When you see a leader delivering a lecture to the masses it is a different face. When you see a priest in the temple worshipping it is a different face. When you fall in love with a woman it is a different face. She is trying to be as good as possible, but that is not the reality, that is a managed reality. She cannot manage it forever – that's why wives are not very beautiful, that's why husbands are ugly. You know them. You have seen them on their holidays.

Morality creates a division – the inner, the real, becomes hidden and the outer, the false, becomes manifested. This is one of the greatest calamities that has happened to humanity.

Religion makes you one. It spreads the inner to the outer. Religion makes you healthy – then you taste the same always and you are never on a holiday because you are always on a holiday. It is your natural quality.

The fourth thing: a tree is alive, a machine only exists, it is not alive. A man of morality only exists, he is not really alive. You will not find vitality, you will not find radiance, you will not find a surging energy, you will not find a flood of life coming from him. He has to curb his being and cut his energies continuously. He has to live at the minimum, he is never aflame. He is always afraid. If he becomes too much alive then that which is repressed will start asserting itself. So he is always afraid. He keeps himself pulled down. He goes on holding onto himself. He never allows himself a total let-go because a total let-go will naturally mean that that which is repressed will suddenly erupt on the surface. It will be like a volcano erupting. So he has to keep himself at the minimum, he has to allow only minimum energy – only then can he control himself. With the maximum energy flowing he will be out of control; he will be off-balance.

A man of morality just appears to be living; it is an appearance. Only a man of religion is alive. A man of religion lives at the optimum and the man of morality lives at the minimum. Naturally, at the minimum you live like an impotent person. You cannot be angry so you cannot love either because there is always the fear that if you love too much sometimes anger may come. When one energy is allowed total expression, other energies also get freedom. When you open your door for one thing, other things will also escape. You cannot open your door, you have to be always on guard. Just think of the misery of a man who is always on guard, who cannot relax. A man who is always on guard is a tense man.

A moral man is never happy. He may not be sad at the most, but he is never happy, he is never ecstatic. For millions of years man has existed on the earth but a single exception has never been seen. Never has a moral man been found who is ecstatic. He cannot dance, he cannot sing, he cannot rejoice. Joy is freedom, and he does not know what freedom is. Ecstasy is going beyond oneself, and that is possible only when you move through your optimum, when you are aflame with a great passion to live, when you love totally, when you are flooded with God. Only then is ecstasy possible.

Ecstasy is not yours; ecstasy is God dancing in you. You cannot allow God to dance in you because you cannot allow nature to dance in you. You have not even been natural, how can you be spiritual?

Remember, spirituality is a higher stage of being natural; spirituality is the ultimate flowering of being spontaneous.

A moral person is never spontaneous. A moral person lives through the past. He has a character and he has to follow the character. He has a blueprint, he has a map, and he always looks at the map and functions through it. He never functions in the present, he is a dead man, he carries his character around with him. His response is never a real response, it is only a reaction. A man of religion is responsive not reactive.

And because he has a character, a man of morality is predictable. You can depend on him, you know that he will be honest tomorrow because he has been always honest. He will be honest even in circumstances where honesty is going to harm the other person. Where honesty is going to be destructive, even then he is going to be honest – you can depend on that. He has no freedom, he has no eyes to look into things, he does not respond to reality. He responds to principles. When you respond to principles you are simply reacting, you have a program in your mind, you are like a computer. You go according to the program – right or wrong is not the question.

And the circumstances of life change every moment – but your principles are rigid, your principles remain the same. Naturally a man of morality never fits anywhere; he is a misfit. It is very difficult to live with a moral man because he is always a misfit. He does not look at the reality, at what reality is. He simply lives through his principles; principles are more important than the reality.

A religious man has no principles. Let it sink deep into your heart. A religious man has no principles whatsoever, he has only an awareness.

He looks into reality and whatsoever is required he responds accordingly. His response is spontaneous, not dominated by the past – hence a religious person is not predictable. You don't know what he will do. Not even he can say what he will do because it will depend on the circumstances. If there is a slight difference in the circumstances the response will be different.

A religious man has no character – it will be difficult for you to get that. A religious man has no character, because character comes from the past.

A religious man has consciousness instead.

Osho – "Tao the Pathless Path", Volume 2, Discourse 7

"THE ATTRACTION FOR DRUGS IS SPIRITUAL"

Drugs are as old as humanity itself, and they certainly fulfill something of immense value. I am against drugs, but my being against drugs is for the same reason as for thousands of years people have been addicted to the drugs.

It may look very strange. The drugs are capable to give you a hallucinatory experience beyond the mundane world. That is the experience that is being searched through meditation.

Meditation brings you to the real experience, and drug gives you just a hallucination, a dream-like experience but very similar. To meditate is difficult. The drug is cheap, but the attraction for drugs is spiritual.

Man is not satisfied with his mundane existence. He wants to know something more. He wants to be something more. Just the ordinary life seems so flat, so meaningless, that if this is all then suicide seems to be the only way out of it. It gives no ecstasy, no joy. On the contrary, it goes on piling you up with more and more misery, anxiety, disease, old age and, finally, death.

From the cradle to the grave, the ordinary life is just a drag. People go on living it because they are cowards. Otherwise, they will commit suicide. They don't have the courage enough to commit suicide. But this is not something one can rejoice in. You can drag on but you cannot call it living. There is no dance in it, no color in it. It is just a vast desert spreading as far as you can see, with no oasis anywhere.

Drugs have attracted man since the very beginning, and they have at least given him a temporary relief. Only few people tried meditation. And my own understanding is, these people also tried meditation because drugs at a point become useless. You become immune: in the beginning they give you tremendous experiences, but soon they become almost part of your body chemistry. Then if you don't take them you are in trouble. Your whole chemistry wants them. If you take them, you gain nothing. You go on increasing the doses.

For 90,000 years Hindus have accepted drugs almost as part of their religious ceremonies. It was only under British regime that drugs created trouble, but because they were part of a religious ritual - which is the ancient most religion in the world - even the British government was afraid to interfere with it. It continued. Even in my childhood all drugs were available in the market. There was no question of any illegality. And every school of Hindu religion was using drugs, but they were using it in a very scientific way.

They will give the drug in a certain quantity, create a certain experience in the man, and then when he will come out of it, will tell him that, "This was only an illusion. It was simply because of the drug, because of the chemistry, your mind experienced. Would you like to experience it in its reality? If the illusion is so beautiful, you can think how much more the reality would be. And the experience created by the drug lasts for a few hours, and again you are back to the same old rotten world. But if the experience is real, it is yours forever. You never lose it. It is not something that has happened to you, it is something that was already in you; you have discovered it."

So I don't see that it was wrong to use drugs in this way. In fact, this should be the approach around the world for the modern man. And now we have more advanced drugs, synthetically made, and we are capable to purify them more. We can make drugs which have no bad effects at all. We can make drugs which are not addictive. And we can have in every hospital, in every university, a certain department which teaches people how to move from drug to meditation.

Just to talk about meditation remains simply verbal. There is no way through the words to give you any experience. But drugs are immensely useful. The words can explain to you what meditation is, the drug can give you an hallucinatory experience of it. And then you can be initiated into a method. And now you will not be moving in darkness. Now you know that if an ordinary drug can do so much, then there must be some way to find an authentic transformation, to experience it without any dependence on anything.

So the drug simply opens up a door and helps you to understand that man's life and his experience need not be confined to the ordinary mundane world - he can fly high towards the stars - that he is capable of knowing things which are not ordinarily available.

Under proper guidance - medical, meditational - drugs can be of immense help.

I said I am against drugs because if they become addictive then they will be the most destructive for your journey towards the self. Then you become enchanted into hallucinations. And because it is cheap - no effort has to be done, just you have to go on taking bigger and bigger doses.

For thousands of years people have been using drugs. Moralists, religious people, governments have been trying prohibition absolutely unsuccessfully. And I don't see that they can ever succeed. The only way to succeed is what I am suggesting. Rather than prohibiting drugs, let the scientists find out better drugs which give deeper and more psychedelic, more colorful, more ecstatic experiences and without any side effects, and without any addiction. And these should be available in the universities, in the colleges, in the hospitals - wherever some kind of guidance is possible, that the person is not prohibited, is allowed total freedom to use anything that he wants. And we use his experience to help him grow towards some authentic process so that he can start experiencing something far greater than any drug can give.

And only then he can compare that...'The first one was just a dream, and this is a reality. And the first one was just cheating myself through chemistry, and the first one was not helping me in my spiritual growth; it was in fact preventing the growth, keeping me addicted and retarded'. The second one goes on growing, and now he starts gathering courage to explore more. He was never aware that these experiences are possible, that these experiences are not just fiction.

So drug can be used in a very beneficial way, to make the person realize that this is hallucination, and the hallucination is so satisfying, would not you like to try the real?

We have the real drug also. I call it meditation. And it takes you to the uttermost blissful experience possible. Then only drugs become useless for you.

If we want humanity to get free of drugs, then meditation is the way. But before we can get free of them, they are very important and can be used to introduce people to meditation.

So this paranoia about drugs is not helpful to humanity. You can make drugs illegal, it makes no change. In fact, they become more attractive, more exciting. Particularly to the youth they become a challenge.

I am amazed sometimes: Is man going ever to learn even the ABC of human psychology? The same stupidity goes on which God did with Adam and Eve - prohibition: "Don't eat the fruit of this tree." But that becomes an invitation.

There are many drugs which have less bad after-effects, particularly synthetic drugs taken in a right atmosphere, in a right mood; for example, LSD. It simply enhances your mood, it does not do anything to you. If you are in a despair the LSD experience will become a nightmare. But if you are feeling a wellbeing, that is the time to take LSD. Then it can give you a really positive ecstatic experience, although it will be hallucinatory.

But if you don't know the real, it looks almost the real. Even a man like Aldous Huxley, one of the most intelligent men of this generation, thought that through LSD he has achieved the same experience as Gautam Buddha, Kabir, Ramakrishna. If you don't know the real, naturally you cannot call it hallucinatory. It is so real. Huxley had no experience of meditation. He has really no right to say such a thing. You can say such a thing only when you have experienced both, that it is the same experience as Kabir.

Kabir never used any drug. His experience was purely of meditation. On what grounds Huxley can say it is the same experience? He does not know the experience of Kabir. I can understand that he has been through a tremendously beautiful experience, but that experience disappears as the effect of the LSD goes out of the system. But Kabir's experience remains 24 hours, day in, day out, his whole life. Once it happens, it is always there. This is a simple criterion.

But Huxley was so much fascinated by the experience, and he corrupted almost a whole generation. They thought that if a man like Huxley says that LSD can give you *samadhi*, then what is the need of going into so much trouble for meditation with no guarantee whether you will be able to succeed or not?

I am against drugs because they can become addictive and they can prevent your spiritual growth. You can start thinking that you have achieved what you were seeking, and your hands are empty. You are just dreaming. But, on the other hand, I am a very scientific mind. On the other hand, I would like drugs to be used, not to be prohibited - but used under proper guidance as a steppingstone towards meditation.

If something even hallucinatory happens to a person, meditation becomes easier. Something in him becomes certain. Something in him is now perfectly guaranteed that meditation is not just fiction. And the hallucinatory experience also opens some doors. The guidance can be of very much importance.

All the efforts of scientists and the government should be to understand that if a certain thing has been so attractive for the whole history of man, and no government has ever been successful to prohibit it, then there must be certain need that it fulfills. And unless that need is fulfilled in some other way, drugs are going to remain in the world. And they are destructive, and the more governments are against them, more destructive they are, because nobody can make any refinements on them, nobody can make any experiments on them, nobody is even allowed to say what I am saying. But I can say it because I am against drugs. But that does not mean they cannot be used. They can be used as a means, they are not the end.

If a child finds his father is meditating, his mother is meditating, everybody is meditating, he will start being curious about it. He also wants to meditate. And that is the age when meditation is very simple because he is not yet corrupted by the society. Yet he is innocent. And if everybody around him is doing something and enjoying in doing it, he cannot remain behind. He will sit with them with closed eyes. First they may laugh at him, that it is not possible for children. But they do not understand. It is more possible for children than for the so-called grownups. Just the atmosphere of meditation in schools, in colleges, in universities - wherever the person goes he finds that atmosphere which nourishes his own meditativeness.

I would love to see that no drugs are needed in the world. But not through prohibition, but through creating something better, something real.

Osho – "The Last Testament", Volume 4, Chapter 6

LOVE, LIGHT AND LIFE ARE ILLOGICAL

Love, life, light. These three l's are the most mysterious. And the mystery is this – that you cannot understand them logically. If you are illogical you can penetrate them; if you are simply logical you cannot understand, because the whole phenomenon depends on a paradox.

When you love someone, two are needed: I and thou. Without two how can love be possible? If you are alone how can you relate, how can you love? If you are alone there can be no love. Love is possible only when there are two; this is the base.

But if they remain two, love is again impossible. If they continue to be two then again love is impossible. Two are needed for love to exist, and then there is a second need: that the two must merge and become one. This is the paradox.

'I' and 'thou' is a basic requirement for love to exist but this is only the base. The temple can come only when these two merge into one. And the mystery is that somehow you remain two and somehow you become one. This is illogical. Two lovers are two and still one. They have found a bridge somewhere where 'I' disappears, 'thou' disappears; where a unity is formed, a harmony comes into being.

Two are needed to create that harmony, but two are needed to dissolve into it.

It is just like this: a river flows, two banks are needed. A river cannot flow with only one bank, it is impossible; the river cannot exist. Two banks are needed for the river to flow. But if you look a little deeper those two banks are joined together just below the river. If they are not joined then also the river cannot exist, it will simply drop into the abyss. Two banks, apparently two on the surface, are one deep down.

Love exists like a river between two persons who on the surface remain two, but deep down have become one. That's why I say it is paradoxical. Two are needed just to be dissolved into one.

So love is a deep alchemy and very delicate. If you really become one, love will disappear, the river cannot flow. If you really remain two, love will disappear, because there can be no river in an abyss if the two banks are really separate.

So lovers create a game in which on the surface they remain two and deep down they become one. Sometimes they fight also, sometimes they are angry also, sometimes in every way they separate – but this is only on the surface. Their separation is just to get married again, their fight is just to create love again. They go a little away from each other just to come and meet again, and the meeting after the separation is beautiful.

They fight to love again. They are intimate enemies. Their enmity is a play, they enjoy it. If there is really love you can enjoy the fight.

In India we have pictured Shiva as *Ardhanarishwar* – half-man, half-woman. That is the only symbol of its type all over the world. Shiva – half is man, half is woman; half Shiva and half Parvati, his consort. Half the body is of man and half of woman: *Ardhanarishwar*, half-man, half-woman. That is the symbol.

Lovers join together but on the surface they remain two. Shiva is one, the body is two – half comes from Parvati, half he contributes. The body is two, on the surface the banks are two; in the depth the souls have mingled and become one.

Or look at it in this way: the room is dark, you bring two lamps into it, two candles into it. Those two candles remain two, but their light has mingled and become one. You cannot separate the light; you cannot say, "This light belongs to this candle and that light belongs to that candle." Light has mingled and become one.

The spirit is like light, the body is the candle. Two lovers are only two bodies, but not two souls. This is very difficult to achieve. That's why love is one of the most difficult things to achieve, and if even for moments you can achieve, it is worth it. If even only for moments in your whole life, if even for moments you can achieve this oneness with someone, this oneness will become the door for the divine.

Love achieved becomes the door for the divine, because then you can feel how this universe exists in the many and remains one.

But this can come only through experience – if you love a person and you feel that you are two and still one. And this should not be just a thought but an experience. You can think, but thinking is of no use. This must be an experience: how the bodies have remained two and the inner beings have merged, melted into each other – the light has become one.

Once experienced, then the whole philosophy of the Upanishads becomes exactly clear, absolutely clear. The many are just the surface; behind each individual is hidden the non-individual, behind each part is hidden the Whole.

And if two can exist as two on the surface, why not many? If two can remain two and still one, why can't many remain many and still one? One in the many is the message of the Upanishads, and this will remain only theoretical if you have never been in love.

But people go on confusing love with sex. Sex may be part of love, but sex is not love. Sex is just a physical, biological attraction, and in sex you remain two. In sex you are not concerned with the other, you are concerned with yourself. You are simply exploiting the other, you are simply using the other for some biological satisfaction of your own, and the other is using you.

That's why sexual partners never feel any deep intimacy. They are using the other. The other is not a person, the other is not a 'thou'; the other is just an 'it', a thing you can use, and the other is using you. Deep down it is mutual masturbation and nothing else. The other is used as a device. It is not love, because you don't care for the other.

Love is totally different. It is not using the other, it is caring for the other, it is just being happy in the other. It is not your happiness that you derive from the other; if the other is happy you are happy, and the other's happiness becomes your happiness. If the other is healthy you feel healthy. If the other is dancing you feel a dance inside. If the other is smiling the smile penetrates you and becomes your smile.

Love is the happiness of the other; sex is happiness of your own, the other has to be used. In love the other's happiness has become even more significant than your own. Lovers are each other's servants, sex partners are each other's exploiters.

Sex can exist in the milieu of love, but then it has a different quality; it is not sexual at all. Then it is one of the many ways of merging into each other. One of the many: not the only, not the sole, not the supreme. Many are the ways to merge into each other. Two lovers can sit silently with each other, and the silence can become the merger. Really only lovers can sit silently.

If two can exist as one, then many can exist as one. Love becomes the door for meditation, prayer. That is the meaning when Jesus goes on insisting that love is God – because love becomes the door, the opening towards the divine.

So to conclude: love is a relationship and yet not a relationship. Love exists between two, that's why you can call it a relationship. And still, if love exists at all it is not a relationship, because the two must disappear and become one.

Osho – "Vedanta, Seven Steps to Sammadhi", Discourse 11

SOCIETY, A FOUNDATION FOR ENLIGHTENMENT

Every child is born natural, loose; then the society comes in, has to come in for certain reasons. Nothing is wrong in it, because if the child is left to himself or herself the child will never grow, and the child will never be able to become religious, he will become just like an animal.

The society has to come in; the society has to be passed through – it is needed. The only thing to remember is: it is just a passage to pass through; one should not make one's house in it. The only thing to remember is: the society has to be followed and then transcended; the rules have to be learned and then unlearned.

The rules will come in your life because there are others, you are not alone. When the child is in the mother's womb he is absolutely alone, no rules are needed. Rules come only when the other comes into relationship; the rules come with relationship – because you are not alone you have to think of others and consider others.

In the mother's womb the child is alone; no rules, no morality, no discipline is needed, no order; but the moment he is born, even the first breath he takes is social. If the child is not crying, the doctors will force him to cry immediately, because if he doesn't cry for a few minutes then he will be dead. He has to cry because the cry opens the passage through which he will be able to breathe, it clears the throat. He has to be forced to cry.

Even the first breath is social; others are there and the molding has started. Nothing is wrong in it. It has to be done, but it has to be done in such a way that the child never loses his awareness, does not become identified with the cultured pattern, remains deep inside still free, knows that rules have to be followed but rules are not life, and knows this also and has to be taught. And that's what a good society will do: "These rules are good because there are others; but these rules are not absolute, and you are not expected to remain confined to them; one day you must transcend them."

A society is good if it teaches its members civilization *and* transcendence; then the society is religious. If it never teaches transcendence then that society is simply secular and political; it has no religion in it.

You have to listen to others up to an extent, and then you have to start listening to yourself. You must come back to the original state in the end. Before you die you must become an innocent child again – loose, natural; because in death again you are entering the dimension of being alone. Just as you were in the womb, in death again you will enter in the realm of being alone. No society exists there.

The whole of your life you have to find a few spaces in your life, a few moments like oases in deserts, where you simply close your eyes and go beyond society, move into yourself, in your own womb.

This is what meditation is: the society is there; you simply close your eyes and forget the society and become alone. No rules exist there, no character is needed, no morality, no words, no language. You can be loose and natural inside.

Grow into that loose-and-naturalness. Even if there is a need for outer discipline, inside you remain wild. If one can remain wild inside and still practicing things which are needed in the society, then soon one can come to a point where one simply transcends.

Osho – "Tantra the Supreme Understanding", Discourse 10

FANATICISM vs EXISTENTIAL OPENNESS

Fanaticism came out of the Judaic mind; it was never part of the Hindu mind or the Chinese mind or the Greek mind. It came out of the Jews. And it spread to Christians and Mohammedans because both are offshoots of Judaism.

The idea that "We are the chosen people of God" is dangerous. It creates fanaticism. The idea that "We have the truth, and nobody else" is dangerous. That "There is only one God and no other Gods" is dangerous - because that one God is going to be *my* God. And then what will happen to *your* God?

Then you are wrong, then you are a sinner. Then you have to be persuaded, converted. If you allow easily, okay; otherwise you have to be forced and coerced so that you can drop the wrong God.

There are many paths by which to reach the peak. The mountain has many paths, but they all reach the same peak. You can go from the south or from the north or from the east or from the west. You can follow a very rocky track, or you can follow a very different track. There are many alternatives.

Wherever you are, watch the people, respect their prayer, respect their God, respect their vision. It may be only one aspect, but it is an aspect of God himself. It may be only one face - God has many faces - but all the manifestations are his. In one way he descends in Krishna, in another he descends in Christ, in still another he descends into Moses. All prophets are his, all messengers are his.

And whatsoever you believe, don't just believe it - consecrate it, make it holy by living. Let it not remain just an intellectual belief in the head: it has to become existential. Then it is consecrated, then you have made it holy and sacred.

Osho – "Philosophia Perennis", Discourse 1

ESSENTIAL QUALITIES CAN BE SHARED

I don't give you any tradition.

I don't give you any scripture.

I don't give you any discipline.

Those are all non-essentials. I simply concentrate my whole work on making you more conscious. Consciousness is the key to transform the whole of humanity.

And yes, Gurdjieff is right: if even 200 people are aflame, enlightened, the whole world will become enlightened, because these two hundred torches can give fire to millions of people. Those people are also carrying torches, but without any fire. They have everything, just the fire is missing. And when fire passes from one torch to another, the first torch is not losing anything at all.

The enlightened consciousness is an infinite reservoir: it can give to you and yet it remains the same. Its quantity does not decrease, because it is not a question of quantity at all; it is a question of quality.

Qualities can be shared without losing anything. You can love as many people as you want – that does not mean one day you will go bankrupt, and you will have to declare, "Now I have no love." You cannot go bankrupt as far as love is concerned.

Yes, you can go bankrupt as far as money is concerned. Money is a quantity; love is a quality. What to say of enlightened consciousness? It is the highest quality possible; there is nothing higher than that.

Osho – "From the False to the Truth", Discourse 16

EXISTENCE IS PURPOSELESS

It is very difficult, particularly for the Western mind, to understand that life is purposeless. And it is beautiful that it is purposeless. If it is purposeful then the whole thing becomes absurd – then who will decide the purpose? Then some God has to be conceived who decides the purpose, and then human beings become just puppets; then no freedom is possible. And if there is some purpose then life becomes businesslike, it cannot be ecstatic. Whenever something is achieved the achieving mind will feel frustrated, because now new goals have to be invented.

This is happening in America. Many of the goals of the past century have been achieved, so America is in a deep frustration. All the goals of the founding fathers who created America and the American constitution are almost achieved. In America the society has become affluent for the first time in the whole history of mankind. Almost everybody is rich. The poor man in America is a rich man here in India.

The goals have almost been achieved – now what to do? Society has become affluent: food is there, shelter is there, everybody has got a car, radio, refrigerator, TV – now what to do? A deep frustration is felt, some other goals are needed. And there seem to be no goals. Instead of one car you can have two cars – a two-car garage has become the goal – or you can have two houses, but that will be achieved within ten years. Whatsoever the goal it can be achieved. Then the achieving mind feels frustrated. What to do now? It again needs a goal, and you have to invent a goal.

So the whole of American business now depends on inventing goals. Give people goals – that's what advertisements and the whole business of advertising is doing. Create goals, seduce people: 'Now this is the goal! You must have this, otherwise life is purposeless!' They start running, because they have an achieving mind. But where does it lead? It leads into more and more neurosis.

Only a non-achieving mind can be at peace. But a non-achieving mind is possible only with the background of a cosmic purposelessness. If the whole existence is purposeless then there is no need for you to be purposeful. Then you can play, you can sing and dance, you can enjoy, you can love and live, and there is no need to create any goal. Here and now, this very moment, the ultimate is present. If you are available the ultimate can enter you. But you are not available here, your mind is somewhere in the future, in some goal.

Life has got no purpose and this is the beauty of it. If there was some purpose life would have been mean – just futile. It is not a business, it is a play. In India we have been calling it *leela*. *Leela* means a cosmic play, as if God is playing. Energy overflowing, not for some purpose, just enjoying itself; just a small child playing – for what purpose? Running after butterflies, collecting colored stones on the beach, dancing under the sun, running under the trees, collecting flowers – for what purpose? Ask a child. He will look at you as if you are a fool. There is no need for purpose.

Your mind has been corrupted. Universities, colleges, education, society, have corrupted you. They have made it a conditioning deep down within you that unless something has a purpose it is useless – so everything must have a purpose.

A child playing has no purpose. At the most, if the child could explain he would say, "Because I feel good. Running, I feel more alive. Collecting flowers, I enjoy, it is ecstatic." But there is no purpose. The very act in itself is beautiful, ecstatic. To be alive is enough, there is no need for any purpose. Why ask for anything else? Can't you be satisfied just by being alive? It is such a phenomenon.

Just think of yourself being a stone. You could have been, because many are still stones. You must have been somewhere in the past, sometime, a stone. Think of yourself being a tree. You must have been somewhere a tree, a bird, an animal, an insect. And then think of yourself being a man – conscious, alert, the peak, the climax of all possibilities. And you are not content with it. You need a purpose, otherwise life is useless.

Your mind has been corrupted by economists, mathematicians, theologians. They have corrupted your mind, because they all talk about purpose. They say, "Do something if something is achieved through it. Don't do anything which leads nowhere."

But I tell you that the more you can enjoy things which are useless, the happier you will be. The more you can enjoy things which are purposeless, the more innocent and blissful you will be. When you don't need any purpose you simply celebrate your being. You feel gratitude just that you are, just that you breathe. It is such a blessing that you can breathe, that you are alert, conscious, alive, aflame. Is it not enough? Do you need something to achieve so that you can feel good, so that you can feel valued, so that you can feel life is justified? What more can you achieve than what you are? What more can be added to your life? What more can you add to it?

Nothing can be added, and the effort will destroy you – the effort to add something. But for many centuries all over the world they have been teaching every child to be purposive. "Don't waste your time! Don't waste your life!" And what do they mean? They mean, "Transform your life into a bank balance. When you die you must die rich. That is the purpose."

Here in the East – particularly the mystics we are talking about, the Upanishads – they say, "Live richly." In the West they say, "Die a rich man." And these are totally different things. If you want to live richly you have to live here and now, not a single moment is to be lost. If you want to achieve something, you will die a rich man – but you will live a poor man, your life will be poor.

Look at rich people: their life is absolutely poor, because they are wasting it transforming it into bank balances, changing their life into money, into big houses, big cars. Their whole effort is that life has to be changed for some things. When they die you can count their things.

Buddha became a beggar. He was born a king, he became a beggar. Why? Just to live richly...because he came to understand that there are two ways to live: one is to die richly, the other is to live richly. And any man who has any understanding will choose to live richly, because dying a rich man doesn't mean anything; you simply wasted yourself for nothing.

But this is possible only if you can conceive that the whole existence is purposeless. It is a cosmic play, a continuous beautiful game, a beautiful hide-and-seek not leading anywhere. Nowhere is the goal. If this is the background, then you need not be worried about individual purposes, evolution, progress.

This word progress is the basic disease of the modern age. What is the need? All that can be enjoyed is available, all that you need to be happy is here and now. But you create conditions and you say that unless these conditions are fulfilled you cannot be happy.

You say, "These conditions must be fulfilled first: this type of house, this type of clothes, this type of car, this type of wife, this type of husband. All these conditions have to be fulfilled first, then I can be happy." As if by being happy you are going to oblige the whole universe.

And who is going to fulfill your conditions? Who is worried? But you will try for those conditions, and the effort is going to be so long that they can never be fulfilled really, because whenever something is fulfilled, by the time it is fulfilled the goal has shifted.

A meditator needs a non-achieving mind, but a non-achieving mind is possible only if you can be content with purposelessness. Just try to understand the whole cosmic play and be a part in it. Don't be serious, because a play can never be serious. And even if the play needs you to be serious, be playfully serious, don't be really serious. Then this very moment becomes rich. Then this very moment you can move into the ultimate.

The ultimate is not in the future, it is the present, hidden here and now. So don't ask about purpose – there is none, and I say it is beautiful that there is none. If there was purpose then your God would be just a managing director or a big businessman, an industrialist, or something like that.

Jesus says.... Somebody asked him, "Who will be able to enter into the kingdom of your God?" Jesus said, "Those who are like small children." This is the secret.

What is the meaning of being a small child? The meaning is that the child is never businesslike, he is always playful.

Osho – "Vedanta, Seven Steps to Samadhi", Discourse 11

BEING A DISCIPLE, A SANNYASIN

To me, sannyas is not something very serious. Life itself is not very serious, and one who is serious is always dead. Life is just an overflowing energy without any purpose, and to me sannyas is to lead life purposelessly. Live life as a play and not as work. The so-called serious mind, which is diseased, will in fact convert play into work. The sannyasins are to do the very opposite - to convert work into play. If you can take this whole life just as a dream, a dream act, then you are a sannyasin.

One who considers life as a dream, a dream-drama, has renounced. Renunciation is not leaving the world, but changing the attitude. An attitude of changing the world is something serious. That is why I can initiate anyone into sannyas. To me, initiation itself is a play. I will not ask for any qualification, whether you are qualified or not, because qualifications are asked where something serious is done. So everyone, by just being in existence, is qualified enough to be at play. He can play, and even if he is unqualified, it makes no difference, because the whole thing is just a play. That is why I will not ask for any qualifications.

And my sannyas does not involve any obligation either - the moment you are a sannyasin, you are totally free. It means now you have taken a decision, and this is the last decision. Now you have not to take any decision anymore. You have taken the last decision now - to live in indecision, to live in freedom.

One who lives decidedly can never be free. He is always bound by the past, because the decision was taken in the past. You can never take any decision for the future, because the future is unknown and whatever decision is taken is bound up with the past. The moment you are initiated into sannyas, you are initiated into an uncharted, unplanned future. Now you are not tethered by the past. You will be free to live. That means to act, to play, and to be whatever happens to you. This is insecurity.

To renounce a name, to renounce a property, is not really insecurity, it is very superficial insecurity. And the mind remains the same, the mind that was thinking about the property as security. Even property is no security at all: you will die with all your property. Even a home is not security at all: you will die in it. So the false notion that property, home, friends and family are securities is still prevailing in the mind which thinks, "I have renounced; now I am insecure."

Only that mind, only that person lives in insecurity who lives untethered to the past. Insecurity means untethered to the past; and it has so many meanings, because all that you know comes from the past. Even your mind is of the past.

Sannyas means throwing all claims of being somebody. Now you are going into no-identity, nobody-ness. So this is the last decision of your mind, with which the past is closed. The identity is broken, the continuity is not there. You are new; you are reborn.

Everyone who is alive is qualified to live in insecurity. If one is really to live, one has to live in insecurity. Every arrangement of security is renounced living. The more you are secure, the less you are living. The more you are dead, the more secure, and *vice versa* also.

For example, a dead man cannot die again, he is death-proof. A dead man cannot be ill, so he is disease-proof. A dead man is so secure that those who go on living may seem foolish to him - they live in insecurity.

If you are alive at all, then you are insecure. The more insecure, the more alive. So a sannyasin to me is a person who decides to live to the utmost, to the optimum, to the maximum; it is just like a flame burning from both poles. Moment to moment you live, moment to moment you act. Each moment is complete in itself. You do not decide for it. You have no decision how to act. The moment comes to you, and you act. There is no pre-determination, there is no pre-plan.

The moment comes to you. You happen to the moment, and whatever comes out, let it come. More and more you will feel a new discipline arising in you, a moment-to-moment discipline.

Osho – "I Am the Gate", Discourse 2

HUMAN BEING vs HUMANOID

Question: *After nearly 3 months, I am still thinking about taking sannyas and I don't understand why I have so much resistance to it while it seems so easy for so many others. Can you say something about this?*

We will have to go deep into this problem. You have become incapable of willing; you have forgotten how to will on your own. And this happens to almost everybody in this world. From your very childhood, parents start deciding for you; they don't allow you to decide. They don't allow you to will on your own: they will for you, they think for you, they decide for you.

And I can understand. The child is helpless; it is bound to be so, the parents have to decide for him. Otherwise the child will not survive. It is the obligation of the parents to think, will, and decide for the child.

But there is another obligation also, which all the parents down the ages have remained oblivious of - and the other is far more important. When the child has become capable of deciding, willing, thinking, they should relax with him. They should allow him to decide on his own - they should help, in fact they should support, provoke, they should tempt the child, to think on his own.

But no parents do it. They enjoy the idea that the child is still dependent on them; they enjoy the idea that the child is obedient. They enjoy the idea that the child always looks up to them - it is very ego-fulfilling. They fulfill the first duty, which is necessary - but they never fulfill the second necessity, which is far more important.

If the parents really love the child they will be very alert. The moment they see that the child can decide about something on his own, they will leave the child alone. They will not enforce anything upon him. But this does not happen. This society is very ill - and the reason for its illness is because nobody is ever allowed to will and think on his own. So everybody is looking for somebody to be ordered by.

"For three months," you say, "I have been thinking and thinking about taking sannyas." For three months? You can go on thinking for three years and three lives - but you have forgotten how to think, and you don't know how to take a step into the unknown. You have not been supported in your childhood to will, to experiment.

Even if sometimes the experiment takes you into errors and mistakes, then too it is worth it - because one learns only through errors. There is no other way of learning, there is no safer way of learning. Learning comes only through this dangerous path: you have to try and experiment. Remembering always, whatsoever you are doing may be wrong - there is no guarantee.

How can the new be guaranteed? And your parents are not here, and your teachers are not here, and your priests are not here, and your so-called leaders are not here. You are left alone here, in a very new situation, and you don't know what to do. You have never tackled, it seems, any problem on your own.

This is what Thomas Hanna has called "the state of a humanoid". Very rarely will you find a human being in the world. The people who are known as human beings are humanoids. A humanoid is a person who has never been allowed to will on his own and has become crippled, paralyzed, and is always in search of somebody to command him. The humanoid is a person who is always seeking some tyrant - who needs a tyrant to say what to do and what not to do, who is always seeking a leader, who is always seeking a state of slavery where he can throw his responsibility of thinking. Thinking is a burden to a humanoid; it is not a joy, he is not exhilarated by it. He feels anxious. He cannot take any decision, he is afraid he may go wrong.

A humanoid is a person who has not really become a grownup. And that's what the whole world is full of: humanoids. Nobody is really a grownup person; everybody is seeking a father figure.

Stand on your own feet. And I am not saying take sannyas or don't take sannyas. Who am I to say? Stand on your own feet: meditate over it. And there is nobody else to order you. Take the whole responsibility on your own shoulders. That's what being grownup means: "I take the responsibility. I go into this experience, knowing fully that I may be moving in a wrong direction, or I may be moving in a right direction - who knows?" It is always a perhaps.

And the humanoid is very much afraid of the perhaps. He needs guarantees; he is always looking for somebody to say it is so. And then he can go to foolish extremes - he can consult tarot cards to decide what to do and what not to do. He can go to an astrologer or a palmist. But he wants somebody else to decide for him. He wants to throw the responsibility on somebody else. If something goes wrong he can always say, "What can I do? That tarot reader was wrong. What can I do? That palmist was stupid."

You want somebody else to take responsibility for your life. Then how are you going to grow? And how will you become a freedom? You will remain encaged. Drop this state of being a humanoid. And the only way to drop it is to start willing on your own, deciding on your own. And whenever you make some mistake, take the responsibility. And there is nothing wrong in making a mistake. It is only by committing mistakes that one knows what is right. By knowing the false, one knows what the true is. By falling again and again one knows how not to fall. By going astray again and again one comes to recognize how not to go astray again. There is no other way.

But you have been brought up with a wrong conditioning - and everybody has been brought up in that way. Your parents, your teachers, your leaders, your priests, are humanoids - because their parents, their teachers and their priests were humanoids, and so on and so forth...you can go back. And every humanoid turns other people into humanoids.

When a child is born to you, you will make the same mistake that your parents have made with you. You will not allow the child to function on his own. Otherwise, you will be surprised - children are so intelligent. Yes, they need your guidance and they need your help - they are helpless, but they are utterly intelligent too. So the parent has to be very, very alert how far to help and when to stop helping. It is good to hold your child's hand when he is learning to walk, but don't go on holding his hand for his whole life.

And this is what is happening psychologically. Even if your parents are gone, you are still walking with your hands in their hands; you are still leaning, clinging to them. And if you cannot find your father you immediately go to the priest. It is not accidental that you call the priest 'father'. He is not a father at all, particularly the Catholic priest - it is so stupid and foolish to call him a father. What kind of father is he? He is a celibate monk! How can he be a father? But you call him a father.

You call God also 'father'. And where is the mother? In your whole trinity not a single woman: God the father, Christ the son, and the Holy Ghost...unless the Holy Ghost is a woman. Or maybe the whole trinity is just gay. Why do you call God 'the father'? A search, a deep psychological search, to have a father who is always there protecting you, safeguarding you, guiding you, sending commandments: do this, don't do that. You can rely on him - and the more you rely on him, the less you are.

And the tendency has become so deep-rooted, you have become so habituated to it that you are not even aware of what you are doing. This bondage has to be dropped. And that's what sannyas is all about! It is not a new prison. I am not here to function as your father.

Do you remember one very strange statement of Jesus? Christians don't pay much attention to it - in fact they feel embarrassed. Jesus said to his disciples, "Unless you hate your father and your mother, you cannot follow me." Does not look like a Jesus statement - a man of love, of tremendous love, who says, "God is love," who teaches love, is saying, "Hate your father and your mother - only then can you follow me."

If you show it to a Christian priest, he feels embarrassed. I have done it many times, and they feel very embarrassed, and they want to get out of it somehow. But you cannot get out of it: it is there. But it is a tremendously significant statement.

Jesus does not mean your actual father or your actual mother, but the psychological search for the father and the mother. The psychological search to depend on something or somebody - that has to be dropped. You have to start hating this dependence, you have to start hating this slavery. But if somebody helps you to drop this slavery you will fight with him - because you think this slavery is something very valuable.

You fought with Jesus, you fought with Socrates, you are fighting with me. And the only thing that is disturbing you is that I am trying to take all the chains off you. But you don't think those chains are chains - you think they are great ornaments, golden, very valuable, that if they are taken you will be naked, you will be poorer.

This is the state of a humanoid. And each humanoid has to become a human being. Each child is born as a human being but the society cripples him and creates a very artificial being: the humanoid. And all the societies do it - Christians, Hindus, Mohammedans, Buddhists,

Jainas - all the societies do it. The whole history of humanity up to now has been a history of great slavery.

Only once in a while has a man escaped out of the wheel of slavery - a Buddha, a Krishna, a Bahauddin, a Pythagoras, a Zarathustra - but only once in a while. It is really surprising how these people managed to escape and became real, authentic human beings, because the wheel is big and the structure is immense and very complicated. And the society takes the grip of you so greatly, and from every nook and corner of your being, and from such an early age, that its slavery penetrates, permeates your very unconscious.

You are not aware of what the society has done to you. Your society has made you very ill at ease, it has made you very miserable. That's why you like these things - when somebody says life is suffering, you immediately agree. Not because life is suffering, not because this statement that life is suffering has any logical support to it - no logical support is there. But why do people immediately agree? Because their experience supports it. They know only misery, they know suffering - they immediately agree. "Yes," they say, "life is a misery. How to get rid of it?"

I declare to you: Life is bliss! You need not get rid of life - you have to get rid of the way that you have learnt to be. You have to get rid of your humanoidness; you have to get rid of all that has been imposed upon your nature and is foreign to you. You have to become an authentic human being.

Becoming a sannyasin is a simple gesture that you are ready to become free. Free from nationality: the sannyasin will not think of himself as an Indian or a German or an Italian. Even if he has to carry a passport, he will not think deep down in his consciousness that he is an Italian. He is simply universal.

A sannyasin will not think of himself as a Christian or a Hindu or a Mohammedan - although there is no need to go on telling people about it, because I don't want you to create unnecessary troubles for yourselves. As it is, you have enough troubles. But deep down you will know, "I am now just a human being." You will transcend all barriers of nation, race, color, religion.

Osho – "Philosophia Perennis", Volume 1, Discourse 10

THE MASTER-DISCIPLE LOVE AFFAIR

Masters don't teach the Truth; there is no way to teach it. It is a transmission beyond scriptures, beyond words. It is a transmission. It is energy provoking energy in you. It is a kind of synchronicity. The Master has disappeared as an ego; he is pure joy. And the disciple sits by the side of the Master, slowly, slowly partaking of his joy, of his being, eating and drinking out of that eternal, inexhaustible source. And one day suddenly it has happened: a process has started in you which reveals the truth of your being to you. You come face to face with yourself. God is not somewhere else: he is now, here.

The Masters illuminate and confirm realization. They illuminate in a thousand and one ways. They go on pointing towards the Truth: fingers pointing to the moon. But there are many fools who start clinging to the fingers. By clinging to the fingers you will not see the moon, remember. There are even greater fools who start biting the fingers. That is not going to give you any nourishment. Forget the finger and look at where it is pointing.

The Masters illuminate. They shower great light - they are light - they shower great light on your being. They are like a searchlight: they focus their being on your being. You have lived in darkness for centuries, for millions of lives. Suddenly a Master's searchlight starts revealing a few forgotten territories in you. They are within you; the Master is not bringing them - he is simply bringing his light, he is focusing himself on you. And the Master can focus only when the disciple is open, when the disciple is surrendered, when the disciple is ready to learn, not to argue, when the disciple has come not to accumulate knowledge but to know Truth, when the disciple is not only curious but is a seeker and is ready to risk all. Even if life has to be risked and sacrificed the disciple is ready. In fact, when you risk your sleepy life, you sacrifice your sleepy life, you attain to a totally different quality of life: the life of light, of love, the life which is beyond death, beyond time, beyond change. They illuminate and confirm realization.

First the Master illuminates the way, the Truth that is within you. And secondly: when you realize it, when you recognize it, it is very difficult for you to believe that you have attained it. The most unbelievable thing is when realization of Truth happens to you, because you have been told that it is very difficult, almost impossible, and that it takes millions of lives to arrive at it. And you have been told it is somewhere else - maybe in heaven - and when you recognize it within yourself, how can you believe it?

The Master confirms it. He says, "Yes, this is it!" His confirmation is as much needed as his illumination. He begins by illuminating and ends by confirming. The Masters are evidence of Truth, not its proof.

Meditate over the subtle difference between evidence and proof. The Master is an evidence; he is a witness. He has seen, he has known, he has become. You can feel it; the evidence can be felt. You can come closer and closer; you can allow the fragrance of the Master to penetrate to the innermost core of your being. The Master is only evidence; he is not proof. If you want any proof...there is no proof.

God can neither be proved nor disproved; it is not an argument. God is not a hypothesis, it is not a theory: it is experience. The Master is living evidence. But to see it you will need a different approach than you are accustomed to. You know how to approach a teacher, how to approach a professor, how to approach a priest. They don't require much because they simply impart information which can be done even by a tape recorder or by a computer or by a gramophone record or by a book.

You know how to approach a teacher, you know how to approach a book, you know how to approach dead information, but you don't know how to approach a Master. It is a totally different way of communing. It is not communication, it is communion - because the Master is not a proof but an evidence. He is not an argument for God, he is a witness for God. He does not possess great knowledge about God, he knows. He is not knowledgeable, he simply knows.

Remember, to know *about* is worthless. The word 'about' means around. To know about something means to go on moving in circles, around and around. The word 'about' is beautiful. Whenever you read 'about', read 'around'. When somebody says, "I know *about* God," read: he knows *around* God. He goes in a circle. And real knowing is never about, never around; it is direct, it is a straight line.

Jesus says, "Straight is the path...." It does not go in circles; it is a jump from the periphery to the center. The Master is an evidence of that jump, that quantum leap, that transformation. You have to approach the Master with great love, with great trust, with an open heart. You are not aware who you are. He is aware who he is, he is aware who you are.

The caterpillar might be said to be unaware that it may become a butterfly. You are caterpillars - *bodhisattvas*. All caterpillars are bodhisattvas and all bodhisattvas are caterpillars. A bodhisattva means one who can become a butterfly, who can become a buddha, who is a buddha in the seed, in essence.

But how can the caterpillar be aware that he can become a butterfly?

The only way is to commune with butterflies, to see butterflies moving in the wind, in the sun. Seeing them soaring high, seeing them moving from one flower to another flower, seeing their beauty, their color, maybe a deep desire, a longing arises in the caterpillar: "Can I also be the same?" In that very moment the caterpillar has started awakening, a process has been triggered.

The Master-disciple relationship is the relationship between a caterpillar and a butterfly, a friendship between a caterpillar and a butterfly. The butterfly cannot prove that the caterpillar can become a butterfly; there is no logical way. But the butterfly can provoke a longing in the caterpillar - that is possible.

The Master helps you to reach your own experience. He does not give you the Vedas, the Koran, the Bible; he throws you to yourself. He makes you aware of your inner sources. He makes you aware of your own juice, of your own godliness.

Osho – "Ah, This!", Discourse 1

"YOU ARE NOT ENLIGHTENED, RELAX!"

Question: *Beloved Osho, I was one of those who was taken for a ride when the list of enlightened people was announced, because I thought, 'If Osho says I'm enlightened, why not try it out?' I enjoyed it: I threw a party for a hundred or so friends, and for the next six months – until I became 'endarkened' again – tried to use what I saw as a really potential situation. The main thing I saw was that I really am okay. Am I kidding myself about that experience?"*

No, if you can understand it, you cannot be kidding. First let me explain a few other things…

After I declared a few people enlightened - Santosh was also one of them. He wrote me a letter saying, "Your declaration of my enlightenment gives me no excitement, but my being accepted as a member of the committee of the enlightened ones makes me feel very great."

I sent him the message: "Why does your being enlightened not make you feel excited? The reason is that you think that you are already enlightened - and that is not true. That's why your becoming a member of the committee of the enlightened ones makes you feel great: at last your enlightenment has been recognized. It is not a declaration for you but a recognition that you have been enlightened long before.

"But if enlightenment is not an excitement, then how can it be a great thing to be a member of the party, or the committee, of enlightened people? If enlightenment itself makes no sense to you, then being the member of the committee cannot make any sense, except this: that it fulfills your ego. You were enlightened, and nobody was taking note of it. Finally I have recognized it, and now you are part of the committee of enlightened people, so it is sealed.

"But you are wrong - because it was all a joke! The committee was a joke, the declaration was a joke. And it was a device."

Somendra immediately sent a telegram to Teertha, saying, "I have got it - what about you?" He was continuously in competition - that was his problem: that he should be higher than Teertha. And this was a good chance. He has dropped sannyas, he has not been in any contact with us, but my declaration of his enlightenment - that he accepts. Sannyas he has dropped - he is no longer part of my family - but enlightenment.... Immediately a telegram: "I have got it - what about you?"

It was a device to see how people would react.

Your response to it was perfectly beautiful. Your response was, "If Osho says I am enlightened, I must be." It simply shows trust, love. It has nothing to do with ego. And throwing a party and rejoicing the moment with your friends was perfectly right. And when I said it was a joke, you were not angry. You simply took it again the same way: "If Osho says I am not enlightened, and it was a joke, perhaps I am not enlightened and it was really a joke." And the six months that you lived as enlightened, the joy and the peace and the serenity that you felt was not of enlightenment - it was of trust and love. It was a good experience for you.

But different experiences happen to different people.

There were only two Indians in the group who were declared enlightened, and they understand traditionally what enlightenment means. One was Vinod Bharti. He became very nervous, was crying, came to Vivek to give me the message, "Osho, I am not enlightened. And you have created a trouble for me: I cannot say you are wrong, and I know perfectly well myself that I am not enlightened. So what am I supposed to do? I am just torn apart. You just tell me the truth!"

He knows about enlightenment. He knows that for centuries in India enlightenment has been the ultimate peak of spiritual search. In the West the very idea has never existed. So he cannot conceive of himself as Gautam Buddha, and he cannot deny me because he loves me and trusts me. So I can see his trouble. So I sent him the message, "Don't be worried, it was just a joke. You are not enlightened, relax!"

Until he heard that he was not enlightened, he could not sleep for two days. Then he relaxed - he is not enlightened; there is no problem.

The other man was Swami Anand Maitreya, who was the only one who understood the joke immediately, because as he left the room he said, "Osho is really a rascal! Saying to me that I am enlightened, proves it!"

But he was also an Indian and particularly comes from Bihar where most of the enlightened people happened in India - Gautam Buddha,

Mahavira, Parsunatha, Naminatha, Adinatha - a long series of enlightened people. All 24 enlightened masters of the Jainas - Gautam Buddha – they all happened in Bihar. Bihar has the deepest understanding and experience of enlightenment. So naturally he said, "Osho is a rascal." But it was also his love. He was not disturbed, because once you know that it is a joke, there is no question of any difficulty about it.

A few people simply remained silent: they neither reacted this way or that. That too is good. They were not affected by it; they simply remained themselves, as they were. "If Osho says it is enlightenment, it may be; if he says it is not, it may not be." But it did not make any difference to them; they remained aloof and detached.

And it was a good experience to see how people react to a single idea, with their different minds. Those who were not included in the committee were angry. I received a few letters saying, "If these people have become enlightened, then why have I not become enlightened?" As if it were something: "You have given it to these people. Why have you not given it to me?"

Somebody wrote, "I have been with you longer than these people, and I am not enlightened yet. Have you forgotten me or what?"

But it was good to know how people react.

Your reaction was perfectly beautiful on both ends. "If Osho says it is enlightenment, it must be" – that is a simple trust. "And if he says it is not…" – then you don't feel any contradiction or inconsistency, you simply accept it: "If he says it is not, then it must not be." You have transcended the world of consistencies, inconsistencies.

Love knows no contradiction. It knows no comparison. Each moment it is available.

Osho – "Beyond Psychology", Discourse 10

EVERYBODY WANTS TO BE A MASTER

You have accumulated fragments of knowledge from here and there; you may have become a great encyclopedia, but that is not the point; and particularly for those who are in search of Truth, that is a barrier, not a help. Knowledge has to be transcended.

When there is no knowledge, knowing happens, because knowing is your quality, the quality of consciousness. It is just like a mirror: the mirror reflects whatsoever is there; consciousness reflects the Truth that is always in front of you, just at the tip of your nose.

Nobody can give you the Truth, nobody, not even a Buddha, a Jesus, a Krishna - nobody can give it to you. And it is beautiful that nobody can give it to you, otherwise it would become a commodity in the market. If it can be given, then it can be sold also. If it can be given, then it can be stolen also. If it can be given, then you can take it from your friend, borrow it.

It is beautiful that Truth is not transferable in any way. Unless *you* reach it, you cannot reach. Unless you *become* it, you never have it. In fact, it is not something you can have. It is not a commodity, a thing, a thought. You can *be* it, but you cannot have it.

In the world, in *this* world, we can have everything - everything can become part of our possessions. Truth can never be possessed, because there are two commodities which can be possessed: thoughts and things. Things can be possessed, thoughts can be possessed - Truth is neither. Truth is being. You can become it, but you cannot possess it. You cannot have it in your safe, you cannot have it in your book, you cannot have it in your hand. When you have it, you *are* it. You become Truth. It is not a concept, it is a being itself.

Second thing to remember: this is a human tendency, to try to show you have that which you don't have. If you have it, you don't try to show it, there is no point. If you don't have it you try to show it, as if you have it. So remember, whatsoever you want to show to people, that is the thing you don't have.

If you go to a rich man's house, become his guest - nothing changes; if he is really rich nothing changes, he simply accepts you. Go to a poor man's house - he changes everything. He may borrow furniture from his neighbor, a carpet from somebody else, curtains from somebody else. He would like to impress you that he is rich. If you are not rich you would like to impress people that you are rich. And if you don't know, you would like people to think that you know. Whenever you want to impress somebody, remember this: it is a human tendency to impress, because nobody wants to look poor - and more so where things of the other world are concerned.

You can be a poor man as far as things of this world are concerned, that is not much of a poverty; but as far as God, the soul, liberation, Truth are concerned - it is too much to bear, to be poor is too much to bear. You would like to impress people that you have something, and it is difficult to impress them as far as things of this world are concerned, because those things are visible. It is easy to impress people about things of the other world because they are not visible. You can impress people that you know, without knowing.

The problem arises because when you impress others, there is a possibility that you may be impressed yourself by their eyes and their convictions that you have something. If many people are convinced that you know, by and by *you* will be convinced that you know. There is the problem, because deceiving others is not much of a problem, but if you are deceived by your own effort, then it will be almost impossible to bring you out of your sleep, because you think it is not a sleep at all. You think you are fully awake. It will be difficult to bring you out of your ignorance because you think you are enlightened already. It will be difficult to bring you out of your disease because you believe that you are healthy and whole already!

The greatest barrier that stands between you and the Truth is that you have convinced yourself via others that you already have it. So it is a vicious circle. First: you try to convince others - and you *can* convince others because the thing is invisible.

Second: others don't have it either, so they don't know. If you go and start talking about God, and go on talking, sooner or later people will start thinking that you know about God - because they don't know either. Except for the word 'God' they don't know anything about it, and you can be very clever and cunning, cunning about theories and philosophies, argumentative. And if you go on and on, just out of sheer boredom they will say, "Yes, we believe that you know, but be finished!"

Be happy if you think you know, but you are creating such a stone wall it will be difficult for you to break it - because if you convince others, you become convinced that, "Yes, I know". That's how there are so many so-called masters. They don't know anything, but they have followers, and because of the followers they are convinced that they know. Take away their followers and you will see their confidence is gone.

Deep down, depth psychologists say that people accumulate followers just to convince themselves that they know. Without followers, how will you convince yourself? There is no way - you are alone! And it is difficult to deceive oneself directly, it is easy to deceive oneself via others. When you talk to someone and you see the light in his eyes, you are convinced that you must have something, otherwise, "Why did this light come to his eyes, his face? He was impressed." That's why we hanker so much to impress people.

The mind wants to impress people so that it can be impressed via them, and can then believe in its borrowed knowledge as if it is a revelation. Beware of this. This is one of the trickiest traps. Once you fall into it, it will be difficult for you to come out.

A sinner can reach the truth more easily than a scholar, because a sinner feels deep down that he is guilty, he can repent, and he feels he has done something wrong. You cannot find a sinner who is basically happy. He feels the guilt; he has done something wrong and he repents in the unconscious; he wants to undo whatsoever he has done to bring about the balance in his life, and some day or other he will bring the balance. But if you are a scholar, a man of words, theories and philosophies, a great pundit, then it is difficult, because you never feel guilty about your scholarship, you feel happy and egoistic about it.

Remember one thing: whatsoever gives you a feeling of ego is a barrier; whatsoever gives you a feeling of egolessness is the way. If you are a sinner and you feel guilty, that means your ego is shaken.

Through sin you cannot accumulate ego. It has happened many times that a sinner has taken the jump in a moment and has become a saint. It happened to Valmiki, an Indian saint, the first to tell the story of Rama. Valmiki was a robber and a murderer, and in a single moment the transformation happened. It has never happened like that to any pundit ever - and India is a great country of pundits: the brahmins, the scholars.

You cannot compete with Indian scholars - they have a long heritage of thousands of years, and they have lived on words and words and words. But it has never happened that a scholar in a single moment took a jump, exploded, was broken from the past and became totally new. It has never happened that way. But it has happened many times with sinners, in a single moment, because deep down they were never able to make arrangements in their ego with whatsoever they were doing. Whatsoever they were doing was ego-shattering - and ego is the wall, the stone wall.

If you feel you are a moralist, a puritan, you will create a subtle ego. If you think you are a knower, you will create a subtle ego. Remember, there is no sin except the ego, so don't accumulate it; and it is always accumulated through false things, because real things always shatter it. If you *really* know, the ego disappears; if you don't know, it accumulates and becomes bigger and bigger and stronger. If you are really a pure man, a religious man, ego disappears; but if you are a puritan, a moralist, then ego is strengthened.

This should always be the criterion to judge whether whatsoever you are doing is good or wrong: judge it by the ego. If ego is strengthened, then it is wrong: drop it as soon as you can, drop it immediately! If ego is not strengthened, it is good.

If you go to the temple every day, or to church every Sunday, and you feel ego is strengthened, don't go to church - stop; don't go to the temple, it is not helping you, it is a poison. If you feel by going to church that you are religious, you are something extraordinary, greater, purer than others, holier-than-thou; if this attitude comes to you, holier-than-thou, then drop it, because this attitude is the only sin in the world that exists. All else is child's play. This is the only sin - this attitude of holier-than-thou.

Do only that which doesn't strengthen your ego, and sooner or later you will become enlightened, because when the ego is not, if even for a single moment it leaves you - suddenly the eyes open and you have seen it. Once seen, it is never forgotten. Once glimpsed, it becomes such a powerful magnet in your life that it goes on drawing you nearer and nearer to the center of the world. Sooner or later you will be merged into it.

But the ego resists, the ego resists surrender. It resists love, it resists prayer, it resists meditation, it resists God. Ego is a resistance, a fight against the Whole; that's why it is a sin. And ego is always interested in impressing people. The more you can impress people, the more ego gets food. This is a fact. If you cannot impress anybody, the supports are withdrawn and the ego starts trembling. It has no base in reality, it depends on others' opinions.

A student cannot be impudent, he cannot be rude, he cannot be an egoist. If he is he cannot be a student, because to be a student means to be receptive, to be ready to learn. And what is readiness to learn? Readiness to learn means: I know that I am ignorant. If I know that I know, how can I learn? The doors are closed, I am not ready to learn; really, I am ready to teach.

It happened once in a Zen monastery: a man came; he wanted to be initiated. The Master said, "We have two categories of initiates here. I have 500 inmates in the ashram, in the monastery, and we have two categories: one is that of disciple, and one that of Master. So which category would you like to join?"

The man was absolutely new, he even felt a little hesitation. He said, "If it is possible then I would like to be initiated as a Master."

The Master was just joking and wanted to look to the deeper unconscious. Everybody would like to be a Master, and even if you become a disciple you become one only as a means, just as a means to become a Master: you have to pass through it, it is a compulsion; otherwise how can you become a Master? So you have to be a disciple, but the search of the ego is to be the Master.

The ego would like to teach, not to learn, and even if you learn it is learning with the idea of how to get ready to teach.

You listen to me. With listening I have two categories also: you can listen like a disciple; you can listen like a would-be Master. If you listen like a would-be Master you will miss, because you cannot listen with that attitude. If you are just waiting, getting ready, and wondering how to jump into being a Master and teach others, you cannot be receptive. You can learn only if you are a disciple with no thought of becoming a Master. This was one of the oldest traditions in the East - that a person would not start teaching unless his Master told him to.

There was one disciple of Buddha who remained for many years with him; his name was Purna. He became enlightened, and he still remained with Buddha. After his enlightenment he would also come every day in the morning to listen to Buddha. He himself was now a buddha; nothing was lacking, he stood now in his own right, but he continued to come.

One day Buddha asked Purna, "Why do you go on coming? Now you can stop." And Purna said, "Unless you say so, how can I stop? If you say so, it is okay." Then he stopped coming to Buddha's lectures, but he remained just like a shadow moving with the *sangha*, with the Order.

Then after a few years, again Buddha said, "Purna, why do you go on following me? You go and teach people! You need not be here with me."

Purna said, "I was waiting. When you say so, I will go. I am a disciple, so whatsoever you say I will do. If you say so, it's okay. So where should I go? Which direction should I go? Whom should I teach? You simply direct me and I will follow! I am a follower."

This man must have listened to Buddha totally, because even when he becomes enlightened he remains a disciple. And there are people who are absolutely ignorant - and they are already 'Masters'. Even if they are listening, they are listening with an attitude that sooner or later they have to teach. You listen just to tell others what you have learned! Drop that idea completely from the mind, because if that idea is there, if the would-be Master is there, the disciple cannot exist with that idea; they never coexist.

A disciple is simply a disciple. One day it happens that he becomes a Master - but that is not the end, that is just a consequence. Just by being a learner one becomes wise. That is a consequence, not the goal.

If you learn simply to become wise you will never learn, because to be wise is an ego-goal, an ego-trip. And if you are just waiting to ripen, mature, and become a Master, and this disciplehood is just a passage to be passed through - the sooner the better, it has to be finished, you are not happy in it, you would like to end it - then you are not a disciple, and you will never be a Master. Because when a disciple ripens, he becomes a Master spontaneously. That is not a goal to be followed, it happens as a byproduct.

Osho – "And the Flowers Showered", Discourse 2

THE INDIVIDUAL IS THE REALITY

Sir Thomas More wrote a book called "Utopia", in which he hopes for everything that man has always aspired to but has never been able to achieve. There have been revolutions, there have been attempts to make alternative societies; all have failed. But that does not mean that we have made every possible effort.

I am reminded of Thomas Alva Edison. He was working on the electric bulb for five years continuously. All his colleagues were tired, bored, but they were puzzled and amazed that the old man would come to the lab before everybody else, full of zest, enthusiasm, hoping that it was going to happen today.

Finally they said, "Three years we have been hearing about it; 900 experiments have been made – all have failed. But you seem to be absolutely unaffected by the failures."

Edison said, "No, I am not unaffected. I am immensely inspired. If 900 attempts have failed, it means now we are coming closer and closer every day to that attempt which is going to succeed. How long can it elude us? It is a challenge."

Do you see his point? He is saying 900 doors are closed. We have enquired: they are wrong doors, they lead nowhere. Now the number of doors is reduced. There are 900 doors less. We are succeeding; we are coming closer and closer to the door that will lead to the successful experiment.

Slowly, slowly his colleagues deserted him, his friends left him. But he continued, and one day he succeeded. It was late at night; it must have been three o'clock in the morning...the first light bulb! And he was so enchanted by it that he simply went on sitting under the light, looking at it. For five years he had been working.

And his wife shouted from the bedroom, "Are you mad or something? Put off that light and come to bed." And he said to her, "You don't know what you are talking about. To put on this light I have wasted five years, lost all my friends and colleagues, and you are telling me to put it off. Just come and see the miracle."

I am a utopian. I am very optimistic. I trust in the inspirations, in the hopes of man. We have just been doing something wrong to materialize them. The basic thing that I want to point out to you is that we have always been thinking of changing the society.

The communists, the fascists, the socialists, the Fabians, the anarchists, all kinds of utopians have one single thing in common, which is the cause of their failure: They all have tried to change the society.

The society does not exist anywhere. What exists is the individual. Society is only a name. Have you ever come across society? Have you ever met society and said, "Hello", shaken hands with society? Whenever you come across anybody, it is the individual. The individual is the reality. Society is only a name. They all tried to change the society to change the individual. That was their wrong approach.

My effort is to change the individual. The society will change by itself; it is simply a name. And to change the individual is not difficult, because each individual desires to be changed. No individual is satisfied as he is. He wants to be more conscious, to be more peaceful, to be more loving, to be more loved. He wants a life full of flowers and fragrance. What he finds is just misery, anxiety, anguish, meaninglessness. What the individual is missing is a very simple thing: a certain methodology to make him more centered, more silent, more serene, more collected, more together.

The name of the methodology is what I call meditation. The individual needs something more than the mind; it is already in him, but he is entangled with the mind. His entanglement with the mind prevents him from seeing beyond it to his real self. Just a little effort for watching the mind, sitting silently, looking at the mind, as if it does not belong to you – and it does not belong to you.

You are the watcher; the mind is the watched.

You are the observer; the mind is the observed.

You are the subject; the mind is the object – you are not one.

Your subjectivity is your liberation – liberation from the mind. And once you are liberated from the mind, once you know that you are beyond the mind, miraculously a great mastery arises in you. The mind cannot pull you this way and that, it simply becomes a humble servant.

The very presence of the master is enough for the mind to become an obedient servant. You can use it if you want. If you do not want to you can say, "Shut up!", and you can remain in eternal peace and silence. The mind is a good mechanism, a biocomputer, but it is not the master.

This is the change that has to be spread to every individual on the earth, and then utopia is just around the corner of the road. Then it is not something which cannot be achieved. It can be achieved, and it should be achieved.

The people who have been calling me a utopian must be thinking that they are condemning me. They are wrong. I take it as a compliment. Give my thanks to them and tell them that I am an utopian, my people are utopians, and I want the whole world to become utopians.

Osho – "Socrates Poisoned After 25 Centuries", Discourse 11

BODY, MIND, HEART PEOPLE

Something very deep has happened to man; a wound, an accident – he has lost the touch of feelings.

If you talk to trees, to birds, to animals, long enough, and you don't feel foolish - because the mind will interfere and say that this is foolish - if you don't listen to the mind and by and by you bypass it and connect directly, a tremendous energy of feeling will be released in you. You will become totally a new sort of being. You had never known these ways were possible to be.

You will become sensitive – sensitive to pain and pleasure. That's why humanity has stopped the functioning of feeling: because when you become sensitive to pleasure, you also become sensitive to pain. The more you can feel happy the more you can feel unhappy also.

That fear, that one can become very unhappy, has closed you, has helped human mind to create barriers so that you cannot feel. When you cannot feel, both ways are closed: you cannot become unhappy, you cannot become happy.

But try! It is a prayer. Because it is heart to heart. First try with human beings – just with your own child, sit silently with the child. Allow feeling. Don't bring the mind in. Sit with your wife, or with your friend, or your husband, holding hands together in a dark room, not doing anything, just trying to feel each other. In the beginning it will be difficult, but by and by you will have a different mechanism functioning within you: you will start feeling.

Almost one third of persons, that is 33% of persons, can revive their heart very easily. It is not dead in them. For the remaining others it may be difficult.

One third of all people are body oriented, one third are heart oriented, one third are head oriented. Those who are heart oriented, 33%, they can revive prayer very easily. Those who are head oriented, it will be difficult for them to have any feeling. For them prayer does not exist.

Buddha himself, and Mahavir, are head oriented people. That's why prayer was not a part of their religions. They have not taught about prayer. They were intelligent people, well-trained intellectually, logically. They developed meditation but they have not talked about prayer.

Nothing like prayer exists in Jainism, cannot exist. It exists in Islam – Mohammed is a heart oriented person, he has a different quality. It exists in Christianity – Jesus is a heart oriented person. It exists in Hinduism, but not in Buddhism or Jainism, nothing like prayer there.

And one third of people are body oriented. They are the potential *charwakas*. For them no prayer, no meditation – only indulgence, only indulgence in the body, that is their only way of being happy, their only way of being.

So if you are a heart oriented person, if you feel more than you think, if music gives you deep stirrings, if poetry touches you, if beauty surrounds you, and you can feel, then prayer is for you – you have to go through prayer. Then start talking to birds and trees – and the sky, it will be helpful. But don't make it a mind talk, let it be heart to heart. Be related.

That's why people of the heart think about God as father or as beloved, some relation. The head oriented people are always laughing – what nonsense you are talking! God, the father? Then where is the mother? They always make a joke out of it because they cannot understand. For them God is truth. For the people of the heart God is love. And for the people of the body, the world is God: their money, their house, their car, their power, their prestige.

A man who is body oriented needs a different type of religion. In fact only just now in the West, particularly in America, a new sort of work has started which is for the body oriented man. That work is towards body sensitivity. Many sensitivity training groups are working. A new sort of religion is being born – for the first time.

In the past there have been two types of religion: meditation oriented – Buddha and Mahavir; prayer oriented – Mohammed, Jesus, Krishna and Ram. But there has never been a body oriented religion. There have been body oriented people but they have always said that there is no religion, because they denied prayer, they denied meditation. These are the epicureans, *charwakas,* the atheists who say there is no God, only this body and this life is all. But they never created a religion.

For the first time in America now a new approach towards entering into the innermost core of life, is gaining hold, and that is body-sensitivity training. It is good, it is beautiful, because there are body oriented people, they need a different type of religion. They need a religion which allows their body to function in a religious way. For these people Tantra can be very helpful. For these people prayer and meditation will not be helpful. But there must be a way from the body also towards God, has to be, because God has come to the body; the body must have a way to reach to God.

These are the three types of religions. You have to find out what type you belong to. And this is not very difficult; if you watch for three weeks continuously in different ways, you can have the feel of it.

If you are body oriented, don't be discouraged, there are ways you can reach towards God through the body, because the body also belongs to God, you can reach through it. If you feel you are heart oriented – then prayer. If you feel you are intellect oriented – then meditation.

But my meditations are different in a way. I have tried to devise methods which can be used by all three types. Much of the body is used in them, much of the heart, and much intelligence. All the three are joined together, and they work on different people in a different way.

If a body oriented person comes to me he immediately loves the methods – but he loves the active parts, and he comes to see me and he says, "Wonderful, active parts are wonderful, but when I have to stand silently – then there is nothing." He feels very healthy through them; he feels more rooted in the body.

If a heart oriented person comes to me the cathartic part becomes more important for him; the heart is released, relieved of burdens, and it starts functioning in a new way.

And when a third type, the type who belongs to intelligence, comes, he loves the last parts when he is just sitting or standing silently, when it becomes meditation.

Body, heart, mind – all my meditations move in the same way: they start from the body, they move through the heart, they reach to the mind – and then they go beyond.

Through body you can relate to existence. You can go to the sea and enjoy swimming in it – but just become the body: without feeling, no thinking, just being 'of the body'. Lie down on the sands and let the body feel the sands, the coolness, the texture. Run – just now I was reading a very beautiful book, "Zen of Running" – that is for body oriented people. One man has discovered that by running there is no need to meditate, just by running meditation happens. He must be absolutely body oriented. Nobody has ever thought that by running meditation is possible – but I know, I used to love running myself. It happens. If you go on running, if you run fast, thinking stops, because thinking cannot possibly continue when you are running very fast.

For thinking an easy chair is needed, that's why we call thinkers armchair philosophers; they sit and relax in a chair, the body completely relaxed, then the whole energy moves into the mind.

If you are running then the whole energy moves into the body, then there is no possibility for the mind to think. And when you run fast, you breathe deep, you exhale deep, you become just the body. A moment comes when you *are* the body, nothing else. In that moment you become one with the universe because there is no division. The air running past you and your body become one. A deep rhythm happens.

That's why games have always been so attractive to people, and athletics. And that's why children love so much dancing, running, jumping. They are bodies! The mind has not yet developed.

If you feel you are the body type, then running can be very beautiful for you: a four, five mile run every day. And make it a meditation. It will transform you completely.

But if you feel you are a heart oriented person then prayer will be needed. Talk to birds, try to have a communion. Watch! Just wait, sit silently with a deep prayer that they should come to you, and they will start coming by and by. By and by they will be sitting on your shoulders.

Accept them. Talk to trees, to rocks, but let it be a heart talk, emotional. Cry and weep and laugh. Tears can be more prayerful than words, and laughter can be more prayerful than words, because they come deep down from the heart.

No need to verbalize – just feel. Embrace the tree and *feel* as if you are becoming one with it. And soon you will feel that the sap is not running only in the tree, it has started to run in you. And your heart is not beating only in you; deep down in the tree there is a response. One has to do it to feel it.

But if you feel that you are a third type, then meditation is for you. Running won't help. Then you will have to sit like Buddha, silently, just sitting doing nothing. Sitting so deeply that even thinking looks like a doing, and you drop it. For a few days the thoughts will continue, but if you go on sitting, just watching them, without any judgement for or against, they stop visiting you. They stop by and by, gaps come, intervals happen. In those intervals you will have the glimpses of your being.

Those glimpses can be had from the body, they can be had from the heart, they can be had from the head. All the possibilities are there because your being is in all the three and yet beyond the three. It is the same distance from all the three points – and it is the fourth point; that's why in the East we call it *turiya*, the fourth.

You can approach it from anywhere. So when somebody comes to me and says, "I don't believe in God", I say, "Don't worry. Do you believe in your body? That will do. Because the body belongs to God."

And I cannot see that there is any possibility of the fourth type. There is not.

Religion becomes universal, available to everybody. Wherever you are the door is open; and *no door is closed!* In the past the tendency has been to deny the other – if Buddha thinks that by meditation, a no-thought state of mind, one reaches, then he will deny the possibility of heart. The possibility of the body has always been denied.

I don't deny anything. I look at you – wherever you are you are related to God. Some possibility is there, some door opens exactly where you stand. Nobody can be out of the possibility. Everybody can start working in himself. No belief is needed; as you are you are accepted.

That's why it becomes a little difficult for people to understand me, because I go on accepting. I have no condemnation and no rejection. Because I see that God accepts you, then who am I to reject you? He goes on breathing in you, he goes on living in you; you may be an alcoholic or a drug taker and he has not left you yet, so whom am I to tell you that you are not accepted?

You may be a thief, you may be immoral, but as I see it God has become a thief in you, that is all. Between the thief and the God there must be a bridge, otherwise how can you exist? And you have been existing beautifully. So there must be a way – it has to be found, that's all.

Nobody is rejected, and for everybody there is every possibility to grow. You have to find out your type; and if you cannot find out your type, that too is not to be made into a worry. That means you can do a synthesis of meditation techniques, in which body, heart and mind are all involved.

But start feeling, being. Start on the way.

Osho – "Tao the Three Treasures", Volume 4, Discourse 8

CONSCIOUS ECOLOGY

Friends, today I am going to talk first about religion and the crime that it has committed against humanity, nature, environment, ecology. Religion's crimes are many, innumerable, but the worst crime is that it has placed man at the center of existence. It has given the idea to the whole of humanity that the whole existence is for your use: you are God's greatest creation.

A man-oriented vision of existence is bound to create catastrophes in nature, it is bound to destroy the ecological balance, it is bound to give man the strange idea of an ego. The Bible says God created man in his own image, and man has believed it. Just look at your face in the mirror: Is it God's face in the mirror?

The truth is that Christianity has been befooling humanity. It is not that God made man in his own image, it is man who has made God in his own image. And all the scriptures of all the religions have given man a strange licentiousness over nature, over animals and birds. That has culminated in destroying many species of animals, birds. It has destroyed millions of trees for no reason.

Every second that passes, one football ground is cleaned of all greenery, all trees. When India became independent, it had 33,000,000 hectares of trees. Today it has only11,000,000 hectares. This man-centered view begins with Genesis, in the Bible. In Genesis it says: "Be fruitful and multiply, and replenish the earth and subdue it; and have dominion over the fish of the sea and over the fowl of the air and over every living thing that moves upon the earth."

This is the ultimate crime that has made man violent against nature, given him the freedom to conquer innocent animals, to destroy them. It has made man barbarous. Now we are suffering because all those trees have been destroyed and more are being destroyed continuously. There is a certain balance in existence. These trees are your brothers and your sisters, there is no question of dominion. You exhale carbon dioxide, they inhale it. They exhale oxygen, you inhale it. Such a deep relationship. You cannot exist without trees, nor can trees exist without you; your existence is so deeply rooted in each other.

Osho – "One Seed Makes the Whole Earth Green", Discourse 3

LET-GO

Your let-go is not my let-go; your let-go is simply a defeatist attitude. Basically you want to fight, but there are situations where you cannot fight, or perhaps you have come to the very end of your energy for fighting. Then, to cover up your defeat, you start thinking of let-go. Your let-go is not true, it is phony.

Real let-go is not against fight. Real let-go is absence of fighting. And you cannot mix real let-go with fighting attitudes, for the simple reason that the presence of let-go means the absence of a fighting attitude. How can you mix something which is present with something which is absent? Just as you cannot mix light and darkness, however great an artist you may be - you cannot mix light and darkness for the simple reason that darkness is only an absence of light. You cannot bring them together; only one can be present.

So the first thing to remember is that the basic attitude of every human being is to fight. So don't think of it particularly as your problem. It will help you immensely to understand that it is a human problem. Then you can stand aloof and watch it, observe it, understand it.

Let-go means no competition, no struggle, no fight; just relaxing with Existence, wherever it leads. Not trying to control your future, not trying to control consequences, but allowing them to happen...not even thinking about them.

Let-go is in the present; consequences are tomorrow. And let-go is such a delightful experience, a total relaxation, a deep synchronicity with Existence. Every act is part of the world of fight. That which you have to do is going to be a fight.

Let-go is simply understanding. And then a silent relaxation, flowing with the river, unconcerned where it is going, unworried that you can get lost...no anxiety, no anguish, because you are not separate from the totality, so whatever is going to happen is going to be good.

Osho – "Beyond Psychology", Discourse 14

SITTING IN THE FRIDGE

Question: *Osho, why should I take sannyas?*

Because tomorrow you may not be. The next moment you may not be. And sannyas is nothing but a vision of living this moment utterly, totally, absolutely.

Sannyas simply means that you will not postpone life anymore. Sannyas simply means that you will not live in dreams anymore, that you will take hold of this moment and squeeze the whole juice out of it right now. That's what sannyas is: it is a way of intense living, of sensitive living. And remember, life is very accidental. One never knows. Listen to this story…

A salesman came home unexpectedly one day, and the first words he said when he came in the door were, "Where is he? I know he is here! I can feel it in my bones!"

His wife, who was cleaning the dishes at the time said, "Who are you looking for?"

Salesman: "Don't give me that. You know who I am looking for, and I will find him!"

He looked in the closet, under the bed, and in the attic. He happened to glance out of the second floor apartment window and saw a young light-haired man get into a red convertible.

"There he is!" he said, and grabbed the refrigerator and rolled it to the window and pushed it out. He crushed the fellow in the car and died of a heart attack himself.

Saint Peter: "What happened to you, young man?"

Young man: "I got crushed to death by a fridge."

Saint Peter: "And you?"

Salesman: "While pushing a fridge through a window I died of a heart attack."

Saint Peter to the third man: "What did you die of?"

Third man: "Well, I was sitting in this fridge, minding my own business, and..."

Life is very accidental. One never knows from where the fridge will come. Somebody may be sitting in it, minding his own business...

That's why I say become a sannyasin: this is the only moment to live, and there is no other moment.

Osho – "The Heart Sutra", Discourse 8

CREATE THE EFFECT

Seek ye first the end - end means the effect, the result – and the cause will follow.

This is as it should be. It is not only that you place a seed in the soil and the tree follows; let there be a tree and there are millions of seeds. If cause is followed by effect, effect is again followed by cause. This is the chain! Then it becomes a circle – start from anywhere, create the cause or create the effect.

And I tell you it is easier to create the effect because the effect depends totally upon you; the cause may not be so dependent on you.

If I say I can only be happy when a certain friend is there, then it depends on a certain friend, whether he is there or not. If I say I cannot be happy until I attain this much wealth, then it depends on the whole world and the economic situations and everything. It may not happen, and then I cannot be happy.

Cause is beyond me. Effect is within me. Cause is in the surroundings, in the situations – cause is without. Effect *is* me!

If I can create the effect, the cause will follow.

Choose happiness – that means you are choosing the effect – and then see what happens. Choose ecstasy and see what happens. Choose to be blissful and see what happens. Your whole life will change immediately and you will see miracles happening around you – because now you have created the effect and causes will have to follow.

This will look magical; you can even call it the law of magic. The first is the law of science and the second is the law of magic. Religion is magic, and you can be the magician. That's what I teach you: to be the magician, to know the secret of magic.

Try it! You have been trying the other your whole life – not only this but many other lives also. Now listen to me! Try this magic formula, this mantra I give to you. Create the effect and see what happens; causes immediately surround you. They follow.

Osho – "My Way: The Way of the White Clouds", Discourse 3

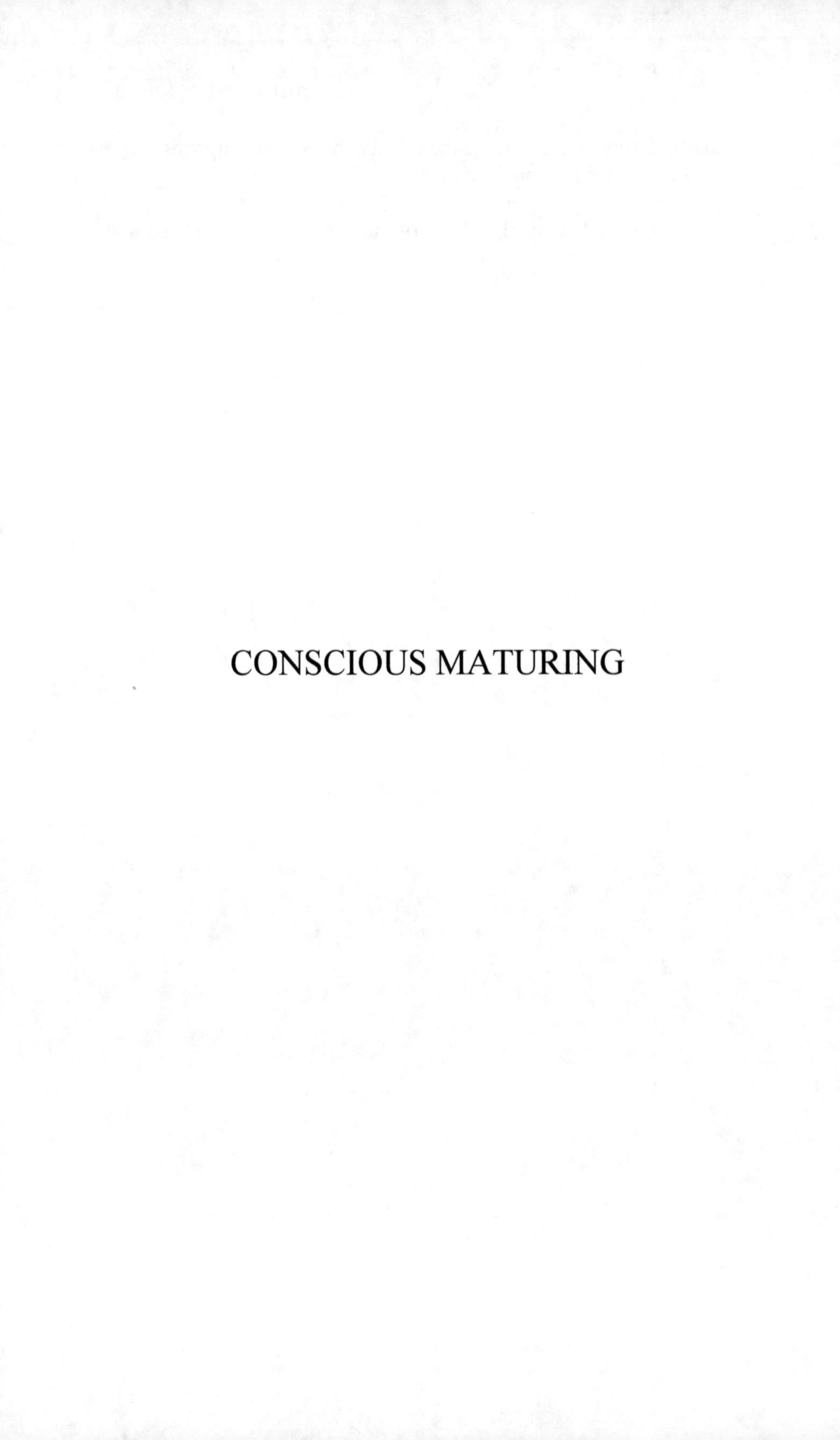

CONSCIOUS MATURING

CONSCIOUS MATURING
by
Swami Shunyo Mahom

Osho shared his experiential understanding of how to mature from sex to love to enlightenment, but how can an ignorant child begin to explore the mysteries of existence from an unconscious state and mature to superconsciousness?

Osho said, "If you become aware that the Whole is doing everything, you are being possessed by the Whole, breathed by it, you are just a hollow bamboo, a flute, the sound comes from the Whole, the whole life comes from it - then you live a life of enlightenment. This is the only difference between ignorance and enlightenment. One step in error that 'I have done it' - and the whole journey goes wrong. One step right that: 'The Whole has been doing it in me; I am not the doer, I am just the field of his play, a flute of his songs, a reed, nothing more, an emptiness in which he flows, moves, lives' - then you live a totally different life, a life of light and bliss."

Although we are born ignorant of who we are and how we got here, it is my personal experience that deep inside my navel center is a connection to a spiritual source of pulsing energy which activates physical breathing. I know that a human being does not need to do anything to be spiritual: we are already spiritual at our center inside.

It is not that we breathe; Existence is breathing us. We are loved, cared for by Existence *as we are*, and the experience of the mystery of breathing can become the foundation for trust and love for oneself, and for other humans and nature.

Thus, the first step in maturing consciously is to experientially value the riches of the inner world by being conscious of how breathing is a mysterious happening sourced at our navel center. By being guided to experience the mystery of breathing, even a child can slowly become conscious of a connection to an invisible source of life energy and is already one with Existence. Slowly fear dissolves and love evolves.

In his last public discourse Osho said, "Zen has to be transformed in a way that the contemporary man can be interested in it. It has to be easy, relaxed, it has not to be hard. That old traditional type is no longer possible, nor is it needed. Once it has been explored, once a single man has become enlightened, the path becomes easy."

A playful attitude is helpful for children and adults when experimenting with breathing. It is best to introduce the mystery of breathing to a child just before the child goes to sleep, so the experience goes deep into the unconscious during sleep.

All around the world children play the game of hide and seek for hours. Why for hours? Because it is fun! Playing hide and seek with conscious breathing, letting the process be fun, the child's feeling of being separate from Existence slowly dissolves. The child begins to tacitly understand that all the manifest world is connected to this same source of life energy: animals, trees, other humans. Love evolves naturally.

Osho said, "The secret to transform life into eternal life is love…and on the path of love, trust is the most essential thing."

An experiential understanding that one is naturally connected to a cosmic source of life energy is the foundation for trusting that everyone and everything in existence is connected with this energy. The flower of love can grow from the roots of this trust. By exploring the mystery of breathing on a daily basis, trust in oneself and existence deepens.

Vipassana is the name of the essential conscious breathing meditation: just sitting silently watching the breath go in and out. By breathing consciously on a daily basis, trust evolves, and a child can then be slowly guided to value other treasures in their inner world.

The fundamental problem a human infant faces in the maturing process is that the child's parents may be as young as 13 and are still immature themselves - or the child's parents may be 30 years old and psychologically and emotionally still 13 years old. In either case, most children are going to stagnate during the maturing process. This is a fact; I was one of those children - until I began to mature by listening to Osho's discourses and experimenting with his cathartic meditations.

During World War One the average physical age of USA soldiers was 24. Psychological tests were done on 1,700,000 soldiers and the average mental age was found to be 13.8. Yes, the average mental age of *half* of those soldiers was *below* 13.8. And these immature 'adults' are legally eligible to vote for 'leaders' of a country.

Today the situation may even be worse. Many children raised in affluent societies are spoiled. Psychologists term such a child 'entitled'. Entitlement usually begins with over-parenting, over-indulging, over-protecting, over-pampering, over-praising in order to meet the endless demands of a child. Many of today's parents are overly invested in a child's happiness, comfort and success. Overly involved parents try to eliminate potential obstacles in a child's path. In their attempt to shelter kids from adversity, they rob them of the opportunity to make decisions, learn from their mistakes, and develop the resilience needed to thrive through the ups and downs of life. This is all done in the name of love—but too much of a good thing can result in kids who always expect to get what they want when they want it. They expect others to make them happy instead of maturing to the point when they take full responsibility for their growth process.

Signs of a Child's or Adult's Entitlement Issue:

1. Expects bribes or rewards for 'good' behavior.
2. Rarely lifts a finger to help.
3. Passes blame when things go wrong.
4. Can't handle disappointment.
5. Expects to be rescued from their mistakes.
6. Feels like the rules don't apply.
7. Constantly wants more...and more.

My personal experience is that daily conscious breathing and enjoying other Osho meditations can change this situation in the future.

A child can be guided to play hide and seek with the mystery of breathing even before language is fully developed. Then at a certain point the education of the child can begin in a conscious way.

The Latin root of the word 'education' means *'to draw out, as water from a well'*, and a parent or guardian can begin to draw out what is inside a child's mind by asking simple questions on a daily basis. For example, "What are you feeling? What are you thinking?" and so on. Slowly a child can begin to feel loved and respected as he or she is.

Parenthood can be an opportunity for a man or woman to accelerate their personal maturing process - or not. Most educational systems stuff the minds of potential parents with an overemphasis on science and dehumanizing history, but utterly fail to *draw out* the merits and strengths latent in young adults which prepare these potential parents for the ability to respond to the challenges of helping a newborn child to consciously mature.

Osho said, "Cleanse people's unconscious with meditation, fill their inner being with light. It is only meditation that gives you a clean heart which cannot be corrupted. Then power can never be misused, then power can be a blessing; it is going to be creative. The essential has to come from the inner, the essential has to grow like a tree, the essential is alive. Then you are going to do something to make life more lovable, more livable; to make existence a little more beautiful."

In "Walking in Zen, Sitting in Zen", Discourse 4, Osho said, "In a better world, in a more human world, at least up to the age of 21, children should not be taught any Christianity, Jainism, Hinduism, Judaism, no. Up to the age of 21 - when they become capable of voting – they should be left to inquire on their own. Yes, parents need to feed you, to clothe you, to support you, to make you strong in body, to support you in your inquiry, in your questioning, to give you every kind of support and protection, so that you can freely inquire. Then the whole world will be full of agnostics, inquirers, and that will be the beginning of a true religion on earth."

It took me 25 years to heal the personal damage caused by my pseudo-religious-educational experience, but each culture presents unique challenges, and ultimately, it's up to each individual to consciously mature in their own way and then share their experiential understanding with children.

A boy's physical body is aggressive, active, and girl's physical body is passive, receptive. But within each boy is a receptive feminine energy body, and within each girl is a positive energetic male body.

Thus, the ages from 7 to 14 are critical for the flower of love to grow in a healthy way because it is during this period that a child's intellect and emotional body slowly develop and sex becomes active.

With conscious guidance, if a child is encouraged to become conscious of the fragrances of *feeling* from 7 to 14, a teenage boy or girl can mature in a healthy way. That is, the energetic and psychological differences between boys and girls can be understood and sex can be explored in respectful loving ways. The foundation for a loving being is then established, and love flows naturally from this being to others.

In the "Seven Bodies of Men and Women" chapter of this book, Osho said, "From 7 years to 14 years the etheric body develops. These 7 years are years of emotional growth of the individual. This is why sexual maturity, which is the most intense form of emotion, is reached at the age of 14. Now some people stagnate at this stage. Their physical bodies grow but they are stuck with the first two bodies."

"Some people stagnate at this age." Why? Because the adults who raise a child – parents and others – have themselves stagnated at this stage and have no experiential understanding of how to support a child to consciously mature during this critical stage of growth. This is especially true in Western cultures where intellect, logic, and science are valued more than qualities of love, intuition, and acceptance of nature's illogical dialectical ways.

Osho said, "Intellect is something pseudo, something false. It is a sub-stitute for intelligence. Intelligence is a totally different phenomena, the real thing. Intelligence needs tremendous courage. Intelligence needs an adventurous life. Intelligence needs you to always go into the unknown, into the uncharted sea. Then intelligence grows, it becomes sharpened. It grows only when it encounters the unknown every moment."

Obviously, intellect and language are needed to communicate and need to be taught to a child. But in addition to teaching language, an adult can help a child bring awareness to their etheric body simply by asking questions like, "What are you feeling?" - then listening from the heart and responding to their answer. And children can be encouraged to question adults: "Is what you are teaching me your experience or just a borrowed belief?" (More in "Creativity and Education" chapter.)

In the third seven-year period, between the ages of 14 and 21, the astral body develops. In this third body reasoning, thinking and intellect are developed. This is an outcome of education, civilization, and culture, and it is important during this period to educate young adults on the principles of conscious relating.

The years from birth to age 21 are critical when establishing a foundation for conscious maturing. During these years the maturing of the body and mind need to be *balanced* with the maturing of the emotional body so that the knack of witnessing the mind and feelings can evolve naturally.

By experimenting with Osho's meditations, I developed the knack of witnessing the body-heart-mind's dualistic nature and consciously responding to situations moment to moment. These experiments also helped me to consciously heal and mature my fourth subtle body.

Witnessing consciousness is the foundation for "The Psychology of the Buddhas Meditation". Osho said, "The Psychology of the Buddhas does not work within the mind. It has no interest in analyzing or synthesizing. It simply helps you get out of the mind so that you can have a look from the outside. And that very look is transformation."

Ma Prem Kaveesha was a devotee of Osho who developed Osho's transformational insights into "The Psychology of the Buddhas Meditation", and I would like to share the essence of this practical meditation with you now.

THE PSYCHOLOGY OF THE BUDDHAS MEDITATION

The Psychology of the Buddhas Meditation is based on the science of the inner world. It is a psychiatry for the meditator, and some familiarity with meditation – not as a practice but as a state of being – is necessary as a foundation on which to build this new understanding.

This is a psychology which is beyond psychology, since one cannot observe something which he is not *in some way* separate from. It is this separation from the mind which is the unique distinction of the meditative state, and in this separation a new world opens up and a new sense of freedom arises.

This is a very specific, definable, and real benefit of meditation, and because of it something can happen with ease to the meditator which would be difficult or impossible otherwise.

The universal experience of the meditator is that the condition of separation from the mind is ineffable and fleeting. You cannot *make* it happen. It happens when it happens. But of course, we don't want it to be so. It is such an extraordinary state of clarity and tranquility that we want it to be permanent. We want it to remain, to be our usual state of affairs. Still, it remains fleeting.

The 'job' of the meditator then is to become grounded, rooted in this state. When that happens, we become rooted in clarity. We see people, situations, and things as they actually are, and it is always very different from what we thought.

The Psychology of the Buddhas Meditation provides a way of helping you to become grounded and settled in a state where there is separation from the mind by providing a simple but revolutionary meditation technique for creating a little space from the mind. This 'little space' is profoundly important; it becomes the source point for a new consciousness, becomes like a little garden inside where new flowers can grow.

The word personality in the Psychology of the Buddhas can be referred to by another term: 'the parts' - the parts of the mind with which we may be identified at any single moment. One moment we may be spiritually asleep and identified with a part of the mind which is a role we are playing - for example, "I am a male," and we behave the way we have been *conditioned* to believe a male *should* act.

Another time we may be identified with a part that is a behavior or action. There are a multitude of potential parts: roles we play ("meditation center leader"); emotions (fear, greed); beliefs ("I need to save money to survive"); body sensations (tiredness, sexual pleasure); diseases, traumatic events (menstrual pain, overeating, rape); talents, gifts and essential qualities of life ("I'm good at organizing"; psychic gifts); body movement or lethargy (speediness, laziness).

Osho said, "My way is simple: to be silent, to experience in oneself that which is always the observer, and never the observed; to know the knower, and forget the known."

During my first 15 years as a sannyasin it was helpful to practice meditation techniques for an hour or two each day to develop the knack of witnessing. But during that time a subtle spiritual ego had begun to creep in the back door, and I knew I needed help. Then in 1996 I was taught the Psychology of the Buddhas Meditation and learned to witness a 'part' moment to moment. This meditation gives me the opportunity to witness the body, mind, and feelings 24 hours a day, 7 days a week, and meditation as a state of being is deepening.

I invite you to try the Osho Psychology of the Buddhas Meditation now. Close your eyes and look inside at what the mind is saying.

Ask yourself, "WHO IS IN?"

Do any words in the following sample selection of 'parts' help you see what the mind may be identified with now?

A Desire	Bragging	Complaining	Denial
Greed	Guilt	Victim	Tyrant
Jealous	*My* religión	*My* Occupation	Judging
Revenge	Excessive Talking	Blaming	Controlling
Angry	Seeking Approval	*My* Family	In Shock
Friend	Abuse of Power	Male	Superior
Possessive	*My* Caste	Rationalizing	Female
Fear	*My* Country	Loving	Enemy
Rescuer	Inferior	Attachment	Sick
My Skin Color	Sex	Daydreaming	"I'm spiritual"

Be a witness.

Bring awareness to actions of the body, thoughts in the mind, and feelings in the moment. Especially watch the feelings, as feelings are closer to your center of being than the mind.

The Psychology of the Buddhas Meditation is that simple. It is another name for Vipassana Meditation.

In the following excerpt from "The Heart Sutra", Discourse 8, Osho describes why it is necessary to thoroughly explore the intricacies of the body-mind-heart moment to moment:

"An intelligent person does not escape from any fact. If it is fear he will go into it - because the way out is through. If he feels fear and trembling arising in him, he will leave everything aside: first this fear has to be gone through. He will go into it, he will try to understand. He will not try how not to be afraid; he will not ask that question. He will simply ask one question: 'What is this fear? It is there, it is part of me, it is my reality. I have to go into it, I have to understand it. If I don't understand it then a part of me will always remain unknown to me. And how am I going to know who I am if I go on avoiding parts? I will not understand fear, I will not understand death, I will not understand anger, I will not understand my hatred, I will not understand my jealousy, I will not understand this and that...' Then how are you going to know yourself?

"All these things are you! This is your being. You have to go into everything that is there, every nook and corner. You have to explore fear. Even if you are trembling it is nothing to be worried about: tremble, but go in. It is far better to tremble than to escape, because once you escape, that part will remain unknown to you, and you will become more and more afraid to look at it because that fear will go on accumulating. It will become bigger and bigger if you don't go into it right now, this moment. Tomorrow it will have lived twenty-four hours more. Beware! - it will have got more roots in you, it will have bigger foliage, it will become stronger; and then it will be more difficult to tackle. It is better to go right now, it is already late.

"And if you go into it and you see it... And seeing means without prejudice. Seeing means that you don't condemn fear as bad from the very beginning. Who knows? - it is not bad. Who knows that it is? The explorer has to remain open to all the possibilities; he cannot afford a closed mind. A closed mind and exploration don't go together. He will go into it. If it brings suffering and pain, he will suffer the pain, but he will go into it. Trembling, hesitant, but he will go into it: 'It is my territory, I have to know what it is. Maybe it is carrying some treasure for me? Maybe the fear is only there to protect the treasure.'

"That's my experience, that's my understanding: if you go deep into your fear, you will find love. That's why it happens that when you are in love, fear disappears. And when you are afraid you cannot be in love. What does this mean? A simple arithmetic - fear and love don't exist together. That means it must be the same energy that becomes fear; then there is nothing left to become love. It becomes love; then there is nothing left to become fear. Hidden behind fear is love, and hidden behind anger is compassion, and hidden behind sex is samadhi.

"Go into each negative thing and you will find the positive. And knowing the negative and the positive, the third, the ultimate happens - the transcendental."

Daily conscious breathing and integrating the Psychology of the Buddhas Meditation into your life are keys to maturing consciously.

The ultimate potential of every human is realized by simultaneously witnessing inner thoughts and feelings and outer physical phenomenon. Slowly, slowly, we become centered in our essential nature, our being, witnessing consciousness.

CONSCIOUS RELATING

No matter what age you are now, you can begin to explore body-mind-feeling 'parts' by answering the 'parts' questions listed below.

With proper guidance, even a young adult can become conscious enough to witness natural animal instincts and not react unconsciously to an external disturbance. This ability to consciously respond to new situations heralds a new way of being, a way to consciously relate.

External relationships mirror our inner world, our feelings and mind. Our old mind projects itself, filters our perception of the external world and keeps us immature prisoners of childhood conditioning – that is, *until* we develop the knack of consciously responding to new situations moment to moment.

So, whenever a person or situation disturbs you, take the time to answer the following questions with paper and pen or in an electronic journal <u>before responding</u>:

1) What did this person or situation do or say that disturbed me?
2) What did you feel after the incident?
3) What did your mind say to do or not do?
4) What did you do or not do?
5) What did you desire in that instance that was denied you?
6) If your desire had been fulfilled, what need of yours would have been met?

Then ask "WHO IS IN?" - and answer the following questions to determine the nature of the 'part' which was mirrored by this incident.

1) What is the name of part which triggered this reaction?
2) List the main characteristics of the part.
3) Describe the situations when this part expresses itself or hides. How does it do this? If it relates with people or groups, name them, and describe how it relates.
4) What do you like and dislike about the part?
5) What emotions does this part feel?
6) What do its inner voices say?
7) What does it say to others?
8) How should it behave or not behave?
9) What are its beliefs about itself and life?
10) How does this part relate with other parts of the mind?

Finally, when you FEEL clear enough to respond to the person who disturbed you, place a hand on your heart and ask, "Why did you say (or do) that?" and listen to their response from the heart.

THE PSYCHOLOGY OF THE BUDDHAS MEDITATION

A) Recognize the part: husband, greed, victim, etc.
B) Allow the part to be so. *Do not change anything!*
C) Wake up in the moment. Be a witness and respond.

Remember, you are not your parts. Parts do not change. Parts do not hear. Parts do not see things as they are. Parts do not go away. Parts love the power of running you.

When you find yourself in a part trying to change someone else's part, hopefully you can wake up in the moment and see the hopelessness, ridiculousness and futility of trying to change another person. You just let your "change others" part be so and have a good laugh!

I have been experimenting with the Osho Psychology of the Buddhas Meditation for 26 years, and now when I wake up in the moment to a part, disidentification happens immediately, naturally, through grace.

Developing the knack of consciously responding to life moment to moment takes practice. But with patience, soon you will be able to see a part and spontaneously become alert that, "Ah-ha! That part again!" - and let the part be so. In that moment you are a master and the mind is a servant. You are awake, present, whole: a person without ego parts, centered, with Existence taking care in mysterious ways.

In the following excerpt from "Vedanta: Seven Steps to Samadhi", Chapter 17, Osho describes how patience can be an important factor in the conscious maturing of a young adult:

"Every young man and woman should be allowed to move for a few years carelessly, without any responsibility, because soon responsibilities will happen, will come. They will have to settle, and they will have to carry many burdens. Before this happens, they must be allowed a floating life, just to know whatsoever exists on earth – the bad and the good, the establishment and the anti-establishment – they must know everything.

"The more you have moved around the richer becomes your consciousness. But this cannot be the whole pattern of life, this can be just a training, because wandering gives many things and then settling in a family life also gives many things that no wanderer can know. Both have their own richness.

"While making friendships and love with many women and men, you may come to know many techniques, many experiences of sex, but you will not be able to know love, what love is, because love needs seasoning. Just a hit-and-run experience cannot be of much depth – it cannot be. When you live with a person, and not only outward but inward wandering also has ceased, and nobody can create the craving in you, now this person is the sole and whole, then a depth starts happening. Then you start mingling, merging into each other, and higher peaks of love will be available to you. And a moment comes when two persons become one.

"It is better if the first wandering part is done when you are not responsible. It must precede, and the latter part should succeed. And you will have your experience with many persons, many places, which will help you to settle somewhere, to choose the right person.

"The first love can almost never be the right love. It is bound to be childish; it is a baby love. You don't know anything about love. When you have loved many persons, you know what love is. You know the misery and the bliss both, the expectations and frustrations both, and then you can choose.

"There is a time to experiment; when you are young, experiment. Know many persons, allow many happenings, don't be shy, don't feel guilty, let life flow so you can become acquainted with it. And when you feel that now you are acquainted, you have known, you have a certain experience to settle with, then settle, and then settle forever. Both these things will give you the highest peaks possible.

"And this is my attitude in every dimension of life: allow both the opposites to happen. Don't choose between the opposites, allow both the opposites to happen. Then you have depth, then you have height, and you will have a growth."

NEEDS vs DESIRES

Needs are of the body: food, shelter, the need to love and be loved. Desires are of the mind and can be infinite; so an expectation that another person should fulfill a desire of ours is foolish. But we all have simple human needs, and most basic human needs can be easily fulfilled.

When you are clear what your basic need is in a certain situation, let the need in: absorb, digest, and feel the need. Find creative ways for the need to be met; and if needed, ask for the need to be met. You can even be silently present to the need without doing anything about it, without repressing it or having it met right away.

If you need to communicate a specific need to another person, you can begin by saying, "I have a need concerning you. Is it possible for you to be open to listening to my need?"

If the person says "Yes", you can begin to state your need by sharing what you are feeling in that moment: "I am feeling…" then state what you need from the other person: "I need (such and such) from you."

If the person says "No", simply feel the rejection and respond.

In summary, awareness evolves through meditation and the conscious maturing techniques, and in time techniques evolve into spontaneous responses as choiceless awareness illuminates situations moment to moment.

MEDITATION

Meditation is a natural silent state of the consciousness which exists in seed form in every human infant. As a child matures into an adult, the seed of consciousness can sprout and flower by experimenting with meditation techniques and by witnessing inner thoughts, feelings, and outer phenomena.

Osho created meditations for the modern man, and most of the following Osho meditations are accompanied by music and are available in CD and DVD forms.

VIPASSANA MEDITATION

Question: Beloved Osho, If I look at my death, or your death, one thing I could never forgive myself for is to miss you. I used to think: if my life has a purpose, you are the purpose – and if there is a destiny, you are my destiny. Now I see things a little differently. The most beautiful gift my life can give to you is not to worship you or help your work on this earth. It is not even to love you. Out of your compassion, as I understand it, the most beautiful gift my life can give to you is my enlightenment. Please, Osho, give me a technique to prepare my meditation.

OSHO RESPONSE:

The way your understanding has been growing is perfectly the right way and the right direction. The only thing you should think of is enlightenment. Yes, that is the only gift you can give to me: your enlightenment. Everything else is trivia. So your conclusion has my absolute, categorical approval. Once you are committed, once you have decided wholeheartedly that enlightenment is the only purpose of being here in the world, of being alive, then a single pointed awareness – just like an arrow moving towards its target – begins in you.

You are asking for the right meditation. Meditation is a beautiful word; hiding behind it is a very dangerous reality. The dangerous reality is: if you want to be deeply in meditation, you will have to pass through almost a death – the death of the old, the death of all that you used to be, a discontinuity with the past – and a rebirth.

The place where your meditation is going to descend is the place occupied by your mind and your past. So the first and primary work is to clean your interior being of all thoughts. There is no question of choosing to keep the good thoughts in and to throw the bad thoughts out. For a meditator, all thoughts are simply junk; there is no question of good and bad. They all occupy the space inside you, and because of their occupation, your inner being cannot become absolutely silent. So good thoughts are as bad as bad thoughts; don't make any discrimination between them. Throw the baby out with the bath water!

Meditation needs absolute quiet, a silence so deep that nothing stirs within you. Once you understand exactly what meditation means, it is not difficult to attain it. It is our birthright; we are absolutely capable of having it. But you cannot have both: the mind and meditation. Mind is a disturbance. Mind is nothing but a normal madness. You have to go beyond the mind into a space where no thought has ever entered, where no imagination functions, where no dream arises, where you simply are – just a nobody.

It is more an understanding than a discipline. It is not that you have to do much; on the contrary, you don't have to do anything except clearly understand what meditation is. That very understanding will stop the functioning of the mind. That understanding is almost like a master before whom the servants stop quarreling with each other, or even talking with each other; suddenly the master enters the house and there is silence.

Understanding what meditation is, is inviting the master in. Mind is a servant. The moment the master comes in with all its silence, with all its joy, suddenly the mind falls into absolute silence. Once you have achieved a meditative space, enlightenment is only a question of time. You cannot force it. You have to be just a waiting, an intense waiting, with a great longing – almost like thirst, hunger, not a word...

It is like the experience of people who have sometimes got lost in a desert. At first, thirst is a word in their mind: "I am feeling thirsty and I am looking for water." But as time goes on, and there is no sign of any oasis – and as far as the eyes can see, there is no possibility of finding water – the thirst goes on spreading all over the body. From the mind, from just a word, 'thirst', it starts spreading to every cell and fiber of the body. Now it is no longer a word, it is an actual experience. Your every cell – and there are seven million cells in the body – is thirsty. Those cells don't know words, they don't know language, but they know that they need water; otherwise, life is going to be finished.

In meditation, the longing becomes just a thirst for enlightenment and a patient awaiting, because it is such a great phenomenon, and you are so tiny. Your hands cannot reach it; it is not within your reach. It will come and overwhelm you, but you cannot do anything to bring it down to you. You are too small; your energies are too small. But whenever you are really waiting with patience and longing and passion, it comes. In the right moment, it comes. It has always come.

You are asking what meditation will be helpful to you. All meditations ... hundreds of techniques are available, but the essence of all those techniques is the same, just their forms differ. And the essence is contained in the meditation vipassana. That is the meditation that has made more people in the world enlightened than any other, because it is the very essence. All other meditations have the same essence, but in different forms; something nonessential is also joined with them. But vipassana is pure essence. You cannot drop anything out of it, and you cannot add anything to improve it.

Vipassana is such a simple thing that even a small child can do it. In fact, the smallest child can do it better than you, because he is not yet filled with the garbage of the mind; he is still clean and innocent.

I would suggest vipassana as the technique for you. Vipassana can be done in three ways – you can choose which one suits you the best. The first is: Awareness of your actions, your body, your mind, your heart.

Walking, you should walk with awareness. Moving your hand, you should move with awareness, knowing perfectly that you are moving the hand. You can move it without any consciousness, like a mechanical thing. You are on a morning walk; you can go on walking without being aware of your feet. Be alert of the movements of your body. While eating, be alert of the movements that are needed for eating. Taking a shower, be alert of the coolness that is coming to you, the water falling on you and the tremendous joy of it .... Just be alert. It should not go on happening in an unconscious state.

And the same about your mind: whatever thought passes on the screen of your mind, just be a watcher. Whatever emotion passes on the screen of your heart, just remain a witness – don't get involved, don't get identified, don't evaluate what is good, what is bad; that is not part of your meditation. Your meditation has to be choiceless awareness.

You will be able one day even to see very subtle moods: how sadness settles in you just like the night is slowly, slowly settling around the world, how suddenly a small thing makes you joyous. Just be a witness. Don't think, "I am sad." Just know, "There is sadness around me, there is joy around me. I am confronting a certain emotion or a certain mood." But you are always far away: a watcher on the hills, and everything else is going on in the valley. This is one of the ways vipassana can be done.

And for a woman, my feeling is that it is the easiest, because a woman is more alert of her body than a man. It is just her nature. She is more conscious of how she looks; she is more conscious of how she moves, she is more conscious of how she sits; she is always conscious of being graceful. And it is not only a conditioning; it is something natural and biological. Mothers who have experienced having at least two or three children, start feeling after a certain time whether they are carrying a boy or girl in their womb. The boy starts playing football; he starts kicking here and there, he starts making himself felt – he announces that he is here. The girl remains silent and relaxed; she does not play football, she does not kick, she does not announce. She remains as quiet as possible, as relaxed as possible.

So it is not a question of conditioning, because even in the womb you can see the difference between the boy and the girl. The boy is hectic; he cannot sit in one place. He is all over the place. He wants to do everything; he wants to know everything. The girl behaves in a totally different way.

(Editor's note: The above first form of Vipassana is precisely "The Psychology of the Buddhas Meditation")

OSHO CONTINUES RESPONDING:

The second form is breathing, becoming aware of breathing. As the breath goes in, your belly starts rising up, and as the breath goes out, your belly starts settling down again. So the second method is to be aware of the belly, its rising and falling. Just the very awareness of the belly rising and falling...

And the belly is very close to the life sources because the child is joined with the mother's life through the navel. Behind the navel is his life's source. So when the belly rises up, it is really the life energy, the spring of life that is rising up and falling down with each breath. That too is not difficult, and perhaps may be even easier, because it is a single technique.

In the first, you have to be aware of the body, you have to be aware of the mind, you have to be aware of your emotions, moods. So it has three steps. The second sort has a single step: just the belly, moving up and down. And the result is the same. As you become more aware of the belly, the mind becomes silent, the heart becomes silent, the moods disappear.

And the third is to be aware of the breath at the entrance, when the breath goes in through your nostrils. Feel it at that extreme – the other polarity from the belly – feel it from the nose. The breath going in gives a certain coolness to your nostrils. Then the breath going out ... breath going in, breath going out .... That too is possible. It is easier for men than for women. The woman is more aware of the belly.

In the night it happens when you sleep: you don't breathe from the chest, you breathe from the belly. That's why the night is such a relaxed experience. After your sleep, in the morning you feel so fresh, so young, because the whole night you were breathing naturally.

These are the two points: if you are afraid that breathing from the belly and being attentive to its rising and falling will destroy your athletic form ... men may be more interested in that athletic form. Then for them it is easier to watch near the nostrils where the breath enters. Watch, and when the breath goes out, watch.

These are the three forms. Any one will do. And if you want to do two forms together, you can do two forms together; then the effort will become more intense. If you want to do all three forms together, you can do all three forms together. Then the process will be quicker. But it all depends on you, whatever feels easy.

Remember: easy is right.

As meditation becomes settled, mind silent, the ego will disappear. You will be there, but there will be no feeling of "I." Then the doors are open. Just wait with a loving longing, with a welcome in the heart for that great moment, the greatest moment in anybody's life – enlightenment. It comes ... it certainly comes. It has never delayed for a single moment. Once you are in the right tuning, it suddenly explodes in you, transforms you. The old man is dead and the new man has arrived.

Osho - "The New Dawn", Discourse 16

DYNAMIC MEDITATION

This meditation is be done in a group or alone at sunrise. It is best to wear loose clothing and a blindfold.

First Stage: 10 minutes. Deep, fast, **chaotic** breathing through the nose, allowing the body to move in rhythm with the breathing.
Second Stage*: 10 minutes. Catharsis. Let go, scream, cry, jump, shake, dance, laugh – whatever helps to release suppressed emotions. Emote into a pillow if necessary. Cooperate with the energy as totally as possible.
Third Stage: 10 minutes. With raised arms, jump up and down, shouting, "Hoo! Hoo! Hoo!" so that the sound hammers deep into the sex center. Exhaust yourself, give all you have!
Fourth Stage: 15 minutes. Stop! Freeze as you are in whatever position you find yourself in. Be a witness to your thoughts and feelings.
Fifth Stage*: 15 minutes. Celebrate! Dance, sing, rejoice in gratitude.

Those unable to make noise during this meditation can keep all the sounds within and still benefit.

KUNDALINI MEDITATION

This meditation releases powerful energies sourced at the naval center and is best done in the afternoon after a day's activities. Each stage lasts 15 minutes.

First Stage: Preferably with a blindfold, stand, close your eyes and let your whole body shake loosely, feeling the energy move up from your feet. Let go and become the shaking.
Second Stage: Dance any way you feel, allowing the body to flow freely.
Third Stage: Stand or sit silently, witnessing the mind and feelings.
Fourth Stage: Lie down and be still while witnessing.

CHAKRA BREATHING AND CHAKRA SOUND MEDITATIONS

Both of these meditations are accompanied by music with the voice of a facilitator who guides the meditator to focus awareness on each of the body's seven chakras in sequence. During the chakra breathing meditation one breathes into each chakra, and during the chakra sound meditation one makes vocal sounds while focusing on each chakra.

First Stage: 45 minutes. The facilitator guides one through 3 cycles of chakra breathing or making vocal sounds into the chakras.
Second Stage: 15 minutes. Sit or lie down and silently witness thoughts and feelings.

NATARAJ MEDITATION

First Stage: 40 minutes. Allow spontaneous freedom to take over completely while dancing to abandon. Do not control your movements or be a witness during this stage - just be the dance.
Second Stage: 20 minutes. Lie down, silent and still. Allow the music and the vibrations inside to penetrate your subtle layers of being.
Third Stage: 5 minutes. Dance, celebrate, enjoy.

NADABRAHMA I

This meditation is best done on an empty stomach before going to bed, or early in the morning followed by 15 minutes of rest.

First Stage: 30 minutes. Sit in a relaxed position with eyes closed and lips together. Hum loudly enough to create a vibration throughout the whole body. Inhale naturally and allow the body to move slowly. Visualize your body as an empty vessel filled with the vibrations of humming.

Second Stage: total 15 minutes. Move the hands, slowly, palms up, in a circular outward motion, the right hand to the right and the left hand to the left. After 7.5 minutes the music will change; and then for another 7.5 minutes, move the hands in the opposite direction; that is, with palms down, moving in circular motions inwards towards the body, taking the energy in. Make the circles large, moving as slowly, naturally as possible.

NADABRAHMA II for COUPLES

Osho created a beautiful Tantra variation of Nadabrahma for couples. The room should be fairly dark with four candles and incense burning. With only a bedsheet covering each other's bodies, partners sit facing each other, holding one another's crossed hands. With the eyes closed, they continue humming in sync for at least 30 minutes. At this point the humming and breathing will merge into unison and energies will be felt to meet and unite.

LAUGHING MEDITATION

This meditation can be done any time day or night, and especially upon waking up in the morning, as follows:

Upon waking up each morning, before opening your eyes, stretch like a cat, then begin to laugh. For 5 or more minutes lose yourself in laughter. Then silently witness your thoughts and feelings.

After a few days you will notice that laughing like this changes the whole nature of your day.

CREATE YOUR SUPPORT GROUP

In the past seekers have isolated themselves in mountain caves, monasteries, and exclusive relationships. Osho has suggested that a sincere seeker invite friends and create their own support group to mature together. Do one of Osho's meditations - Dynamic, Kundalini, or another meditation - listen to an Osho discourse, and share the insights gained by exploring the Conscious Maturing processes. Be a light unto yourself and share the light with others.

A list of Osho Meditation Centers and resources - where you can obtain Osho CD and DVD meditations, books and discourses - is included at the end of this book.

HEALTHY SCIENCE

Physical science has made amazing discoveries to help create a comfortable physical environment in many parts of the earth. The discovery and implementation of electrical energy is supreme among those discoveries. Without the benefits of electricity most of the labor-saving and communication devices we have in the 21st century would not exist.

However, this 'progress' has come at a great cost. Electricity produced by fossil fuels and nuclear energy create deadly side effects and waste which threaten to destroy life on planet earth. A new approach to create a healthy physical science is needed for mankind to survive. A balance of the male and female approaches to the inner and outer sciences is desperately needed.

In the "Bardo and Other Mysteries" chapter of this book, Osho describes how the *fourth psychic body* of different scientists in the past revealed medicinal powers in plants, the 700 acupressure points of the body, and other psychic insights into physical phenomena.

In reference to the Mahabharata, an ancient Hindu scripture, Osho said, "The airplane is described with great detail in the Mahabharata, and perhaps a far better version than we know of yet, because it was not fueled by petrol. It used to have a certain precious stone on top of it, which absorbed the sun's rays, and through those sun rays the airplane was fueled. That was a far more developed version than our airplanes. We are wasting all the petrol on airplanes, on cars. In the Mahabharata, which is 5,000 years old, it is shown that they had found how to use solar energy."

Much of mankind's advanced technological wisdom has been lost over time, and the approach of today's physical scientist is through the 'male' principle: to actively, aggressively penetrate matter to forcibly reveal nature's deepest secrets. A sensitive scientist experienced in meditation naturally *balances* this aggressive scientific approach with the 'female' intuitive principle and allows nature's secrets to reveal themselves through *fourth body insights* into physical nature.

Electricity and magnetism are closely related. Flowing electrons produce a magnetic field, and spinning magnets cause an electric current to flow through a metal wire. Electromagnetism is the interaction of these two natural forces.

When natural physical forces like gravity, wind and solar energy are used in combination with wires and magnets to produce electricity, there is little or no pollution side effect.

But when *natural* elements like uranium are made *unnatural* by splitting the natural bonds among electrons, protons and neutrons, nuclear energy is produced with radioactive side effects which cause physical disease and death in humans. The *unnatural* production of nuclear power creates deadly nuclear waste.

Nuclear and fossil fuel electricity production methods can be eliminated by educating scientists to help mature their fourth body from a natural dreaming state to a visionary state. These conscious "neo-scientists" will then be able to translate their *fourth body insights* into methods which produce ecologically healthy electricity.

Anyone who has deeply experienced their inner world intuitively knows that reincarnation is a reality, and that an ecologically healthy earth is needed for us to come back to until we realize our spiritual immortality.

This fragile earth has the potential to be the womb for the ultimate transformation of our immortal being. But only the potential.... If the earth continues to be polluted by human unconsciousness, this womb will cease to exist, and the potential for transformation lost.

An ecologically healthy earth is needed for an individual to mature from a natural unconscious animal state to a superconscious human being.

OSHO'S LEGACY

Osho said that two groups will form after his death: exoteric groups, who are organizers concerned with society and the outside world, and esoteric groups, individuals concerned with their inner world.

Throughout history many enlightened Masters have graced the earth and inspired thousands of seekers to realize their full human potential. Unfortunately, many seekers start out with good intentions then intellectually parrot a Master and organize pseudo-religious sects to exploit gullible believers by inventing dogma and moralistic rules of behavior which have nothing to do with a Master's teachings. Osho emphasized maturing through awareness, not beliefs.

On 18 November 2013 criminal charges were filed in India against six Osho sannyasins accused of forging Osho's signature on a 'will' to try to create a financial monopoly and exclusive copyright of Osho's audio discourses, books, videos, and meditations. Three independent experts – one from Bologna, Italy, and two from India, Aurangabad and New Delhi – all concluded that the signature on the supposed 'will' is the same signature as the one on an unrelated 1976 letter signed by Osho, and that it is impossible for two signatures to be exactly the same. As a result, the three experts concluded with 100% certainty that the alleged 'will' is a forgery, and the six sannyasins eventually withdrew their claim of a 'will' left by Osho.

So it goes… some individuals are still trying to create a monopoly of Osho's wisdom. The fact is, we are born unconscious flawed potential buddhas and the ego is going to assert itself every step of the way to enlightenment. Every human makes mistakes along the way and it's up to each person to learn from mistakes or not. Through the light of awareness, one learns from mistakes and consciously matures.

In his discourse titled, "Om Shanti Shanti Shanti", Osho said, "Things can be copyrighted, thoughts cannot be copyrighted, and certainly meditations cannot be copyrighted. They are not things of the marketplace. Nobody can monopolize anything. But perhaps the West cannot understand the difference between an objective commodity and an inner experience. For 10,000 years the East has been meditating and nobody has put trademarks upon meditations."

Osho emphasized that his relationship is with each sannyasin and that each individual is responsible for their conscious growth process. A psychologically and emotionally healthy human being, someone who has healed wounds from their childhood conditioning and has balanced esoteric and exoteric qualities within themselves, can share love and meditation without exploiting or interfering with other human beings.

Osho said, "You can recognize Jesus only if you have recognized something of the beyond within yourself; otherwise not. You can recognize Buddha only if a part of you has become like Buddha; otherwise, you cannot recognize. You cannot recognize that which has not happened to you."

In this regard, only a psychologically and emotionally healthy human being can recognize another psychologically and emotionally healthy human being, and only if a time comes when a majority of humanoids have the resources and courage to mature into psychologically and emotionally healthy human beings, can the current flaws inherent in democracy evolve into meritocracy as a collective way of governing.

Osho said, "I salute the buddha within you." Osho knew from his own experience that you and I are essentially enlightened as we are, and he has shown us how to awaken the buddha within. Now it is up to each of us to flower in enlightenment, then share the fragrance of love and compassion with others.

Osho is the essential author of the Invitation and Conscious Maturing sections of this book. In these sections I shared with you how Osho's words became a living truth in my life, and I offer the following list of Osho resources - websites, communes and information centers - so that you too can explore the miracle of Osho in your own way.

RESOURCES

www.oshoworld.com, Osho sannyasin center in Delhi, India. Online books, audio discourses, and meditations. All the excerpts from Osho discourses in this book were downloaded FREE from this website.

Osho Tapoban International Commune, Nagarjun Hills, Kathmandu, Nepal. www.tapoban.com.

Osho Nirvana Ashram, Valley Center, California, USA - www.oshonirvana.com

Osho Miasto Institute for Meditation and Spiritual Growth, Tuscany, Italy. https://www.oshomiasto.it/en/

Osho Humaniversity Institute for Therapy and Education, Egmond aan Zee, Netherlands. www.humaniversity.com

www.oshonews.com, a constantly updated website with information about Osho and sannyas.

www.sannyas.wiki, list of sannyasin bios, music and events.

www.shunyo.org, Swami Shunyo Mahom website with resources.

www.oshoviha.org USA, selling Osho Meditation CD's, books, DVD's; publisher of sannyasin magazine, "Viha Connection".

RECOMMENDED BOOKS by OSHO

"The Art of Enlightenment"
"My Way: The Way of the White Clouds"
"Meditation: The First and Last Freedom"
"Tantra the Supreme Understanding"
"Inner War and Peace" - Commentaries on the Bhagavad Gita
"In Search of the Miraculous"
"The Book of Secrets" – 112 Meditations from Vigyan Bhairav Tantra
"Tao the Three Treasures" – Insights on Lao Tzu's "Tao Te Ching"

BOOKS by OSHO SANNYASINS

"Zen Pearls" - Art by Swami Shunyo Mahom, with Osho discourses.
"Deva Leela" – Swami Shunyo Mahom, a novel.
"Mama Llama's Pajamas" – Swami Shunyo Mahom, children's book.
"In Wonder with Osho" – Swami Anand Arun.
"Lone Seeker Many Masters" – Swami Anand Arun.
"Tears of the Mystic Rose" – Ozen Rajneesh Buddha.
"From Fear to Enlightenment" – Mahadevi Buddha.
"ReAwakening of Art" – Ma Meera Hashimoto.

ACKNOWLEDGEMENTS

Life with Osho and his disciples, and my family and friends, has been a blessing. The following is a partial list of beloveds with whom I have shared this amazing journey.

Gratitude for my parents, sisters, brothers; Ryan Curren and family; Swami Anand Arun, Swami Ram Krishnananda, Ma Prem Chandrika, Ma Bodhi Purnima, Swami Atmo Chaitanya, Ma Prem Bhakti, Swami Anand Nijen, Ma Prem Kaveesha, Ma Shantam Avirbhava, Mahadevi Buddha, Ozen Buddha, Swami Anand Bodhichitta, Swami Bodhi Dion, Ma Prem Noori, Ma Anand Meera, Swami Prasad, Ma Leela, Swami Alok Hsu Kwang-han, Swami Anand Vibhavan, Swami Dhyan Yogi, Swami Jivan Prahas, Ma Nimeesha Cohn, Gayle Stachula, Marie Jamison, Bill Doran, Ma Prem Sarito, Frank Castelli, David Krahn, Ma Naveena Shine, Ma Hani Zand, David Mentzer, Swami Dhyan Yatri, Ma Ragini Elizabeth Michaels, Swami Bodhi Raghav, Jeff Biggs, Rose Manandahar, Lynn Ohana, Sandra Bennett, Camille Narle, Swami Chetan Bishal, Swami Ananda Teertha, Swami Anand Nisanga, Ma Yoga Anand Pratima. And gratitude for you, the reader.
With love, Swami Shunyo Mahom